57412

PN
1995   HARRINGTON
.3   Film and / as literature.
.H3

WITHDRAWN

Film And/As Literature

Film And /As Literature

JOHN HARRINGTON, 1942-

California Polytechnic State University
San Luis Obispo, California

PRENTICE-HALL, INC., Englewood Cliffs, New Jersey 07632

Library of Congress Cataloging in Publication Data

HARRINGTON, JOHN, 1942–
   Film and/as literature.

   Bibliography: p.
   Includes index.
   1. Moving-pictures and literature—Addresses, essays,
lectures.   I. Title.
PN1995.3.H3   791.43'01   76-48137
ISBN 0-13-315945-0

© 1977 by Prentice-Hall, Inc., Englewood Cliffs, N.J. 07632

Printed in the United States of America

10   9   8   7   6   5   4   3   2   1

PRENTICE-HALL INTERNATIONAL, INC., *London*
PRENTICE-HALL OF AUSTRALIA PTY. LIMITED, *Sydney*
PRENTICE-HALL OF CANADA, LTD., *Toronto*
PRENTICE-HALL OF INDIA PRIVATE LIMITED, *New Delhi*
PRENTICE-HALL OF JAPAN, INC., *Tokyo*
PRENTICE-HALL OF SOUTHEAST ASIA PTE. LTD., *Singapore*
WHITEHALL BOOKS LIMITED, *Wellington, New Zealand*

Contents

6

MESSAGE, MEDIUM, AND LITERARY ART 255

7

FILM'S LITERARY RESOURCES 315

Preface

Film is a medium which dates back only to the 1890s, and no agreed-upon work of art in the medium exists before the second decade of the twentieth century. While other art forms have taken centuries to develop, the span of a single lifetime has witnessed the birth and maturity of film. It seems axiomatic that such rapid development has occurred because of, not in spite of, the contributions of other art forms. Of these contributors, literature has had a seminal role in cinema's development, and this anthology collects the work of many contemporary thinkers who have reflected on the relationships between the two.

Studying the relationships between film and literature does not, however, imply a critical methodology applicable to individual works, but rather a unique area of study undertaken at the points where two arts or two media intersect and therefore become the subject of inter-disciplinary study. Many literary concerns are irrelevant for responding to film. When a scholar works with words, for example, he or she can open a dictionary to discover a word's present and past meanings, as well as nuances of meaning that might resonate with other words. Similarly, groups of words may have histories or overtones which are discoverable through reference works. But the film scholar has none of this available since he or she labors not with a finite, and hence collect-able and definable, number of words, but with images infinite in source and variation. This and other distinctions between film and literature, which are considered in greater detail in this collection, serve as a caution that separate entities are being compared and that the person undertaking a comparison must establish the specific basis for that comparison.

Many grounds for comparison do, of course, exist. When a film-maker adapts a novel, he or she invites the reader/viewer to examine the relationships between specific works in each medium. The implications for the dramatist of interpreting a text in performance, the novelist's challenge in realizing narrative structure, and the poet's efforts to capture a moment of human experience similarly encourage questions about the filmmaker's approaches to parallel problems. The scholar's critical methodologies also invite comparisons. Archetypal or structural approaches, for instance, show up in criticism of both literature and cinema.

What allows an interpretative tool to be applicable to works in different media? Do specific media define limits for the use of interpretative tools? Does a structural or an archetypal analysis of a novel differ from a structural or an archetypal analysis of a narrative film? What happens when a critical methodology designed for a temporal art, such as literature, is applied to a dominantly spacial art, such as film? These are only some of the basic questions of interest to the student concerned with the intersection of film and literature, and these comparative questions are still largely unexplored.

Comparing film and literature seems an even more intricate task when one attempts to ask precisely what should be treated as "film": educational and training films? home movies? narrative works? newsreels? documentaries? theatrical performances recorded by fixed cameras? concerts? political rallies? abstract forms drawn directly on celluloid? If one is chiefly concerned with questions of communication, then perhaps it matters little what is on the screen. The visual (and perhaps audio) image is all that is needed, and one image can be studied as readily as another. But when most people use the word "film," they do not have in mind a definition so broad that it would include anything and everything recorded on celluloid, and when they go to a film they expect a fictional presentation. Anything else needs further words of qualification. Critics' expectations are similar, and, as one would expect, most of the writers in this anthology focus specifically on fictional presentations to which the brief history of cinema has given some stature.

After the 1890s saw the invention of a new medium, the works of art created by later decades in the medium necessarily grew from artistic roots centuries old. In some cases literary conventions and form were unostentatiously adopted (as in such pleasant fantasies of Georges Melies as "A Trip to the Moon"); in others, established works of literary art were performed directly for the camera. For the latter, the medium did little at first but capture action, such as that of a stage play, directly.

The Film d'Art offered the first attempt to achieve for cinema works of literary merit equivalent to those of the stage. In 1908 a French Film company calling itself the Film d'Art produced "The Assassination of the Duke of Guise," an effort of high seriousness but with excessively theatrical staging and acting, as well as unedited scenes. The Film d'Art quickly revealed that many of the conventions of dramatic performance were not transferable to the newer medium. Gradually, filmmakers learned ways of manipulating the medium—through editing, shot angles, *mise-en-scene,* and so on—which established complex means of expression unique to cinema.

In that synthesis of older artistic traditions and newer means of expression, it may be argued that the artistic traditions weigh most heavily even though cinematic technique remains most visible. The contributions to film of Aristotle, Dickens, Brecht, and countless other writers may be largely unsung or even unknown to most people, but nevertheless these contributions are fundamental. To ignore them would be to ignore the vital continuation of artistic traditions and developments. It is, however, in the tension between media approaches and artistic traditions that much of the concern with—and controversy over—the film-literature relationship lies.

A central concern of this anthology is the interactions between literary form and content and the specific media potentialities of film and print. Since the narrative is the dominant artistic mode of film, the traditions of literature have had the strongest impact on this mode. Direct relationships between narrative works in film or print, which occur during the process of adaptation, represent only one of the more obvious issues of concern to the student of film vis-à-vis printed literature. Other deeper and more subtle areas of shared concern exist: problems of plot, characterization, theme, style, point of view, symbolism; use of tropes, ambiguity, parody, imagery, irony, myth, and allegory; the manipulation and modification of conventions and traditions (comedy, satire, tragedy, melodrama, picaresque); or the standard critical methods (moral-philosophical, textual-linguistic, historical-biographical, genre, formalistic, psychological, mythological-archetypal, Marxian, structural) which seem unable to discern significant impediments to crossing back and forth between fictional works in print and film. A list such as this of shared concerns points out why so many critics address themselves directly or indirectly to film's literary relationships.

The theoretical questions about the nature of film have been anything but stultifying to filmmakers, many of whom move from art form to art form or medium to medium, seemingly growing from the experience. In discussing the variety of his artistic undertakings, Jean Cocteau observed, "I have always been accused of jumping from branch to branch.

Well, I have—but always in the same tree." He viewed himself as a poet creating poetry in a variety of artistic genera: *"poésie, poésie de roman, poésie de théâtre, poésie critique, poésie graphique, and poésie cinématographique."* For Cocteau the medium in which he worked did not define the nature or form taken by his creativity. Poetry was not something confined to print, nor was film incompatible with poetry.

While Cocteau speaks for the creative artist's right to subordinate structures of art to creative purposes, Francois Truffaut insists upon the importance of at least one other art form in creating a viewer of cinema: "I don't want to make films for people who don't read." Truffaut's blunt statement certainly does not refer to the viewer's ability to comprehend subtitles or signs within the cinematographic image. Rather, Truffaut sees a connection between a person's exposure to works of literary art in print and what that person might gain from seeing a film. A person's breadth of experience in printed literature is directly related to his ability to understand, absorb, and respond to cinema.

The openness of Cocteau and Truffaut, along with other film-makers, in looking at the relationships of the various media and art forms is instructive. We have much to discover about the nature of film and of the ways film uses, modifies, avoids, or extends the artistic traditions and conventions of non-cinematic art forms. By comparing and contrasting issues central to both film and literature, we are likely to learn much about both which might otherwise be missed.

The title of this anthology reflects the theorist's two primary ways of approaching film's relationship to literature: "Film *and* literature" suggests the drawing of comparisons and contrasts between two artistic forms or between two media; "film *as* literature" involves an examination of literature as an entity larger than the medium in which it appears, suggesting that many films rely on approaches and traditions held in common with various poems, novels, or plays and that several media (especially print, film, and oral) are capable of communicating works of literature to an audience. Differing points of view toward topics are included, insofar as that has been possible. By examining contrasting or divergent viewpoints, a reader can synthesize ideas, grow familiar with the issues and vocabulary of film and literature, and begin formulating conclusions about the value, purpose, scope, and development of the relationships.

The articles are primarily theoretical, providing a survey of the problems and topics fundamental to an understanding of film's bonds with literature. The essays vary widely in approach, in assumptions of audience sophistication, and in disposition toward both film and literature. In a few cases, articles concentrating on particular films have been included, but these also, and primarily, serve to advance theoretical propositions. Otherwise, length has precluded the many excellent analyses of individual adaptations or of other films interesting for literary reasons. Emphasis has been placed on issues rather than on historicity or on an effort to include only those critics whose perceptions seem accurate in 1976; hence, many of the writers disagree, draw opposite conclusions from similar observations, rely on questionable assumptions, or simply seem outdated in their thinking. The task of the reader is thus to sort through and weigh the strengths and weaknesses of the various arguments.

This book has been divided into seven sections, beginning with film's relationships to specific literary forms and advancing through the larger issues involving film and literature. The first section, "Adaptation," examines the value of adaptation and some of the criteria for looking at a work as an adaptation. "Film and Theater" considers the relationships between dramatic and cinematic form, including the problems specific to adapting plays to the screen. "Film and Novel" similarly probes the resemblances and differences of the two forms and examines what happens when a novel is transferred to the screen. "Film and Poetry" primarily looks at the nature of poetry, comparing its manifestations in print and on film. In "Authorship and Auteurship" the nature and function of the script are examined, along with the question of where artistic credit belongs. Questions of media appear in "Message, Medium, and Literary Art"; various writers explore the different capabilities of words and images and consider the literary ramifications brought about by media relationships. Finally, "Film's Literary Resources" takes up various forms, techniques, and critical concerns shared by film and literature.

For help and advice in preparing this volume, I owe special thanks to David Bernstein, Charles Eidsvik, Tom Erskine, Jack Jorgens, Blanche Lashway, and to my wife, Marie.

JOHN HARRINGTON

Film And/As Literature

1

Adaptation

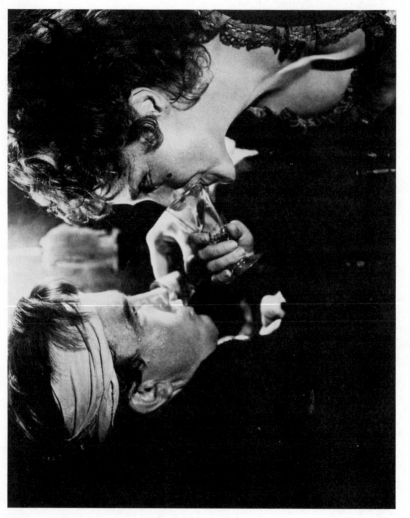

Figure 1.1　The eating scene from Tony Richardson's adaptation of Henry Fielding's Tom Jones. Courtesy, The Museum of Modern Art/Film Stills Archive.

OUTTAKES

Whoever does it, this work of adaptation is subject to the same rule as literary translations from foreign languages: a faithful translation is often a betrayal of the original.

RENE CLAIR

Everything can be transferred to the screen, everything expressed through an image.

JACQUES FEYDER

Obviously, adaptation must occur in an almost biological sense. The book must be anatomized and reassembled so as to produce the same effect in a different medium; to the degree that this second life is achieved, the adaptation is successful.

STANLEY KAUFFMAN

I believe you must say something new about a book, otherwise it is better not to touch it.

ORSON WELLES

To present the play in its own terms is not to adapt it.

A. R. FULTON

Assuming the creative talent, it seems to me two things are extremely important in developing an ability to adapt literary material to film: one, a really deep empathy with the material, the author's theme, intention and view of life; and two, an unblocked imagination which is able to flow freely from the original source, playing, embroidering, ornamenting, extending and, in the most successful adaptations, even enriching the original material.

It has been pointed out that the more "literary" the primary story, the more difficult it is to adapt. A piece which depends for its effect on a brilliant style, on ideas, on interior monologues, on metaphor is often a disappointment on the screen. Similarly excellent films have been made from badly written books. In the first case the adapter has had to subtract, in the second he has added.

ELEANOR PERRY

3

Although the problems of adaptations receive a good deal of casual mention by film reviewers, few detailed considerations exist. Most comments about adaptation tend to be ad hoc, focusing on the problems raised by specific films. Reviewers will complain that a film is unfaithful to its literary source, that an adaptation is uncinematic, or that a director has been overly slavish in an attempt to capture a text. Consequently much confusion exists over how to approach an adaptation.

Since most comments about adaptations concentrate on evaluating specific examples, personal taste precedes and informs critical consideration in all too many cases. In looking at adaptations, most critics and reviewers look first at how successful—how good (or bad)—an adaptation is. The criteria for determining an adaptation's "quality" vary: one critic will focus on whether or not the adaptation recreated his emotional experience with the book; another will consider an adaptation's ability to capture something as abstract and undefinable as the "sweep" of a novel; still another will have a predetermined point of view that no film should be based on a literary source. Seldom are the more probing questions of interpretation asked. The legitimate task of the reviewer is to offer opinions about the merit of works of art, and most people recognize that a reviewer's comments remain opinions and that the winnowing process of time all too often refuses to substantiate those opinions. The mission of criticism, on the other hand, is to illuminate works of art rather than to praise or condemn. Critical attention itself acknowledges excellence, and silence damns. It is the second level, the level of criticism rather than of personal taste and opinion, which is frequently missing from considerations of adaptations.

Much work remains to be done on the problem of adaptations. Each director or screenwriter seriously attempting to adapt a work from one medium to another faces a set of critical and interpretative problems, and critical procedures are needed to illuminate this process. Most of the writers in this section argue against simplistic and formulaic responses to adaptations. Instead they ask us to see adaptations as a fact of cinema, a fact requiring our understanding of adaptation as a phenomenon central to the work of many filmmakers.

In the first selection, Béla Balázs, one of the distinguished early theorists of cinema as well as a scenarist and a director, focuses on the long-standing debate over whether adaptation is a worthwhile and "artistic" endeavor. Tracing the problem to a need for firmer definition of what is meant by "form" and "content," Balázs argues that even though an adaptation takes the subject of another work, the adaptation achieves both a content and a form different from the original. Just as a number of creative artists can realize different works of art from the same event in reality, so another art work can provide the raw material for adapters to create new forms and contents. The artist can form and reform the raw material of life, and apparently of art, to infinite new variations. Hence, in Balazs' view, the filmmaker has little responsibility to a source, but instead shows respect through faithfulness to the nature of the art form.

Andre Bazin, on the other hand, values faithfulness to a source, distinguishing between those who would "ransack other works" and those who would respect them. Bazin faces head on the dependence of film on literary works and does not find the relationship damaging. Second-rate adaptations do no harm and, he believes, can benefit a viewer by both what they offer in themselves and by encouraging the viewer to experience the original work of literature. Further, those filmmakers who do not simplify but instead capture the complexity of a novel or play help extend the art of film. An art secure in the understanding of its own aesthetic has nothing to fear in aspiring to fidelity. The resources of literature, in Bazin's view, are important to the further development of cinema as an art form. Bazin believes that the time for cinema's independence will come, but meanwhile our task as readers and viewers is to come to terms with the potential advances cinema can make by taking advantage of the resources of literature.

Charles Eidsvik extends Bazin's arguments and calls for a "Politique des Adaptations," a policy of adaptations which would recognize the contributions literary materials have made to the advancement of cinematic art. Eidsvik contends that both professional critics and the viewing public apply a double standard to films; adaptations are judged by standards far more rigorous than those applied to non-adaptations. Consequently he calls for a recognition of the realities of film production and hence for a reappraisal of the relationship between literary and cinematic works.

Martin C. Battestin offers a more specific criterion for looking at adaptations than do the other writers in this section, and his notion that "analogy is the key" has gained wide popularity. (Bazin makes a similar, though not central, argument when he asks for "equivalents.") Battestin's criterion applies best to adaptations of novels, and he demonstrates in detail how the makers of the movie *Tom Jones* found techniques analogous to those Henry Fielding used in the novel. Battestin's essay shows how a critical theory about the process of adaptation can be applied to an individual work.

5

BÉLA BALÁZS

Art Form and Material

It is an accepted practice that we adapt novels and plays for the film; sometimes because we think their stories "filmic," sometimes because the popularity they have gained as novels or plays is to be exploited in the film market. Original film stories are very few and far between, a circumstance which undoubtedly points to the undeveloped state and imperfections of script-writing.

There is little point in discussing the practical aspects of this question. Shall we demand original film stories when even all the adaptations taken together are insufficient to satisfy the demand? In practice the law of supply and demand decides the issue. If there were a greater supply of good original film stories, there would probably be less adaptations from other forms.

We however are at the present moment interested in the laws of art and not the law of supply and demand. The method of adapting novels or plays may obey the latter law—but does it not contravene the laws of art? Must not such pandering to a practical demand necessarily be detrimental to the interests of art and the aesthetic culture of the public?

"Necessarily" is the key word here, because on it depends whether the problem is one of principle. For if such adaptations can be good *in principle* then it is for the film critics to decide in each case whether they are well or ill done and there is no theoretical problem.

There is, however, an old—one could almost say classic—aesthetic viewpoint which rejects on principle all adaptations on the grounds that they are necessarily inartistic. Here is a problem that is of the greatest

From Béla Balázs, *Theory of the Film*. Dover Publications, Inc., New York, 1970. Reprinted through the permission of the publisher.

interest for the theory of art because, although the opponents of adaptations base themselves on an undoubtedly correct thesis, they are nevertheless wrong. The history of literature is full of classic masterpieces which are adaptations of other works.

The theoretical reason on which the opposition to adaptations is based is that there is an organic connection between form and content in every art and that a certain art form always offers the most adequate expression for a certain content. Thus the adaptation of a content to a different art form can only be detrimental to a work of art, if that work of art was good. In other words, one may perhaps make a good film out of a bad novel, but never out of a good one.

This theoretically impeccable thesis is contradicted by such realities as these: Shakespeare took the stories of some of his very good plays from certain very good old Italian tales and the plots of the Greek classical drama were also derived from older epics.

Most of the classical dramas used the material of the old epics and if we turn the pages of Lessing's *Hamburgische Dramaturgie* we will find that the very first three reviews in it deal with plays adapted from novels. It should be mentioned that the author of the immortal art philosophy contained in *Laokoon*, whose concern was precisely to find the specific laws governing each form of art, found much to criticize in the plays which he reviewed, but had no objection to their being the adaptations of novels. On the contrary, he proffered much good advice as to how such adaptations could be more skilfully done.

The contradiction appears so obvious that one must wonder why no learned aestheticist ever bothered to clear up this problem. For if the objection on principle to adaptations were merely a theoretical error, the matter would be simple. But it is not an error; it is a logical conclusion from the undeniably correct thesis about the connection between content and form.

It is obvious that the contradiction here is only apparent—an undialectic nailing-down of partial truths. It may be worth while to probe deeper for the source of the error.

To accept the thesis that the content or material determines the form and with it the art form, and nevertheless to admit the possibility of putting the same material into a different form, is thinkable only if the terms used are used loosely, that is if the terms "content" and "form" do not exactly cover what we are accustomed to call material, action, plot, story, subject, etc. on the one hand, and "art form" on the other. There can be no doubt that it is possible to take the subject, the story, the plot of a novel, turn it into a play or a film and yet produce perfect works of art in each case—the form being in each case adequate to the content. How is this possible? It is possible because, while the subject, or story, of both works is identical, their *content* is nevertheless different. It is this different *content* that is adequately expressed in the changed form resulting from the adaptation.

The unsophisticated and naïve believe that life itself provides the writer with ready-made dramas and novels. According to this view every event has an *a priori*, immanent affinity to a certain form of art; that life itself determines what happenings are suitable for a play, for a novel or for a film; the writer is given, as it were, a pre-determined material as a definite subject susceptible of being used in only one way, in only one art form. If a certain subject takes his fancy, he cannot use the art form he pleases—that has been already decided by the artistic predetermination inherent in reality itself.

The world outside us, however, has an objective reality which is independent of our consciousness and hence independent of our artistic ideas. Reality has colours, shapes and sounds but it can have no immanent affinity to paintings, sculpture or music, for these are specifically human activities. Reality does not of itself curdle into any art form, not even into subjects suitable for definite art forms, and waiting like ripe apples for some artist to pick them. Art and its forms are not *a priori* inherent in reality but are methods of human approach to it, although of course this approach and its methods are also elements of reality as a whole.

These methods of approach are naturally neither arbitrary nor is their number unlimited. In the cultural sphere of civilized humanity several such methods of approach (or art forms) have evolved as historically given objective forms of culture, and although they are merely subjective forms by means of which human consciousness approaches reality, they nevertheless appear to the individual as being objectively given. The parallel of the dialectic interaction of river and river-bed could again be quoted here as the model for the mutual relationship of material and art form.

Hence, if there is a "dramatic" theme or subject which appears specific because it already shows the peculiar characteristics of the dramatic art form, then it is already *content* (which really determines the form it can take) and no longer mere "material" i.e. merely the raw material of living reality, which cannot as yet determine its art form and could be the content of any of them not yet being content in its own right.

Such specific themes (or contents) are no longer mere fragments of reality—they are an approach to reality from the viewpoint of a certain form of art. One might call them "semi-fashioned" for they are already prepared to fit into a certain art form. If we call them "themes," "subjects" or "stories," we are already using a correlative term which cannot be conceived in itself, but only as the theme of something, e.g. a drama, as the subject of a novel, as the story on which a film is based. Such can be found only in a reality already regarded from the angle of one or the other of the forms of art.

What is the conclusion from this? That the raw material of reality can be fashioned into many different art forms. But a "content," which determines the form, is no longer such raw material.

Are there not writers who write nothing but plays or nothing but novels? They, too, regard the entire reality of life, but only from the viewpoint of their own form of art, which has become an organic part of their approach. There are others who work in more than one art form; writers who regard life now with the eye of the novelist, now with the eye of the dramatist. So it may happen that they see the same bit of reality more than once; perhaps once as a drama and once as a film. But if this does happen, they would not be adapting their own drama for the screen. They would have gone back to their own basic experience and formed the same raw material once as a play, once as a film. It is quite certain that there are few outstanding events in history which have not served as material for ballads, plays, epics or novels. But a historical event is in itself only material, not theme. Material can still be regarded from the angle of various art forms. But a theme is already something regarded from the viewpoint of one or the other art form, lifted out of a multiform reality and developed into a dominant *motif*. Such themes can be adequately expressed in only one art form; they determine their art form, for they have themselves been determined by it. Such a theme, such a reality, such a material is already "content" and determines its form.

Take a portrait. The reality of the model is as yet only raw material. Is can be painted or drawn in black-and-white or modelled in clay. But if a true painter looks at the model, he will see colours in the first place, the colours will be the dominant characteristic and once this has happened the colours will no longer be raw material—they will be a theme for a painter, a content which determines the form, which is the art form, which is painting. A black-and-white artist will see the lines of the same model. Here, the same material will provide a different artistic theme, and this theme will be the content determining the art form, which will be drawing or etching or some other line technique. A sculptor may see the same model, and yet not the same model, for in his case it will be a model for a sculpture. The same material will provide for him a theme of plastic shapes, and thereby determine the adequate art form, sculpture.

The same applies to the literary forms. One writer may feel the atmosphere, the fleeting moods in a subject and take that for his theme; probably he will make it a short story. Another will see in the same subject a central conflict, an inexorable problem which demands a dramatic approach. The raw material of life may be the same, but the themes of the two writers will be different. And the different themes will give rise to different contents and demand different art forms. A third writer might come across the same event and see in it not the event itself but the inner adventures of human beings interacting with one another and showing the web of their destinies like a multicoloured carpet of life. This third writer would probably write a novel. Thus the same event as raw material regarded from three different angles can result in three themes, three contents, three forms of art. What mostly happens, however, is that a subject already used in one form of art is adapted to another form—in other words, it would not be the same model sitting to three different artists but rather a drawing made after a painting, or a sculpture after a drawing. This is much more problematic than the other case.

If, however, the artist is a true artist and not a botcher, the dramatist dramatizing a novel or a film-script writer adapting a play may use the existing work of art merely as raw material, regard it from the specific angle of his own art form as if it were raw reality, and pay no attention to the form once already given to the material. The playwright, Shakespeare, reading a story by Bandello, saw in it not the artistic form of a masterpiece of story-telling but merely the naked event narrated in it. He saw it isolated from the story form, as raw life-material with all its dramatic possibilities, i.e. possibilities which Bandello could never have expressed in a *novella*.

Thus although it is the raw material of a Bandello story that was given new form in a Shakespeare play, there is no trace of the main content of the play in the Bandello story. In that story Shakespeare saw a totally different theme and therefore the content that determined the art form of his play was also totally different.

I would like to mention here a less well-known adaptation, for the reason that the poet who was its author was at the same time an accomplished theoretician who could explain how and why the adaptation was made. Friedrich Hebbel, the German playwright, wrote plays based on the mighty epic material of the Nibelung saga. It would be quite impossible to accuse Hebbel of insufficient respect for the eternal greatness of the Germanic epic and its peerless formal perfection. Hebbel had no intention of improving on the Nibelung saga, nor can any intention of a popularization for money-making purposes be ascribed to this very serious writer. What then were his motives and his purpose in undertaking such an adaptation?

Hebbel himself gives the reason in his famous diary: "It seems to me that on the foundation of the Nibelung saga one could build a purely human tragedy which would be quite natural in its motivation."

What, then, did Hebbel do? He kept the mythical foundation, that is the skeleton of the story. But he gave it a different interpretation. The actions and events remained largely the same, but were given other motives and explanations.

Thus the same event, being given quite different emphasis, was turned into a different theme. The theme and content of Hebbel's Nibelung trilogy is not identical with that of the Nibelung saga. For although in Hebbel's drama Hagen kills Siegfried, as he does in the saga, he does so from entirely different motives and Kriemhild's vengeance, as depicted in Hebbel's drama, is a tragedy of a quite different order than the same event in the Germanic epic.

Nearly every artistically serious and intelligent adaptation is such a re-interpretation. The same external action has quite different inner motives, and it is these inner motives which throw light on the hearts of the characters and determine the content which determines the form. The material, that is the external events, serve merely as clues, and clues can be interpreted in many ways—as we know from the detective stories.

It often happens that a writer uses a second time, in another art form, the material he himself has once already used in a certain art form. We know that nowadays, especially when it is a question of adapting novels or plays for the films, this is mostly done for financial reasons. A successful novel can be adapted first as a play and then as a film, and thus make money for its author several times over. But sometimes such adaptations are made with quite serious artistic intentions.

Let us take a case in which no suspicion of financial motives can arise. We know that Goethe wanted to make a play out of his very interesting story "The man of fifty," which is a part of his *Wilhelm Meister*. The plan of this play has been preserved—it gives, already divided into acts and scenes, the content of the projected play, which is the content of the story, only told in a different way. This different way very instructively shows why Goethe felt the need of re-writing in another art form the material once already used. We can see in detail how in the projected play he stresses aspects which are scarcely or not at all perceptible in the short story, how he tries to bring to the surface a totally different layer of reality. The course of events is similar, but their significance is different and it contains a quite different inner experience. The reality from which he borrowed his material included this inner experience; but when he shaped his material into a short story, he had to pass by this inner experience; it was for this reason that he felt the urge of dipping once more into the depths of the same life-material by means of another art form.

It may at first sound paradoxical to say that it is often a respect for the laws of style that govern the various art forms which makes adaptations justifiable and even necessary. The severe style of the drama, for instance, demands the omission of the multiple colours and changing moods of real life. The drama is the art form suited to great conflicts and the wealth of detail which a novel may contain finds no room in its severe structure. But sometimes the author is loath to let all the wealth of mood and detail go to waste and so he puts it into a novel rather than impair the pure style of the drama. And if an author wants to pour into a film the colours of life which are barred by the severe style of the drama, he does so not because he does not respect the style of the various art forms, but because he respects them absolutely.

[1945]

ANDRÉ BAZIN

In Defense of Mixed Cinema

A backward glance over the films of the past 10 to 15 years quickly reveals that one of the dominant features of their evolution is the increasingly significant extent to which they have gone for their material to the heritage of literature and the stage.

Certainly it is not only just now that the cinema is beginning to look to the novel and the play for its material. But its present approach is different. The adaptation of *Monte Cristo, Les Misérables,* or *Les Trois Mousquetaires* is not in the same category as that of *Symphonie pastorale, Jacques le fataliste, Les Dames du Bois de Boulogne, Le Diable au corps,* or *Le Journal d'un curé de campagne.* Alexandre Dumas and Victor Hugo simply serve to supply the filmmaker with characters and adventures largely independent of their literary framework. Javert or D'Artagnan have become part of a mythology existing outside of the novels. They enjoy in some measure an autonomous existence of which the original works are no longer anything more than an accidental and almost superfluous manifestation. On the other hand, filmmakers continue to adapt novels that are sometimes first-rate as novels but which they feel justified in treating simply as very detailed film synopses. Filmmakers likewise go to novelists for character, a plot, even—and this is a further stage—for atmosphere, as for example from Simenon, or the poetic atmosphere found in Pierre Véry. But here again, one can ignore the fact that it is a book and just consider the writer a particularly prolix scenarist. This is so true that a great number of American crime novels are clearly written

From André Bazin, *What Is Cinema?* Originally published by the University of California Press; reprinted by permission of The Regents of the University of California.

with a double purpose in view, namely with an eye on a Hollywood adaptation. Furthermore, respect for crime fiction when it shows any measure of originality is becoming more and more the rule; liberties cannot be taken with the author's text with an easy conscience. But when Robert Bresson says, before making *Le Journal d'un curé de campagne* into a film, that he is going to follow the book page by page, even phrase by phrase, it is clearly a question of something quite different and new values are involved. The cinéaste is no longer content, as were Corneille, La Fontaine or Molière before him, to ransack other works. His method is to bring to the screen virtually unaltered any work the excellence of which he decides on a priori. And how can it be otherwise when this work derives from a form of literature so highly developed that the heroes and the meaning of their actions depend very closely on the style of the author, when they are intimately wrapped up with it as in a microcosm, the laws of which, in themselves rigorously determined, have no validity outside that world, when the novel has renounced its epic-like simplicity so that it is no longer a matrix of myths but rather a locus of subtle interactions between style, psychology, morals, or metaphysics.

In the theater the direction of this evolution is more evident still. Dramatic literature, like the novel, has always allowed itself to suffer violence at the hands of the cinema. But who would dare to compare Laurence Olivier's *Hamlet* to the, in retrospect, ludicrous borrowings that the *film d'art* made once upon a time from the repertoire of the Comédie Française? It has always been a temptation to the filmmaker to film theater since it is already a spectacle; but we know what comes of it. And it is with good reason that the term "filmed theater" has become a commonplace of critical opprobrium. The novel at least calls for some measure of creativity, in its transition from page to screen. The theater by contrast is a false friend; its illusory likeness to the cinema set the latter en route to a dead end, luring it onto the slippery slope of the merely facile. If the dramatic repertory of the boulevards, however, has occasionally been the source of a goodish film, that is only because the director has taken the same kind of liberty with the play as he would with a novel, retaining in fact only the characters and the plot. But there again, the phenomenon is radically new and this seems to imply respect for the theatrical character of the model as an inviolable principle.

The films we have just referred to and others the titles of which will undoubtedly be cited shortly, are both too numerous and of too high a quality to be taken as exceptions that prove the rule. On the contrary, works of this kind have for the last 10 years signposted the way for one of the most fruitful trends of contemporary cinema.

"*Ça, c'est du cinéma!*" "That's really cinema!" Georges Altmann long ago proclaimed from the cover of a book dedicated to the glorification of the silent film, from *The Pilgrim* to *The General Line*. Are the dogmas and hopes of the earliest film criticism that fought for the autonomy of the Seventh Art now to be discarded like an old hat? Is the cinema or what remains of it incapable of surviving without the twin crutches of literature and theater? Is it in process of becoming an art derived from and dependent on one of the traditional arts?

The question proposed for our consideration is not so new; first of all, it is the problem of the reciprocal influence of the arts and of adaptations in general. If the cinema were two or three thousand years old we would undoubtedly see more clearly that it does not lie outside the common laws of the evolution of the arts. But cinema is only sixty years old and already its historical perspectives are prodigiously blurred. What ordinarily extends through one or two civilizations is here contained within the life span of a single man.

Nor is this the principal cause of error, because this accelerated evolution is in no sense contemporary with that of the other arts. The cinema is young, but literature, theater, and music are as old as history. Just as the education of a child derives from imitating the adults around him, so the evolution of the cinema has been influenced by the example of the hallowed arts. Thus its history, from the beginning of the century on, is the result of determinants specific to the evolution of all art, and likewise of effects on it of the arts that have already evolved. Again, the confused pattern of this aesthetic complex is aggravated by certain sociological factors. The cinema, in fact, has come to the fore as the only popular art at a time when the theater, the social art *par excellence*, reaches only a privileged cultural or monied minority. It may be that the past 20 years of the cinema will be reckoned in its overall history as the equivalent of five centuries in literature. It is not a long history for an art, but it is for our critical sense. So let us try and narrow the field of these reflections.

First of all let it be said that adaptations which the modern critic looks upon as a shameful way out are an established feature of the history of art. Malraux has pointed out how much the painting of the Renaissance was originally indebted to Gothic sculpture. Giotto painted in full relief. Michelangelo deliberately refused any assistance he might have had from oils, the fresco being more suitable to a style of painting based on sculpture. And doubtless this was a stage quickly passed through on the way to the liberation of "pure painting." But would you therefore say that Giotto is inferior to Rembrandt? And what is the value of such a hierarchy? Can anyone deny that fresco in full relief was a necessary stage in the process of development and hence aesthetically justified? What again does one say about Byzantine miniatures in stone enlarged to the dimensions of a cathedral tympanum? And to turn now to the field of the novel, should one censure preclassical tragedy for adapting the pastoral novel for the stage or Madame La Fayette for her indebtedness to Racinian dramaturgy? Again, what is true technically is even truer of themes which turn up in all kinds and varieties of expression. This is a commonplace of literary history up to the eighteenth century, when the notion of plagiarism appeared for the first time. In the Middle Ages, the great Christian themes are to be found alike in theater, painting, stained-glass windows, and so on.

Doubtless what misleads us about the cinema is that, in contrast to what usually happens in the evolutionary cycle of an art, adaptation, borrowing, and imitation do not appear in the early stages. On the contrary, the autonomy of the means of expression, and the originality of subject matter, have never been greater than they were in the first twenty or thirty years of the cinema. One would expect a nascent art to try to imitate its elders and then, bit by bit, to work out its own laws and select its rightful themes. One finds it less easy to understand that it should place an increased volume of experience at the service of material foreign to its genius, as if its capacity for invention was in inverse proportion to its powers of expression. From there to the position that this paradoxical evolution is a form of decadence is but a step, and one that criticism did not hesitate to take upon the advent of sound.

But this was to misunderstand the basic facts of the history of film. The fact that the cinema appeared after the novel and the theater does not mean that it falls into line behind them and on the same plane. Cinema developed under sociological conditions very different from those in which the traditional arts exist. You might as well derive the *bal-musette* or bebop from classical choreography. The first film-makers effectively extracted what was of use to them from the art with which they were about to win their public, namely the circus, the provincial theater, and the music hall, which provided slapstick films, especially, with both technique and actors. Everyone is familiar with the saying attributed to Zecca when he discovered a certain Shakespeare. "What a lot of good stuff that character passed up!" Zecca and his fellows were in no danger of being influenced by a literature that neither they nor their audience read. On the other hand they were greatly influenced by the popular literature of the time, to which we owe the sublime *Fantômas*, one of the masterpieces of the screen. The film gave a new life to the conditions out of which came an authentic and great popular art. It did not spurn the humbler and despised forms of the theater, of the fairground, or of the penny dreadful. True, the fine gentlemen of the Academy and of the Comédie Française did make an effort to adopt this child that had been brought up in the profession of its parents, but the failure of their efforts only emphasized the futility of this unnatural enterprise. The misfortune of *Oedipus* and *Hamlet* meant about as much to the cinema in its early days as "our ancestors the Gauls" do to Negro elementary school children in the African bush. Any interest or charm that these early films have for us is on a par with those pagan and naïve interpretations practiced by savage tribes that have gobbled up their missionaries. If the obvious borrowings in France—Hollywood unashamedly pillaged the techniques and personnel of the Anglo-Saxon music hall—from what survived of the popular theater, of the fairgrounds, or the boulevard, did not create aesthetic disputes, it was primarily because as yet there was no film criticism properly so called. It was likewise because such reincarnations by these so-called inferior arts did not shock anybody. No one felt any call to defend them except the interested parties who had more knowledge of their trade than they had of filmological preconceptions.

When the cinema actually began to follow in the footsteps of the theater, a link was restored, after a century or two of evolution, with dramatic forms that had been virtually abandoned. Did those same learned historians who know everything there is to be known about farce in the sixteenth century ever make it their business to find out what a resurgence of vitality it had between 1910 and 1914 at the Pathè and Gaumont Studios and under the baton of Mack Sennett?

It would be equally easy to demonstrate that the same process occurred in the case of the novel. The serial film adopting the popular technique of the feuilleton revived the old forms of the *conte*. I experienced this personally when seeing once again Feuillade's *Vampires* at one of those gatherings which my friend Henri Langlois, the director of the Cinémathèque Française, knows how to organize so well. That night only one of the two projectors was working. In addition, the print had no subtitles and I imagine that Feuillade himself would have had difficulty in trying to recognize the murderers. It was even money as to which were the good guys and which the bad. So difficult was it to tell who was which that the apparent villains of one reel turned out to be the victims in the next. The fact that the lights were turned on every ten minutes to change reels seemed to multiply the episodes. Seen under these conditions, Feuillade's *chef d'oeuvre* reveals the aesthetic principle that lies behind its charm. Every interruption evoked an "ah" of disappointment and every fresh start a sigh of hope for a solution. This story, the meaning of which was a complete mystery to the audience, held its attention and carried it along purely and simply by the tension created in the telling. There was no question of preexisting action broken up by intervals, but of a piece unduly interrupted, an inexhaustible spring, the flow of which was blocked by a mysterious hand. Hence the unbearable tension set up by the next episode to follow and the anxious wait, not so much for the events to come as for the continuation of the telling, of the restarting of an interrupted act of creation. Feuillade himself proceeded in the same way in making his films. He had no idea what would happen next and filmed step by step as the morning's inspiration came. Both the author and the spectator were in the same situation, namely, that of the King and Scheherazade; the repeated intervals of darkness in the cinema paralleled the separating off of the Thousand and One Nights. The "to be continued" of the true feuilleton as of the old serial films is not just a device extrinsic to the story. If Scheherazade had told everything at one sitting, the King, cruel as any film audience, would have had her executed at dawn. Both storyteller and film want to test the power of their magic by way of interruption, to know the teasing sense of waiting for the continuation of a tale that is a substitute for everyday living which, in its turn, is but a break in the continuity of a dream. So we see that the so-called original purity of the primitive screen does not stand up under examination. The sound film does not mark the threshold of a lost paradise on the other side of which the muse of the seventh art, discovering her nakedness, would then start to put back the rags of which she had been stripped. The cinema has not escaped a universal law. It has obeyed it in its own way—the only way possible, in view of the combination of technical and sociological circumstances affecting it. . . .

What do we actually mean by "cinema" in our present context? If we mean a mode of expression by means of realistic representation, by a simple registering of images, simply an outer seeing as opposed to the use of the resources of introspection or of analysis in the style of the classical novel, then it must be pointed out that the English novelists had already discovered in behaviorism the psychological justifications of such a technique. But here the literary critic is guilty of imprudently prejudging the true nature of cinema, based on a very superficial definition of what is here meant by reality. Because its basic material is photography it does not follow that the seventh art is of its nature dedicated to the dialectic of appearances and the psychology of behavior. While it is true that it relies entirely on the outside world for its objects it has a thousand ways of acting on the appearance of an object so as to eliminate any equivocation and to make of this outward sign one and only one inner reality. The truth is that the vast majority of images on the screen conform to the psychology of the theater or to the novel of classical analysis. They proceed from the commonsense supposition that a necessary and unambiguous causal relationship exists between feelings and their outward manifestations. They postulate that all is in the consciousness and that this consciousness can be known.

If, a little more subtly, one understands by cinema the techniques of a narrative born of montage and change of camera position, the same statement holds true. A novel by Dos Passos or Malraux is no less different from those films to which we are accustomed than it is from a novel by Fromentin or Paul Bourget. . . . It is nonsense to wax wroth about the indignities practiced on literary works on the screen, at least in the name of literature. After all, they cannot harm the original in the eyes of those who know it, however little they approximate to it. As for those who are unacquainted with the original, one of two things may happen; either they will be satisfied with the film which is as good as most, or they will want to know the original, with the resulting gain for literature. This argument is supported by publishers' statistics that show a rise in the sale of literary works after they have been adapted to the screen. No, the truth is, that culture in general and literature in particular have nothing to lose from such an enterprise.

There now remains the cinema, and I personally feel that there is every reason to be concerned over the way it is too often used in relation to our literary capital because the film-maker has everything to gain from fidelity. Already much more highly developed, and catering to a relatively cultured and exacting public, the novel offers the cinema characters that are much more complex and, again, as regards the relation of form and content, a firmness of treatment and a subtlety to which we are not accustomed on the screen. Obviously if the material on which the scenarist and the director are working is in itself on an intellectual level higher than that usual in the cinema then two things can be done. Either this difference in level and the artistic prestige of the original work serves as a guarantee, a reservoir of ideas and a *cachet* for the film, as is the case with *Carmen, La Chartreuse de Parme*, or *L'Idiot*, or the film-makers honestly attempt an integral equivalent, they try at least not simply to use the book as an inspiration, not merely to adapt it, but to translate it onto the screen as instanced in *La Symphonie Pastorale, Le Diable au corps, The Fallen Idol*, or *Le Journal d'un curé de campagne*. We should not throw stones at the image-makers who simplify in adapting. Their betrayal as we have said is a relative thing and there is no loss to literature. But the hopes for the future of the cinema are obviously pinned to the second group. When one opens the sluice the level of the water is very little higher than that of the canal. When someone makes a film of *Madame Bovary* in Hollywood, the difference of aesthetic level between the work of Flaubert and the average American film being so great, the result is a standard American production that has only one thing wrong with it—that it is still called *Madame Bovary*. And how can it be otherwise when the literary work is brought face to face with the vast and powerful cinematographic industry: cinema is the great leveler. When, on the other hand, thanks to a happy combination of circumstances, the film-maker plans to treat the book as something different from a run-of-the-mill scenario, it is a little as if, in that moment, the whole of cinema is raised to the level of literature. This is the case with the *Madame Bovary* and *Une Partie de campagne* of Jean Renoir. Actually, these are not two very good examples, not because of the quality of the films but precisely because Renoir is more faithful to the spirit than the letter. What strikes us about the fidelity of Renoir is that paradoxically it is compatible with complete independence from the original. The justification for this is of course that the genius of Renoir is certainly as great as that of Flaubert or Maupassant. The phenomenon we face here is comparable then to the translation of Edgar Allen Poe by Baudelaire.

Certainly it would be better if all directors were men of genius; presumably then there would be no problem of adaptation. The critic is only too fortunate if he is confronted merely with men of talent. This is enough however on which to establish our thesis. There is nothing to prevent us from dreaming of a *Diable au corps* directed by Jean Vigo but let us congratulate ourselves that at least we have an adaptation by Claude Autant-Lara. Faithfulness to the work of Radiguet has not only forced the screenwriters to offer us interesting and relatively complex characters, it has incited them to flout some of the moral conventions of the cinema, to take certain risks—prudently calculated, but who can blame them for this—with public prejudices. It has widened the intellectual and moral horizons of the audience and prepared the way for other films of quality. What is more, this is not all; and it is wrong to present fidelity as if it were necessarily a negative enslavement to an alien aesthetic. Undoubtedly the novel has means of its own—language not the image is its material, its intimate effect on the isolated reader is not the same as that of a film on the crowd in a darkened cinema—but precisely for these reasons the differences in aesthetic structure make the search for equivalents an even more delicate matter, and thus they require all the more power of invention and imagination from the film-maker who is truly attempting a resemblance. One might suggest that in the realm of language and style cinematic creation is in direct ratio to fidelity. For the same reasons that render a word-by-word translation worthless and a too free translation a matter for condemnation, a good adaptation should result in a restoration of the essence of the letter and the spirit. But one knows how intimate a possession of a language and of the genius proper to it is required for a good translation. For example, taking the well-known simple past tenses of André Gide as being specifically a literary effect of a style, one might consider them subtleties that can never be translated into the cinema. Yet it is not at all certain that Delannoy in his *Symphonie pastorale* has not found the equivalent. The ever-present snow carries with it a subtle and polyvalent symbolism that quietly modifies the action, and provides it as it were with a permanent moral coefficient the value of which is not so different after all from that which the writer was searching for by the appropriate use of tenses. Yet, the idea of surrounding this spiritual adventure with snow and of ignoring systematically the summery aspect of the countryside is a truly cinematographic discovery, to which the director may have been led by a fortunate understanding of the text. The example of Bresson in *Le Journal d'un curé de campagne* is even more convincing; his adaptation reaches an almost dizzy height of fidelity by way of a ceaselessly created respect for the text. Alfred Beguin has rightly remarked that the violence characteristic of Bernanos could never have the same force in literature and cinema. The screen uses violence in such a customary fashion that it seems somehow like a devalued currency, which is at one and the same time provoking and conventional. Genuine fidelity to the tone set by the novelist calls thus for a kind of conversion of the violence of the text. The real equivalent of the hyperbole of Bernanos lay in the ellipsis and litotes of Robert Bresson's editing. The more important and decisive the literary qualities of the work, the more the adaptation disturbs its equilibrium, the more it needs a creative talent to reconstruct it on a new equilibrium not indeed identical with, but the equivalent of, the old one. To pretend that the adaptation of novels is a slothful exercise from which the true cinema, "pure cinema," can have nothing to gain, is critical nonsense to which all adaptations of quality give the lie. It is those who care the least for fidelity in the name of the so-called demands of the screen who betray at one and the same time both literature and the cinema.

The effective fidelity of a Cocteau or Wyler is not evidence of a backward step, on the contrary, it is evidence of a development of cinematographic intelligence. Whether it is, as with the author of *Les Parents terribles,* the astonishingly perspicacious mobility of the camera or, as with Wyler, the asceticism of his editing, the refining down of the photography, the use of the fixed camera and of deep focus, their success is the result of outstanding mastery; moreover it is evidence of an inventiveness of expression which is the exact opposite of a passive recording of theater. To show respect for the theater it is not enough to photograph it. To create theater of any worthwhile kind is more difficult than to create cinema and this is what the majority of adapters were trying to do up to now.

There is a hundred times more cinema, and better cinema at that, in one fixed shot in *The Little Foxes* or *Macbeth* than in all the exterior travelling shots, in all the natural settings, in all the geographical exoticism, in all the shots of the reverse side of the set, by means of which up to now the screen has ingeniously attempted to make us forget the stage. Far from being a sign of decadence, the mastering of the theatrical repertoire by the cinema is on the contrary a proof of maturity. In short, to adapt is no longer to betray but to respect. Let us take a comparison from circumstances in the material order. In order to attain this high level of aesthetic fidelity, it is essential that the cinematographic form of expression makes progress comparable to that in the field of optics. The distance separating *Hamlet* from the *film d'art* is as great as that separating the complexities of the modern lens from the primitive condenser of the magic lantern. Its imposing complexity has no other purpose than to compensate for the distortions, the aberrations, the diffractions, for which the glass is responsible—that is to say, to render the *camera obscura* as objective as possible. The transition from a theatrical work to the screen demands, on the aesthetic level, a scientific knowledge, so to speak, of fidelity comparable to that of a camera operator in his photographic rendering. It is the termination of a progression and the beginning of a rebirth. If the cinema today is capable of effectively taking on the realm of the novel and the theater, it is primarily because it is sure enough of itself and master enough of its means so that it no longer need assert itself in the process. That is to say it can now aspire to fidelity—not the illusory fidelity of a replica—through an intimate understanding of its own true aesthetic structure which is a prerequisite and necessary condition of respect for the works it is about to make its own. The multiplication of adaptations of literary works which are far from cinematic need not disturb the critic who is concerned about the purity of the seventh art; on the contrary, they are the guarantee of its progress.

"Why then," it will be asked by those nostalgic for cinema with a capital C, independent, specific, autonomous, free of all compromise, "should so much art be placed at the service of a cause that does not need it—why make unauthentic copies of novels when one can read the book, and of *Phèdre* when all you need is to go to the Comédie Française? No matter how satisfying the adaptations may be, you cannot argue that they are worth more than the original, especially not of a film of an equal artistic quality on a theme that is specifically cinematographic? You cite *Le Diable au corps, The Fallen Idol, Les Parents terribles,* and *Hamlet.* Well and good. I can cite in return *The Gold Rush, Potemkin, Broken Blossoms, Scarface, Stagecoach,* or even *Citizen Kane,* all masterpieces which would never have existed without the cinema, irreplaceable additions to the patrimony of art. Even if the best of adaptations are no longer naive betrayals or an unworthy prostitution, it is still true that in them a great deal of talent has gone to waste. You speak of progress but progress which can only render the cinema sterile in making it an annex of literature. Give to the theater and to the novel that which is theirs and to the cinema that which can never belong elsewhere."

This last objection would be valid in theory if it did not overlook historical relativity, a factor to be counted when an art is in full evolution. It is quite true that an original scenario is preferable to an adaptation, all else being equal. No one dreams of contesting this. You may call

Charlie Chaplin the Molière of the cinema, but we would not sacrifice *Monsieur Verdoux* for an adaptation of *Le Misanthrope*. Let us hope, then, to have as often as possible films like *Le Jour se lève, La Règle du jeu,* or *The Best Years of Our Lives*. But these are platonic wishes, attitudes of mind that have no bearing on the actual evolution of the cinema. If the cinema turns more and more to literature—indeed to painting or to drama—it is a fact which we take note of and attempt to understand because it is very likely that we cannot influence it. In such a situation, if fact does not absolutely make right, it requires the critic at least to be favorably predisposed. Once more, let us not be misled here by drawing an analogy with the other arts, especially those whose evolution towards an individualistic use has been made virtually independent of the consumer. Lautréamont and Van Gogh produced their creative work while either misunderstood or ignored by their contemporaries. The cinema cannot exist without a minimum number, and it is an immense minimum, of people who frequent the cinema here and now. Even when the film-maker affronts the public taste there is no justification for his audacity, no justification except insofar as it is possible to admit that it is the spectator who misunderstands what he should and someday will like. The only possible contemporary comparison is with architecture, since a house has no meaning except as a habitation. The cinema is likewise a functional art. If we take another system of reference we must say of the cinema that its existence precedes its essence; even in his most adventurous extrapolations, it is this existence from which the critic must take his point of departure. As in history, and with approximately the same reservations, the verification of a change goes beyond reality and already postulates a value judgment. Those who damned the sound film at its birth were unwilling to admit precisely this, even when the sound film held the incomparable advantage over the silent film that it was replacing.

Even if this critical pragmatism does not seem to the reader sufficiently well-founded, he must nevertheless admit that it justifies in us a certain humility and thoughtful prudence when faced with any sign of evolution in the cinema. It is in this frame of mind that we offer the explanation with which we would like to end this essay. The masterpieces to which we customarily refer as examples of true cinema—the cinema which owes nothing to the theater and literature because it is capable of discovering its own themes and language—these masterpieces are probably as admirable as they are inimitable. If the Soviet cinema no longer gives us the equivalent of *Potemkin* or Hollywood the equivalent of *Sunrise, Hallelujah, Scarface, It Happened One Night,* or even of *Stagecoach* it is not because the new generation of directors is in any way inferior to the old. As a matter of fact, they are very largely the same people. Nor is it, we believe, because economic and political factors of production have rendered their inspiration sterile. It is rather that genius and talent are relative phenomena and only develop in relation to a set of historical circumstances. It would be too simple to explain the theatrical failures of Voltaire on the grounds that he had no tragic sense; it was the age that had none. Any attempt to prolong Racinian tragedy was an incongruous undertaking in conflict with the nature of things. There is no sense in asking ourselves what the author of *Phèdre* would have written in 1740 because he whom we call Racine was not a man answering that identity, but "the-poet-who-had-written-*Phèdre*." Without *Phèdre* Racine is an anonymity, a concept of the mind. It is equally pointless in the cinema to regret that we no longer have Mack Sennett to carry on the great comic tradition. The genius of Mack Sennett was that he made his slapstick comedies at the period when this was possible. As a matter of fact, the quality of Mack Sennett productions died before he did, and certain of his pupils are still very much alive; Harold Lloyd and Buster Keaton, for example, whose rare appearances these past fifteen years have been only painful exhibitions in which nothing of the verve of yesteryear has survived. Only Chaplin has known how to span a third of a century of cinema, and this because his genius was truly exceptional. But at the price of what reincarnations, of what a total renewal of his inspiration, of his style and even of his character! We note here—the evidence is overwhelming—that strange acceleration of aesthetic continuity which characterizes the cinema. A writer may repeat himself both in matter and form over half a century. The talent of a film-maker, if he does not evolve with his art, lasts no more than five or ten years. This is why genius, less flexible and less conscious than talent, has frequent moments of extraordinary failure; for example, Stroheim, Abel Gance, Pudovkin. Certainly the causes of these profound disagreements between the artist and his art, which cruelly age genius and reduce it to nothing more than a sum of obsessions and useless megalomania, are multiple, and we are not going to analyze them here. But we would like to take up one of them which is directly related to our purpose.

Up till about 1938 the black-and-white cinema made continuous progress. At first it was a technical progress—artificial lighting, panchromatic emulsions, travelling shots, sound—and in consequence an enriching of the means of expression—close-up, montage, parallel montage, ellipsis, re-framing, and so on. Side by side with this rapid evolution of the language and in strict interdependence on it, film-makers discovered original themes to which the new art gave substance. "That is cinema!" was simply a reference to this phenomenon, which dominated the first thirty years of the film as art—that marvelous accord between a new technique and an unprecedented message. This phenomenon has taken on a great variety of forms: the star, reevaluation, the rebirth of the epic, of the *Commedia dell'Arte*, and so on. But it was directly attributable to technical progress —it was the novelty of expression which paid the price for new themes. For thirty years the history of cinematographic technique, in a broad sense, was bound up in practice with the development of the scenario. The great directors are first of all creators of form; if you wish, they are rhetoricians. This in no sense means that they supported the theory of "art for art's sake," but simply that in the dialectic of form and content, form was then the determining factor in the same way that perspective or oils turned the pictorial world upside down.

We have only to go back 10 or 15 years to observe evidence of the aging of what was the patrimony of the art of cinema. We have noted the speedy death of certain types of film, even major ones like the slapstick comedy, but the most characteristic disappearance is undoubtedly that of the star. Certain actors have always been a commercial success with the public, but this devotion has nothing in common with the socio-religious phenomenon of which Rudolph Valentino and Greta Garbo were the golden calves. It all seemed as if the area of cinematic themes had exhausted whatever it could have hoped for from technique. It was no longer enough to invent quick cutting or a new style of photography, in order to stir people's emotions. Unaware, the cinema had passed into the age of the scenario. By this we mean a reversal of the relationship between matter and form. Not that form has become a matter of indifference, quite the opposite. It had never been more rigorously determined by the content or become more necessary or a matter of greater subtlety. But all this knowledge that we have acquired operates against the intrusion of form, rendering it virtually invisible before a subject that we appreciate today for its own sake and concerning which we become more and more exacting. Like those rivers which have finally hollowed out their beds and have only the strength left to carry their waters to the sea, without adding one single grain of sand to their banks, the cinema approaches its equilibrium-profile. The days are gone when it was enough to "make cinema" in order to deserve well of the seventh art. While we wait until color or stereoscopy provisionally return its primacy to form and create a new cycle of aesthetic erosion, on the surface cinema has no longer anything to conquer. There remains for it only to irrigate its banks, to insinuate itself between the arts among which it has so swiftly carved out its valleys, subtly to invest them, to infiltrate the subsoil, in order to excavate invisible galleries. The time of resurgence of a cinema newly independent of novel and theater will return. But it may then be because novels will be written directly onto film. As it awaits the dialectic of the history of art which will restore to it this desirable and hypothetical autonomy, the cinema draws into itself the formidable resources of elaborated subjects amassed around it by neighboring arts during the course of the centuries. It will make them its own because it has need of them and we experience the desire to rediscover them by way of the cinema.

This being done, cinema will not be a substitute for them, rather will the opposite be true. The success of filmed theater helps the theater just as the adaptation of the novel serves the purpose of literature. *Hamlet* on the screen can only increase Shakespeare's public and a part of this public at least will have the taste to go and hear it on the stage. *Le Journal d'un curé de campagne*, as seen by Robert Bresson, increased Bernanos' readers tenfold. The truth is there is here no competition or substitution, rather the adding of a new dimension that the arts had gradually lost from the time of the Reformation on: namely a public.

Who will complain of that?

[1958]

CHARLES EIDSVIK

Toward a
"Politique des Adaptations"

Expectations have a lot to do with how we react to movies. The higher our expectations, the more frequent our disappointment. Usually we do not feel cheated if a film has only ten or twenty good minutes in it; a few really good moments are enough to make a film worthwhile and twenty good minutes is rather a treat. Moreover, if we do get twenty good minutes we are willing to put up with a lot during the other hour or two that the film runs. But such is not the case if the film is an adaptation of a book or a play, especially if that book or play is well known and highly regarded. Not only are our expectations higher for adaptations; what we are willing to put up with is radically less. If adaptations reached the level we expected—not wanted, but *expected*—they would all be masterpieces. Most adaptations are not, of course, masterpieces. Rather they are, on the average, average, which is to say that they have a few good moments, enough to justify our evening. Except that our sense of the work adapted makes us feel betrayed, and therefore blind to the good moments. If there *are* ten or twenty or even thirty good minutes, we are still unsatisfied and come out of the theatre feeling ambivalent or even cheated and utterly blind to the ways in which twenty good minutes *in an adaptation* can contain more originality than one is apt to find in whole masterpieces.

Masterpieces, as Picasso pointed out, are seldom very original; truly original works are seldom well enough done to be masterpieces. Masterpieces are (after our critical rhetoric is exhausted) no more or less than works so successful that they transcend or make us forgive their limitations. But originality and success are rare bedfellows; a whole platoon of

Reprinted by permission of Charles Eidsvik.

ambitious failures and lucky breakthroughs usually precedes and lays the groundwork for each recognizable masterpiece. The failures and break-throughs attempt newness. When twenty minutes of originality occurs in film history—even when twenty minutes of innovative excellence happens —I am so startled I want to wake my friends to tell them. I have, over a dozen years as a film connoisseur, found that the urge to wake my friends occurs most frequently after I have seen an adaptation. I refuse to believe that is because I have a soft spot for adaptations. I habitually sneer at adaptations and quote Alain Resnais to the effect that they are "warmed-over meals." It's just that experience forces me to admit that adaptations frequently provide major advances in the art of film. The art of film, after all, does not proceed from masterpiece to masterpiece; art advances twenty minutes at a time and is only consolidated in its successes by works we consider masterful. There is no *single* good reason why adaptations should provide newness; each film has *its* reasons. But it seems that the attempt to adapt a work which is not "cinematically-conceived" into "cine-matic terms" forces film-makers into attempting original solutions. Some-times the attempted solutions expose "cinematic terms" for the cliched conventions they so frequently are; sometimes the solutions are successful because they show us new cinematic terms; and sometimes the solutions work for no known reason at all except that response to films is as per-verse as human response itself.

I do not wish to present a pantheon of films crucial to the cinema's growth, and then play a "look fellas!" game of showing that the films are, indeed, adaptations. Though I enjoy their contents pantheons give me indigestion. Moreover I am unwilling to call very many films (or books or plays or paintings) "masterpieces." I would rather say "these are some very interesting films." Which is what I will do later in this essay. But first I feel it necessary to briefly point out attitudes which obscure our perceptions of originality in adaptations. They are attitudes I myself have habituated; I confess what I attack. First: film critics want desperately for film to be an "original" art form. Not paying attention to the fact that original scripts, scripts with originality, and original films (made from whatever sources) are three quite different things, critics have enforced an almost ideological preference for movies not made from books or plays. There exists a cult of the original script with its attendent imposition of Romantic Genius on whoever happens to write one. I subscribe to the cult myself; I will go to anything Ben Hecht ever wrote, and admire a good director doubly if he writes his own material. But the cult of the original script ought not be confused with sharp viewing habits. Nor should other cults, such as the cult of original works of literature, con-fuse our perceptions. But it's difficult to see an adaptation in a straight-forward way. Even John Simon, the most literate of American film critics and the friendliest to adaptations, manages to put his eyeballs in crooked when seeing some adaptations.[1]

> For his newest film, Welles has picked Kafka's *The Trial*, and if ever two temperaments were polar opposites, they are the delicately devious Kafka, whose meanings seem one great iridescent elusiveness, and the assertive Welles, who loves the stridently grandiose, the unmistakable effect. The only trait shared by them is irony, but where Kafka's irony hovers in disturbing suspension over ego and universe, Welles's crashes down so heavily on a specific, and sometimes questionable, target that it tends to annihilate itself along with its object.
>
> There are so many things wrong with *The Trial* that I shall have to limit myself to a few principal objections. The gravest of these is that Kafka's work has to be perceived on at least three levels—psychological, political, religious—whereas Welles, with typical oversimplification, makes it purely political. No less improper is the turning of the protagonist K. into someone who is manifestly free of guilt and never doubts his blamelessness; as W. H. Auden points out in *The Dyer's Hand*, "If the K. of *The Trial* were innocent, he would cease to be K. and become nameless . . ." Concomitantly Kafka's world is irrational, pettifogging, dilatory, unsympathetic, ugly, and worst of all, incomprehensible. But it is not, like the world in the film, grossly vicious and, in its lack of shading, dull.

I appreciate Simon's perceptions about Kafka but not about Welles' film. Simon posits an exalted, absolute, and ideal vision of the novel and then judges Welles' film by that vision; anything other than Simon's absolute is necessarily less than it. Result: automatic condemnation of Welles' film. Or of any interpretation of Kafka which differs from Simon's view. Simon implies that Kafka has been maligned and we, cheated. But faithfulness frequently comes off as badly for Simon as does unfaithfulness. For example, Simon's review of Sidney Lumet's *Long Day's Journey into Night*:[2]

> Here a very great play has not been translated to the screen but reverently put behind glass—it matters little whether the plate glass around the stuffed fauna of museums or the glass of lenses encasing live theatre in inanimate images. . . . The problem is that a stage masterpiece can be put on the screen only if the author or some scenarist of genius recreates it in cinematic terms. Here, out of monumental but pedestrian veneration, we have characters and camera pacing restlessly around a small enclosure like so many caged panthers, or, in the case of Ralph Richardson, polar bears. . . . [Lumet's] endlessly receding camera . . . merely draws attention to unresolved incompatibilities between two art forms . . . neither peripheral pluses nor minuses can much affect the respectful leadenness at the center.

[1]John Simon, *Private Screenings* (New York: Berkley, 1971), pp. 68–69.
[2]*Ibid*, pp. 51–52.

The double bind Simon imposes is almost marital: to be unfaithful is to be a heel and to be faithful, dull. Condemnation comes not because a film does something but rather because of what a film does not do; Simon has expectations so rigorous that sins of omission are inevitable. I am not claiming the films are masterpieces; both are flawed. But Simon's attitude prevented him from seeing that Welles' film hardly attempts Kafka at all but rather is a remarkably original presentation of a Camus-style existential rebel caught in a Kafkaesque world comprised of *Symboliste* paranoid nightmares and Gestapo memories, seen as actuality. I never expected Welles to do Kafka straight; what I wanted to know is what Welles would make *after* brooding about Kafka. I see about twenty-five very original minutes in *The Trial*. On Lumet, Simon is more accurate: the film *is* slow. But so is the play. My buttocks cringe at mere mention of the title. No matter: buttocks and brains are as far apart as ordinary movie fare and Lumet's treatment of O'Neil. There just isn't any way of doing *Journey* in the usual movie terms of Chase, Kissyface, and Shootemdead. *Journey* is about being stuck in a place with a junky, a juicer, and a loudmouthed charlatan, but it's the only family you've got. Except for a *very* few adaptations like *Journey* there are *no* honest treatments of family disintegration in American film. Lumet attempts not only to tell it "like it is"—He tells it "where it is," that is to say, in a remarkably unmovielike house. Lumet put over two hours of attempted honesty on the screen and (if my memory and research are correct) that was the only time a commercial American film attempted unleavened naturalism in that year (1962). I wish a film of equally serious intent and execution had been made from an original script; instinctively I would rather praise the seriousness of non-adapted films. I will, however, willingly accept good serious films wherever I can get them and, if it is the medium of film that has to be adapted to a play rather than a play adapted to film's conventions, I really see nothing wrong with that. Good drama is so hard to come by that it seems silly to complain if it doesn't look like the movies you're used to seeing. Sure, Sidney Lumet gave us a second-hand stage play. Second-hand is not the same thing as second-rate. Second-hand has to be judged by what it is that is second-hand. There's a lot of difference between a second-hand Rolls Royce in good shape and a second-hand sandwich. The Lumet *Journey* resembles the former a lot more than it does the latter.

I wonder how much our sniffing at adaptations stems from our desire to keep movies at a *kitsch* level? We prefer movies in their place and enjoy keeping them there. For example, this story by George Garrett:[3]

---

[3]George Garrett, "Don't Make Waves," in *Man and the Movies*, ed. W. R. Robinson (Baltimore: Penguin, 1969), p. 246.

> Story is that when Peter Lorre first came to this country and did his first, successful picture, he was asked by the Big Boss what he wanted to do next. He suggested *Crime and Punishment*. Boss said: "Gimme a one-page synopsis and we'll see." Lorre looked around studio until he found a near moron working in the accounting office. Offered the man fifty bucks if he could deliver a one-page synopsis of *Crime and Punishment* the next day. Just skimming, hitting the high spots. Done. The synopsis read like an old-fashioned thriller (truth in that). Boss read it and, in those days when the Industry was prospering and they were making four or five times as many pictures as they do now (though no more *good* ones), Boss says to get started. Picture was almost finished before Boss got around to reading the "property" and realized, raging, he had been had.

I enjoy Garrett's little tale immensely. The crassness, vulgarity, and pragmatic lunacy of Hollywood is fully a part of movie mythology. But Garrett's story does reinforce our literary snobbery, our sense of difference between what is appropriate to literature and what, to film. Snobbery seldom works against films from a popular genre tradition. When we go to a gangster film we slum along, wantonly craving a good wallow in precisely what the "Boss" is used to delivering. But when movies get "uppity" —as they frequently do when they are adaptations—the Garrett-type tale comes into force and functions in the same way as an ethnic or racial joke. We want to keep Hollywood secure as a singing-and-dancing place that is crass-but-happy. Kael is right; "trashy" is a word we relish if we love movies. We would be offended if Lorre's "Boss" had gotten "pretentious" enough to really have a go at adapting *Crime and Punishment*. Though we expect and demand high-quality adaptations our sense of propriety is a little bit offended when we do get them.

Dostoyevski Meets The Boss is not apt to be a masterpiece, but it might have some very unique minutes in it. Eisenstein tells us that "A" plus "B" can (if the two collide hard enough) equal "C." When two radically disparate entities collide the result is a third entity with properties not contained in either original. The process of adaptation is, like the process of Eisensteinian montage, a matter of bisociation. As Arthur Koestler points out, bisociation is the core process in both humor and creativity. Sometimes the attempt to adapt books into films produces the ludicrous. At other times it is fair to say that adaptation is montage writ large. I disagree with conventional bisociation theory, however, in my assessment of the effects of collisions. The originals are altered, at least after a time: films and books have a social and historical dimension. There are four reasons adaptations are good for literature, and five why they are good for film. First, the literary.

One. Movies work as introductions to books. Books sell better if they have been filmed, and read better, because the film aids the imagination.

Books (and their authors) can use all the help they can get. A movie is a ninety-minute free "ad" circulated to millions of people. What's more, the movie people *pay* to advertise books. Advertisement tends to make a book into a temporary folk-myth, or undergraduate cult piece. That social importance is otherwise virtually unattainable because of the difficulties of advertising books by ordinary methods. Movies make books "stand out" as important and, secondarily, remind us that dramatic literature was meant to be acted.

Two. Movies help get books out of college classrooms and into the streets where they can do some good. There is a sense in which literature is defused by its respectability. Shakespeare's original popularity was attained in a theatre in London's red-light district; his audience had in it whores and pickpockets and vagabonds. Dickens circulated originally by means of newspaper serialization; his work was by no means designed as the subject of seminars. Literature loses its "presence," its virility, when given no other environment than library or classroom; movie adaptations help restore literature's significance. I have a great deal more faith in the potency of a book first encountered via a movie adaptation than in its power if it is first encountered in a college classroom.

Three. Movies help restore literature's links with its past. The modern novel and modern theatre have gone experimental and thereby rejected the easy-access melodramatic modes of popular Victorian drama and fiction, modes which connect literature to its roots in popular storytelling. Movies are, in an important sense, the extension of Victorian melodrama. The joycean-faulknerian modernist novel, left to its own devices, would leave us all brain, and with restricted carotid and jugular at that. Movies connect us with literature's gutty past, a past which, like it or not, is necessary to the nourishment even of the brainy present. Were I to be isolated on a desert island for a month, I would take along Joyce's *Ulysses*, but that book is a hell of a way to spend Saturday night.

Four. Movies help make writers self-conscious, nervous, and aggressively experimental. Movies are, after all, a co-opting medium, a great middle-class sponge of ideas, plots, and characters. Writers hate being co-opted; they hate the fact that movies can reach audiences better than books; they hate taking money to see their creative offspring gang-raped in a screenwriters' conference room; they hate the formulaic-cliché side of Hollywood. I tend to think that hate helps reinforce the paranoiac love of romantic individuality necessary to literary genius. Except for Joyce and Dos Passos, who loved movies, just about everyone involved in inventing literary modernism hated film. Dislike of the movies has been useful to the advance of literature. The whole Lawrencean-Joycean-Millerian thrust of modern literature has been to explore the dangerous, to keep from being co-opted by the *kitsch* trade, to stay authentic. I believe film has kept modern literature pure by producing adaptations which serve as cautionary tales about what will happen to your work if you sell out, if you popularize. Reason four of course contradicts reason three, but that contradiction points to the fact that movies, by carrying on literature's popular traditions, free serious writers from having to carry on those traditions themselves.

The five reasons why adaptations are good for movies are less subtle than the reasons adaptations are good for books. The first reason is so unsubtle I blush to mention it. Books are almost the only source of intelligence to be found in Los Angeles County. They *are* the only source of new ideas. I am not trying to offend movie lovers. I am merely trying to describe the process of making a commercial film. Films are not written; they are produced. A book can start with a tantalizing image which slowly grows until it becomes a novel. But a Hollywood film starts with a producer wanting to make a movie, then deciding what sort of movie he wants to make, and then going out and getting the materials, "properties" and personnel to do the job. To get the money to make a film, a producer must convince his backers that the odds are good for making a profit. There are only two ways of doing that: dominoes and adaptations. In dominoes, the producer shows that his movie is just like other money-making movies and will therefore topple audience resistance. Lining up stars, genre, plotline, theme, and approach, the producer attempts to cash in on a proven formula. The only other way is adaptations, where the fact that a book sold well proves that an audience exists for something outside the formula. It's a choice between Lumiere's train coming into the station one more time, but *this* time with *two headlights* to make it *really* exciting!!) and the adaptation. That choice being a little too much for financiers to make, producers frequently make a synthesis of formulaic elements with adapted story-material and, in the resulting films, create successes which then can be formulized and mixed with new adaptation-material in an ever-evolving way.

Two. Literature provides raw material for film. Even if filmmakers wanted to work purely from formulaic, non-literary sources, they couldn't. Film is an industrial institution with raw-material needs far beyond the native resources of Hollywood. Literature is a source of high-grade ore which can be cheaply turned into "product."

Three. Adaptations keep the middle class in shape. The middle class has always relied on being able to co-opt fringe fantasies; the ability to co-opt is necessary to its survival. Hollywood, as the mouthpiece of middle-classness, must be able to co-opt whatever artistic ideas are new and dangerous, if middle-class fantasies are to be kept safe. By turning dangerous books into Consumer Romance (the genre which subsumes most Hollywood genres) our institutions are protected. To someone like me with two cars and a banking habit, it is very reassuring to know Hollywood is protecting us. In an age in which Blacks have *Ebony* and the Women's movement has Virginia Slims, one ought not let literature run loose, beyond the bourgeois pale.

Four. Adaptations present film with technical challenges. Film, more than any other medium, depends on technical flexibility. Film technology is, as a standardized system, only as good as it has to be; adaptations, by presenting technical problems, help keep the equipment from rigidifying. I don't think we would have the sound film if it were not for the desire to put adapted plays and dialogue-dependent novels onto film. The widely variegated conventions of the novel have dictated the use of adaptable equipment for novel adaptations. Technical advances allow the art to advance.

Five. Literature gives filmmakers an inferiority complex. Culturally and in terms of respectability, the novel and theatre are ranked above the cinema. Without the adaptation to keep literature's quality-standards clearly in view, Hollywood's anti-intellectual biases would be given freer reign. The social dimension is important in the production of art. The first wish of the producer or director is, of necessity, to make money; he has to do that to keep working. But the *nouveaux-riches* have a compulsion to legitimize themselves, to social-climb above the level of money-grubbers. Becoming artists or backing artistic projects is, for the filmmaker, the route to respectability. The process is no different than the way the bourgeoisie usually buys its way into the aristocracy, but when a filmmaker social-climbs, we benefit.

The five reasons for film lovers to be grateful for the adaptation are, like the reasons given for literature-lovers, both contradictory and overlapping. That is precisely because the marriage of literature and film has nothing to do with logic as philosophy departments teach it; rather, it has to do with the irrational logics of economics, art history, and the processes of creation. The forces the adaptation sets in motion are by no means conducive to a happy marriage between book culture and the film world; the opposite is the case. But we benefit from the lousy marriage between literature and film, a marriage in which the battleground is, often as not, the process of adaptation. All good marriages more or less resemble one another. It is the bad ones which are interesting and from which grow offspring strong enough and violent enough to create new directions in evolution.

I have repeatedly argued that adaptations advance the art of film. To give all the examples available would be to write yet one more film history. I would like, however, to mention a few films for those who, like myself, have difficulty recalling specific works while reading essays awash with theory. First a list of scenes and what I think is important in them.

No order or organization is intended. The graveyard scene in *Great Expectations* by David Lean does the best job of its period at treating the fear of a kid. Lean's desert stuff in *Lawrence of Arabia* and his snow scenes in *Zhivago* still amaze me. Lean chooses books with that kind of epic landscape to them and then tries to do with lenses and landscape what the authors did with words. Magnificent results. Nearly as memorable: the flood in Ken Miles' *The Virgin and the Gipsy*. I've never seen anything like it in film; it follows the book closely, though. In *Women in Love* the two men wrestling, Birkin in the woods naked, and Gudrun's odd ballet with the cattle provide lyric moments totally original to film. *The Hireling* does the best job in film history of presenting lower class pride. *Jules and Jim* gives us an ironic mode of narration new in film. *Blow-Up* takes the cinema into mental ranges it (or *Blow-Up's* maker, Antonioni) had not reached before. The witch scenes in Polanski's *Macbeth* gives us the human body as no filmmaker had previously the guts to show it. Peter Brook's *King Lear* does things with cold and stormy weather beyond anything else in film history. Peter Hall's *Midsummer Night's Dream* proves that the techniques used in *Marienbad* could be made coherent by a lucid text; Hall does what Resnais does, but so smoothly that audiences don't even notice anything's offbeat. *Adrift* by Jan Kadar makes the cinema as sophisticated at handling consciousness as is the novel. Last, one should mention *This Sporting Life*, which has the best subjective violence and pain I have ever seen in an "action" film. David Storey's novel is about a man who feels flaming lungs and battered ribs and broken teeth every time he goes to make a living at rugby. Storey's screenplay and Lindsay Anderson's directing turn the subjective anguish of a professional jock into montage and sound track combinations more effective than anything in "original" action-genre films I have seen. Is it odd that adaptations are frequently the best examples of genre-related streams like the "action" picture? I think not. Originals like Storey's novel force the director into finding techniques beyond the ordinary conventions of cinema. When the directors are as talented as Anderson, extraordinary films are the result.

I am not arguing that extraordinary films are not made by means other than adapting books, or that films from original scripts are not apt to be innovative. Though it has been convenient in this brief essay to equate film with Hollywood, that equation has never been true. In Europe the traditions of film are different from those in America and one encounters individual directors like Bergman and Fellini who need no help from literature in order to create quality cinema. Even in America independently-produced films somehow manage to get made; those films are frequently from original scripts and frequently provide cutting edges for film history (I am thinking of Cassavetes). But creators like Bergman,

Fellini, and Cassavetes are rare and are exceptions to the rule that without adaptation, cinema would be a phenomenally illiterate art form. By illiterate I mean not only unaware of literature; I mean dumb. The modes which Hollywood has succeeded in formulating into genres are usually part of what Northrop Frye calls "romance." Romance is characterized by its structure, the quest, and by its trait of summerness; only one of the seasons of man will fit into it. Romantic genres tend toward shallowness: musical, gangster, detective, and young-love-makes-happy-family formulaic stories generally involve a quest for nothing deeper than the good bourgeois life. Romance is a pleasant genre. There just isn't much range or depth to it. For depth the cinema relies on its masters and independents—its Bergmans and Cassaveteses—and on adaptations. Bergman's depth is greater than that of any adaptation I have ever seen. But Bergman is unique. What the adaptation helps do is to deepen the average depth to the point where an intelligent person can with regularity go to the cinema and not be restricted to skimming the surfaces of existence.

Ideally the cinema would be created by genius directors working from original scripts they thought up themselves. But that ideal assumes the existence of a sufficient quantity of those geniuses, and it assumes a degree of production integrity simply not extant today. Today an original script is a hired script designed to exploit a currently popular star, a currently popular genre and a currently popular theme. The ideal world is one hell of a walk from the movie world as it now exists, so we are faced with a choice between trying to criticize on the basis of phantom desires and learning to appreciate what is best about movies as they now exist. I prefer working with the realities of film, and think it is important to probe what it is that makes good movies good. It is for the purpose of praising reality's excellences that it might be useful to propose a *Politique des Adaptations*, a policy designed explicitly to promote analysis of films adapted from books.

A policy is not a theory. It does not say that in the best of all worlds one would even want movies to be adaptations. It does not form a basis for the pretentious to love the second-rate or for the second-rate to love the pretentious. Rather it insists—like the *Politique des Auteurs* before it—that the business of movie criticism is to find ways of describing what makes good movies good. The auteurists found a number of good directors working in popular genres who could impose their intelligence on hack formats. Further the auteurists found ways of talking about intelligent popular directors, and got otherwise neglected films to be taken seriously. I think the adaptation is as or more important in film history than the *film d'auteur*. What I envision as the practice of an adaptations policy is no more or less than a revamping of film history by reexamining the sources of film's growth as an art form. Each time film is seen to advance, three questions should be asked. What does a film owe (directly or indirectly) to works or kinds of literature or drama? What does a film owe to film history? What syntheses, breakthroughs, and new forms come from the rubbing together or collision of a film's component cultures? Carried out vigorously *Une Politique des Adaptations* just might make film critics examine their values and the values of the works they admire. I am quite sure that old notions of cinema's uniqueness as an art form are bound to fall and that new masterpieces, previously unrecognized, will be discovered. And I am sure that the adaptation's contribution to film's uniqueness will be better recognized. I do not believe we can afford to continue to belittle the adaptation. To do so would be to distort a good part of the meaning of cinema's evolution and to ignore the true genius of cinema as a synthetic art form.

[1975]

MARTIN C. BATTESTIN

Osborne's Tom Jones: Adapting a Classic

. . . Analogy is the key. To judge whether or not a film is a successful adaptation of a novel is to evaluate the skill of its makers in striking analogous attitudes and in finding analogous rhetorical techniques. From this point of view Osborne and Richardson produced in *Tom Jones* one of the most successful and imaginative adaptations in the brief history of film. This, as we have seen, is less true with regard to the authorial attitudes and ultimate thematic intentions of the two works. The real genius of the film as adaptation is in its brilliantly imaginative imitation of the *art* of the novel. Those "gimmicks" that so much surprised and delighted audiences may be seen as technical analogues of Fielding's own most distinctive devices.

Consider, for example, the opening sequence of the film. Before the title and credits we are presented with a rapid succession of scenes done in affected mimicry of the manner of the silent film, with subtitles supplying both commentary and dialogue (even Mrs. Wilkins' "aah!" as she sees Allworthy in his nightshirt), and with John Addison's spirited harpsichord setting the mood in the manner of the upright of the old "flicker" days. The device serves several practical purposes, of course: exposition which required the better part of two books in the novel is presented here swiftly and economically; a playful comic tone is at once established; and the reminiscence of the earliest era of the cinema also serves to remind us that Fielding's book appeared at a comparable moment in the history of that other peculiarly modern genre, the novel. Less obviously, in the use of outdated acting styles, exaggerated reactions and posturing, and sub-titles, Richardson and Osborne have translated into the medium of the cinema two aspects of Fielding's technique which contribute to the comic effect and distance. The overstated acting of the silent-film era is analo-gous to what may be called the "Hogarthian" manner (Fielding himself often made the comparison) of characterization in the novel. Even after spoken dialogue has been introduced (after the credits) and the need for pantomime is no longer present, Richardson continues to elicit heightened and hyperbolic performances from his actors—a style which, as in Hogarth and Fielding, serves not only to amuse, as caricature does, but also to reveal and accentuate the essential natures of the characters. As Fielding declared in *Joseph Andrews* (III, i), he describes "not men, but manners; not an individual, but a species." Richardson's actors rarely behave in the under-stated, naturalistic manner of the conventional film: smiles become leers, glances become ogles, gestures are heightened into stances, posturings. Similarly Fielding's characters, like Hogarth's, verge on caricature: they do not ask, as Moll Flanders or Clarissa Harlowe or Dorothea Brooke or Emma Bovary asks, to be accepted as real people, but rather as types and emblems of human nature; they have the reality of symbol rather than of fact.

Just as the miming of the actors during the opening sequence estab-lishes the hyperbolic style of the performances throughout, so Osborne's initial use of subtitles prepares us for the spoken commentary of the nar-rator, whose voice is the first we hear in the film and who will accompany us throughout as an invisible guide and observer. Osborne's commentator is a clever adaptation of Fielding's celebrated omniscient narrator, whose presence is constantly felt in *Tom Jones*, describing the action, making apposite observations on the characters' motives and deeds, entertaining us with his wit and learning, controlling our attitudes and responses. It has been remarked that the most important "character" in Fielding's novel is the author-narrator himself, whose genial and judicious spirit pervades the entire work, presiding providentially over the world of the novel and reminding us at every point that the creation we behold is his own. He it is who, more than any character in the story itself—more than Tom, more even than Allworthy—provides the moral center of the book. Osborne's commentator functions correspondingly: when first we see Tom, now a full-grown young scamp prowling for nocturnal sport in the woods, the over-voice of the commentator informs us that Tom is "far happier in the woods than in the study," that he is "as bad a hero as may be," that he is very much a member of the generation of Adam. Like Fielding's, Osborne's narrator presents his fallible hero, but the tone of wry amuse-ment and clear affection for the character controls our own attitude, estab-lishes that tolerant morality which makes Tom's peccadilloes far less important than his honest, warm-hearted zest for life. Though Fielding's narrator has the advantage of being continually present, Osborne's commentator is heard often enough so that his own relationship with the audience is sustained, and with each intrusion his own "personality" becomes more sharply defined: in matters of morality he is tolerant of everything but hypocrisy and inhumanity; he knows his Bible and his Ovid; he can recite a verse or apply an adage; he has a becoming sense of decorum in turning the camera away from a bawdy tumble in the bushes. Though necessarily a faint echo, he is very much the counterpart of Fielding's authorial voice.

A further effect of the constant intrusion of the narrator in both the film and the novel is to insure that the audience remains aloof and detached from the drama. We are never allowed to forget that this is not a slice of life, but only a tale told (or shown). The narrator is always there between the audience and the images on the screen, preventing the sort of empathic involvement which generally occurs in movies, or in fiction. Such detachment is very much a part of Fielding's comic purpose: his fictional world never pretends to be an imitation of life in any realistic sense, but is offered to us as a consciously contrived and symbolic representation of human nature and society. We are asked to behold it from a distance, at arm's length, as it were, to enjoy it and to learn from it.

The use of type characters and a self-conscious narrator are, moreover, only two of the means by which Fielding achieves this comic distance. The style of *Tom Jones* is itself highly mannered, not unlike the artful compositions of Hogarth, and it is often deliberately "rhetorical," not unlike the poetic diction of Pope and Gay. To reproduce this feature of Fielding's book, Osborne and Richardson similarly flaunt every conceivable device in the rhetoric of their own medium. Just as Fielding indulges in amplifications, ironies, similes, mock-heroics, parodies, etc., so the film exploits for comic effect a circusful of wipes, freezes, flips, speed-ups, narrowed focuses—in short, the entire battery of camera tricks. The effect of this is again to call attention to the skill of the artist, to the intelligence manipulating the pen or the camera, as the case may be. Particularly remarkable in this respect is the most celebrated of Richardson's tricks—his deliberate violation of the convention that actors must never take notice of the camera, because to do so is to dispel the illusion of life on the screen, to call attention to the fact that what the audience is seeing is a play being acted before a camera. But Richardson's actors are constantly winking at us, appealing to us to settle their disputes, thrusting their hats before our eyes, etc. The effect, paradoxically, is not to involve us in their dramas, but to remind us of the presence of the camera and, consequently, to prevent us, in our darkened seats, from achieving that customary magical identification with the vicarious world unfolding on the screen. In just this way Fielding's rhetorical somersaults keep us aware that his own fictional world, like the macrocosm itself, is being supervised and manipulated by a controlling and ultimately benign intelligence. This, though tacitly achieved, is the supreme statement of his comedy.

The brilliance of Osborne's adaptation may be seen not only in the general handling of character, narrator, and rhetoric, but in his treatment of particular scenes from the novel as well. Certainly one of the most delightful and significant of these is the sequence in which Tom, concerned that he has got Molly Seagrim with child, pays an unexpected visit to her in her garret bedroom, only to find that he has been sharing her favors with the philosopher Square. At the critical moment a curtain falls away and the august metaphysician—who has made a career of denouncing the body—stands revealed in his hiding place, clad only in a blush and Molly's nightcap. In both the novel and the film this scene is shaped as a sort of parabolic dramatization of Fielding's satiric theory and practice: satire, as he had pointed out in the preface to *Joseph Andrews*, deals with "the true Ridiculous," which was his term for affectation and pretense— for those whose deeds did not match their professions. As a graphic enactment of this comic theory—the hilarious revelation of the naked truth behind the drapery—the exposure of Square is the quintessential scene in all of Fielding's fiction.

But the most impressive single instance of Osborne's and Richardson's genius in translating Fielding's style, attitudes, and intentions into their own medium is the famous eating scene at Upton. It may surprise those whose memory of the novel is vague that virtually every gesture and every grimace in the film sequence—and, indeed, its basic metaphorical equation of lust and appetite—originated with Fielding. The passage in question is Book IX, Chapter V, entitled "An apology for all heroes who have good stomachs, with a description of a battle of the amorous kind." The chapter begins with the reluctant admission that even the most accomplished of heroes have more of the mortal than the divine about them: even Ulysses must eat. When Jones and Mrs. Waters sit down to satisfy their appetites—he by devouring three pounds of beef to break a fast of twenty-four hours, she by feasting her eyes on her companion's handsome face—Fielding proceeds to define love, according to the modern understanding of the word, as "that preference which we give to one kind of food rather than to another." Jones loved his steak and ale; Mrs. Waters loved Jones. During the course of the meal the temptress brings to bear on her companion "the whole artillery of love," with an efficacy increasing in direct proportion to Jones's progress in appeasing his hunger. Fielding, invoking the Graces, describes the lady's artful seduction of his hero in the amplified, hyperbolic terms of a mock-epic battle: "First, from two lovely blue eyes, whose bright orbs flashed lightning at their discharge, flew forth two pointed ogles: but happily for our hero, hit only a vast piece of beef which he was then conveying into his plate, and harmless spent their force. . . ." Mrs. Waters heaves an epic sigh, but this is lost in "the coarse bubbling of some bottled ale." The assault continues as, "having planted her right eye sidewise against Mr. Jones, she shot from its corner a most penetrating glance. . . ." Perceiving the effect of this ogle, the fair one coyly lowers her glance and then, having made her meaning clear even to the unassuming Jones, lifts her eyes again and discharges "a voley of small charms at once from her whole countenance" in an affectionate smile which our hero receives "full in his eyes." Jones, already staggering, succumbs when his delicious adversary unmasks "the royal battery, by carelessly letting her handkerchief drop from her neck. . . ." No one who has seen the film will need to be reminded how brilliantly Joyce Redman and Finney conveyed, in images only, the sense of Fielding's metaphor of lust and appetite and how well Miss Redman visually rendered the epic sighs and ogles and leers of Mrs. Waters. This scene is not only the funniest in the film; it is a triumph of the art of cinematic translation. Both the form of the adaptation and the supremely comic effect could have been achieved in this way in no other genre: they are, in other words, the result of the collaborative exploitation (by writer, director, photographer, actors, and editor) of peculiarly cinematographic techniques—here, specifically, a series of close-ups arranged and controlled by expert cutting. An entirely verbal effect in the novel has been rendered in the film entirely in terms of visual images.

Consideration of the ways in which the film is a successful imitation of Fielding's novel can go no farther than this scene of amorous gastronomics at Upton. Let us turn, then, briefly, to an analysis of the film as a skillful work of art in its own right, for ultimately, of course, it is meant to be judged as such. Here perhaps it will be best to discuss those elements and techniques for which there is only the barest suggestion in the book. Most impressive of these is the use of visual contrasts in setting and situation for symbolic purposes. For instance, to establish at once the difference in nature between Jones and Blifil—the one free and wild and open-hearted, the other stiff and artful and cold—Osborne introduces each character in diametrically opposing situations. We first see Jones as he prowls in the wild woods at night, breaking the game laws and tumbling in the bushes with Molly: Tom is at home with the fox and the beaver; he returns the wink of an owl; and Molly, dark and dishevelled, flips a fern as she lures him to another kind of illicit sport. Blifil, on the other hand, is first seen in Allworthy's sun-drenched formal garden: he is dressed in formal frock coat and walks sedately, holding a book in his fastidious hands and obsequiously following those twin custodians of virtue and religion, the deist Square and Thwackum the divine. The contrast between Tom's two sweethearts, the profane and the sacred, is equally deliberate. After we have been shown another night scene of Tom and Molly among the bushes, the camera shifts abruptly to a bright, idyllic setting: we see Sophie's image reflected in a pond; swans swim gracefully about, and Sophie is as fair and white as they are. When Tom appears, bringing her a caged song bird (nature not wild, but tame and lovely), the lovers run from opposite sides of the water to meet at the center of a bridge. Sophie has been presented as the very image of purity and light, the proper emblem of that chastity of spirit which (in Fielding's story at least) Tom must learn to seek and find. The film is visually organized according to a scheme of such contrasts—Allworthy's formal estate with Western's sprawling, boisterous barnyard; Molly's disordered bedroom with Sophie's chaste boudoir. Even such a fundamental element as the color itself is varied in this way to signal the shift from the naturalness and simplicity of the country to the affectation and luxury, and man-made squalor, of London: the scenes in the country are done predominantly in greens and browns, and in black, grey, and white; but London is revealed in a shock of violent colors. The entry of Tom and Partridge into town is meant to recall the stark and vicious scenes of Hogarth's "Rake's Progress" and "Gin Lane." And soon thereafter the screen is flushed with reds, purples, and oranges as Tom enters the gaudy masquerade at Vauxhall, where he will meet Lady Bellaston.

Such contrasts are based, of course, on similar oppositions, thematic and structural, in the novel. For two of the film's most effective sequences, however, Osborne had scarcely any help from Fielding at all, and yet both these scenes serve independently to convey attitudes and themes consonant with Fielding's intentions and essential to the film Osborne is making. The first of these sequences is the stag hunt, for which there was no basis in the novel, except for the fact that Fielding represents Squire Western as almost monomaniacal in his devotion to the chase. In general effect the hunt serves a function similar to the shots at Western's licentious table manners or of the gastronomic encounter between Tom and Mrs. Waters: it serves, in other words, visually to emphasize the brutal, predatory, appetitive quality of life in the provinces two centuries ago. It is, as Osborne meant it to be, "no pretty Christmas calendar affair." No one who has seen this chase will forget the furious pace of it, the sadistic elation of the hunters—the lashing of horses, the spurt of crimson as spur digs into flesh, the tumbling of mounts and riders, the barnyard and the broken-necked goose trampled in the pursuit, the uncontrollable surge of the dogs as they tear the stag's throat out, and Western's triumphant display of the bloody prey. This, surely, is one of the most perfectly conceived and skillfully realized sequences in the film.

In sharp antithesis to the violence of this passage is the lyricism of the montage sequence portraying the courtship and deepening love of Tom and Sophie as Tom recovers from his broken arm on Western's estate. Richardson has achieved here a sense of arcadia—an unfallen, Edenic world of bright flowers and placid waters, of gaiety and innocence. The growing intimacy and communion of the lovers is expressed in a series of playful images in which their roles are interchanged or identified: first, Sophie poles Tom around the lake while he lolls and smokes a pipe, then their positions are reversed; Sophie appears on horseback followed by Tom awkwardly straddling an ass, then vice versa, then they both appear on the same horse; Sophie shaves Tom, and Tom later wades into mud chest-deep to fetch her a blossom. They sing, skip, and lark about together. When at length they do silently declare their love with a deep exchange of glances and a kiss, the tone of the sequence is softly modulated from the frivolous to the sincere. The entire passage is altogether brilliant, done with exquisite sensitivity and a nice control. Richardson has managed to communicate in a few frames skillfully juxtaposed the way it feels to fall in love. From this moment we can never doubt the rightness and warmth of Tom and Sophie's affection—not even when, afterwards, Tom will succumb to the temptations of Molly, Mrs. Waters, and the demi-rep Lady Bellaston.

It is pleasant to think of this film, a comic masterpiece of our new Age of Satire, standing in the same relation to Fielding's classic as, say, Pope's free imitations of Horace stand in relation to their original. In an impressive variety of ways, both technical and thematic, Osborne and Richardson's *Tom Jones* is a triumph in the creative adaptation of a novel to the very different medium of the cinema. Ultimately, of course, the film is not the novel, nor, doubtless, was it meant to be. It does capture an essential part of Fielding's spirit and intention in its depiction of the sweep and quality of eighteenth-century English life, in its celebration of vitality and an open heart, and in its ridicule of vanity and sham. But Osborne's vision is narrower than Fielding's: this is a function partly of the necessary limitations of scope in the film, partly of commercial pressures precluding "moral seriousness" in a work designed to entertain millions, and partly of the different *Weltanschauung* of the twentieth century. We are not left with a sense of Fielding's balanced and ordered universe, nor are we made aware of the lesson Fielding meant to impart in the progress of his lovable, but imperfect hero. And because the vision behind the film is different in kind, even those techniques of characterization, narration, and rhetoric which have been so effectively adapted from the novel do not serve, as they do in Fielding, as the perfect formal expression of theme. Despite these limitations and discrepancies, however, Osborne's *Tom Jones* is a splendid illustration of what can be done in the intelligent adaptation of fiction to the screen.

[1967]

2

Film and Theater

The action moves from within the artificial setting of "This Wooden O" to the realism of an exterior location in Sir Laurence Oliver's 1944 version of Shakespeare's *Henry V* (figures 2.1 and 2.2).

Figure 2.1   Museum of Modern Art/Film Stills Archive.

Figure 2.2   Museum of Modern Art/Film Stills Archive.

Three adaptations of Shakespeare's Hamlet *(figures 2.3, 2.4, 2.5).*

Figure 2.3   This 1922 version of Hamlet *(starring Asta Nielsen) relies on conventional theatrical staging, simple lines of composition, and the perspective of a normal lens shooting from slightly low angle (an audience's angle of perception during a stage drama). Courtesy, The Museum of Modern Art/Film Stills Archive.*

Figure 2.4 Mass, lighting, and deep focus are used to comment upon Hamlet's relationship to the king in Sir Laurence Olivier's 1948 adaptation of Hamlet. *Museum of Modern Art/Film Stills Archive.*

Figure 2.5 Another sense of Hamlet's relationship to the king is conveyed in Griggori Kozintsev's 1964 adaptation; the courtiers and the tapestry combine with costuming and placement to establish meaning. Museum of Modern Art/Film Stills Archive.

OUTTAKES

The motion picture is filmed theater; it is an extension of the literary art of the stage, with some limitations removed.

GEORGE BERNARD SHAW

I saw how film technique could set me free in so many ways I still feel bound down—free to realize a real Elizabethan treatment and get the whole meat out of a theme. . . . As for the objection to the "talkies" that they do away with the charm of the living, breathing actor, that leaves me completely cold, "the play's the thing," and I think in time plays will get across for what their authors intended much better in this medium than in the old.

EUGENE O'NEILL

To be successfully adapted to the screen a play must give up its characteristic unity.

A. R. FULTON

The novel is concerned with *what has happened.* The theater asks *what is about to happen.* The screen tells us *what is happening* is all-important because it is not isolated—it is part of the past and future.

JOHN HOWARD LAWSON

It was a theatrical sin when the old-fashioned stage actor was rendered unimportant by his scenery. But the motion picture actor is but the mood of the mob or the landscape or the department store behind him, reduced to a single hieroglyphic.

VACHEL LINDSAY, 1915

Cinema, even where fantasy is introduced, is much more realistic than the stage. Especially in an historical picture, the setting, the costume, and the way of life represented have to be accurate. Even a minor anachronism is intolerable. On the stage much more can be overlooked or forgiven; and indeed, an excessive care for accuracy of historical detail can become burdensome and distracting. In watching a stage performance, the member of the audience is in direct contact with the actor playing a part. In looking at a film, we are much more passive; as audience, we contribute less. We are seized with the illusion that we are observing an actual event, or at least a series of photographs of the actual event; and nothing must be allowed to break this illusion. Hence the precise attention to detail.

T. S. ELIOT

And the film has, quite specifically, nothing to do with the drama. It is narrative in pictures. That these faces are present to your sight does not prevent their greatest effectiveness from being in its nature epic; and in this sphere, if in any, the film approaches literary art. It is much too genuine to be theater. The stage setting is based upon delusion, the scenery of the film is nature itself, just as the fancy stimulated by the story creates it for the reader. Nor have the protagonists in a film the bodily presence and actuality of the human figures in the drama. They are living shadows. They speak not, they are not, they merely were—and were precisely as you see them—and that is narrative. The film possesses a technique of recollection, of psychological suggestion, a mastery of detail in men and in things, from which the novelist, though scarcely the dramatist, might learn much. That the Russians, who have never been great dramatists, are supreme in this field, rests, without any doubt in my mind, upon their narrative skill.

THOMAS MANN

At an early point in cinema's history, filmmakers attempted to capture stage drama on film, but early adapters relied on a dramatic, rather than a cinematic, visual aesthetic. For that they have never been forgiven. In their hands, film remained merely a medium used to make a visual record of a play. As filmmakers became aware of their medium's potentials for storytelling, the relationship between films and plays became more subtle and complex.

Critical responses to the film-theater liaison experienced a parallel genesis. Early critics witnessed efforts to reproduce, in an entirely visual medium, dramatic works which were created for the predominantly verbal situation of the stage. Most early adaptations were one reel long (less than twenty minutes) with titles furnishing all "spoken" content. Critics could only dismiss such condensed efforts, perhaps pausing occasionally to compliment the motions of an interesting performance. Nevertheless, filmmakers still produced these adaptations in quantity; by 1920, for example, there were at least nine versions of *Hamlet*, including one by Melies and two with female Hamlets (Sarah Bernhardt and Asta Nielsen). The coming of sound allowed the use of the words of the original, and critics could begin focusing on the relationships between spoken words (as well as other sounds) and visual performances. And the audio-visual experiences of stage and of screen could be compared. The essays in this section include responses from writers at various time periods (scholars, active critics, and creative writers), revealing the spectrum of available attitudes toward film and theater.

In a short statement, Henry Arthur Jones, a British dramatist, sums up the response of much of the intelligentsia to film during the early 1920s. ("The Dramatist and the Photoplay" appeared in 1921; sound did not come to the movies until 1928.) Jones posits that film cannot provide the pleasures available in literature. Words furnish man's noblest form of expression, and words were unavailable to the moviegoer in 1921. At the same time Jones is taken with film's ability to focus audience attention and to achieve dramatic speed through editing.

Writing five years before Jones, Hugo Munsterberg provides the careful analysis of the scholar. Munsterberg blends a consideration of aesthetics with the psychological implications of the two forms, taking into account the work and audience views, as well as the dynamics of the process of audience perception. Concerned chiefly with the differences between the events of reality and the unreality of events perceived on stage and screen, Munsterberg concludes that film provides an art form farther from reality than does the stage. He finds, for example, that while theater is controlled by nature's laws of causality, the camera defeats laws of space, time, and causality. Among the other issues Munsterberg raises is that of which form can best develop character and which must rely on types, a question addressed by several later thinkers.

Writing in 1937, Allardyce Nicoll reaches conclusions quite different from Munsterberg's. Nicoll believes that effective stage characters are types, while cinema relies on individualization. Where Munsterberg finds film the form most stimulating to the individual imagination, Nicoll proposes that dramatic illusion is the chief challenge to the imagination and that film audiences think they are seeing reality revealed by a camera incapable of lying (despite the audience's intellectual knowledge that the camera can deceive). Both men are also interested in the need for psychological or critical distance, but again the two men reach different conclusions. Nicoll's book, *Film and Theater*, remains the most comprehensive work on the subject, although many of his conclusions have been challenged by more recent thinkers.

Foremost among Nicoll's challengers is Susan Sontag. She points out the obvious but highly important notion that cinema is both a medium and an art, while theater is only an art and not a medium. She also insists that there is no reason to insist on a single model for film, a critical error made by far too many film theorists who would justify one kind of film at the expense of others. Avoiding dogmatic statements, and broad, unsupported generalizations about each form, Sontag leads the reader to understand more fully the complexity and importance of the relationship between film and theater. (Her argument is also directed against Edwin Panofsky's classic essay "Style and Medium in the Motion Pictures." This essay is reprinted in Section 6, "Message, Medium, and Literary Art.")

Unlike Sontag, Andre Bazin does not seek to challenge Nicoll directly; instead Bazin considers the two art forms within his developing aesthetic. Consequently, he takes up issues somewhat different from those addressed by Sontag and Nicoll. Premising his ideas on the objectivity of cinema, Bazin considers the images realized in both forms. Unlike the visual reproductions found in art forms such as painting or sculpture, cinema makes a mold of light which Bazin suggests carries a kind of identity with the person or thing filmed. This identity leads him to explore the notion of "presence" in both cinema and theater. In addition to considering the formal relationships of film and theater, Bazin continues on to examine adaptation and what contributes to a successful adaptation, from decor to dialogue.

George Garrett offers the perspective of a contemporary creative writer. (He has written novels, film scripts, short stories, poems, and a play.) In his lively article, Garrett touches the problems a writer faces in films and plays, such as focusing the audience's attention and developing character. Like Munsterberg, he makes a case that "a large part of the experience of a movie is imaginative," but unlike Munsterberg he finds that the imaginative element lessens aesthetic distance. Finally, Garrett provides a light and entertaining amble through several of the problems faced by film and theater.

HENRY ARTHUR JONES

The Dramatist and
the Photoplay

The dramatist wins enduring renown by his dialogue, and by his dialogue alone. To write a successful play he must of course have other gifts and acquirements. Me must call in the scene-painter, the upholsterer, the costumer, the electrician, and other adjutants to help him to express himself. But his dialogue alone has permanent value; all the rest of his trappings are perishable. The difference between *Macbeth* or *Hamlet* and a stock melodrama is that *Macbeth* and *Hamlet* can be read and studied as literature. That is the reason they have held their place in our theater for three hundred years. That is also the chief reason why they often fail on our modern stage. They are literature. They demand serious thought and feeling from an audience. They ask for examination, and offer emotional and intellectual enjoyment on these grounds.

It is clear that the film cannot afford the quality and kind of pleasure that spoken drama can give—the pleasure of literature.

Again, the voice has always been the chief gift of the actor, his chief means of swaying his audience and stirring their emotions. It is mainly by the voice that the actor gets his finest and worthiest effects. What the dramatist has written falls dead upon the stage unless it is vitalized by the actor.

It is clear that, as the film play forbids the dramatist to use his chief and highest means of expression, so also it forbids the actor to use his chief and highest means of expression.

What balancing advantages and compensations has the film to offer to the actor and the dramatist? To the film actor and actress it offers universal, though not immortal, fame, by displaying their pictures in every city of the civilized world, perhaps in five hundred theaters on the same night. It further offers to star performers an enormous salary.

53

What are the advantages offered the dramatist? In the volume, variety, and impetus of its action—that is, in the very essence of drama—in its swift, vivid, multiple transformations, its startling command of contrasts, its power of concentration on valuable minutiae, its capacity for insinuation and flashing suggestion—in all these truly dramatic qualities the film play offers to the dramatist an infinitude of opportunity compared with the spoken drama.

Aristotle compared the limitations of the drama with the expanses of the epic. But, compared with the film, even the epic, the novel, becomes a tedious chronicler of events.

The film is a bungler at comedy, except of the rude and boisterous kind which Thalia reproves. But the film invites and welcomes Romance and Imagination and opens a large field for their exploits. Now, imagination, from Shakespeare downwards, is largely shut out from our modern stage, with its pert vulgarity and dictionary of slang. Tongue-tied already, and almost banished from the spoken drama, imagination may perhaps find a home in the film theater. She will be deprived of speech, but how rarely she is allowed to open her lips upon the regular stage! May not Imagination find utterance in the vast pictorial resources and devices of the film theater, throw her magic beams amongst its fascinating lights and shadows, and employ the quick vibrations and successions of the screen to tell larger stories of human life than are being told today upon the stage of the spoken drama.

[1921]

HUGO MUNSTERBERG

The Means of the Photoplay

We have now reached the point at which we can knot together all our threads, the psychological and the esthetic ones. If we do so, we come to the true thesis of this whole book. Our esthetic discussion showed us that it is the aim of art to isolate a significant part of our experience in such a way that it is separate from our practical life and is in complete agreement within itself. Our esthetic satisfaction results from this inner agreement and harmony, but in order that we may feel such agreement of the parts we must enter with our own impulses into the will of every element, into the meaning of every line and color and form, every word and tone and note. Only if everything is full of such inner movement can we really enjoy the harmonious cooperation of the parts. The means of the various arts, we saw, are the forms and methods by which this aim is fulfilled. They must be different for every material. Moreover the same material may allow very different methods of isolation and elimination of the insignificant and reenforcement of that which contributes to the harmony. If we ask now what are the characteristic means by which the photoplay succeeds in overcoming reality, in isolating a significant dramatic story and in presenting it so that we enter into it and yet keep it away from our practical life and enjoy the harmony of the parts, we must remember all the results to which our psychological discussion in the first part of the book has led us.

We recognized there that the photoplay, incomparable in this respect with the drama, gave us a view of dramatic events which was completely shaped by the inner movements of the mind. To be sure, the events in the photoplay happen in the real space with its depth. But the spectator feels that they are not presented in the three dimensions of the outer world, that they are flat pictures which only the mind molds

55

into plastic things. Again the events are seen in continuous movement; and yet the pictures break up the movement into a rapid succession of instantaneous impressions. We do not see the objective reality, but a product of our own mind which binds the pictures together. But much stronger differences came to light when we turned to the processes of attention, of memory, of imagination, of suggestion, of division of interest and of emotion. The attention turns to detailed points in the outer world and ignores everything else: the photoplay is doing exactly this when in the close-up a detail is enlarged and everything else disappears. Memory breaks into present events by bringing up pictures of the past; the photoplay is doing this by its frequent cut-backs, when pictures of events long past flit between those of the present. The imagination anticipates the future or overcomes reality by fancies and dreams; the photoplay is doing all this more richly than any chance imagination would succeed in doing. But chiefly, through our division of interest our mind is drawn hither and thither. We think of events which run parallel in different places. The photoplay can show in intertwined scenes everything which our mind embraces. Events in three or four or five regions of the world can be woven together into one complex action. Finally, we saw that every shade of feeling and emotion which fills the spectator's mind can mold the scenes in the photoplay until they appear the embodiment of our feelings. In every one of these aspects the photoplay succeeds in doing what the drama of the theater does not attempt.

If this is the outcome of esthetic analysis on the one side, of psychological research on the other, we need only combine the results of both into a unified principle: *the photoplay tells us the human story by overcoming the forms of the outer world, namely, space, time, and causality, and by adjusting the events to the forms of the inner world, namely, attention, memory, imagination, and emotion.*

We shall gain our orientation most directly if once more, under this point of view, we compare the photoplay with the performance on the theater stage. We shall not enter into a discussion of the character of the regular theater and its drama. We take this for granted. Everybody knows that highest art form which the Greeks created and which from Greece has spread over Asia, Europe, and America. In tragedy and in comedy from ancient times to Ibsen, Rostand, Hauptmann, and Shaw we recognize one common purpose and one common form for which no further commentary is needed. How does the photoplay differ from a theater performance? We insisted that every work of art must be somehow separated from our sphere of practical interests. The theater is no exception. The structure of the theater itself, the framelike form of the stage, the difference of light between stage and house, the stage setting and costuming, all inhibit in the audience the possibility of taking the action on the stage to be real life. Stage managers have sometimes tried the experiment of reducing those differences, for instance, keeping the audience also in a fully lighted hall, and they always had to discover how much the dramatic effect was reduced because the feeling of distance from reality was weakened. The photoplay and the theater in this respect are evidently alike. The screen too suggests from the very start the complete unreality of the events.

But each further step leads us to remarkable differences between the stage play and the film play. In every respect the film play is further away from the physical reality than the drama and in every respect this greater distance from the physical world brings it nearer to the mental world. The stage shows us living men. It is not the real Romeo and not the real Juliet; and yet the actor and the actress have the ringing voices of true people, breathe like them, have living colors like them, and fill physical space like them. What is left in the photoplay? The voice has been stilled: the photoplay is a dumb show. Yet we must not forget that this alone is a step away from reality which has often been taken in the midst of the dramatic world. Whoever knows the history of the theater is aware of the tremendous role which the pantomime has played in the development of mankind. From the old half-religious pantomimic and suggestive dances out of which the beginnings of the real drama grew to the fully religious pantomimes of medieval ages and, further on, to many silent mimic elements in modern performances, we find a continuity of conventions which make the pantomime almost the real background of all dramatic development. We know how popular the pantomimes were among the Greeks, and how they stood in the foreground in the imperial period of Rome. Old Rome cherished the mimic clowns, but still more the tragic pantomimics. "Their very nod speaks, their hands talk and their fingers have a voice." After the fall of the Roman empire the church used the pantomime for the portrayal of sacred history, and later centuries enjoyed very unsacred histories in the pantomimes of their ballets. Even complex artistic tragedies without words have triumphed on our present-day stage. L'Enfant Prodigue which came from Paris, Sumurun, which came from Berlin, Petroushka which came from Petrograd, conquered the American stage; and surely the loss of speech, while it increased the remoteness from reality, by no means destroyed the continuous consciousness of the bodily existence of the actors.

Moreover the student of a modern pantomime cannot overlook a characteristic difference between the speechless performance on the stage and that of the actors of a photoplay. The expression of the inner states, the whole system of gestures, is decidedly different: and here we might say that the photoplay stands nearer to life than the pantomime. Of course, the photoplayer must somewhat exaggerate his natural expression.

The whole rhythm and intensity of his gestures must be more marked than it would be with actors who accompany their movements by spoken words and who express the meaning of their thoughts and feelings by the content of what they say. Nevertheless the photoplayer uses the regular channels of mental discharge. He acts simply as a very emotional person might act. But the actor who plays in a pantomime cannot be satisfied with that. He is expected to add something which is entirely unnatural, namely a kind of artificial demonstration of his emotions. He must not only behave like an angry man, but he must behave like a man who is consciously interested in his anger and wants to demonstrate it to others. He exhibits his emotions for the spectators. He really acts theatrically for the benefit of the bystanders. If he did not try to do so, his means of conveying a rich story and a real conflict of human passions would be too meager. The photoplayer, with the rapid changes of scenes, has other possibilities of conveying his intentions. He must not yield to the temptation to play a pantomime on the screen, or he will seriously injure the artistic quality of the reel.

The really decisive distance from bodily reality, however, is created by the substitution of the actor's picture for the actor himself. Lights and shades replace the manifoldness of color effects and mere perspective must furnish the suggestion of depth. We traced it when we discussed the psychology of kinematoscopic perception. But we must not put the emphasis on the wrong point. The natural tendency might be to lay the chief stress on the fact that those people in the photoplay do not stand before us in flesh and blood. The essential point is rather that we are conscious of the flatness of the picture. If we were to see the actors of the stage in a mirror, it would also be a reflected image which we perceive. We should not really have the actors themselves in our straight line of vision; and yet this image would appear to us equivalent to the actors themselves, because it would contain all the depth of the real stage. The process which leads from the living men to the screen is more complex than a mere reflection in a mirror, but in spite of the complexity in the transmission we do, after all, see the real actor in the picture. The photograph is absolutely different from those pictures which a clever draughtsman has sketched. In the photoplay we see the actors themselves and the decisive factor which makes the impression different from seeing real men is not that we see the living persons through the medium of photographic reproduction but that this reproduction shows them in a flat form. The bodily space has been eliminated. We said once before that stereoscopic arrangements could reproduce somewhat this plastic form also. Yet this would seriously interfere with the character of the photoplay. We need there this overcoming of the depth, we want to have it as a picture only and yet as a picture which strongly suggests to us the actual depth of the real world. We want to keep the interest in the plastic world and want to be aware of the depth in which the persons move, but our direct object of perception must be without the depth. That idea of space which forces on us most strongly the idea of heaviness, solidity and substantiality must be replaced by the light flitting immateriality.

But the photoplay sacrifices not only the space values of the real theater; it disregards no less its order of time. The theater presents its plot in the time order of reality. It may interrupt the continuous flow of time without neglecting the conditions of the dramatic art. There may be twenty years between the third and the fourth act, inasmuch as the dramatic writer must select those elements spread over space and time which are significant for the development of his story. But he is bound by the fundamental principle of real time, that it can move only forward and not backward. Whatever the theater shows us now must come later in the story than that which it showed us in any previous moment. The strict classical demand for complete unity of time does not fit every drama, but a drama would give up its mission if it told us in the third act something which happened before the second act. Of course, there may be a play within a play, and the players on the stage which is set on the stage may play events of old Roman history before the king of France. But this is an enclosure of the past in the present, which corresponds exactly to the actual order of events. The photoplay, on the other hand, does not and must not respect this temporal structure of the physical universe. At any point the photoplay interrupts the series and brings us back to the past. We studied this unique feature of the film art when we spoke of the psychology of memory and imagination. With the full freedom of our fancy, with the whole mobility of our association of ideas, pictures of the past flit through the scenes of the present. Time is left behind. Man becomes boy; today is interwoven with the day before yesterday. The freedom of the mind has triumphed over the unalterable law of the outer world.

It is interesting to watch how playwrights nowadays try to steal the thunder of the photoplay and experiment with time reversals on the legitimate stage. We are esthetically on the borderland when a grandfather tells his grandchild the story of his own youth as a warning, and instead of the spoken words the events of his early years come before our eyes. This is, after all, quite similar to a play within a play. A very different experiment is tried in *Under Cover*. The third act, which plays on the second floor of the house, ends with an explosion. The fourth act, which plays downstairs, begins a quarter of an hour before the explosion. Here we have a real denial of a fundamental condition of the theater. Or if we stick to recent products of the American stage, we may think of *On Trial*, a play which perhaps comes nearest to a dramatic usurpation of the rights of the photoplay. We see the court scene and as one witness after another begins to give his testimony the courtroom is replaced by the scenes of the actions about which the witness is to report. Another clever play, *Between the Lines,* ends the first act with a postman bringing three letters from the three children of the house. The second, third, and fourth acts lead us to the three different homes from which the letters came and the action in the three places not only precedes the writing of the letters, but goes on at the same time. The last act, finally, begins with the arrival of the letters which tell the ending of those events in the three homes. Such experiments are very suggestive but they are not any longer pure dramatic art. It is always possible to mix arts. An Italian painter produces very striking effects by putting pieces of glass and stone and rope into his paintings, but they are no longer pure paintings. The drama in which the later event comes before the earlier is an esthetic barbarism which is entertaining as a clever trick in a graceful superficial play, but intolerable in ambitious dramatic art. It is not only tolerable but perfectly natural in any photoplay. The pictorial reflection of the world is not bound by the rigid mechanism of time. Our mind is here and there, our mind turns to the present and then to the past: the photoplay can equal it in its freedom from the bondage of the material world.

But the theater is bound not only by space and time. Whatever it shows is controlled by the same laws of causality which govern nature. This involves a complete continuity of the physical events: no cause without following effect, no effect without preceding cause. This whole natural course is left behind in the play on the screen. The deviation from reality begins with that resolution of the continuous movement which we studied in our psychological discussions. We saw that the impression of movement results from an activity of the mind which binds the separate pictures together. What we actually see is a composite; it is like the movement of a fountain in which every jet is resolved into numberless drops. We feel the play of those drops in their sparkling haste as one continuous stream of water, and yet are conscious of the myriads of drops, each one separate from the others. This fountainlike spray of pictures has completely overcome the causal world.

In an entirely different form this triumph over causality appears in the interruption of the events by pictures which belong to another series. We find this whenever the scene suddenly changes. The processes are not carried to their natural consequences. A movement is started, but before the cause brings its results another scene has taken its place. What this new scene brings may be an effect for which we saw no causes. But not only the processes are interrupted. The intertwining of the scenes which we have traced in detail is itself such a contrast to causality. It is as if different objects could fill the same space at the same time. It is as if the resistance of the material world had disappeared and the substances could penetrate one another. In the interlacing of our ideas we experience this superiority to all physical laws. The theater would not have even the technical means to give us such impressions, but if it had, it would have no right to make use of them, as it would destroy the basis on which the drama is built. We have only another case of the same type in those series of pictures which aim to force a suggestion on our mind. We have spoken of them. A certain effect is prepared by a chain of causes and yet when the causal result is to appear the film is cut off. We have the causes without the effect. The villain thrusts with his dagger—but a miracle has snatched away his victim.

While the moving pictures are lifted above the world of space and time and causality and are freed from its bounds, they are certainly not without law. We said before that the freedom with which the pictures replace one another is to a large degree comparable to the sparkling and streaming of the musical tones. The yielding to the play of the mental energies, to the attention and emotion, which is felt in the film pictures, is still more complete in the musical melodies and harmonies in which the tones themselves are merely the expressions of the ideas and feelings and will impulses of the mind. Their harmonies and disharmonies, their fusing and blending, is not controlled by any outer necessity, but by the inner agreement and disagreement of our free impulses. And yet in this world of musical freedom, everything is completely controlled by esthetic necessities. No sphere of practical life stands under such rigid rules as the realm of the composer. However bold the musical genius may be he cannot emancipate himself from the iron rule that his work must show complete unity in itself. All the separate prescriptions which the musical student has to learn are ultimately only the consequences of this central demand which music, the freest of the arts, shares with all the others. In the case of the film, too, the freedom from the physical forms of space, time, and causality does not mean any liberation from this esthetic bondage either. On the contrary, just as music is surrounded by more technical rules than literature, the photoplay must be held together by the esthetic demands still more firmly than is the drama. The arts which are subordinated to the conditions of space, time, and causality find a certain firmness of structure in these material forms which contain an element of outer connectedness. But where these forms are given up and where the freedom of mental play replaces their outer necessity, everything would fall asunder if the esthetic unity were disregarded.

This unity is, first of all, the unity of action. The demand for it is the same which we know from the drama. The temptation to neglect it is nowhere greater than in the photoplay where outside matter can so easily be introduced or independent interests developed. It is certainly true for the photoplay, as for every work of art, that nothing has the right to existence in its midst which is not internally needed for the unfolding of the unified action. Wherever two plots are given to us, we receive less by far than if we had only one plot. We leave the sphere of valuable art entirely when a unified action is ruined by mixing it with declamation, and propaganda which is not organically interwoven with the action itself. It may be still fresh in memory what an esthetically intolerable helter-skelter performance was offered to the public in *The Battlecry of Peace*. Nothing can be more injurious to the esthetic cultivation of the people than such performances which hold the attention of the spectators by ambitious detail and yet destroy their esthetic sensibility by a complete disregard of the fundamental principle of art, the demand for unity. But we recognized also that this unity involves complete isolation. We annihilate beauty when we link the artistic creation with practical interests and transform the spectator into a selfishly interested bystander. The scenic background of the play is not presented in order that we decide whether we want to spend our next vacation there. The interior decoration of the rooms is not exhibited as a display for a department store. The men and women who carry out the action of the plot must not be people whom we may meet tomorrow on the street. All the threads of the play must be knotted together in the play itself and none should be connected with our outside interests. A good photoplay must be isolated and complete in itself like a beautiful melody. It is not an advertisement for the newest fashions.

This unity of action involves unity of characters. It has too often been maintained by those who theorize on the photoplay that the development of character is the special task of the drama, while the photoplay, which lacks words, must be satisfied with types. Probably this is only a reflection of the crude state which most photoplays of today have not outgrown. Internally, there is no reason why the means of the photoplay should not allow a rather subtle depicting of complex character. But the chief demand is that the characters remain consistent, that the action be developed according to inner necessity, and that the characters themselves be in harmony with the central idea of the plot. However, as soon as we insist on unity we have no right to think only of the action which gives the content of the play. We cannot make light of the form. As in music the melody and rhythms belong together, as in painting not every color combination suits every subject, and as in poetry not every stanza would agree with every idea, so the photoplay must bring action and pictorial expression into perfect harmony. But this demand repeats itself in every single picture. We take it for granted that the painter balances perfectly the forms in his painting, groups them so that an internal symmetry can be felt and that the lines and curves and colors blend into a unity. Every single picture of the sixteen thousand which are shown to us in one reel ought to be treated with this respect of the pictorial artist for the unity of the forms.

The photoplay shows us a significant conflict of human actions in moving pictures which, freed from the physical forms of space, time, and causality, are adjusted to the free play of our mental experiences and which reach complete isolation from the practical world through the perfect unity of plot and pictorial appearance.

[1916]

ALLARDYCE NICOLL

Film Reality:
The Cinema and the Theater

When we witness a film, do we anticipate something we should
not expect from a stage performance, and, if so, what effect has this upon
our appreciation of film acting? At first we might be tempted to dismiss
such a query or to answer it easily and glibly. There is no essential difference, we might say, save insofar as we expect greater variety and movement on the screen than we do on the stage; and for acting, that, we
might reply, is obviously the same as stage acting although perhaps more
stabilized in type form. Do we not see Charles Laughton, Cedric Hardwicke, Ernest Thesiger, Elisabeth Bergner now in the theater, now in the
cinema? To consider further, we might say, were simply to indulge in useless and uncalled-for speculation.

Nevertheless, the question does demand just a trifle more of investigation. Some few years ago a British producing company made a film of
Bernard Shaw's *Arms and the Man*. This film, after a few exciting shots
depicting the dark streets of a Balkan town, the frenzied flight of the
miserable fugitives and the clambering of Bluntschli onto Raina's window
terrace, settled down to provide what was fundamentally a screen picture
of the written drama. The dialogue was shortened, no doubt, but the shots
proceeded more or less along the dramatic lines established by Shaw and
nothing was introduced which he had not originally conceived in preparing his material for the stage. The result was that no more dismal film
has ever been shown to the public. On the stage *Arms and the Man* is
witty, provocative, incisively stimulating; its characters have a breath of

genuine theatrical life; it moves, it breathes, it has vital energy. In the screen version all that life has fled, and, strangest thing of all, those characters—Bluntschli, Raina, Sergius—who are so exciting on the boards looked to the audience like a set of wooden dummies, hopelessly patterned. Performed by a third-rate amateur cast their lifeblood does not so ebb from them, yet here, interpreted by a group of distinguished professionals, they wilted and died—died, too, in such forms that we could never have credited them with ever having had a spark of reality. Was there any basic reason for this failure?

THE CAMERA'S TRUTH

The basic reason seems to be simply this—that practically all effectively drawn stage characters are types and that in the cinema we demand individualization, or else that we recognize stage figures as types and impute greater power of independent life to the figures we see on the screen. This judgment, running so absolutely counter to what would have been our first answer to the original question posited, may seem grossly distorted, but perhaps some further consideration will demonstrate its plausibility. When we go to the theater, we expect theater and nothing else. We know that the building we enter is a playhouse; that behind the lowered curtain actors are making ready, dressing themselves in strange garments and transforming their natural features; that the figures we later see on the boards are never living persons of king and bishop and clown, but merely men pretending for a brief space of time to be like these figures. Dramatic illusion is never (or so rarely as to be negligible) the illusion of reality; it is always imaginative illusion, the illusion of a period of make-believe. All the time we watch Hamlet's throes of agony we know that the character Hamlet is being impersonated by a man who presently will walk out of the stage door in ordinary clothes and an autograph-signing smile on his face. True, volumes have been written on famous dramatic characters—Greek, Elizabethan English and modern Norwegian— and these volumes might well seem to give the lie to such assumptions. Have not Shakespeare's characters seemed so real to a few observers that we have on our shelves books specifically concerned with the girlhood of his heroines—a girlhood the dramas themselves denied us?

These studies, however, should not distract us from the essential truth that the greatest playwrights have always aimed at presenting human personality in bold theatric terms. Hamlet seizes on us, not because he is an individual, not because in him Shakespeare has delineated a particular prince of Denmark, but because in Hamlet there are bits of all men; he is a composite character whose lineaments are determined by dramatic necessity, and through that he lives. Fundamentally, the truly vital theater deals in stock figures. Like a child's box of bricks, the stage's material is limited; it is the possibilities in arrangement that are well-nigh inexhaustible. Audiences thrill to see new situations born of fresh sociological conditions, but the figures set before them in significant plays are conventionally fixed and familiar. Of Romeos there are many, and of Othellos legion. Character on the stage is restricted and stereotyped and the persons who play upon the boards are governed not by the strangely perplexing processes of life but by the established terms of stage practice. Bluntschli represents half a hundred similar rationalists; the idealism of thousands is incorporated in Sergius; and Raina is an eternal stage type of the perplexing female. The theater is populated, not by real individuals whose boyhood or girlhood may legitimately be traced, but by heroes and villains sprung full-bodied from Jove's brain, by clowns and pantaloons whose youth is unknown and whose future matters not after the curtain's fall.

In the cinema we demand something different. Probably we carry into the picture house prejudices deeply ingrained in our beings. The statement that "the camera cannot lie" has been disproved by millions of flattering portraits and by dozens of spiritualistic pictures which purport to depict fairies but which mostly turn out to be faintly disguised pictures of ballet dancers or replicas of figures in advertisements of night lights. Yet in our heart of hearts we credit the truth of that statement. A picture, a piece of sculpture, a stage play—these we know were created by man; we have watched the scenery being carried in backstage and we know we shall see the actors, turned into themselves again, bowing at the conclusion of the performance. In every way the "falsity" of a theatrical production is borne in upon us, so that we are prepared to demand nothing save a theatrical truth. For the films, however, our orientation is vastly different. Several periodicals, it is true, have endeavored to let us into the secrets of the moving-picture industry and a few favored spectators have been permitted to make the rounds of the studios; but for ninety per cent of the audience the actual methods employed in the preparation of a film remain far off and dimly realized. . . .

The strange paradox, then, results that, although the cinema introduces improbabilities and things beyond nature at which any theatrical director would blench and murmur soft nothings to the air, the filmic material is treated by the audience with far greater respect (in its relation to life) than the material of the stage. Our conceptions of life in Chicago gangsterdom and in distant China are all colored by films we have seen. What we have witnessed on the screen becomes the "real" for us. In moments of sanity, maybe, we confess that of course we do not believe this or that, but, under the spell again, we credit the truth of these pictures even as, for all professed superiority, we credit the truth of newspaper paragraphs.

TYPE CASTING

This judgment gives argument for Pudovkin's views concerning the human material to be used in a film—but that argument essentially differs from the method of support which he utilized. His views may be briefly summarized thus: Types are more desirable in film work because of the comparative restrictions there upon make-up; the director alone knows the complete script and therefore there is little opportunity for an individual actor to build up a part intelligently and by slow gradations; an immediate, vital and powerful impression, too, is demanded on the actor's first entrance; since the essential basis of cinematic art is montage of individual shots and not the histrionic abilities of the players, logic demands the use of untrained human material, images of which are wrought into a harmony by the director.

Several of the apparent fallacies in Pudovkin's reasoning have been discussed above. There is, thus, no valid objection to the employment of trained and gifted actors, provided that these actors are not permitted to overrule other elements in the cinematic art and provided the director fully understands their essential position. That casting by type is desirable in the film seems, however, certain. Misled by theatrical ways, we may complain that George Arliss is the same in every screenplay he appears in; but that is exactly what the cinema demands. On the stage we rejoice, or should rejoice, in a performer's versatility; in the cinema unconsciously we want to feel that we are witnessing a true reproduction of real events, and consequently we are not so much interested in discerning a player's skill in diversity of character building. Arliss and Rothschild and Disraeli and Wellington are one. That the desire on the part of a producing company to make use of a particular star may easily lead to the deliberate manufacturing of a character to fit that star is true; but, after all, such a process is by no means unknown to the theater, now or in the past. Shakespeare and Molière both wrote to suit their actors, and Sheridan gave short sentimental scenes to Charles and Maria in *The School for Scandal* because, according to his own statement, "Smith can't make love —and nobody would want to make love to Priscilla Hopkins."

To exemplify the truth of these observations no more is demanded than a comparison of the stage and screen versions of *The Petrified Forest*. As a theatrical production this play was effective, moving and essentially harmonized with the conventions applying to its method of expression; lifeless and uninteresting seemed the filming of fundamentally the same material. The reasons for this were many. First was the fact that the film attempted to defy the basic law which governs the two forms; the theater rejoices in artistic limitation in space while the film demands movement and change in location. We admire Sherwood's skill in confining the whole of his action to the Black Mesa but we condemn the same confining process when we turn to see the same events enacted on the screen. Secondly, since a film can rarely bear to admit anything in the way of theatricality in its settings, those obviously painted sets of desert and mountain confused and detracted from our appreciation of the narrative. A third reason may be sought for in the dialogue given to the characters. This dialogue, following the lines provided for the stage play, showed itself as far too rich and cumbersome for cinematic purposes; not only was there too much of it, but that which sounded exactly right when delivered on the boards of the theater (because essentially in tune with theatrical conventions) seemed ridiculous, false and absurd when associated with the screen pictures. Intimately bound up with this, there has to be taken into account both the nature and the number of the dramatis personae. Sherwood's stage characters were frankly drawn as types—an old pioneer, a killer, an unsuccessful littérateur, an ambitious girl, a veteran, a businessman, a businessman's wife—each one representative of a class or of an ideal. Not for a moment did we believe that these persons were real, living human beings; they were typical figures outlining forces in present-day society. This being so, we had no difficulty in keeping them all boldly in our minds even when the whole group of them filled the stage. When transferred to the screen, however, an immediate feeling of dissatisfaction assailed us; these persons who had possessed theatrical reality could have no reality in the film; their vitality was fled; they seemed false, absurd, untrue. Still further, their number became confusing. The group of representative types which dominated the stage proved merely a jumbled mass on the screen, for the screen, although it may make use of massed effects of a kind which would be impossible in the theater, generally finds its purposes best served by concentration on a very limited number of major figures. The impression of dissatisfaction thus received was increased by the interpretation of these persons. Partly because of the words given to them, all the characters save Duke Mantee seemed to be actors and nothing else. There was exhibited a histrionic skill which might win our admiration but which at the same time was alien to the medium through which it came to us. A Leslie Howard whose stage performance was right and just became an artificial figure when, before the camera, he had to deliver the same lines he had so effectively spoken on the stage. From the lack of individualization in the characters resulted a feeling of confusion and falsity; because of the employoment of conventions suited to one art and not to another vitality, strength and emotional power were lost.

PSYCHOLOGICAL PENETRATION

The full implications of such individualization of film types must be appreciated, together with the distinct approach made by a cinema audience to the persons seen by them on the screen. Because of these things, allied to its possession of several technical devices, the cinema is given the opportunity of coming into closer accord with recent tendencies in other arts than the stage. Unquestionably, that which separates the literature of today from yesterday's literature is the former's power of penetrating, psychoanalytically, into human thought and feeling. The discovery of the subconscious has opened up an entirely fresh field of investigation into human behavior, so that whereas a Walter Scott spread the action of a novel over many years and painted merely the outsides of his characters, their easily appreciated mental reactions and their most obvious passions, James Joyce has devoted an extraordinarily lengthy novel to twenty-four hours in the life of one individual. By this means the art of narrative fiction has been revolutionized and portraiture of individuals completely altered in its approach.

Already it has been shown that normally the film does not find restrictions in the scope of its material advantageous; so that the typical film approaches outwardly the extended breadth of a Scott novel. In dealing with that material, however, it is given the opportunity of delving more deeply into the human consciousness. By its subjective method it can display life from the point of view of its protagonists. Madness on the stage, in spite of Ophelia's pathetic efforts, has always appeared rather absurd, and Sheridan was perfectly within his rights when he caricatured the convention in his Tilburnia and her address to all the finches of the grove. On the screen, however, madness may be made arresting, terrifying, awful. The mania of the lunatic in the German film *M* held the attention precisely because we were enabled to look within his distracted brain. Seeing for moments the world distorted in eccentric imaginings, we are moved as no objective presentation of a stage Ophelia can move us.

Regarded in this way, the cinema, a form of expression born of our own age, is seen to bear a distinct relationship to recent developments within the sphere of general artistic endeavor. While making no profession to examine this subject, one of the most recent writers on *This Modern Poetry*, Babette Deutsch, has expressed, *obiter dicta*, judgments which illustrate clearly the arguments presented above.

> The symbolists [she says] had telescoped images to convey the rapid passage of sensations and emotions. The metaphysicians had played in a like fashion with ideas. Both delighted in paradox. The cinema, and ultimately the radio, made such telescopy congenial to the modern poet, as the grotesqueness of his environment made paradox inevitable for him.

And again:

> The cinema studio creates a looking-glass universe where, without bottles labeled "Drink me" or cakes labeled "Eat me" or keys to impossible gardens, creatures are elongated or telescoped, movements accelerated or slowed up, in a fashion suggesting that the world is made of India rubber or collapsible tin. The ghost of the future glimmers through the immediate scene, the present dissolves into the past.

Akin to these marvels is the poetry of such a man as Horace Gregory. In his *No Retreat: New York, Cassandra,* "the fluent images, the sudden close-ups, the shifting angle of vision, suggest the technique of the cinema." The method of the film is apparent in such lines as these:

> Give Cerberus a nonemployment wage, the dog is hungry.
> This head served in the war, Cassandra, it lost an eye;
> That head spits fire, for it lost its tongue licking the paws
> of lions caged in Wall Street and their claws
> were merciless.
> Follow, O follow him, loam-limbed Apollo, crumbling before
> Tiffany's window: he must buy
> himself earrings for he meets his love tonight,
> (Blossoming Juliet
> emptied her love into her true love's lap)
> dies in his arms.

If the cinema has thus influenced the poets, we realize that inherently it becomes a form of art through which may be expressed many of the most characteristic tendencies in present-day creative endeavor. That most of the films so far produced have not made use of the peculiar methods inherent in the cinematic approach need not blind us to the fact that here is an instrument capable of expressing through combined visual and vocal means something of that analytical searching of the spirit which has formed the pursuit of modern poets and novelists. Not, of course, that in this analytic and realistic method are to be enclosed the entire boundaries of the cinema. The film has the power of giving an impression of actuality and it can thrill us by its penetrating truth to life; but it may, if we desire, call into existence the strangest of visionary worlds and make these too seem real. The enchanted forest of *A Midsummer Night's*

Dream will always on the stage prove a thing of lath and canvas and paint; an enchanted forest in the film might truly seem haunted by a thousand fears and supernatural imaginings. This imaginary world, indeed, is one that our public has cried for and demanded, and our only regret may be that the producers, lacking vision, have compromised and in compromising have descended to banalities. Taking their sets of characters, they thrust these, willy-nilly, into scenes of ornate splendor, exercising their inventiveness not to create the truly fanciful but to fashion the exaggeratedly and hyperbolically absurd. Hotels more sumptuous than the Waldorf-Astoria or the Ritz; liners outvying the pretentions of the *Normandie;* speed that sets Malcolm Campbell to shame; melodies inappropriately rich—these have crowded in on us again and yet again. Many spectators are becoming irritated and bored with scenes of this sort, for mere exaggeration of life's luxuries is not creative artistically.

That the cinema has ample opportunities in this direction has been proved by Max Reinhardt's *A Midsummer Night's Dream,* which, if unsatisfactory as a whole and if in many scenes tentative in its approach, demonstrated what may be done with imaginative forms on the screen. Apart from the opportunity offered by Shakespeare's theme for the presentation of the supernatural fairy world, two things were specially to be noted in this film. The first was that certain passages which, spoken in our vast modern theaters with their sharp separation of audience and actors, become mere pieces of rhetoric devoid of true meaning and significance were invested in the film with an intimacy and directness they lacked on the stage. The power of the cinema to draw us near to an action or to a speaker served here an important function, and we could at will watch a group of players from afar or approach to overhear the secrets of soliloquy. The second feature of interest lay in the ease with which the cinema can present visual symbols to accompany language. At first, we might be prepared to condemn the film on this ground, declaring that the imaginative appeal of Shakespeare's language would thereby be lost. Again, however, second thoughts convince us that much is to be said in its defense; reference once more must be made to a subject already briefly discussed. Shakespeare's dialogue was written for an audience not only sympathetic to his particular way of thought and feeling, but gifted with certain faculties which today we have lost. Owing to the universal development of reading, certain faculties possessed by men of earlier ages have vanished from us. In the sixteenth century, men's minds were more acutely perceptive of values in words heard, partly because their language was a growing thing with constantly occurring new forms and strange applications of familiar words, but largely because they had to maintain a constant alertness to spoken speech. Newspapers did not exist then; all men's knowledge of the larger world beyond their immediate ken had to come from hearing words uttered by their companions. As a result, the significance of words was more keenly appreciated and certainly was more concrete than it is today. When Macbeth, in four lines, likened life to a brief candle, to a walking shadow and to a poor player, one may believe that the ordinary spectator in the Globe Theater saw in his mind's eye these three objects referred to. The candle, the shadow and the player became for him mental realities.

The same speech uttered on the stage today can hardly hope for such interpretation. Many in the audience will be lulled mentally insensible to its values by the unaccustomed movement of the lines, and others will grasp its import, not by emotional imaginative understanding, but by a painful, rational process of thought. A modern audience, therefore, listening to earlier verse drama, will normally require a direct stimulus to its visual imagination—a thing entirely unnecessary in former times. Thus, for example, on the bare Elizabethan platform stage the words concerning dawn or sunlight or leafy woods were amply sufficient to conjure up an image of these things; latter-day experiments in the production of these dramas in reconstructed "Shakespearean" theaters, interesting as these may be and refreshing in their novelty, must largely fail to achieve the end so easily and with such little effort reached among sixteenth-century audiences. We need, now, all the appurtenances of a decorated stage to approach, even faintly, the dramatist's purpose. This is the justification for the presentation of Shakespeare's tragedies and comedies, not in a reconstructed Globe Theatre, but according to the current standards of Broadway or of Shaftesbury Avenue.

The theater, however, can do only so much. It may visually create the setting, but it cannot create the stimulus necessary for a keener appreciation of the magic value of Shakespeare's lines. No method of stage representation could achieve that end. On the screen, on the other hand, something at least in this direction may be accomplished. In *A Midsummer Night's Dream* Oberon's appearance behind dark bespangled gauze, even although too much dwelt on and emphasized, gave force to lines commonly read or heard uncomprehendingly—"King of Shadows," he is called; but the phrase means little or nothing to us unless our minds are given such a stimulus as was here provided. Critics have complained that in the film nothing is left to the imagination, but we must remember that in the Shakespearean verse there is a quality which, because of changed conditions, we may find difficulty in appreciating. Its strangeness to us demands that an attempt be made to render it more intelligible and directly appealing. Such an attempt, through the means of expression granted to the cinema, may merely be supplying something which will bring us nearer to the conditions of the original spectators for whom Shakespeare wrote.

Normally, however, verse forms will be alien to the film. Verse in itself presupposes a certain remoteness from the terms of ordinary life, and the cinema, as we have seen, usually finds its most characteristic expression in the world that immediately surrounds us. The close connection, noted by Babette Deutsch, between cinematic expression and tendencies in present-day poetry will declare itself, not in a utilization of rhythmic speech, but in a psychological penetration rendered manifest through a realistic method. . . .

THE WAY OF THE FILM

For the film are reserved things essentially distinct. Possibility of confusion between the two has entered in only because the playhouse has not been true to itself. To the cinema is given a sphere where the subjective and objective approaches are combined, where individualization takes the place of type characterization, where reality may faithfully be imitated and where the utterly fantastic equally is granted a home, where Walt Disney's animated flowers and flames exist alongside the figures of men and women who may seem more real than the figures of the stage, where a visual image in moving forms may thrill and awaken an age whose ears, while still alert to listen to poetic speech based on or in tune with the common language of the day, has forgotten to be moved by the tones of an earlier dramatic verse. Within this field lies the possibility of an artistic expression equally powerful as that of the stage, though essentially distinct from that. The distinction is determined by the audience reactions to the one and to the other. In the theater the spectators are confronted by characters which, if successfully delineated, always possess a quality which renders them greater than separate individuals. When Clifford Odets declares that by the time he came to write his first play, *Awake and Sing!* he understood clearly that his interest

> was not in the presentation of an individual's problems, but in those of a whole class. In other words, the task was to find a theatrical form with which to express the mass as hero . . .

he is doing no more than indicate that he has the mind and approach of a dramatist. All the well-known figures created in tragedy and comedy since the days of Aristophanes and Aeschylus have presented in this way the lineaments of universal humanity. If the theater stands thus for mankind, the cinema, because of the willingness on the part of spectators to accept as the image of truth the moving forms cast on the screen, stands for the individual. It is related to the modern novel in the same respect that the older novel was related to the stage. Impressionistic and expressionistic settings may serve for the theater—even may we occasionally fall back on plain curtains without completely losing the interest of our audiences; the cinema can take no such road, for, unless in frankly artificially created films (such as the Walt Disney cartoon), we cling to our preconceived beliefs and clamor for the three-dimensional, the exact and the authentic. In a stage play such as *Yellow Jack* we are prepared to accept a frankly formal background, because we know that the actors are actors merely; but for the treatment of similar material in *The Prisoner of Shark Island* and *The Story of Pasteur* cinematic authenticity is demanded. At first glance, we might aver that, because of this, the film had fewer opportunities for artistic expression than the stage; but further consideration will demonstrate that the restrictions are amply compensated for by an added scope. Our illusion in the picture house is certainly less "imaginative" than the illusion which attends us in the theater, but it has the advantage of giving increased appreciation of things which are outside nature. Through this the purely visionary becomes almost tangible and the impossible assumes shapes easy of comprehension and belief. The sense of reality lies as the foundation of the film, yet real time and real space are banished; the world we move in may be far removed from the world ordinarily about us; and symbols may find a place alongside common objects of little or no importance. If we apply the theory of "psychological distance" to theater and the film we realize the force of each. For any kind of aesthetic appreciation this distance is always demanded; before we can hope to feel the artistic qualities of any form we must be able to set ourselves away from it, to experience the stimulus its contemplation creates and at the same time have no call to put the reactions to that stimulus into play. This distance obviously may be of varying degrees; sometimes it is reduced, sometimes it provides a vast gulf between the observer and the art object. Furthermore the variation may be of two kinds—variation between one art and another, and variation between forms within the sphere of a single art. Music is further removed from reality than sculpture, but in music there may be an approach toward commonly heard sounds and in sculpture abstract shapes may take the place of familiar forms realistically delineated. Determination of the proper and legitimate approach will come from a consideration of the sense of distance between the observer and the object; the masterpieces in any art will necessarily be based on an adaptation of the particular requirements of their own peculiar medium of expression.

Applying this principle to theater and cinema, we will recognize that whereas there is a strong sense of reality in audience reactions to the film, always there is the fact that the pictures on the screen are two-dimensional images and hence removed a stage from actual contact with the spectators. What may happen if successful three-dimensional projection is introduced we cannot tell; at present we are concerned with a flat screen picture. This gulf between the audience and the events presented to them will permit a much greater use of realism than the stage may legitimately employ. The presence of flesh-and-blood actors in the theater means that it is comparatively easy to break the illusion proper to the theater and in doing so to shatter the mood at which any performance ought to aim. This statement may appear to run counter to others made above, but there is no essential contradiction involved. The fact remains that, when living person is set before living person—actor before spectator—a certain deliberate conventionalizing is demanded of the former if the aesthetic impression is not to be lost, whereas in the film, in which immediately a measure of distance is imposed between image and spectator, greater approaches to real forms may be permitted, even though these have to exist alongside impossibilities and fantastic symbols far removed from the world around us. This is the paradox of cinematic art.

Herein lies the true filmic realm and to these things the cinema, if it also is to be true to itself, must tend, just as toward the universalizing and toward conventionalism must tend the theater if it is to find a secure place among us. Fortunately the signs of the age are propitious; experiments in poetic drama and production of films utilizing at least a few of the significant methods basically associated with cinematic art give us authority for believing that within the next decade each will discover firmer and surer foothold and therefore more arresting control over their material. Both stage and cinema have their particular and peculiar functions; their houses may stand side by side, not in rivaling enmity, but in that friendly rivalry which is one of the compelling forces in the wider realm of artistic achievement.

[1936]

SUSAN SONTAG

Theater and Film

Does there exist an unbridgeable gap, even opposition, between the two arts? Is there something genuinely "theatrical," different in kind from what is genuinely "cinematic"?

Virtually all opinion holds that there is. A commonplace of discussion has it that film and theatre are distinct and even antithetical arts, each giving rise to its own standards of judgment and canons of form. Thus Erwin Panofsky argues in his celebrated essay "Style and Medium in the Motion Pictures" (1934, rewritten in 1956) that one of the criteria for evaluating a movie is its freedom from the impurities of theatricality, and that, to talk about film, one must first define "the basic nature of the medium." Those who think prescriptively about the nature of live drama, less confident in the future of that art than the *cinéphiles* in theirs, rarely take a comparably exclusivist line.

The history of cinema is often treated as the history of its emancipation from theatrical models. First of all from theatrical "frontality" (the unmoving camera reproducing the situation of the spectator of a play fixed in his seat), then from theatrical acting (gestures needlessly stylized, exaggerated—needlessly, because now the actor could be seen "close up"), then from theatrical furnishings (unnecessary distancing of the audience's emotions, disregarding the opportunity to immerse the audience in reality). Movies are regarded as advancing from theatrical stasis to cinematic fluidity, from theatrical artificiality to cinematic naturalness and immediateness. But this view is far too simple.

Such oversimplification testifies to the ambiguous scope of the camera eye. Because the camera *can* be used to project a relatively passive, unselective kind of vision—as well as the highly selective ("edited") vision generally associated with movies—cinema is a medium as well as an art, in the sense that it can encapsulate any of the performing arts and render it in a film transcription. (This "medium" or non-art aspect of film attained its routine incarnation with the advent of television. There, movies themselves became another performing art to be transcribed, miniaturized on film.) One *can* film a play or ballet or opera or sporting event in such a way that film becomes, relatively speaking, a transparency, and it seems correct to say that one is seeing the event filmed. But theatre is never a "medium." Thus, because one can make a movie of a play but not a play of a movie, cinema had an early but fortuitous connection with the stage. Some of the earliest films were filmed plays. Duse and Bernhardt are on film—marooned in time, absurd, touching; there is a 1913 British film of Forbes-Robertson playing Hamlet, a 1923 German film of *Othello* starring Emil Jannings. More recently, the camera has preserved Helene Weigel's performance of *Mother Courage* with the Berliner Ensemble, the Living Theatre production of *The Brig* (filmed by the Mekas brothers), and Peter Brook's staging of Weiss' *Marat/Sade*.

But from the beginning, even within the confines of the notion of film as a "medium" and the camera as a "recording" instrument, other events than those occurring in theatres were taken down. As with still photography, some of the events captured on moving photographs were staged but others were valued precisely because they were *not* staged—the camera being the witness, the invisible spectator, the invulnerable voyeuristic eye. (Perhaps public happenings, "news," constitute an intermediate case between staged and unstaged events; but film as "newsreel" generally amounts to using film as a "medium.") To create on film a *document* of a transient reality is a conception quite unrelated to the purposes of theatre. It only appears related when the "real event" being recorded happens to be a theatrical performance. In fact, the first use of the motion-picture camera was to make a documentary record of unstaged, casual reality; Lumière's films from the 1890's of crowd scenes in Paris and New York antedate any filming of plays.

The other paradigmatic non-theatrical use of film, which dates from the earliest period of movie-making with the celebrated work of Méliès, is the creation of illusion, the construction of fantasy. To be sure, Méliès (like many directors after him) conceived of the rectangle of the screen on analogy with the proscenium stage. And not only were the events staged; they were the very stuff of invention: impossible journeys, imaginary objects, physical metamorphoses. But this, even adding the fact that Méliès situated his camera in front of the action and hardly moved it, does not make his films theatrical in an invidious sense. In their treatment of persons as things (physical objects) and in their disjunctive presentation of time and space, Méliès' films are quintessentially "cinematic"—so far as there is such a thing.

If the contrast between theatre and films doesn't lie in the materials represented or depicted in a simple sense, this contrast survives in more generalized forms.

According to some influential accounts, the boundary is virtually an ontological one. Theatre deploys artifice while cinema is committed to reality, indeed to an ultimately physical reality which is "redeemed," to use Siegfried Kracauer's striking word, by the camera. The aesthetic judgment that follows from this venture in intellectual map-making is that films shot in real-life settings are better (i.e., more cinematic) than those shot in a studio. Taking Flaherty and Italian neo-realism and the *cinéma-vérité* of Rouch and Marker and Ruspoli as preferred models, one would judge rather harshly the era of wholly studio-made films inaugurated around 1920 by *The Cabinet of Dr. Caligari*, films with ostentatiously artificial décor and landscapes, and applaud the direction taken at the same period in Sweden, where many films with strenuous natural settings were being shot on location. Thus, Panofsky attacks *Dr. Caligari* for "pre-stylizing reality," and urges upon cinema "the problem of manipulating and shooting unstylized reality in such a way that the result has style."

But there is no reason to insist on a single model for film. And it is helpful to notice how the apotheosis of realism in cinema, which gives the greatest prestige to "unstylized reality," covertly advances a definite political-moral position. Films have been rather too often acclaimed as the democratic art, the preeminent art of mass society. Once one takes this description seriously, one tends (like Panofsky and Kracauer) to wish that movies continue to reflect their origins in a vulgar level of the arts, to remain loyal to their vast unsophisticated audience. Thus, a vaguely Marxist orientation collaborates with a fundamental tenet of romanticism. Cinema, at once high art and popular art, is cast as the art of the authentic. Theatre, by contrast, means dressing up, pretense, lies. It smacks of aristocratic taste and the class society. Behind the objection of critics to the stagy sets of *Dr. Caligari*, the improbable costumes and florid acting of Renoir's *Nana*, the talkiness of Dreyer's *Gertrud* as "theatrical" lay the judgment that such films were false, that they exhibited a sensibility both pretentious and reactionary which was out of step with the democratic and more mundane sensibility of modern life.

Anyway, whether aesthetic defect or no in the particular case, the synthetic "look" in films is not necessarily a misplaced theatricalism.

From the beginning of film history, there were painters and sculptors who claimed that cinema's true future resided in artifice, construction. Not figurative narration or storytelling of any kind (either in a relatively realistic or in a "surrealistic" vein) but abstraction was film's true destiny. Thus, Theo van Doesburg in his essay of 1929, "Film as Pure Form," envisages film as the vehicle of "optical poetry," "dynamic light architecture," "the creation of a moving ornament." Films will realize "Bach's dream of finding an optical equivalent for the temporal structure of a musical composition." Though only a few film-makers—for example, Robert Breer—continue to pursue this conception of film, who can deny its claim to be cinematic?

Could anything be more alien to the nature of the theatre than such a degree of abstraction? Let's not answer that question too quickly.

Panofsky derives the difference between theatre and film as a difference between the *formal* conditions of seeing a play and those of seeing a movie. In the theatre, "space is static, that is, the space represented on the stage, as well as the spatial relation of the beholder to the spectacle, is unalterably fixed," while in the cinema, "the spectator occupies a fixed seat, but only physically, not as the subject of an aesthetic experience." In the theatre, the spectator cannot change his angle of vision. In the cinema, the spectator is "aesthetically . . . in permanent motion as his eye identifies with the lens of the camera, which permanently shifts in distance and direction."

True enough. But the observation does not warrant a radical dissociation of theatre and film. Like many critics, Panofsky has a "literary" conception of the theatre. In contrast to theatre, conceived of as basically dramatized literature (texts, words), stands cinema, which he assumes to be primarily "a visual experience." This means defining cinema by those means perfected in the period of silent films. But many of the most interesting movies today could hardly be described adequately as images with sound added. And the most lively work in the theatre is being done by people who envisage theatre as more than, or different from, "plays" from Aeschylus to Tennessee Williams.

Given his view, Panofsky is as eager to hold the line against the infiltration of theatre by cinema as the other way around. In the theatre, unlike movies, "the setting of the stage cannot change during one act (except for such incidentals as rising moons or gathering clouds and such illegitimate reborrowings from film as turning wings or gliding backdrops)." Not only does Panofsky assume that theatre means plays, but by the aesthetic standard he tacitly proposes, the model play would approach the condition of *No Exit*, and the ideal set would be either a realistic living room or a blank stage. No less arbitrary is his complementary view of what is illegitimate in film: all elements not demonstrably subordinate to the image, more precisely, the *moving* image. Thus Panofsky asserts: "Wherever a poetic emotion, a musical outburst, or a literary conceit (even, I am grieved to say, some of the wisecracks of Groucho Marx) entirely loses contact with visible movement, they strike the sensitive spectator as, literally, out of place." What then of the films of Bresson and Godard, with their allusive, thoughtful texts and their characteristic refusal to be primarily a visual experience? How could one explain the extraordinary rightness of Ozu's relatively immobilized camera?

Part of Panofsky's dogmatism in decrying the theatrical taint in movies can be explained by recalling that the first version of his essay appeared in 1934 and undoubtedly reflects the recent experience of seeing a great many bad movies. Compared with the level that film reached in the late 1920's, it is undeniable that the average quality of films declined sharply in the early sound period. Although a number of fine, audacious films were made during the very first years of sound, the general decline had become clear by 1933 or 1934. The sheer dullness of most films of this period can't be explained simply as a regression to theatre. Still, it's a fact that film-makers in the 1930's did turn much more frequently to plays than they had in the preceding decade—filming stage successes such as *Outward Bound, Rain, Dinner at Eight, Blithe Spirit, Faisons un Rêve, Twentieth Century, Boudu Sauvé des Eaux,* the Pagnol trilogy, *She Done Him Wrong, Der Dreigroschen Oper, Anna Christie, Holiday, Animal Crackers, The Petrified Forest,* and many, many more. Most of these films are negligible as art; a few are first-rate. (The same can be said of the plays, though there is scant correlation between the merits of the movies and of the stage "originals.") However, their virtues and faults cannot be sorted out into a cinematic versus a theatrical element. Usually, the success of movie versions of plays is measured by the extent to which the script rearranges and displaces the action and deals less than respectfully with the spoken text—as do certain English films of plays by Wilde and Shaw, the Olivier Shakespeare films (at least *Henry V*), and Sjöberg's *Miss Julie.* But the basic disapproval of films which betray their origins in plays remains. (A recent example: the outrage and hostility which greeted Dreyer's masterly *Gertrud,* because of its blatant fidelity to the 1904 Danish play on which it is based, with characters conversing at length and quite formally, with little camera movement and most scenes filmed in medium shot.)

My own view is that films with complex or formal dialogue, films in which the camera is static or in which the action stays indoors, are not necessarily theatrical—whether derived from plays or not. *Per contra,* it is no more part of the putative "essence" of movies that the camera must rove over a large physical area than it is that the sound element in a film must always be subordinate to the visual. Though most of the action of Kurosawa's *The Lower Depths,* a fairly faithful transcription of Gorky's play, is confined to one large room, this film is just as cinematic as the same director's *Throne of Blood,* a very free and laconic adaption of *Macbeth.* The claustrophobic intensity of Melville's *Les Enfants Ter- ribles* is as peculiar to the movies as the kinetic élan of Ford's *The Searchers* or the opening train journey in Renoir's *La Bête Humaine.*

A film does become theatrical in an invidious sense when the nar- ration is coyly self-conscious. Compare Autant-Lara's *Occupe-toi d'Amélie,* a brilliant cinematic use of the conventions and materials of boulevard theatre, with Ophuls' clumsy use of similar conventions and materials in *La Ronde.*

In his book *Film and Theatre* (1936), Allardyce Nicoll argues that the difference between the two arts, both forms of dramaturgy, is that they use different kinds of characters. "Practically all effectively drawn stage characters are types [while] in the cinema we demand individuali- zation . . . and impute greater power of independent life to the figures on the screen." (Panofsky, by the way, makes exactly the same contrast but in reverse: that the nature of films, unlike that of plays, requires flat or stock characters.)

Nicoll's thesis is not as arbitrary as it may at first appear. A little- remarked fact about movies is that the moments that are plastically and emotionally most successful, and the most effective elements of characteri- zation, often consist precisely of "irrelevant" or unfunctional details. (One random example: the ping-pong ball the schoolmaster toys with in Ivory's *Shakespeare Wallah.*) Movies thrive on the narrative equivalent of a technique familiar from painting and photography: off-centering. Hence, the pleasing disunity or fragmentariness of the characters of many of the greatest films, which is probably what Nicoll means by "individuali- zation." In contrast, linear coherence of detail (the gun on the wall in the first act that must go off by the end of the third) is the rule in Occidental narrative theatre, and gives rise to the impression of the unity of the characters (a unity that may be equivalent to the construction of a "type").

But, even with these adjustments, Nicoll's thesis doesn't work so far as it rests on the idea that "when we go to the theatre, we expect theatre and nothing else." For what is this theatre-and-nothing-else if not the old notion of artifice? (As if art were ever anything else, some arts being artificial but others not.) According to Nicoll, when we sit in a theatre "in every way the 'falsity' of a theatrical production is borne in upon us, so that we are prepared to demand nothing save a theatrical truth." Quite a different situation obtains in the cinema, Nicoll holds.

Every member of the movie audience, no matter how sophisticated, is on essentially the same level; we all believe that the camera cannot lie. As the film actor and his role are identical, the image cannot be dissociated from what is imaged. We experience what cinema gives us as the truth of life.

But couldn't theatre dissolve the distinction between the truth of artifice and the truth of life? Isn't that just what theatre as ritual seeks to do? Isn't that the aim of theatre conceived as an *exchange* with an audience?—something that films can never be.

Panofsky may be obtuse when he decries the theatrical taint in movies, but he is sound when he points out that, historically, theatre is only one of the arts feeding into cinema. As he remarks, it is apt that films came to be known popularly as moving pictures rather than "photoplays" or "screen plays." Cinema derives less from the theatre, from a performance art, an art that already moves, than it does from forms of art which were stationary. Nineteenth-century historical paintings, sentimental postcards, the museum of wax figures à la Madame Tussaud, and comic strips are the sources Panofsky cites. Another model, which he surprisingly fails to mention, is the early narrative uses of still photography—like the family photo album. The stylistics of description and scene-building developed by certain nineteenth-century novelists, as Eisenstein pointed out in his brilliant essay on Dickens, supplied still another prototype for cinema.

Movies are images (usually photographs) that move, to be sure. But the distinctive cinematic unit is not the image but the principle of connection between the images: the relation of a "shot" to the one that preceded it and the one that comes after. There is no peculiarly "cinematic" as opposed to "theatrical" mode of linking images.

If an irreducible distinction between theatre and cinema does exist, it may be this. Theatre is confined to a logical or *continuous* use of space. Cinema (through editing, that is, through the change of shot—which is the basic unit of film construction) has access to an alogical or *discontinuous* use of space.

In the theatre, actors are either in the stage space or "off." When "on," they are always visible or visualizable in contiguity with each other. In the cinema, no such relation is necessarily visible or even visualizable. (Example: the last shot of Paradjanov's *Shadows of Our Forgotten Ancestors*.) Some of the films considered objectionably theatrical are those which seem to emphasize spatial continuities, like Hitchcock's virtuoso *Rope* or the daringly anachronistic *Gertrud*. But closer analysis of both these films would show how complex their treatment of space is. The long takes increasingly favored in sound films are, in themselves, neither more nor less cinematic than the short takes characteristic of silents.

Thus, cinematic virtue does not reside in the fluidity of the movement of the camera or in the mere frequency of the change of shot. It consists in the arrangement of screen images and (now) of sounds. Méliès, for example, though he didn't go beyond the static positioning of his camera, had a very striking conception of how to *link* screen images. He grasped that editing offered an equivalent to the magician's sleight of hand—thereby establishing that one of the distinctive aspects of film (unlike theatre) is that anything can happen, that there is nothing that cannot be represented convincingly. Through editing, Méliès presents discontinuities of physical substance and behavior. In his films, the discontinuities are, so to speak, practical, functional; they accomplish a transformation of ordinary reality. But the continuous *re*invention of space (as well as the option of temporal indeterminacy) peculiar to film narration does not pertain only to the cinema's ability to fabricate "visions," to show the viewer a radically altered world. The most "realistic" use of the motion-picture camera also involves a discontinuous account of space, insofar as all film narration has a "syntax," composed of the rhythm of associations and disjunctions. (As Cocteau has written, "My primary concern in a film is to prevent the images from flowing, to oppose them to each other, to anchor them and join them without destroying their relief." But such a conception of film syntax need hardly entail, as Cocteau thinks, rejecting movies as "mere entertainment instead of a vehicle for thought.")

In marking the boundary between theatre and film, the issue of the continuity of space seems to me more fundamental than the obvious contrast between theatre as an organization of movement in three-dimensional space (like dance) and cinema as an organization of plane space (like painting). The theatre's capacities for manipulating space and time are simply much cruder and more labored than those of film. Theatre cannot equal the cinema's facilities for the strictly controlled repetition of images, for the duplication or matching of word and image, and for the juxtaposition and overlapping of images. (With advanced lighting techniques and an adept use of scrim, one can now "dissolve in" or "dissolve out" on the stage. But no technique could provide an equivalent on the stage of the "lap dissolve.")

Sometimes the division between theatre and film is located as the difference between the play and the film script. Theatre has been described as a mediated art, presumably because it usually consists of a pre-existent play mediated by a particular performance which offers one of many possible interpretations of the play. Film, in contrast, is regarded as unmediated—because of its larger-than-life scale and more unrefusable impact on the eye, and because (in Panofsky's words) "the medium of the movies is physical reality as such" and the characters in a movie "have no aesthetic existence outside the actors." But there is an equally valid sense which shows movies to be the mediated art and theatre the un-mediated one. We see what happens on the stage with our own eyes. We see on the screen what the camera sees.

In the cinema, narration proceeds by ellipsis (the "cut" or change of shot); the camera eye is a unified point of view that continually displaces itself. But the change of shot can provoke questions, the simplest of which is: from *whose* point of view is the shot seen? And the ambiguity of point of view latent in all cinematic narration has no equivalent in the theatre. Indeed, one should not underestimate the aesthetically positive role of *disorientation* in the cinema. Examples: Busby Berkeley dollying back from an ordinary-looking stage already established as some thirty feet deep to disclose a stage three hundred feet square; Resnais panning from character X's point of view a full 360 degrees to come to rest upon X's face.

Much also may be made of the fact that, in its concrete existence, cinema is an *object* (a product, even) while theatre results in a *performance*. Is this so important? In a way, no. Art in all its forms, whether objects (like films or painting) or performances (like music or theatre), is first a mental act, a fact of consciousness. The object aspect of film and the performance aspect of theatre are only means—means to the experience which is not only "of" but "through" the film and the theatre event. Each subject of an aesthetic experience shapes it to his own measure. With respect to any *single* experience, it hardly matters that a film is identical from one projection of it to another while theatre performances are highly mutable.

The difference between object art and performance art underlies Panofsky's observation that "the screenplay, in contrast to the theatre play, has no aesthetic existence independent of its performance," so that characters in movies *are* the stars who enact them. It is because each film is an object, a totality that is set, that movie roles are identical with the actors' performances; while in the theatre (in the Occident, an artistic totality that is generally additive rather than organic) only the written play is "fixed," an object (literature) and therefore existing apart from any staging of it.

But these qualities of theatre and film are not, as Panofsky apparently thought, unalterable. Just as movies needn't necessarily be designed to be shown at all in theatre situations (they can be intended for more continuous and casual viewing: in the living room, in the bedroom, or on public surfaces like the façades of buildings), so a movie *may* be altered from one projection to the next. Harry Smith, when he runs off his films, makes each projection an unrepeatable performance. And, again, theatre is not just about preexisting plays which get produced over and over, well or badly. In Happenings, street or guerrilla theatre, and certain other recent theatre events, the "plays" are identical with their productions in precisely the same sense as the screenplay is identical with the unique film made from it.

Despite these developments, however, a large difference still remains. Because films are objects, they are totally manipulable, totally calculable. Films resemble books, another portable art-object; making a film, like writing a book, means constructing an inanimate thing, every element of which is determinate. Indeed, this determinacy has or can have a quasi-mathematical form in films, as it does in music. (A shot lasts a certain number of seconds, "matching" two shots requires a change of angle of so many degrees.) Given the total determinacy of the result on celluloid (whatever the extent of the director's conscious intervention), it was inevitable that some film directors would want to devise schemas to make their intentions more exact. Thus, it was neither perverse nor primitive of Busby Berkeley to have used only one camera to shoot the whole of each of his mammoth dance numbers. Every "set-up" was designed to be shot from only one, exactly calculated angle. Working on a far more self-conscious level of artistry than Busby Berkeley, Bresson has declared that, for him, the director's task consists in finding the single way of doing each shot that is correct. No image is justified in itself, according to Bresson, but rather in the exactly specifiable relation it bears to the chronologically adjacent images—which relation constitutes its "meaning."

But theatre allows only the loosest approximation to this sort of formal concern and to this degree of aesthetic responsibility on the part of the director, which is why French critics justly speak of the director of a film as its "author." Because they are performances, events that are always "live," what takes place on a theatre stage is not subject to an equivalent degree of control and cannot admit a comparably exact integration of effects.

It would be foolish to conclude that superior films are those resulting from the greatest amount of conscious planning on the part of the director or those which objectify a complex plan (though the director may not have been aware of it, and proceeded in what seemed to him an intuitive or instinctive way). Plans may be faulty or ill-conceived or sterile. More important, the cinema admits of a number of quite different kinds of sensibility. One gives rise to the kind of formalized art to which cinema (unlike theatre) is naturally adapted. Another has produced an impressive body of "improvised" cinema. (This should be distinguished from the work of some filmmakers, notably Godard, who have become fascinated with the "look" of improvised, documentary cinema, used for formalistic ends.)

Nevertheless, it seems indisputable that cinema, not only potentially but by its nature, is a more rigorous art than theatre. This capacity for formal rigor, combined with the accessibility of mass audiences, has given cinema an unquestioned prestige and attractiveness as an art form. Despite the extreme emotional resources of "pure theatre" demonstrated by Julian Beck and Judith Malina's Living Theatre and Jerzy Grotowski's Theatre Laboratory, theatre as an art form gives the general impression of having a problematic future.

More than a failure of nerve must account for the fact that theatre, this seasoned art, occupied since antiquity with all sorts of local offices—enacting sacred rites, reinforcing communal loyalty, guiding morals, provoking the therapeutic discharge of violent emotions, conferring social status, giving practical instruction, affording entertainment, dignifying celebrations, subverting established authority—is now on the defensive before movies, this brash art with its huge, amorphous, passive audience. But the fact is undeniable. Meanwhile, movies continue to maintain their astonishing pace of formal articulation. (Take the commercial cinema of Europe, Japan, and the United States since 1960, and consider what the audiences of these films in less than a decade have become habituated to in the way of increasingly elliptical storytelling and visualization.)

But note: this youngest of the arts is also the most heavily burdened with memory. Cinema is a time machine. Movies preserve the past, while theatres—no matter how devoted to the classics, to old plays—can only "modernize." Movies resurrect the beautiful dead; present, intact, vanished or ruined environments; embody without irony styles and fashions that seem funny today; solemnly ponder irrelevant or naïve problems. The historical particularity of the reality registered on celluloid is so vivid that practically all films older than four or five years are saturated with pathos. (The pathos I am describing is not simply that of old photographs, for it overtakes animated cartoons and drawn, abstract films as well as ordinary movies.) Films age (being objects) as no theatre event does (being always new). There is no pathos of mortality in theatre's "reality" as such, nothing in our response to a good performance of a Mayakovsky play comparable to the aesthetic role of the emotion of nostalgia when we see in 1966 a film by Pudovkin.

Also worth noting: compared with the theatre, innovations in cinema seem to be assimilated more efficiently, seem altogether more sharable—among other reasons, because new films are quickly and widely circulated. And, partly because virtually the entire body of accomplishment in film can be consulted in the present (in film libraries, of which the most celebrated is the Cinemathèque Française), most filmmakers are more knowledgeable about the entire history of their art than most theatre directors are about even the very recent past of theirs.

The key word in most discussions of cinema is "possibility." There is a merely classifying use of the word, as in Panofsky's engaging judgment that "within their self-imposed limitations the early Disney films . . . represent, as it were, a chemically pure distillation of cinematic possibilities." But behind this relatively neutral usage lurks a more polemical sense of cinema's possibilities, in which what is regularly intimated is the obsolescence of theatre and its supersession by films.

Thus, Panofsky describes the mediation of the camera eye as opening "up a world of possibility of which the stage can never dream." Already in 1924, Artaud declared that motion pictures had made the theatre obsolete. Movies "possess a sort of virtual power which probes into the mind and uncovers undreamt-of possibilities . . . When this art's exhiliration has been blended in the right proportions with the psychic ingredient it commands, it will leave the theatre far behind and we will relegate the latter to the attic of our memories." (When sound came in, though, Artaud became disenchanted with films and returned to theatre.)

Meyerhold, facing the challenge head on, thought the only hope for theatre lay in a wholesale emulation of the cinema. "Let us 'cinematify' the theatre," he urged, meaning that the staging of plays should be "industrialized," theatres must accommodate audiences in the tens of thousands rather than in the hundreds. Meyerhold also seemed to find some relief in the idea that the coming of sound signaled the downfall of movies. Believing that the international appeal of films depended entirely on the fact that screen actors (unlike theatre actors) didn't have to speak any particular language, he was unable to imagine in 1930 that technology (dubbing, subtitling) could solve the problem.

Is cinema the successor, the rival, or the revivifyer of the theatre?

Sociologically, it is certainly the rival—one of many. Whether it is theatre's successor depends partly on how people understand and use the decline of theatre as an art form. One can't be sure that theatre is not in a state of irreversible decline, spurts of local vitality notwithstanding. And art forms *have* been abandoned (though not necessarily because they become "obsolete").

But why should theatre be rendered obsolete by movies? Predictions of obsolescence amount to declaring that a something has one particular task (which another something may do as well or better). But has theatre one particular task or aptitude? One which cinema is better able to perform?

Those who predict the demise of the theatre, assuming that cinema has engulfed its function, tend to impute a relation between films and theatre reminiscent of what was once said about photography and painting. If the painter's job really had been no more than fabricating likenesses, then the invention of the camera might indeed have made painting obsolete. But painting is hardly just "pictures," any more than cinema is just theatre democratized and made available to the masses (because it can be reproduced and distributed in portable standardized units).

In the naïve tale of photography and painting, painting was reprieved when it claimed a new task: abstraction. As the superior realism of photography was supposed to have liberated painting, allowing it to go abstract, cinema's superior power to represent (not merely to stimulate) the imagination may appear to have similarly emboldened the theatre, inviting the gradual obliteration of the conventional "plot."

This was how it was supposed to be, but not how it in fact turned out. Actually, painting and photography evidence parallel development rather than a rivalry or a supersession. And, at an uneven rate, so do theatre and film. The possibilities for theatre that lie in going beyond psychological realism, thereby achieving greater abstractness, are equally germane to the future of narrative films. Conversely, the idea of movies as witness to real life, testimony rather than invention or artifice, the treatment of collective historical situations rather than the depiction of imaginary personal "dramas," seems equally relevant to theatre. Alongside documentary films and their sophisticated heir, *cinéma-vérité*, one can place the new documentary theatre, the so-called "theatre of fact," exemplified in plays by Hochhuth, in Weiss' *The Investigation*, in Peter Brook's recent projects for a production called *US* with the Royal Shakespeare company in London.

Despite Panofsky's strictures, there seems no reason for theatre and film not to exchange with each other, as they have been doing right along.

The influence of the theatre upon films in the early years of cinema history is well known. According to Kracauer, the distinctive lighting of *Dr. Caligari* (and of many German films of the early 1920's) can be traced to an experiment with lighting that Max Reinhardt made shortly before on the stage in his production of Sorge's *The Beggar*. Even in this period, however, the impact was reciprocal. The accomplishments of the "expressionist film" were immediately absorbed by the expressionist theatre. Stimulated by the cinematic technique of the "iris-in," stage lighting took to singling out a lone player or some segment of the scene, masking out the rest of the stage. Rotating sets tried to approximate the instantaneous displacement of the camera eye. (More recently, reports have come of ingenious lighting techniques used by the Gorky Theatre in Leningrad, directed since 1956 by Georgy Tovstonogov, which allow for incredibly rapid scene changes taking place behind a horizontal curtain of light.)

Today traffic seems, with few exceptions, entirely one way: film to theatre. Particularly in France and in Central and Eastern Europe, the staging of many plays is inspired by the movies. The aim of adapting neo-cinematic devices for the stage (I exclude the outright use of films within the theatre production) seems mainly to tighten up the theatrical experience, to approximate the cinema's absolute control of the flow and location of the audience's attention. But the conception can be even more directly cinematic. An example is Josef Svoboda's production of *The Insect Play* by the Capek brothers at the Czech National Theatre in Prague (recently seen in London), which frankly attempted to install a mediated vision upon the stage, equivalent to the discontinuous intensifications of the camera eye. According to a London critic's account, "the set consisted of two huge, faceted mirrors slung at an angle to the stage, so that they reflect whatever happens there defracted as if through a decanter stopper or the colossally magnified eye of a fly. Any figure placed at the base of their angle becomes multiplied from floor to proscenium; further out, and you find yourself viewing it not only face to face but from overhead, the vantage point of a camera slung to a bird or a helicopter."

Marinetti was perhaps the first to propose the use of films as one element in a theatre experience. Writing between 1910 and 1914, he envisaged the theatre as a final synthesis of all the arts; and as such it had to draw in the newest art form, movies. No doubt the cinema also recommended itself for inclusion because of the priority Marinetti gave to existing forms of popular entertainment, such as the variety theatre and the *café chantant*. (He called his projected total art form "the Futurist Variety Theatre.") And at that time scarcely anyone considered cinema anything but a vulgar art.

After World War I, similar ideas appear frequently. In the total-theatre projects of the Bauhaus group in the 1920's (Gropius, Piscator, etc.) film had an important place. Meyerhold insisted on its use in the theatre, describing his program as fulfilling Wagner's once "wholly utopian" proposals to "use all means available from the other arts." Alban Berg specified that a silent film of the developing story was to be projected in the middle of Act 2 of his opera *Lulu*. By now, the employment of film in theatre has a fairly long history which includes the "living newspaper" of the 1930's, "epic theatre," and Happenings. This year marked the introduction of a film sequence into Broadway-level theatre. In two successful musicals, London's *Come Spy with Me* and New York's *Superman*, both parodic in tone, the action is interrupted to lower a screen and run off a movie showing the pop-art hero's exploits.

But thus far the use of film within live theatre events has tended to be stereotyped. Film is often employed as *document*, supportive of or redundant to the live stage events (as in Brecht's productions in East Berlin). Its other principal use is as *hallucinant;* recent examples are Bob

Whitman's Happenings, and a new kind of nightclub situation, the mixed-media discothèque (Andy Warhol's The Plastic Inevitable, Murray the K's World). From the point of view of theatre, the interpolation of film into the theatre experience may be enlarging. But in terms of what cinema is capable of, it seems a reductive, monotonous use of film.

What Panofsky perhaps could not have realized when he wrote his essay is that much more than the "nature" of a specific art "medium" is at stake. The relation between film and theatre involves not simply a static definition of the two arts, but sensitivity to the possible course of their radicalization.

Every interesting aesthetic tendency now is a species of radicalism. The question each artist must ask is: What is *my* radicalism, the one dictated by *my* gifts and temperament? This doesn't mean all contemporary artists believe that art progresses. A radical position isn't necessarily a forward-looking position.

Consider the two principal radical positions in the arts today. One recommends the breaking down of distinctions between genres; the arts would eventuate in one art, consisting of many different kinds of behavior going on at the same time, a vast behavioral magma or synesthesia. The other position recommends the maintaining and clarifying of barriers between the arts, by the intensification of what each art distinctively is; painting must use only those means which pertain to painting, music only those which are musical, novels those which pertain to the novel and to no other literary form, etc. The two positions are, in a sense, irreconcilable—except that both are invoked to support the perennial modern quest for the definitive art form.

An art may be proposed as definitive because it is considered the most rigorous or most fundamental. For these reasons, Schopenhauer suggested and Pater asserted that all art aspires to the condition of music. More recently, the thesis that all the arts are leading toward one art has been advanced by enthusiasts of the cinema. The candidacy of film is founded on its being both so exact and, potentially, so complex a combination of music, literature, and the image.

Or, an art may be proposed as definitive because it is held to be most inclusive. This is the basis of the destiny for theatre held out by Wagner, Marinetti, Artaud, Cage—all of whom envisaged theatre as a total art, potentially conscripting all the arts into its service. And as the ideas of synesthesia continue to proliferate among painters, sculptors, architects, and composers, theatre remains the favored candidate for the role of summative art. In this conception, theatre's role must disparage the claims of cinema. Partisans of theatre would argue that while music, painting, dance, cinema, and utterance can all converge on a "stage," the film object can only become bigger (multiple screens, 360 degree projection, etc.) or longer in duration or internally more articulated and complex. Theatre can be anything, everything; in the end, films can only be more of what they specifically (that is to say, cinematically) are.

Underlying the more grandiose apocalyptic expectations for both arts is a common animus. In 1923 Béla Balázs, anticipating in great detail the thesis of Marshall McLuhan, described movies as the herald of a a new "visual culture" which will give us back our bodies, and particularly our faces, which have been rendered illegible, soulless, unexpressive by the centuries-old ascendancy of "print." An animus against literature, against the printing press and its "culture of concepts," also informs most interesting thinking about the theatre in our time.

No definition or characterization of theatre and cinema can be taken for granted—not even the apparently self-evident observation that both cinema and theatre are temporal arts. In theatre and cinema, like music (and unlike painting), everything is *not* present all at once. But there are significant developments today pointing up the atemporal aspect of these forms. The allure of mixed-media forms in theatre suggests not only a more elongated and more complex "drama" (like Wagnerian opera) but also a more compact theatre experience which approaches the condition of painting. This prospect of compactness is broached by Marinetti; he calls it simultaneity, a leading notion of Futurist aesthetics. As the final synthesis of all the arts, theatre "would use the new twentieth century devices of electricity and the cinema; this would enable plays to be extremely short, since all these technical means would enable the theatrical synthesis to be achieved in the shortest possible space of time, as all the elements could be presented simultaneously."

The source of the idea of art as an act of violence pervading cinema and theatre is the aesthetics of Futurism and of Surrealism; its principal texts are, for theatre, the writings of Artaud and, for cinema, two films of Luis Buñuel, *L'Age d'Or* and *Un Chien Andalou*. (More recent examples: the early plays of Ionesco, at least as conceived; the "cinema of cruelty" of Hitchcock, Clouzot, Franju, Robert Aldrich, Polanski; work by the Living Theatre; some of the neo-cinematic light shows in experimental theatres and discothèques; the sound of late Cage and LaMonte Young.) The relation of art to an audience understood to be passive, inert, surfeited, can only be assault. Art becomes identical with aggression.

However understandable and valuable this theory of art as an assault on the audience is today (like the complementary notion of art as ritual), one must continue to question it, particularly in the theatre. For it can become as much a convention as anything else and end, like all theatrical conventions, by reinforcing rather than challenging the deadness of the audience. (As Wagner's ideology of a total theatre played its role in confirming the philistinism of German culture.)

Moreover, the depth of the assault must be assessed honestly. In the theatre, this means not "diluting" Artaud. Artaud's writings express the demand for a totally open (therefore flayed, self-cruel) consciousness of which theatre would be one adjunct or instrument. No work in the theatre has yet amounted to this. Thus, Peter Brook has astutely and forthrightly disclaimed that his company's work in the "Theatre of Cruelty," which culminated in his celebrated production of *Marat/Sade*, is genuinely Artaudian. It is Artaudian, he says, in a trivial sense only. (Trivial from Artaud's point of view, not from ours.)

For some time, all useful ideas in art have been extremely sophisticated. Take, for example, the idea that everything is what it is and not another thing: a painting is a painting; sculpture is sculpture; a poem is a poem, not prose. Or the complementary idea: a painting can be "literary" or sculptural, a poem can be prose, theatre can emulate and incorporate cinema, cinema can be theatrical.

We need a new idea. It will probably be a very simple one. Will we be able to recognize it?

[1966]

ANDRÉ BAZIN

Theater and Cinema

The leitmotiv of those who despise filmed theater, their final and apparently insuperable argument, continues to be the unparalleled pleasure that accompanies the presence of the actor. "What is specific to theater," writes Henri Gouhier, in *The Essence of Theater*, "is the impossibility of separating off action and actor." Elsewhere he says, "the stage welcomes every illusion except that of presence; the actor is there in disguise, with the soul and voice of another, but he is nevertheless there and by the same token space calls out for him and for the solidity of his presence. On the other hand and inversely, the cinema accommodates every form of reality save one—the physical presence of the actor." If it is here that the essence of theater lies then undoubtedly the cinema can in no way pretend to any parallel with it. If the writing, the style, and the dramatic structure are, as they should be, rigorously conceived as the receptacle for the soul and being of the flesh-and-blood actor, any attempt to substitute the shadow and reflection of a man on the screen for the man himself is a completely vain enterprise. There is no answer to this argument. The successes of Laurence Olivier, of Welles, or of Cocteau can only be challenged—here you need to be in bad faith—or considered inexplicable. They are a challenge both to critics and philosophers. Alternatively one can only explain them by casting doubts on that commonplace of theatrical criticism "the irreplacable presence of the actor."

From André Bazin, *What Is Cinema?* Originally published by the University of California Press; reprinted by permission of The Regents of the University of California.

THE CONCEPT OF PRESENCE

At this point certain comments seem called for concerning the concept of "presence," since it would appear that it is this concept, as understood prior to the appearance of photography, that the cinema challenges.

Can the photographic image, especially the cinematographic image, be likenend to other images and in common with them be regarded as having an existence distinct from the object? Presence, naturally, is defined in terms of time and space. "To be in the presence of someone" is to recognize him as existing contemporaneously with us and to note that he comes within the actual range of our senses—in the case of cinema of our sight and in radio of our hearing. Before the arrival of photography and later of cinema, the plastic arts (especially portraiture) were the only intermediaries between actual physical presence and absence. Their justification was their resemblance which stirs the imagination and helps the memory. But photography is something else again. In no sense is it the image of an object or person, more correctly it is its tracing. Its automatic genesis distinguishes it radically from the other techniques of reproduction. The photograph proceeds by means of the lens to the taking of a veritable luminous impression in light—to a mold. As such it carries with it more than mere resemblance, namely a kind of identity—the card we call by that name being only conceivable in an age of photography. But photography is a feeble technique in the sense that its instantaneity compels it to capture time only piecemeal. The cinema does something strangely paradoxical. It makes a molding of the object as it exists in time and, furthermore, makes an imprint of the duration of the object.

The nineteenth century with its objective techniques of visual and sound reproduction gave birth to a new category of images, the relation of which to the reality from which they proceed requires very strict definition. Even apart from the fact that the resulting aesthetic problems cannot be satisfactorily raised without this introductory philosophical inquiry, it would not be sound to treat the old aesthetic questions as if the categories with which they deal had in no way been modified by the appearance of completely new phenomena. Common sense—perhaps the best philosophical guide in this case—has clearly understood this and has invented an expression for the presence of an actor, by adding to the placards announcing his appearance the phrase "in flesh and blood." This means that for the man in the street the word "presence," today, can be ambiguous, and thus an apparent redundancy is not out of place in this age of cinema. Hence it is no longer as certain as it was that there is no middle stage between presence and absence. It is likewise at the ontological level that the effectiveness of the cinema has its source. It is false to say that the screen is incapable of putting us "in the presence of" the actor. It does so in the same way as a mirror—one must agree that the mirror relays the presence of the person reflected in it—but it is a mirror with a delayed reflection, the tin foil of which retains the image.* It is true that in the theater Molière can die on the stage and that we have the privilege of living in the biographical time of the actor. In the film about Manolete however we are present at the actual death of the famous matador and while our emotion may not be as deep as if we were actually present in the arena at that historic moment, its nature is the same. What we lose by way of direct witness do we not recapture thanks to the artificial proximity provided by photographic enlargement? Everything takes place as if in the time-space perimeter which is the definition of presence. The cinema offers us effectively only a measure of duration, reduced but not to zero, while the increase in the space factor reestablishes the equilibrium of the psychological equation.

OPPOSITION AND IDENTIFICATION

An honest appraisal of the respective pleasures derived from theater and cinema, at least as to what is less intellectual and more direct about them, forces us to admit that the delight we experience at the end of a play has a more uplifting, a nobler, one might perhaps say a more moral, effect than the satisfaction which follows a good film. We seem to come away with a better conscience. In a certain sense it is as if for the man in the audience all theater is "Corneillian." From this point of view one could say that in the best films something is missing. It is as if a certain inevitable lowering of the voltage, some mysterious aesthetic short circuit, deprived us in the cinema of a certain tension which is a definite part of theater. No matter how slight this difference it undoubtedly exists, even between the worst charity production in the theater and the most

*Television naturally adds a new variant to the "pseudopresences" resulting from the scientific techniques for reproduction created by photography. On the little screen during live television the actor is actually present in space and time. But the reciprocal actor-spectator relationship is incomplete in one direction. The spectator sees without being seen. There is no return flow. Televised theater, therefore, seems to share something both of theater and of cinema: of theater because the actor is present to the viewer, of cinema because the spectator is not present to the actor. Nevertheless, this state of not being present is not truly an absence. The television actor has a sense of the millions of ears and eyes virtually present and represented by the electronic camera. This abstract presence is most noticeable when the actor fluffs his lines. Painful enough in the theater, it is intolerable on television since the spectator who can do nothing to help him is aware of the unnatural solitude of the actor. In the theater in similar circumstances a sort of understanding exists with the audience, which is a help to an actor in trouble. This kind of reciprocal relationship is impossible on television.

brilliant of Olivier's film adaptations. There is nothing banal about this observation and the survival of the theater after fifty years of cinema, and the prophecies of Marcel Pagnol, is practical proof enough. At the source of the disenchantment which follows the film one could doubtless detect a process of depersonalization of the spectator. As Rosenkrantz wrote in 1937, in *Esprit*, in an article profoundly original for its period, "The characters on the screen are quite naturally objects of identification, while those on the stage are, rather, objects of mental opposition because their real presence gives them an objective reality and to transpose them into beings in an imaginary world the will of the spectator has to intervene actively, that is to say, to will to transform their physical reality into an abstraction. This abstraction being the result of a process of the intelligence that we can only ask of a person who is fully conscious." A member of a film audience tends to identify himself with the film's hero by a psychological process, the result of which is to turn the audience into a "mass" and to render emotion uniform. Just as in algebra if two numbers equal a third, then they are equal to one another, so here we can say, if two individuals identify themselves with a third, they identify themselves with one another. Let us compare chorus girls on the stage and on the screen. On the screen they satisfy an unconscious sexual desire and when the hero joins them he satisfies the desire of the spectator in the proportion to which the latter has identified himself with the hero. On the stage the girls excite the onlooker as they would in real life. The result is that there is no identification with the hero. He becomes instead an object of jealousy and envy. In other words, Tarzan is only possible on the screen. The cinema calms the spectator, the theater excites him. Even when it appeals to the lowest instincts, the theater up to a certain point stands in the way of the creation of a mass mentality.* It stands in the way of any collective representation in the psychological sense, since theater calls for an active individual consciousness while the film requires only a passive adhesion.

These views shed a new light on the problem of the actor. They transfer him from the ontological to the psychological level. It is to the extent to which the cinema encourages identification with the hero that it conflicts with the theater. Put this way the problem is no longer basically insoluble, for it is a fact that the cinema has at its disposal means which favor a passive position or on the other hand, means which to a greater or lesser degree stimulate the consciousness of the spectator. Inversely the theater can find ways of lessening the psychological tension between spectator and actor. Thus theater and cinema will no longer be separated off by an unbridgeable aesthetic moat, they would simply tend

---

*Crowd and solitude are not antinomies: the audience in a movie house is made up of solitary individuals. Crowd should be taken here to mean the opposite of an organic community freely assembled.

to give rise to two attitudes of mind over which the director maintains a wide control.

Examined at close quarters, the pleasure derived from the theater not only differs from that of the cinema but also from that of the novel. The reader of a novel, physically alone like the man in the dark movie house, identifies himself with the character.* That is why after reading for a long while he also feels the same intoxication of an illusory intimacy with the hero. Incontestably, there is in the pleasure derived from cinema and novel a self-satisfaction, a concession to solitude, a sort of betrayal of action by a refusal of social responsibility.

The analysis of this phenomenon might indeed be undertaken from a psychoanalytic point of view. Is it not significant that the psychiatrists took the term catharsis from Aristotle? Modern pedagogic research on psychodrama seems to have provided fruitful insights into the cathartic process of theater. The ambiguity existing in the child's mind between play and reality is used to get him to free himself by way of improvised theater from the repressions from which he suffers. This technique amounts to creating a kind of vague theater in which the play is of a serious nature and the actor is his own audience. The action that develops on these occasions is not one that is divided off by footlights, which are undoubtedly the architectural symbol of the censor that separates us from the stage. We delegate Oedipus to act in our guise and place him on the other side of a wall of fire—that fiery frontier between fantasy and reality which gives rein to Dionysiac monsters while protecting us from them.** These sacred beasts will not cross this barrier of light beyond which they seem out of place and even sacrilegious—witness the disturbing atmosphere of awe which surrounds an actor still made up, like a phosphorescent light, when we visit him in his dressing room. There is no point to the argument that the theater did not always have footlights. These are only a symbol and there were others before them from the cothurnus and mask onwards. In the seventeenth century the fact that young nobles sat up on the stage is no denial of the role of the footlights, on the contrary, it confirms it, by way of a privileged violation so to speak, just as when today Orson Welles scatters actors around the auditorium to fire on the audience with revolvers. He does not do away with the footlights, he just crosses them. The rules of the game are also made to be broken. One expects some players to cheat.† With regard to the objection based on

---

*Cf. Cl. E. Magny, *L'Age du roman américain*, ed. Du Seuil.

**Cf. P. A. Touchard, *Dionysos*, ed. Du Seuil.

†Here is a final example proving that presence does not constitute theater except in so far as it is a matter of a performance. Everyone either at his own or someone else's expense has known the embarrassment of being watched without knowing it or in spite of knowing it. Lovers who kiss on public benches offer a spectacle to the passerby, but they do not care. My concierge who has a feeling for the *mot juste* says, when she sees them, that it is like being at the movies. Each of us has sometimes found himself forced to his annoyance to do something absurd before other people. On those occa-

presence and on that alone, the theater and the cinema are not basically in conflict. What is really in dispute are two psychological modalities of a performance. The theater is indeed based on the reciprocal awareness of the presence of audience and actor, but only as related to a performance. The theater acts on us by virtue of our participation in a theatrical action across the footlights and as it were under the protection of their censorship. The opposite is true in the cinema. Alone, hidden in a dark room, we watch through half-open blinds a spectacle that is unaware of our existence and which is part of the universe. There is nothing to prevent us from identifying ourselves in imagination with the moving world before us, which becomes *the* world. It is no longer on the phenomenon of the actor as a person physically present that we should concentrate our analysis, but rather on the ensemble of conditions that constitute the theatrical play and deprive the spectator of active participation. We shall see that it is much less a question of actor and presence than of man and his relation to the decor.

BEHIND THE DOOR

The human being is all-important in the theater. The drama on the screen can exist without actors. A banging door, a leaf in the wind, waves beating on the shore can heighten the dramatic effect. Some film masterpieces use man only as an accessory, like an extra, or in counterpoint to nature which is the true leading character. Even when, as in *Nanook* and *Man of Aran*, the subject is man's struggle with nature, it cannot be compared to a theatrical action. The mainspring of the action is not in man but in nature. As Jean-Paul Sartre, I think it was, said, in the theater the drama proceeds from the actor, in the cinema it goes from the decor to man. This reversal of the dramatic flow is of decisive importance. It is bound up with the very essence of the *mise-en-scène*. One must see here one of the consequences of photographic realism. Obviously, if the cinema makes use of nature it is because it is able to. The camera puts at the disposal of the director all the resources of the telescope and the microscope. The last strand of a rope about to snap or an entire army making an assault on a hill are within our reach. Dramatic causes and effects have no longer any material limits to the eye of the camera. Drama

---

sions, we experience a sense of angry shame which is the very opposite of theatrical exhibitionism. Someone who looks through a keyhole is not at the theater; Cocteau has rightly demonstrated in *Le sang d'un poète* that he was already at the cinema. And nevertheless there are such things as "shows," when the protagonists are present to us in flesh and blood but one of the two parties is ignorant of the fact or goes through it reluctantly. This is not "play" in the theatrical sense.

is freed by the camera from all contingencies of time and space. But this freeing of tangible dramatic powers is still only a secondary aesthetic cause, and does not basically explain the reversal of value between the actor and the decor. For sometimes it actually happens that the cinema deliberately deprives itself of the use of setting and exterior nature . . . while the theater in contrast uses a complex machinery to give a feeling of ubiquity to the audience. Is *La Passion de Jeanne d'Arc* by Carl Dreyer, shot entirely in close-up, in the virtually invisible and in fact theatrical settings by Jean Hugo, less cinematic than *Stagecoach?* It seems to me that quantity has nothing to do with it, nor the resemblance to certain theater techniques. The ideas of an art director for a room in *Les Dames aux camélias* would not noticeably differ whether for a film or a play. It's true that on the screen you would doubtless have some close-ups of the blood-stained handkerchief, but a skillful stage production would also know how to make some play with the cough and the handkerchief. All the close-ups in *Les Parents terribles* are taken directly from the theater where our attention would spontaneously isolate them. If film direction only differed from theater direction because it allows us a closer view of the scenery and makes a more reasonable use of it, there would really be no reason to continue with the theater and Pagnol would be a true prophet. For it is obvious that the few square yards of the decor of Vilar's *La Danse de la mort* contributed as much to the drama as the island on which Marcel Cravene shot his excellent film. The fact is that the problem lies not in the decor itself but in its nature and function. We must therefore throw some light on an essentially theatrical notion, that of the dramatic place.

There can be no theater without architecture, whether it be the cathedral square, the arena of Nîmes, the palace of the Popes, the trestle stage on a fairground, the semicircle of the theater of Vicenza that looks as if it were decorated by Bérard in a delirium, or the rococo amphitheaters of the boulevard houses. Whether as a performance or a celebration, theater of its very essence must not be confused with nature under penalty of being absorbed by her and ceasing to be. Founded on the reciprocal awareness of those taking part and present to one another, it must be in contrast to the rest of the world in the same way that play and reality are opposed, or concern and indifference, or liturgy and the common use of things. Costume, mask, or make-up, the style of the language, the footlights, all contribute to this distinction, but the clearest sign of all is the stage, the architecture of which has varied from time to time without ever ceasing to mark out a privileged spot actually or virtually distinct from nature. It is precisely in virtue of this *locus dramaticus* that decor exists. It serves in greater or less degree to set the place apart, to specify. Whatever it is, the decor constitutes the walls of this three-sided box opening onto the auditorium, which we call the stage. These false perspectives, these façades, these arbors, have another side which is cloth and nails and wood. Everyone knows that when the actor "retires to his apartment" from the yard or from the garden, he is actually going to his dressing room to take off his make-up. These few square feet of light and illusion are surrounded by machinery and flanked by wings, the hidden labyrinths of which do not interfere one bit with the pleasure of the spectator who is playing the game of theater. Because it is only part of the architecture of the stage, the decor of the theater is thus an area materially enclosed, limited, circumscribed, the only discoveries of which are those of our collusive imagination.

Its appearances are turned inward facing the public and the footlights. It exists by virtue of its reverse side and of anything beyond, as the painting exists by virtue of its frame. Just as the picture is not to be confounded with the scene it represents and is not a window in a wall. The stage and the decor where the action unfolds constitute an aesthetic microcosm inserted perforce into the universe but essentially distinct from the Nature which surrounds it.

It is not the same with cinema, the basic principle of which is a denial of any frontiers to action.

The idea of a *locus dramaticus* is not only alien to, it is essentially a contradiction of the concept of the screen. The screen is not a frame like that of a picture but a mask which allows only a part of the action to be seen. When a character moves off screen, we accept the fact that he is out of sight, but he continues to exist in his own capacity at some other place in the decor which is hidden from us. There are no wings to the screen. There could not be without destroying its specific illusion, which is to make of a revolver or of a face the very center of the universe. In contrast to the stage the space of the screen is centrifugal. It is because that infinity which the theater demands cannot be spatial that its area can be none other than the human soul. Enclosed in this space the actor is at the focus of a two-fold concave mirror. From the auditorium and from the decor there converge on him the dim lights of conscious human beings and of the footlights themselves. But the fire with which he burns is at once that of his inner passion and of that focal point at which he stands. He lights up in each member of his audience an accomplice flame. Like the ocean in a sea shell the dramatic infinities of the human heart moan and beat between the enclosing walls of the theatrical sphere. This is why this dramaturgy is in its essence human. Man is at once its cause and its subject.

On the screen man is no longer the focus of the drama, but will become eventually the center of the universe. The impact of his action may there set in motion an infinitude of waves. The decor that surrounds him is part of the solidity of the world. For this reason the actor as such can be absent from it, because man in the world enjoys no a priori privilege over animals and things. However there is no reason why he should not be the mainspring of the drama, as in Dreyer's *Jeanne d'Arc*, and in this respect the cinema may very well impose itself upon the theater. As actions *Phèdre* or *King Lear* are no less cinematographic than theatrical, and the visible death of a rabbit in *La Règle du jeu* affects us just as deeply as that of Agnès' little cat about which we are merely told.

But if Racine, Shakespeare, or Molière cannot be brought to the cinema by just placing them before the camera and the microphone, it is because the handling of the action and the style of the dialogue were conceived as echoing through the architecture of the auditorium. What is specifically theatrical about these tragedies is not their action so much as the human, that is to say the verbal, priority given to their dramatic structure. The problem of filmed theater at least where the classics are concerned does not consist so much in transposing an action from the stage to the screen as in transposing a text written for one dramaturgical system into another while at the same time retaining its effectiveness. It is not therefore essentially the action of a play which resists film adaptation, but above and beyond the phases of the intrigue (which it would be easy enough to adapt to the realism of the screen) it is the verbal form which aesthetic contingencies or cultural prejudices oblige us to respect. It is this which refuses to let itself be captured in the window of the screen. "The theater," says Baudelaire, "is a crystal chandelier." If one were called upon to offer in comparison a symbol other than this artificial crystal-like object, brilliant, intricate, and circular, which refracts the light which plays around its center and holds us prisoners of its aureole, we might say of the cinema that it is the little flashlight of the usher, moving like an uncertain comet across the night of our waking dream, the diffuse space without shape or frontiers that surrounds the screen.

The story of the failures and recent successes of theater on film will be found to be that of the ability of directors to retain the dramatic force of the play in a medium that reflects it or, at least, the ability to give this dramatic force enough resonance to permit a film audience to perceive it. In other words, it is a matter of an aesthetic that is not concerned with the actor but with decor and editing. Henceforth it is clear that filmed theater is basically destined to fail whenever it tends in any manner to become simply the photographing of scenic representation even and perhaps most of all when the camera is used to try and make us forget the footlights and the backstage area. The dramatic force of the text, instead of being gathered up in the actor, dissolves without echo into the cinematic ether. This is why a filmed play can show due respect to the text, be well acted in likely settings, and yet be completely worthless. This is what happened, to take a convenient example, to *Le Voyageur sans bag-gages.* The play lies there before us apparently true to itself yet drained of every ounce of energy, like a battery dead from an unknown short. But over and beyond the aesthetic of the decor we see clearly both on the screen and on the stage that in the last analysis the problem before us is that of realism. This is the problem we always end up with when we are dealing with cinema.

THE SCREEN AND THE REALISM OF SPACE

The realism of the cinema follows directly from its photo-graphic nature. Not only does some marvel or some fantastic thing on the screen not undermine the reality of the image, on the contrary it is its most valid justification. Illusion in the cinema is not based as it is in the theater on convention tacitly accepted by the general public; rather, con-trariwise, it is based on the inalienable realism of that which is shown. All trick work must be perfect in all material respects on the screen. The "invisible man" must wear pajamas and smoke a cigarette.

Must we conclude from this that the cinema is dedicated entirely to the representation if not of natural reality at least of a plausible reality of which the spectator admits the identity with nature as he knows it? The comparative failure of German expressionism would seem to confirm this hypothesis, since it is evident that *Caligari* attempted to depart from realistic decor under the influence of the theater and painting. But this would be to offer an oversimplified explanation for a problem that calls for more subtle answers. We are prepared to admit that the screen opens upon an artificial world provided there exists a common denominator between the cinematographic image and the world we live in. Our experi-ence of space is the structural basis for our concept of the universe. We may say in fact, adapting Henri Gouhier's formula, "the stage welcomes every illusion except the illusion of presence," that "the cinematographic image can be emptied of all reality save one—the reality of space."

It is perhaps an overstatement to say "all reality" because it is diffi-cult to imagine a reconstruction of space devoid of all reference to na-ture. The world of the screen and our world cannot be juxtaposed. The screen of necessity substitutes for it since the very concept of universe is spatially exclusive. For a time, a film is the Universe, the world, or if you like, Nature. We will see how the films that have attempted to substitute a fabricated nature and an artificial world for the world of experience have not all equally succeeded. Admitting the failure of *Caligari* and *Die Nibelungen* we then ask ourselves how we explain the undoubted success of *Nosferatu* and *La Passion de Jeanne d'Arc,* the criterion of success being that these films have never aged. Yet it would seem at first sight that the methods of direction belong to the same aesthetic family, and that viewing the varieties of temperament and period, one could group these four films together as expressionist as distinct from realist. However, if we examine them more closely we see that there are certain basic differences between them. It is clear in the case of R. Weine and Murnau. *Nosferatu* plays, for the greatest part of the time, against natural settings whereas the fantastic qualities of *Caligari* are derived from deformities of lighting and decor. The case of Dreyer's *Jeanne d'Arc* is a little more subtle since at first sight nature plays a nonexistent role. To put it more directly, the decor by Jean Hugo is no whit less artificial and theatrical than the settings of *Caligari;* the systematic use of close-ups and unusual angles is well calculated to destroy any sense of space. Regular cinéclub goers know that the film is unfailingly introduced with the famous story of how the hair of Falconetti was actually cut in the interests of the film and likewise, the actors, we are told, wore no make-up. These references to history ordinarily have no more than gossip value. In this case, they seem to me to hold the aesthetic secret of the film; the very thing to which it owes its continued survival. It is precisely because of them that the work of Dreyer ceases to have anything in common with the theater, and indeed one might say, with man. The greater recourse Dreyer has exclusively to the human "expression," the more he has to reconvert it again into Nature. Let there be no mistake, that prodigious fresco of heads is the very opposite of an actor's film. It is a documentary of faces. It is not important how well the actors play, whereas the pockmarks on Bishop Cauchon's face and the red patches of Jean d'Yd are an integral part of the action. In this drama-through-the-microscope the whole of nature palpitates beneath every pore. The movement of a wrinkle, the pursing of a lip are seismic shocks and the flow of tides, the flux and reflux of his human epidermis. But for me Dreyer's brilliant sense of cinema is evidenced in the exterior scene which every other director would assuredly have shot in the studio. The decor as built evoked a Middles Ages of the theater and of miniatures. In one sense, nothing is less realistic than this tribunal in the cemetery or this drawbridge, but the whole is lit by the light of the sun and the gravedigger throws a spadeful of real earth into the hole.*

It is these "secondary" details, apparently aesthetically at odds with with the rest of the work, which give it its truly cinematic quality.

If the paradox of the cinema is rooted in the dialectic of concrete

---

*This is why I consider the graveyard scene in *Hamlet* and the death of Ophelia bad mistakes on Olivier's part. He had here a chance to introduce sun and soil by way of counterpoint to the setting of Elsinore. Does the actual shot of the sea during the soliloquy of Hamlet show that he had sensed the need for this? The idea, excellent in itself, is not well handled technically.

and abstract, if cinema is committed to communicate only by way of what is real, it becomes all the more important to discern those elements in filming which confirm our sense of natural reality and those which destroy that feeling. On the other hand, it certainly argues a lack of perception to derive one's sense of reality from those accumulations of factual detail. It is possible to argue that *Les Dames du Bois de Boulogne* is an eminently realistic film, though everything about it is stylized. Everything, except for the rarely noticeable sound of a windshield-wiper, the murmur of a waterfall, or the rushing sound of soil escaping from a broken vase. These are the noises, chosen precisely for their "indifference" to the action, that guarantee its reality.

The cinema being of its essence a dramaturgy of Nature, there can be no cinema without the setting up of an open space in place of the universe rather than as part of it. The screen cannot give us the illusion of this feeling of space without calling on certain natural guarantees. But it is less a question of set construction or of architecture or of immensity than of isolating the aesthetic catalyst, which it is sufficient to introduce in an infinitesimal dose, to have it immediately take on the reality of nature.

The concrete forest of *Die Nibelungen* may well pretend to be an infinite expanse. We do not believe it to be so, whereas the trembling of just one branch in the wind, and the sunlight, would be enough to conjure up all the forests of the world.

If this analysis be well founded, then we see that the basic aesthetic problem of filmed theater is indeed that of the decor. The trump card that the director must hold is the reconversion into a window onto the world of a space oriented toward an interior dimension only, namely the closed and conventional area of the theatrical play.

It is not in Laurence Olivier's *Hamlet* that the text seems to be rendered superfluous or its strength diminished by directional interpretations, still less in Welles' *Macbeth*, but paradoxically in the stage productions of Gaston Baty, to the precise extent that they go out of their way to create a cinematographic space on the stage; to deny that the settings have a reverse side, thus reducing the sonority of the text simply to the vibration of the voice of the actor who is left without his "resonance box" like a violin that is nothing else but strings. One would never deny that the essential thing in the theater is the text. The latter conceived for the anthropocentric expression proper to the stage and having as its function to bring nature to it cannot, without losing its raison d'être, be used in a space transparent as glass. The problem then that faces the film-maker is to give his decor a dramatice opaqueness while at the same time reflecting its natural realism. Once this paradox of space has been dealt with, the director, so far from hesitating to bring theatrical conventions and faithfulness to the text to the screen will find himself now, on the contrary, completely free to rely on them. From that point on it is no longer a matter of running away from those things which "make theater" but in the long run to acknowledge their existence by rejecting the resources of the cinema, as Cocteau did in *Les Parents terribles* and Welles in *Macbeth,* or by putting them in quotation marks as Laurence Olivier did in *Henry V*. The evidence of a return to filmed theater that we have had during the last ten years belongs essentially to the history of decor and editing. It is a conquest of realism—not, certainly, the realism of subject matter or realism of expression but that realism of space without which moving pictures do not constitute cinema. . . .

MORALITY

Thus the practice (certain) like the theory (possible) of successful filmed theater reveals the reasons for former failures. Straightforward animated photography of theater is a childish error recognized as such these thirty years and on which there is no point in insisting further. The heresy of film adaptation has taken longer to smoke out. It will continue to have its dupes but we now know where it leads—to aesthetic limbos that belong neither to film nor to theater, to that "filmed theater" justly condemned as the sin against the spirit of cinema. The true solution, revealed at last, consists in realizing that it is not a matter of transferring to the screen the dramatic element—an element interchangeable between one art and another—of a theatrical work, but inversely the theatrical quality of the drama. The subject of the adaptation is not that of the play, it is the play precisely in its scenic essence. . . .

[1958]

GEORGE GARRETT

"Don't Make Waves"

. . . Except for the fact that both forms are dramatic, writing for films is very different from writing for the stage.

Very different. At least insofar as our present concept of the stage permits. And here I am speaking of our present *stage* and its conventions, not of the marketplace, its conditions and subjects. Except to say that if one does consider the marketplace, the gap between stage and film is much wider.

To talk, even briefly, of difference, I must begin with some of the similarities. Both involve directed actors speaking lines of dialogue and performing dramatic actions. Meaning that many of the tools are the same. And we can't ignore the simple fact that the structure of the modern three-act play has had a considerable influence on the way a film script is put together. Before talkies the influence would appear to have been much less. But with the introduction of real spoken and heard dialogue the influence became stronger. For one thing a great many playwrights were hired to write pictures. Testimony to this can be found in the files of old scripts in the studios. Frequently they were divided into three acts and so labeled on the typescript. To this day a great many people who make movies or work on movies speak of the structure of a movie in terms of three acts. Asked where he begins work on a script, Billy Wilder has said that he begins with "a good second act curtain."

Yet it is possible to see this, by analogy, as a little like the evolution of the automobile from a horseless carriage with an engine to a thing in itself. Yes, it has wheels and runs something like a carriage, and yes its power is still measured in horsepower. But a car, for better or worse, is not a carriage any more.

Some of the differences between stage and screen help define the screenwriter's job and craft. One of the most obvious differences in the craft is a result of the singular trickery of the film. What is seen and shown, whether large or small, is perfectly controlled. By the camera. When something happens on stage we may look at it and react if we choose, but we don't have to. We can look at the set, at other actors, or anything else. Which means, among other things, that the playwright and/or the director have got to focus audience attention in a different way. One of the simplest problems of drama, getting people on and off stage credibly and reasonably, simply does not exist for the screenwriter. In that medium he need only put the camera on what he wants the audience to see, and all else vanishes. It is in the nature of the rhetoric of the medium that *nothing except what we see (and whatever is evoked by that sight) exists at any given moment.*

From crowded room full of people to close-up on a couple of characters. The crowded room, though the characters may indeed be in it, vanishes.

Once movements and transitions, movement in place or time for example, were emphasized as they have to be on stage. In the older picture, somebody says, "Let's go to the beach." You then have shots of the characters loading gear into a car. Shots of the car going along a road. Shots establishing the sea and shore. Finally we find our characters under an umbrella having a picnic. Logical enough. But a logic of rational motivation derived from the stage—"Come and see the azaleas in the garden."

Now it is not even necessary to prepare for such a transition with dialogue or suggested intention. More likely, to return to that crowded room, the camera shows us a close-up of the characters we are concerned with, the scene ends where it ends in fact and not artificially, and the next instant our characters are under an umbrella on the beach eating cucumber sandwiches.

Supremely economical, swift and easy.

As in stage drama much work by the writer is done by *reaction.* But how easily this is conveyed on film. Something happens or is said. We go immediately to the simple, direct, and usually wordless reaction of a character. And this reaction need not take into account the literal context. That is, boy and girl are talking. Obviously girl is eager to make points with boy. Boy says, "See you around." We need not even see the boy walk away. We can go to close-up of the girl looking disappointed. A look she might not, as an actor or in real life either, allow herself precisely at that second and in his presence. His presence is finished, his departure simply assumed when we see the girl's reaction.

Very simple examples. Ordinary. But they tell us something about the different rhetoric of film and stage. Some of these things are true because the audience has seen so many movies and filmed television shows and has become increasingly sophisticated. A condition compounded by the fact that except for wider screens, sound, different kinds of films, etc., the basic elements of film technique were set and established almost from the beginning. A uniform deck of cards which can be dealt out in a number of combinations. The basic conventions are all there. Knife, fork, and spoon. And what else? Every time you see something that appears to be radically new or different in a movie, chances are that any old-timer can give you a list of precedents for whatever it is, a list as long as your arm. It's pretty safe to say that there are no new techniques, neither in the making of pictures nor in the writing of them. The result is that movies are intricately *conventional*. Highly stylized in the use and arrangement of conventions. As much so as No drama. Perhaps more.

So, inevitably with time, with experience in making and the corresponding sophistication of the audience, short cuts and simplicity are possible.

But I think that the evolutionary analogy is only partially useful. For the very characteristics I've mentioned (and will be mentioning) are inherent in the medium and the form. The film is becoming more truly itself. The form is being discovered and rediscovered. And as its singular identity is being discovered it is also being explored and tested.

Moreover, the rhetorical experience of the audience, its side of the dialogue, is quite different in a number of ways. We'd have to admit, I suppose, that both occasions, going to the theater and going to the movies, are unusual, special, ceremonious, different in degree, not kind, these days. With television in the house, with prices high, with the effort of getting out and going to, both are occasions. The theater only more so. The theater experience becoming increasingly rare for many. Both becoming luxuries (remember that in the Depression a part of the relief check was *for* the movies?), but the theater much more so.

Once there, though, and the experience becomes quite different. Both are *group* experiences. Any picture plays better to a full and sympathetic house. But there's a difference in the group experience and reaction. The circumstances, even with the dimming of lights and the old gesture of opening a curtain before the screen, are slightly different. One might be tempted to imagine a kind of passivity not present in a stage performance. After all no two stage performances are quite identical. Whereas the film is set, fixed to the last frame and foot. Nothing will change or happen that has not happened before identically. Nevertheless it is of the magic power of all drama that once in motion and if the original slight spell is cast, it takes a conscious effort of will and mind, a deliberate sort of suppression of the imagination, for the suspense to be dissipated. A second or third time and one is still moved at most of the same places. A condition attested to by the apparent asininity of people who react to animated cartoons and commercials as if they were real events.

There was a moment in one of the old Bob Hope–Bing Crosby *Road* movies where Dorothy Lamour was about to slip out of her cele- brated sarong and go for a skinny dip in a calm lagoon. At precisely the instant that the sarong was shucked and Miss Lamour should have been revealed in all her pristine glory, there was a gag shot—a direct cut to a shot of a train whizzing past a crossing. Then back to Miss Lamour now swimming and decently concealed by the waters of the lagoon. As I re- member it, I also remember Bob Hope got some mileage out of that moment. Something like: "I've been to see the picture eight times now and I'm going again. Sooner or later that train is bound to be late. . . ."

The absurdity was shared, which is why the joke worked. Something atavistic, childlike, archetypal, call it what you will, the spell and magic of the theater and of drama itself in all forms, takes over. All things are possible even in a film.

We'll come back to Miss Lamour and the locomotive. For now a simple distinction between the rhetoric of film and of stage. On stage there are real people, actors in three dimensions, alive and performing. A different kind of encounter with the audience. It would be difficult (and probably tedious) to explain this, but it seems to me that audiences at a movie react if not more quickly, then with more assurance, than audiences at a play. One finds this in one's own reactions. An example. I once sent students to see the movie of *Long Day's Journey Into Night*. They had not seen the play. The movie seemed to be, on the whole, a pretty faithful adaptation of the play. That may have been the trouble with it—maybe the trouble with any *faithful* adaptation of a play. Their unanimous reaction was that it was very boring because they knew the problem and, to an extent, the secret of each character long before it was revealed. The essence of the play was the striptease of character. The lines and situations were the same. But within the context of *cinematic* experi- ence the characters were revealed to the audience before it was time for revelation. Partly due to cinematic convention. Due also, I think, to the simple human reaction of skepticism and the reservation of judgment in a real and personal encounter.

Though movies are not widely noted for subtlety, much that is subtle on stage can in the cold eye of the camera become blatant and bare.

Back to Dorothy. Another difference of rhetoric. The reason why film-watching is less passive than we are usually told. From my very little experience I have discovered that many people see things that were never on the film, hear lines that were never said (or written), etc. This is merely an exaggeration of the sleight-of-hand rhetoric of the film which is already built in. A gun is fired. A man grabs his chest and falls. Two separate camera shots. Most often the audience simply sees one man shoot another. The heroine starts to unbutton her blouse. The hero observes her. We see his reaction. The implication, the heroine's undressing, is *seen* by most of the audience.

Which is why, in spite of its novelty, the direct scene of nudity, in good taste or bad, is less effective than the scene of implied nudity. Point being that a large part of the experience of a movie is imaginative. The audience sees things, makes relationships. The very skillful director, say Alfred Hitchcock, builds his art on the maximum imaginative involvement of the audience, building, working and, if possible, controlling the utmost imaginative involvement. Ironically, this seems to be especially difficult when the subject matter is close to the audience, when it is most *true* and personal. Then group response is dissipated in favor of memory, the individual imagination. Often people (even critics) seem to see a hundred different versions of a single scene.

Which may be why the admirable Mr. Hitchcock prefers to avoid certain kinds of serious subject matter in favor of his fables of suspense.

Difference between the James Bond movies and *The Spy Who Came In from the Cold.* Two ways to work within the same genre.

Which is also why the writer must, from the outset, exercise extreme care and all his craft in scenes and situations which come very close to the life and problems of his audience, to "reality."

It is easier to get away with murder when there is little "aesthetic distance."

Some of the other basic differences from the stage. Films are very much more a drama of *reaction*. To have reaction we have to have, in the context of any given scene, a witness, more or less reliable, in any case known. We can either believe the witness or we can judge his reaction by what we know of him. First a witness is established. Something happens which he sees happen as we do. We then see his reaction. His reaction tells us about him and is a guide to, a control of, chorus-like sometimes, the reactions of the audience. This is much the same thing as, in fiction, the device critics call *point of view*. Except that it may change swiftly from scene to scene.

Maybe Hitchcock was right when he said the *literary* form most analogous to the movie was the short story. In any case, in spite of various kinds and conventions of breaks and transitions, a movie is a continuous and uninterrupted experience. The old three-act structure of the play may be helpful to directors and some writers, but it is not a form that is explicit and discernible. Thus does not really function within the film.

No one has suggested seriously what I sometimes think of as the closest literary analogy to the screenplay. A type, probably the most widely used and known, of modern poem. The contemporary lyric which consists of (quite aside from subject, form, ostensible theme) an initial statement of images, followed by the development, exploitation, and rearrangement of those images in various combinations, ending with some final rearrangement, valid within the context of the poem. The images themselves need not be rational and the logic of their arrangement may be exclusively imaginative, a "poetic" logic. A movie differs in being group rhetoric (only one person can experience a poem or book at a time), in having to be, by virtue of its collaborative creation, supremely rational. Yet the organization and architecture is often quite like that of the prevailing mode of a modern lyric poem. It is possible that poets would make the best screenwriters. . . .

[1967]

3

Film and Novel

Figure 3.1   D. W. Griffith's 1909 adaptation of Charles Dickens's "The Cricket on the Hearth" displays a rich sense of detail in the setting. Museum of Modern Art/Film Stills Archive.

OUTTAKES

[It] seems to me that when a movie is made from a novel the novel is merely raw material, the movie is a new creation, and the novelist can properly attract neither praise nor blame for it.

ROBERT PENN WARREN

For me, I despise [the film] myself—but I love it too. It is not art, it is life, it is actuality. . . . For it is all raw material, it has not been transmuted, it is life at first hand. . . . It is much too genuine to be theater. . . . The film possesses a technique of recollection, of psychological suggestion, a mastery of detail in men and in things, from which the novelist, though scarcely the dramatist, might learn much.

THOMAS MANN

The destruction of the continuity of time and space is a nightmare when applied to the physical world but it is a sensible order in the realm of the mind. The human mind, in fact, stores the experiences of the past as memory traces, and in a storage vault there are no time sequences or spatial connections, only affinities and associations based on similarity or contrast. It is this different but positive order of the mind that novelists and film directors of the last few years have presented as a new reality while demolishing the old. By eliminating the difference between what is presently perceived and what is only remembered from the past, they have created a new homogeneity and unity of all experience, independent of the order of physical things. When in Michael Butor's novel, *La Modification*, the sequence of the train voyage from Paris to Rome constantly interacts with a spray of atomized episodes of the past, the dismemberment of physical time and space creates a new time sequence and a new spacial continuum, namely, those of the mind.

It is the creation and exploitation of this new order of the mind in its independence of the order of physical things which, I believe, will keep the cinema busy while the other visual arts explore the other side of the dichotomy—the world of physical things from which the mind seems to pleasantly absent.

RUDOLF ARNHEIM

One of the most important differences between the novel and the movie is that a character is never explained in terms of description, dialogue or background, but rather in terms of action. If, for instance, it is necessary to show that a middle-aged man is abnormal, the point can be made very well by having him slide down the bannisters without saying a word.

HORTENSE POWDERMAKER

A great novel has yet to make a great film. Rarely, very rarely, an estimable achievement comes along. . . . But always either the book or the film is less than absolutely first-rate.

JOHN SIMON

The film is an art of high points. I think of it as embracing five or six sequences, each one mounting to a climax that rushes the action onward. The novel is an art of high, middle, and low points and, though I believe its form must never be overlooked, it's the sort of form you lock the front door against, knowing full well it will climb into one of the small back-windows thoughtfully left open for it. The film does best when it concentrates on a single character. It tells the "Informer" superbly. It tends to lose itself in the ramifications of "War and Peace." It has no time for what I call the essential digression. The "digression" of complicated, contradictory character. The "digression" of social background. The film must go from significant episode to more significant episode in a constantly mounting pattern. It's an exciting form. But it pays a price for this excitement. It cannot wander as life wanders, or pause as life always pauses, to contemplate the incidental or the unexpected. The film has a relentless form. Once you set it up it becomes your master, demanding and rather terrifying. It has its own tight logic, and once you stray from that straight and narrow path the tension slackens—or, you might say, the air is let out of the balloon.

BUDD SCHULBERG

The short story lends itself readily to motion-picture adaptation. Whereas a novel adapted to the screen must be contracted in scope and a play must be expanded, a short story may be adapted with only slight change in scope, if any at all. Given the usual short story, that is, one dependent largely on narration, an adapter has for the most part only to translate epic terms into cinematic ones. It is not surprising that short stories were popular sources of early films. Many a short story was ready-made for representation in one or two reels.

Although films are now longer, short stories continue to be drawn on as source material. But the increased length of films has resulted in a different treatment. A short story made into a feature-length film must be expanded, although not in the same way as in the adaptation of a novel. For whereas a novel adapted to the screen is expanded in detail and contracted in scope, a short story is made into a feature-length film by an expansion of both scope and detail. A short story so adapted to the screen therefore implies a film more different from the story than a film adapted from a novel is different from the novel. But although this additional difference implies a correspondingly greater freedom in adaptation, the resulting film, if it is to be faithful to its source, must not distort subject, theme, characterizations, etc.

A. R. FULTON

You see, the nearest art form to the motion picture is, I think, the short story. It's the only form where you ask the audience to sit down and read it in one sitting.

ALFRED HITCHCOCK

I saw that the novel, which at my maturity was the strongest and supplest medium for conveying thought and emotion from one human being to another, was becoming subordinate to a mechanical and communal art that, whether in the hands of Hollywood merchants or Russian idealists was capable of reflecting only the tritest thought, the most obvious emotion. It was an art in which words were subordinate to images, where personality was worn down to the inevitable low gear of collaboration. As long past as 1930, I had a hunch that the talkies would make even the best selling novelist as archaic as silent pictures. . . . [This] was a rankling indignity, that to me had become almost an obsession, in seeing the power of the written word subordinated to another power, a more glittering, a grosser power. . . .

F. SCOTT FITZGERALD

Less attention has been paid to the relationship between novel and film than to that between theater and film. No full-length theoretical study has been published in English. (Even George Bluestone's *Novels into Film* confines theory to a long introductory chapter and then pursues a series of individual adaptations.) Yet critics generally hold that most of the memorable adaptations come from novels rather than from plays. Nor does there seem to be the variety of critical concerns characterizing the approaches to the theater and film. At the same time, most adaptations are taken from novels. Perhaps one-third of the films made (estimates vary from less than twenty percent to sixty-five percent or more) have their sources in novels. Any such figures have little meaning, though, since a novel may furnish little more than its title, with no serious at-

117

This sequence of stills (figures 3.2-3.5) shows two styles used to adapt Charles Dickens's novel *Great Expectations* to the screen. The upper stills, from Stuart Walker's 1934 version, use setting primarily to furnish a backdrop to the action. The stills from David Lean's 1946 version reveal a much more complex handling of setting to portray a person's state of mind and to create subtle effects of atmosphere.

Figure 3.3 Pip encounters Magwitch at the graveyard (1946 version). Museum of Modern Art/Film Stills Archive.

Figure 3.2 Pip at the graveyard (1934 version). Museum of Modern Art/Film Stills Archive.

Figure 3.4   Estella and Mrs. Havisham (1934 version). Museum of Modern Art/Film Stills Archive.

Figure 3.5   Estella and Mrs. Havisham (1946 version). Museum of Modern Art/Film Stills Archive.

tempt undertaken to adapt the work to film. Considering the process of adaptation, however, is not the same problem as considering the theoretical relationship between two art forms appearing in different media. Most of the writers in this section are concerned first with the relationship of novel and film, and then they consider how similarities and differences in form affect translation from print to screen.

In his seminal essay on film and literature, "Dickens, Griffith, and the Film Today" (written in 1944), Sergei Eisenstein explores the contribution of novelistic art to a cinematic aesthetic. Working primarily from the perspective of viewers and readers, he investigates the techniques and forms which Griffith borrowed from Charles Dickens. Such cinematic devices as the close-up, montage, parallel action, and the dissolve he traces to Dickens's novels. Eisenstein also compares the forms and functions of narrative as it is manifested in novel and cinema, providing insight into Dickens's methods, style, and use of point of view. Eisenstein offers extensive examples from Dickens's *Oliver Twist* to suggest the relationships between film and novel, and despite the boldness of his writing he warns against the danger of pursuing analogies and resemblances too far.

Although other writers have extended and, in some cases, modified or questioned the conclusions of George Bluestone, *Novels into Film* (1957) remains the primary work in the area. Bluestone concentrates on the differences between "the two media" and upon the mutations and changes which inevitably occur in the movement from a printed linguistic medium to a visual one. He contends that viewers and readers go through different mental processes when experiencing each genus, and "between percept of the visual image and the concept of the mental image lies the root difference between the two media." A film is perceived, not thought, and consequently film cannot effectively reflect the interior processes and thoughts of the mind as the novel can. Thus Bluestone sees adaptation from a perspective similar to that of Béla Balázs: the novel provides raw materials and the filmmaker adapts a "paraphrase" rather than converting the essence of a novel to the screen. Bluestone looks to characters and myths who have achieved a life independent of their source, and these become the wellsprings for adaptation.

A. R. Fulton concentrates on a few basic problems of the relationship between film and novel, furnishing examples from *Great Expectations* to clarify his arguments. Noting that film and novel share similar narrative methods, he paradoxically suggests that novels adapt to the screen more easily than plays since a play can be captured simply by switching on a camera while the novel must first be thought out visually and translated into cinematic terms. Fulton's most interesting notions involve what must be contracted and what must be expanded during the adaptation process.

George Linden, one of the most recent writers on the relationship between film and novel, attempts to sharpen our understanding of the two. Linden takes up the problem of tense, exploring the notion that films operate in a continuous present while novels operate in the past. Linden ranges widely in his examination of film and novel, considering time and space relationships, methods of presenting and representing ideas and physical reality, and the importance of fidelity. Linden reserves some of his most barbed criticism for Marshall McLuhan, disagreeing with many of McLuhan's observations about the relationships between film and literature. Linden maintains that an inverse relationship exists between the greatness of a novel and the chances for a successful adaptation; he further suggests that the best films are not adaptations nor do they depend on novelistic techniques. The distinctions between the two forms require that faithfulness not be the ultimate criterion in an adaptation, which nevertheless must capture the "feeling-tone" of the original.

SERGEI EISENSTEIN

Dickens, Griffith, and the Film Today

People talked as if there had been no dramatic or descriptive music before Wagner; no impressionist painting before Whistler; whilst as to myself, I was finding that the surest way to produce an effect of daring innovation and originality was to revive the ancient attraction of long rhetorical speeches; to stick closely to the methods of Molière; and to lift characters bodily out of the pages of Charles Dickens.

GEORGE BERNARD SHAW

"The kettle began it. . . ."
Thus Dickens opens his *Cricket on the Hearth.*
"The kettle began it. . . ."
What could be further from films! Trains, cowboys, chases . . . And, *The Cricket on the Hearth?* "The Kettle began it!" But, strange as it may seem, movies also were boiling in that kettle. From here, from Dickens, from the Victorian novel, stem the first shoots of American film esthetic, forever linked with the name of David Wark Griffith. . . .
The kettle began it. . . .
As soon as we recognize this kettle as a typical close-up, we exclaim: "Why didn't we notice it before! Of course this is the purest Griffith. How often we've seen such a close-up at the beginning of an episode, a sequence, or a whole film by him!" (By the way, we shouldn't overlook the fact that one of Griffith's earliest films was based on *The Cricket on the Hearth!*)

From *Film Form* by Sergei Eisenstein, translated by Jay Leyda, copyright, 1949, by Harcourt Brace Jovanovich, Inc. and reprinted with their permission.

122

Certainly, this kettle is a typical Griffith-esque close-up. A close-up saturated, we now become aware, with typically Dickens-esque "atmosphere," with which Griffith, with equal mastery, can envelop the severe face of life in *Way Down East*, and the icy cold moral face of his characters, who push the guilty Anna (Lillian Gish) onto the shifting surface of a swirling ice-break.

Isn't this the same implacable atmosphere of cold that is given by Dickens, for example, in *Dombey and Sons?* The image of Mr. Dombey is revealed through cold and prudery. And the print of cold lies on everyone and everything—everywhere. And "atmosphere"—always and everywhere—is one of the most excessive means of revealing the inner world and ethical countenance of the characters themselves.

We can recognize this particular method of Dickens in Griffith's inimitable bit-characters who seem to have run straight from life onto the screen. I can't recall who speaks with whom in one of the street scenes of the modern story of *Intolerance*. But I shall never forget the mask of the passer-by with nose pointed forward between spectacles and straggly beard, walking with hands behind his back as if he were manacled. As he passes he interrupts the most pathetic moment in the conversation of the suffering boy and girl. I can remember next to nothing of the couple, but this passer-by, who is visible in the shot only for a flashing glimpse, stands alive before me now—and I haven't seen the film for twenty years!

Occasionally these unforgettable figures actually walked into Griffith's films almost directly from the street: a bit-player, developed in Griffith's hands to stardom; the passer-by who may never again have been filmed; and that mathematics teacher who was invited to play a terrifying butcher in *America*—the late Louis Wolheim—who ended the film career thus begun with his incomparable performance as "Kat" in *All Quiet on the Western Front*.

These striking figures of sympathetic old men are also quite in the Dickens tradition; and these noble and slightly one-dimensional figures of sorrow and fragile maidens; and these rural gossips and sundry odd characters. They are especially convincing in Dickens when he uses them briefly, in episodes.

> The only other thing to be noticed about [Pecksniff] is that here, as almost everywhere else in the novels, the best figures are at their best when they have least to do. Dickens's characters are perfect as long as he can keep them out of his stories. Bumble is divine until a dark and practical secret is entrusted to him. . . . Micawber is noble when he is doing nothing; but he is quite unconvincing when he is spying on Uriah Heep. . . . Similarly, while Pecksniff is the best thing in the story, the story is the worst thing in Pecksniff. . . .

Free of this limitation, and with the same believability, Griffith's characters grow from episodic figures into those fascinating and finished images of living people, in which his screen is so rich.

Instead of going into detail about this, let us rather return to that more obvious fact—the growth of that second side of Griffith's creative craftsmanship—as a magician of tempo and montage; a side for which it is rather surprising to find the same Victorian source.

When Griffith proposed to his employers the novelty of a parallel "cut-back" for his first version of *Enoch Arden (After Many Years, 1908)*, this is the discussion that took place, as recorded by Linda Arvidson Griffith in her reminiscences of Biograph days:

> When Mr. Griffith suggested a scene showing Annie Lee waiting for her husband's return to be followed by a scene of Enoch cast away on a desert island, it was altogether too distracting. "How can you tell a story jumping about like that? The people won't know what it's about."
>
> "Well," said Mr. Griffith, "doesn't Dickens write that way?"
>
> "Yes, but that's Dickens; that's novel writing; that's different."
>
> "Oh, not so much, these are picture stories; not so different."

But, to speak quite frankly, all astonishment on this subject and the apparent unexpectedness of such statements can be ascribed only to our —ignorance of Dickens.

All of us read him in childhood, gulped him down greedily, without realizing that much of his irresistibility lay not only in his capture of detail in the childhoods of his heroes, but also in that spontaneous, childlike skill for story-telling, equally typical for Dickens and for the American cinema, which so surely and delicately plays upon the infantile traits in its audience. We were even less concerned with the technique of Dickens's composition: for us this was nonexistent—but captivated by the effects of this technique, we feverishly followed his characters from page to page, watching his characters now being rubbed from view at the most critical moment, then seeing them return afresh between the separate links of the parallel secondary plot.

As children, we paid no attention to the mechanics of this. As adults, we rarely re-read his novels. And becoming filmworkers, we never found time to glance beneath the covers of these novels in order to figure out what exactly had captivated us in these novels and with what means these incredibly many-paged volumes had chained our attention so irresistibly.

Apparently Griffith was more perceptive. . . .

The most thrilling figure against this background was Griffith, for it was in his works that the cinema made itself felt as more than an entertainment or pastime. The brilliant new methods of the American cinema were united in him with a profound emotion of story, with human acting, with laughter and tears, and all this was done with an astonishing ability to preserve all that gleam of a filmically dynamic holiday, which had been captured in *The Gray Shadow* and *The Mark of Zorro* and *The House of Hate*. That the cinema could be incomparably greater, and that this was to be the basic task of the budding Soviet cinema—these were sketched for us in Griffith's creative work, and found ever new confirmation in his films.

Our heightened curiosity of those years in *construction and method* swiftly discerned wherein lay the most powerful affective factors in this great American's films. This was in a hitherto unfamiliar province, bearing a name that was familiar to us, not in the field of art, but in that of engineering and electrical apparatus, first touching art in its most advanced section—in cinematography. This province, this method, this principle of building and construction was *montage*.

This was the montage whose foundations had been laid by American film-culture, but whose full, completed, conscious use and world recognition was established by our films. Montage, the rise of which will be forever linked with the name of Griffith. Montage, which played a most vital rôle in the creative work of Griffith and brought him his most glorious successes.

Griffith arrived at it through the method of parallel action. And, essentially, it was on this that he came to a standstill. But we musn't run ahead. Let us examine the question of how montage came to Griffith or—how Griffith came to montage.

Griffith arrived at montage through the method of parallel action, and he was led to the idea of parallel action by—Dickens!

To this fact Griffith himself has testified, according to A. B. Walkley, in *The Times* of London, for April 26, 1922, on the occasion of a visit by the director to London. Writes Mr. Walkley:

> He [Griffith] is a pioneer, by his own admission, rather than an inventor. That is to say, he has opened up new paths in Film Land, under the guidance of ideas supplied to him from outside. His best ideas, it appears, have come to him from Dickens, who has always been his favorite author. . . . Dickens inspired Mr. Griffith with an idea, and his employers (mere "business" men) were horrified at it; but, says Mr. Griffith, "I went home, reread one of Dickens's novels, and came back next day to tell them they could either make use of my idea or dismiss me."
>
> Mr. Griffith found the idea to which he clung thus heroically in Dickens. That was as luck would have it, for he might have found the same idea almost anywhere. Newton deduced the law of gravita-

tion from the fall of an apple; but a pear or a plum would have done just as well. The idea is merely that of a "break" in the narrative, a shifting of the story from one group of characters to another group. People who write the long and crowded novels that Dickens did, especially when they are published in parts, find this practice a convenience. You will meet with it in Thackeray, George Eliot, Trollope, Meredith, Hardy, and, I suppose, every other Victorian novelist. . . . Mr. Griffith might have found the same practice not only in Dumas *père*, who cared precious little about form, but also in great artists like Tolstoy, Turgeniev, and Balzac. But, as a matter of fact, it was not in any of these others, but in Dickens that he found it; and it is significant of the predominant influence of Dickens that he should be quoted as an authority for a device which is really common to fiction at large.

Even a superficial acquaintance with the work of the great English novelist is enough to persuade one that Dickens may have given and did give to cinematography far more guidance than that which led to the montage of parallel action alone.

Dickens's nearness to the characteristics of cinema in method, style, and especially in viewpoint and exposition, is indeed amazing. And it may be that in the nature of exactly these characteristics, in their community both for Dickens and for cinema, there lies a portion of the secret of that mass success which they both, apart from themes and plots, brought and still bring to the particular quality of such exposition and such writing.

What were the novels of Dickens for his contemporaries, for his readers? There is one answer: they bore the same relation to them that the film bears to the same strata in our time. They compelled the reader to live with the same passions. They appealed to the same good and sentimental elements as does the film (at least on the surface); they alike shudder before vice, they alike mill the extraordinary, the unusual, the fantastic, from boring, prosaic and everyday existence. And they clothe this common and prosaic existence in their special vision.

Illumined by this light, refracted from the land of fiction back to life, this commonness took on a romantic air, and bored people were grateful to the author for giving them the countenances of potentially romantic figures.

This partially accounts for the close attachment to the novels of Dickens and, similarly, to films. . . .

Perhaps the secret lies in Dickens's (as well as cinema's) creation of an extraordinary plasticity. The observation in the novels is extraordinary —as is their optical quality. The characters of Dickens are rounded with means as plastic and slightly exaggerated as are the screen heroes of today. The screen's heroes are engraved on the senses of the spectator with clearly visible traits, its villains are remembered by certain facial expressions, and all are saturated in the peculiar, slightly unnatural radiant gleam thrown over them by the screen.

It is absolutely thus that Dickens draws his characters—this is the faultlessly plastically grasped and pitilessly sharply sketched gallery of immortal Pickwicks, Dombeys, Fagins, Tackletons, and others. . . .

Analogies and resemblances cannot be pursued too far—they lose conviction and charm. They begin to take on the air of machination or card-tricks. I should be very sorry to lose the conviction of the affinity between Dickens and Griffith, allowing this abundance of common traits to slide into a game of anecdotal semblance of tokens.

All the more that such a gleaning from Dickens goes beyond the limits of interest in Griffith's individual cinematic craftsmanship and widens into a concern with film-craftsmanship in general. This is why I dig more and more deeply into the film-indications of Dickens, revealing them through Griffith—for the use of future film-exponents. So I must be excused, in leafing through Dickens, for having found in him even—a "dissolve." How else could this passage be defined—the opening of the last chapter of *A Tale of Two Cities:*

> Along the Paris streets, the death-cars rumble, hollow and harsh. Six tumbrils carry the day's wine to La Guillotine. . . .
>
> Six tumbrils roll along the streets. Change these back again to what they were, thu powerful enchanter, Time, and they shall be seen to be the carriages of absolute monarchs, the equipages of feudal nobles, the toilettes of flaring Jezebels, the churches that are not my Father's house but dens of thieves, the huts of millions of starving peasants!

How many such "cinematic" surprises must be hiding in Dickens's pages!

However, let us turn to the basic montage structure, whose rudiment in Dickens's work was developed into the elements of film composition in Griffith's work. Lifting a corner of the veil over these riches, these hitherto unused experiences, let us look into *Oliver Twist.* Open it at the twenty-first chapter. Let's read its beginning:

Chapter XXI*

> 1. It was a cheerless morning when they got into the street; blowing and raining hard; and the clouds looking dull and stormy.
>
> The night had been very wet: for large pools of water had collected in the road: and the kennels were overflowing.
>
> There was a faint glimmering of the coming day in the sky; but it

*For demonstration purposes I have broken this beginning of the chapter into smaller pieces than did its author; the numbering is, of course, also mine.

rather aggravated than relieved the gloom of the scene: the sombre light only serving to pale that which the street lamps afforded, without shedding any warmer or brighter tints upon the wet housetops, and dreary streets.

There appeared to be nobody stirring in that quarter of the town; for the windows of the houses were all closely shut; and the streets through which they passed, were noiseless and empty.

2. By the time they had turned into the Bethnal Green Road, the day had fairly begun to break. Many of the lamps were already extinguished;

a few country waggons were slowly toiling on, towards London; and now and then, a stage-coach, covered with mud, rattled briskly by:

the driver bestowing, as he passed, an admonitory lash upon the heavy waggoner who, by keeping on the wrong side of the road, had endangered his arriving at the office, a quarter of a minute after his time.

The public-houses, with gas-lights burning inside, were already open.

By degrees, other shops began to be unclosed; and a few scattered people were met with.

Then, came straggling groups of labourers going to their work;

then, men and women with fish-baskets on their heads:

donkey-carts laden with vegetables;

chaise-carts filled with live-stock or whole carcasses of meat;

milk-women with pails;

and an unbroken concourse of people, trudging out with various supplies to the eastern suburbs of the town.

3. As they approached the City, the noise and traffic gradually increased;

and when they threaded the streets between Shoreditch and Smithfield, it had swelled into a roar of sound and bustle.

It was as light as it was likely to be, till night came on again; and the busymorning of half the London population had begun. . . .

4. It was market-morning.

The ground was covered, nearly ankle-deep, with filth and mire;

and a thick steam, perpetually rising from the reeking bodies of the cattle,

and mingling with the fog,

which seemed to rest upon the chimney-tops, hung heavily above. . . .

Countrymen,

butchers,

drovers,

hawkers,

boys,

thieves,

idlers,

and vagabonds of every low grade,
were mingled together in a dense mass;

5. the whistling of drovers,
the barking of dogs,
the bellowing and plunging of oxen,
the bleating of sheep,
the grunting and squeaking of pigs;
the cries of hawkers,
the shouts, oaths and quarrelling on all sides;
the ringing of bells
and roar of voices, that issued from every public-house;
the crowding, pushing, driving, beating,
whooping and yelling;
the hideous and discordant din that resounded from every corner of
the market;
and the unwashed, unshaven, squalid, and dirty figures constantly
running to and fro, and bursting in and out of the throng; rendered
it a stunning and bewildering scene, which quite confounded the
senses.

How often have we encountered just such a structure in the work
of Griffith? This austere accumulation and quickening tempo, this gradual play of light: from burning street-lamps, to their being extinguished;
from night, to dawn; from dawn, to the full radiance of day (*It was as
light as it was likely to be, till night came on again*); this calculated transition from purely visual elements to an interweaving of them with aural
elements: at first as an indefinite rumble, coming from afar at the second
stage of increasing light, so that the rumble may grow into a roar, transferring us to a purely aural structure, now concrete and objective (section
5 of our break-down); with such scenes, picked up *en passant*, and intercut
into the whole—like the driver, hastening towards his office; and, finally,
these magnificently typical details, the reeking bodies of the cattle, from
which the steam rises and mingles with the over-all cloud of morning fog,
or the close-up of the legs in the almost ankle-deep filth and mire, all this
gives the fullest cinematic sensation of the panorama of a market.

Surprised by these examples from Dickens, we must not forget one
more circumstance, related to the creative work of Dickens in general.

Thinking of this as taking place in "cozy" old England, we are
liable to forget that the works of Dickens, considered not only against a
background of English literature, but against a background of world literature of that epoch, as well, were produced as the works of a city artist.
He was the first to bring factories, machines, and railways into literature.

But indication of this "urbanism" in Dickens may be found not only in his thematic material, but also in that head-spinning tempo of changing impressions with which Dickens sketches the city in the form of a dynamic (montage) picture; and this montage of its rhythms conveys the sensation of the limits of speed at that time (1838), the sensation of a rushing—stagecoach!

> As they dashed by the quickly-changing and ever-varying objects, it was curious to observe in what a strange procession they passed before the eye. Emporiums of splendid dresses, the materials brought from every quarter of the world; tempting stores of everything to stimulate and pamper the sated appetite and give new relish to the oft-repeated feast; vessels of burnished gold and silver, wrought into every exquisite form of vase, and dish, and goblet; guns, swords, pistols, and patent engines of destruction; screws and irons for the crooked, clothes for the newly-born, drugs for the sick, coffins for the dead, church-yards for the buried—all these jumbled each with the other and flocking side by side, seemed to flit by in motley dance. . . .

Isn't this an anticipation of a "symphony of a big city"?*
But here is another, directly opposite aspect of a city, out-distancing Hollywood's picture of the City by eighty years.

> It contained several large streets all very like one another, inhabited by people equally like one another, who all went in and out at the same hours, with the same sound upon the same pavements, to do the same work, and to whom every day was the same as yesterday and tomorrow, and every day the counterpart of the last and the next.

Is this Dickens's Coketown of 1853, or King Vidor's *The Crowd* of 1928?
If in the above-cited examples we have encountered prototypes of characteristics for Griffith's *montage exposition*, then it would pay us to read further in *Oliver Twist*, where we can find another montage method typical for Griffith—the method of a *montage progression of parallel scenes, intercut into each other.*
For this let us turn to that group of scenes in which is set forth the familiar episode of how Mr. Brownlow, to show faith in Oliver in spite of his pick-pocket reputation, sends him to return books to the book-seller, and of how Oliver again falls into the clutches of the thief Sikes, his sweetheart Nancy, and old Fagin.
These scenes are unrolled absolutely à la Griffith: both in their inner emotional line, as well as in the unusual sculptural relief and delinea-

---

*A reference to the Ruttmann-Freund film, *Berlin: Die Sinfonie der Grosstadt* (1927).

tion of the characters; in the uncommon fullbloodedness of the dramatic as well as the humorous traits in them; finally, also in the typical Griffith-esque montage of parallel interlocking of all the links of the separate episodes. Let us give particuar attention to this last peculiarity, just as unexpected, one would think, in Dickens, as it is characteristic for Griffith!

Chapter XIV

Comprising Further Particulars of Oliver's Stay at Mr. Brownlow's, with the Remarkable Prediction which One Mr. Grimley Uttered Concerning Him, When He Went Out on an Errand.

. . . "Dear me, I am very sorry for that," exclaimed Mr. Brownlow; "I particularly wished those books to be returned tonight."

"Send Oliver with them," said Mr. Grimwig, with an ironical smile; "he will be sure to deliver them safely, you know."

"Yes; do let me take them, if you please, Sir," said Oliver. "I'll run all the way, Sir."

The old gentleman was just going to say that Oliver should not go out on any account; when a most malicious cough from Mr. Grim-wig determined him that he should; and that, by his prompt dis-charge of the commission, he should prove to him the injustice of his suspicions: on this head at least: at once.

[Oliver is prepared for the errand to the bookstall-keeper.]

"I won't be ten minutes, Sir," replied Oliver, eagerly.

[Mrs. Bedwin, Mr. Brownlow's housekeeper, gives Oliver the direc-tions, and sends him off.]

"Bless his sweet face!" said the old lady, looking after him. "I can't bear, somehow, to let him go out of my sight."

At this moment, Oliver looked gaily round, and nodded before he turned the corner. The old lady smilingly returned his salutation, and, closing the door, went back to her own room.

"Let me see; he'll be back in twenty minutes, at the longest," said Mr. Brownlow, pulling out his watch, and placing it on the table. "It will be dark by that time."

"Oh! you really expect him to come back, do you?" inquired Mr. Grimwig.

"Don't you?" asked Mr. Brownlow, smiling.

The spirit of contradiction was strong in Mr. Grimwig's breast, at the moment; and it was rendered stronger by his friend's confident smile.

"No," he said, smiting the table with his fist, "I do not. The boy has a new suit of clothes on his back; a set of valuable books under his arm; and a five-pound note in his pocket. He'll join his old friends the thieves, and laugh at you. If ever that boy returns to this house, Sir, I'll eat my head."

> With these words he drew his chair closer to the table; and there
> the two friends sat, in silent expectation, with the watch between
> them.

This is followed by a short "interruption" in the form of a digression:

> It is worthy of remark, as illustrating the importance we attach to
> our own judgments, and the pride with which we put forth our most
> rash and hasty conclusions, that, although Mr. Grimwig was not by
> any means a bad-hearted man, and though he would have been un-
> feignedly sorry to see his respected friend duped and deceived, he
> really did most earnestly and strongly hope, at that moment, that
> Oliver Twist might not come back.

And again a return to the two old gentlemen:

> It grew so dark, that the figures on the dial-plate were scarcely dis-
> cernible; but there the two old gentlemen continued to sit, in si-
> lence: with the watch between them.

Twilight shows that only a little time has passed, but the *close-up*
of the watch, *already twice* shown lying between the old gentlemen, says
that a great deal of time has passed already. But just then, as in the game
of "will he come? won't he come?", involving not only the two old men,
but also the kind-hearted reader, the worst fears and vague forebodings of
the old housekeeper are justified by the cut to the new scene—Chapter
XV. This begins with a short scene in the public-house, with the bandit
Sikes and his dog, old Fagin and Miss Nancy, who has been obliged to
discover the whereabouts of Oliver.

> "You are on the scent, are you, Nancy?" inquired Sikes, proffering
> the glass.
> "Yes, I am, Bill," replied the young lady, disposing of its contents;
> "and tired enough of it I am, too. . . ."

Then, one of the best scenes in the whole novel—at least one that
since childhood has been perfectly preserved, along with the evil figure of
Fagin—the scene in which Oliver, marching along with the books, is
suddenly

> startled by a young woman screaming out very loud, "Oh, my dear
> brother!" And he had hardly looked up, to see what the matter was,
> when he was stopped by having a pair of arms thrown tight round
> his neck.

With this cunning maneuver, Nancy, with the sympathies of the
whole street, takes the desperately pulling Oliver, as her "prodigal

brother," back into the bosom of Fagin's gang of thieves. This fifteenth chapter closes on the now familiar montage phrase:

> The gas-lamps were lighted; Mrs. Bedwin was waiting anxiously at the open door; the servant had run up the street twenty times to see if there were any traces of Oliver; and still the two old gentlemen sat, perseveringly, in the dark parlour: with the watch between them.

In Chapter XVI Oliver, once again in the clutches of the gang, is subjected to mockery. Nancy rescues him from a beating:

> "I won't stand by and see it done, Fagin," cried the girl. "You've got the boy, and what more would you have? Let him be—let him be, or I shall put that mark on some of you, that will bring me to the gallows before my time."

By the way, it is characteristic for both Dickens and Griffith to have these sudden flashes of goodness in "morally degraded" characters and, though these sentimental images verge on hokum, they are so faultlessly done that they work on the most skeptical readers and spectators!

At the end of this chapter, Oliver, sick and weary, falls "sound asleep." Here the physical time unity is interrupted—an evening and night, crowded with events; but the montage unity of the episode is not interrupted, tying Oliver to Mr. Brownlow on one side, and to Fagin's gang on the other.

Following, in Chapter XVIII, is the arrival of the parish beadle, Mr. Bumble, in response to an inquiry about the lost boy, and the appearance of Bumble at Mr. Brownlow's, again in Grimwig's company. The content and reason for their conversation is revealed by the very title of the chapter: *Oliver's Destiny Continuing Unpropitious, Brings a Great Man to London to Injure His Reputation* . . .

> "I fear it is all too true," said the old gentleman sorrowfully, after looking over the papers. "This is not much for your intelligence; but I would gladly have given you treble the money, if it had been favourable to the boy."
>
> It is not at all improbable that if Mr. Bumble had been possessed of this information at an earlier period of the interview, he might have imparted a very different coloring to his little history. It was too late to do it now, however; so he shook his head gravely; and, pocketing the five guineas, withdrew. . . .
>
> "Mrs. Bedwin," said Mr. Brownlow, when the housekeeper appeared; "that boy, Oliver, is an imposter."
>
> "It can't be, Sir. It cannot be," said the old lady energetically. . . .
>
> "I never will believe it, Sir. . . . Never!"
>
> "You old women never believe anything but quack-doctors, and lying story-books," growled Mr. Grimwig. "I knew it all along. . . ."

"He was a dear, grateful, gentle child, Sir," retorted Mrs. Bedwin, indignantly. "I know what children are, Sir; and have done these forty years; and people who can't say the same, shouldn't say anything about them. That's my opinion!"

This was a hard hit at Mr. Grimwig, who was a bachelor. As it extorted nothing from that gentleman but a smile, the old lady tossed her head, and smoothed down her apron preparatory to another speech, when she was stopped by Mr. Brownlow.

"Silence!" said the old gentleman, feigning an anger he was far from feeling. "Never let me hear the boy's name again. I rang to tell you that. Never. Never, on any pretence, mind! You may leave the room, Mrs. Bedwin. Remember! I am in earnest."

And the entire intricate montage complex of this episode is concluded with the sentence:

There were sad hearts in Mr. Brownlow's that night.

It was not by accident that I have allowed myself such full extracts, in regard not only to the composition of the scenes, but also to the delineation of the characters, for in their very modeling, in their characteristics, in their behavior, there is much typical of Griffith's manner. This equally concerns also his "Dickens-esque" distressed, defenseless creatures (recalling Lillian Gish and Richard Barthelmess in *Broken Blossoms* or the Gish sisters in *Orphans of the Storm*), and is no less typical for his characters like the wto old gentlemen and Mrs. Bedwin; and finally, it is entirely characteristic of him to have such figures as are in the gang of "the merry old Jew" Fagin.

In regard to the immediate task of our example of Dickens's montage progression of the story composition, we can present the results of it in the following table:

1. *The old gentlemen.*
2. Departure of Oliver.
3. *The old gentlemen and the watch. It is still light.*
4. Digression on the character of Mr. Grimwig.
5. *The old gentlemen and the watch. Gathering twilight.*
6. Fagin, Sikes and Nancy in the public-house.
7. Scene on the street.
8. *The old gentlemen and the watch. The gas-lamps have been lit.*
9. Oliver is dragged back to Fagin.
10. Digression at the beginning of Chapter XVII.
11. The journey of Mr. Bumble.
12. *The old gentlemen* and Mr. Brownlow's command to forget Oliver forever.

As we can see, we have before us a typical and, for Griffith, a model of parallel montage of two story lines, where one (the waiting gentlemen) emotionally heightens the tension and drama of the other (the capture of Oliver). It is in "rescuers" rushing along to save the "suffering heroine" that Griffith has, with the aid of parallel montage, earned his most glorious laurels!

Most curious of all is that in the *very center* of our breakdown of the episode, is wedged another "interruption"—a whole digression at the beginning of Chapter XVII, on which we have been purposely silent. What is remarkable about this digression? It is Dickens's own "treatise" on the principles of this montage construction of the story which he carries out so fascinatingly, and which passed into the style of Griffith. Here it is:

> It is the custom on the stage, in all good murderous melodramas, to present the tragic and the comic scenes, in as regular alternation, as the layers of red and white in a side of streaky well-cured bacon. The hero sinks upon his straw bed, weighed down by fetters and misfortunes; and, in the next scene, his faithful but unconscious squire regales the audience with a comic song. We behold, with throbbing bosoms, the heroine in the grasp of a proud and ruthless baron: her virtue and her life alike in danger; drawing forth her dagger to preserve the one at the cost of the other; and just as our expectations are wrought up to the highest pitch, a whistle is heard: and we are straightway transported to the great hall of the castle: where a grey-headed seneschal sings a funny chorus with a funnier body of vassals, who are free of all sorts of places from church vaults to palaces, and roam about in company, carolling perpetually.
>
> Such changes appear absurd; but they are not so unnatural as they would seem at first sight. The transitions in real life from well-spread boards to death-beds, and from mourning-weeds to holiday garments, are not a whit less startling; only, there, we are busy actors, instead of passive lookers-on; which makes a vast difference. The actors in the mimic life of the theatre, are blind to violent transitions and abrupt impulses of passion of feeling, which, presented before the eyes of mere spectators, are at once condemned as outrageous and preposterous.
>
> As sudden shiftings of the scene, and rapid changes of time and place, are not only sanctioned in books by long usage, but are by many considered as the great art of authorship: an author's skill in his craft being, by such critics, chiefly estimated with relation to the dilemmas in which he leaves his characters at the end of every chapter: this brief introduction to the present one may perhaps be deemed unnecessary. . . .

There is another interesting thing in this treatise: in his own words, Dickens (a life-long amateur actor) defines his direct relation to the theater melodrama. This is as if Dickens had placed himself in the position of a connecting link between the future, unforeseen art of the cinema, and the not so distant (for Dickens) past—the traditions of "good murderous melodramas."

This "treatise," of course, could not have escaped the eye of the patriarch of the American film, and very often his structure seems to follow the wise advice, handed down to the great filmmaker of the twentieth century by the great novelist of the nineteenth. And Griffith, hiding nothing, has more than once acknowledged his debt to Dickens's memory. . . .

I don't know how my readers feel about this, but for me personally it is always pleasing to recognize again and again the fact that our cinema is not altogether without parents and without pedigree, without a past, without the traditions and rich cultural heritage of the past epochs. It is only very thoughtless and presumptuous people who can erect laws and an esthetic for cinema, proceeding from premises of some incredible virgin-birth of this art!

Let Dickens and the whole ancestral array, going back as far as the Greeks and Shakespeare, be superfluous reminders that both Griffith and our cinema prove our origins to be not solely as of Edison and his fellow inventors, but as based on an enormous cultured past; each part of this past in its own moment of world history has moved forward the great art of cinematography. Let this past be a reproach to those thoughtless people who have displayed arrogance in reference to literature, which has contributed so much to this apparently unprecedented art and is, in the first and most important place: the art of viewing—not only the *eye*, but *viewing*—both meanings being embraced in this term.

[1944]

GEORGE BLUESTONE

The Limits of the Novel
and the Limits of the Film

THE TWO WAYS OF SEEING

Summing up his major intentions in 1913, D. W. Griffith is reported to have said, "The task I'm trying to achieve is above all to make you see."[1] Whether by accident or design, the statement coincides almost exactly with an excerpt from Conrad's preface to *Nigger of the Narcissus* published sixteen years earlier: "My task which I am trying to achieve is, by the power of the written word, to make you hear, to make you feel— it is, before all, to make you *see*."[2] Aside from the strong syntactical resemblance, the coincidence is remarkable in suggesting the points at which film and novel both join and part company. On the one hand, that phrase "to make you see" assumes an affective relationship between creative artist and receptive audience. Novelist and director meet here in a common intention. One may, on the other hand, see visually through the eye or imaginatively through the mind. And between the percept of the visual image and the concept of the mental image lies the root difference between the two media.

Because novel and film are both organic—in the sense that aesthetic judgments are based on total ensembles which include both formal and thematic conventions—we may expect to find that differences in form and theme are inseparable from differences in media. Not only are Conrad

[1]Lewis Jacobs, *The Rise of the American Film* (New York, 1939), p. 119.
[2]Joseph Conrad, *A Conrad Argosy* (New York, 1942), p. 83.

and Griffith referring to different ways of seeing, but the "you's" they refer to are different. Structures, symbols, myths, values which might be comprehensible to Conrad's relatively small middle-class reading public would, conceivably, be incomprehensible to Griffith's mass public. Conversely, stimuli which move the heirs of Griffith's audience to tears, will outrage or amuse the progeny of Conrad's "you." The seeming concurrence of Griffith and Conrad splits apart under analysis, and the two arts turn in opposite directions. That, in brief, has been the history of the fitful relationship between novel and film: overtly compatible, secretly hostile.

On the face of it, a close relationship has existed from the beginning. The reciprocity is clear from almost any point of view: the number of films based on novels; the search for filmic equivalents of literature; the effect of adaptations on reading; box-office receipts for filmed novels; merit awards by and for the Hollywood community.

The moment the film went from the animation of stills to telling a story, it was inevitable that fiction would become the ore to be minted by story departments. Before Griffith's first year as a director was over, he had adapted, among others, Jack London's *Just Meat (For Love of Gold)*, Tolstoy's *Resurrection*, and Charles Reade's *The Cloister and the Hearth*. Sergei Eisenstein's essay, "Dickens, Griffith, and the Film Today,"[3] demonstrates how Griffith found in Dickens hints for almost every one of his major innovations. Particular passages are cited to illustrate the dissolve, the superimposed shot, the close-up, the pan, indicating that Griffith's interest in literary forms and his roots in Victorian idealism[4] provided at least part of the impulse for technical and moral content. . . .

Quantitative analyses have very little to do with qualitative changes. They tell us nothing about the mutational process, let alone how to judge it. In the case of film versions of novels, such analyses are even less helpful. They merely establish the fact of reciprocity; they do not indicate its implications for aesthetics. They provide statistical, not critical data. Hence, from such information the precise nature of the mutation cannot be deduced.

Such statements as: "The film is true to the spirit of the book"; "It's incredible how they butchered the novel"; "It cuts out key passages, but it's still a good film"; "Thank God they changed the ending"—these and similar statements are predicated on certain assumptions which blur the mutational process. These standard expletives and judgments assume, among other things, a separable content which may be detached and reproduced, as the snapshot reproduces the kitten; that incidents and char-

[3]Sergei Eisenstein, *Film Form*, trans. Jay Leyda (New York, 1949), pp. 195–255.
[4]Jacobs, pp. 98–99.

acters in fiction are interchangeable with incidents and characters in the film; that the novel is a norm and the film deviates at its peril; that deviations are permissible for vaguely defined reasons—exigencies of length or of visualization, perhaps—but that the extent of the deviation will vary directly with the "respect" one has for the original; that taking liberties does not necessarily impair the quality of the film, whatever one may think of the novel, but that such liberties are somehow a trick which must be concealed from the public.

What is common to all these assumptions is the lack of awareness that mutations are probable the moment one goes from a given set of fluid, but relatively homogeneous, conventions to another; that changes are *inevitable* the moment one abandons the linguistic for the visual medium. Finally, it is insufficiently recognized that the end products of novel and film represent different aesthetic genera, as different from each other as ballet is from architecture.

The film becomes a different *thing* in the same sense that a historical painting becomes a different thing from the historical event which it illustrates. It is as fruitless to say that film A is better or worse than novel B as it is to pronounce Wright's Johnson's Wax Building better or worse than Tchaikowsky's *Swan Lake*. In the last analysis, each is autonomous, and each is characterized by unique and specific properties. . . .

The Modes of Consciousness

It is a commonplace by now that the novel has tended to retreat more and more from external action to internal thought, from plot to character, from social to psychological realities. Although these conflicting tendencies were already present in the polarity of Fielding and Sterne, it was only recently that the tradition of *Tristram Shandy* superseded the tradition of *Tom Jones*. It is this reduction of the novel to experiences which can be verified in the immediate consciousness of the novelist that Mendilow has called modern "inwardness" and E. M. Forster the "hidden life." Forster suggests the difference when he says that "The hidden life is, by definition, hidden. The hidden life that appears in external signs is hidden no longer, has entered the realm of action. And it is the function of the novelist to reveal the hidden life at its source." But if the hidden life has become the domain of the novel, it has introduced unusual problems.

In a recent review of Leon Edel's *The Psychological Novel: 1900– 1950*, Howard Mumford Jones sums up the central problems which have plagued the modern novelist: the verbal limitations of nonverbal experience; the dilemma of autobiographical fiction in which the novelist must at once evoke a unique consciousness and yet communicate it to others; the difficulty of catching the flux of time in static language. The summary is acutely concise in picking out the nerve centers of an increasingly subjective novel where "after images fished out of the stream of past time . . . substitute a kind of smoldering dialectic for the clean impact of drama."[5]

Béla Belázs has shown us how seriously we tend to underestimate the power of the human face to convey subjective emotions and to suggest thoughts. But the film, being a presentational medium (except for its use of dialogue), cannot have direct access to the power of discursive forms. Where the novel discourses, the film must picture. From this we ought not to conclude like J. P. Mayer that "our eye is weaker than our mind" because it does not "*hold* sight impressions as our imagination does."[6] For sense impressions, like word symbols, may be appropriated into the common fund of memory. Perceptual knowledge is not necessarily different in strength; it *is* necessarily different in kind.

The rendition of mental states—memory, dream, imagination—cannot be as adequately represented by film as by language. If the film has difficulty presenting streams of consciousness, it has even more difficulty presenting states of mind which are defined precisely by the absence in them of the visible world. Conceptual imaging, by definition, has no existence in space. However, once I cognize the signs of a sentence through the conceptual screen, my consciousness is indistinguishable from nonverbal thought. Assuming here a difference between *kinds* of images— between images of things, feelings, concepts, words—we may observe that conceptual images evoked by verbal stimuli can scarcely be distinguished in the end from those evoked by nonverbal stimuli. The stimuli, whether they be the signs of language or the sense data of the physical world, lose their spatial characteristics and become components of the total ensemble which is consciousness.

On the other hand, the film image, being externalized in space, cannot be similarly converted through the conceptual screen. We have already seen how alien to the screen is the compacted luxuriance of the trope. For the same reasons, dreams and memories, which exist nowhere but in the individual consciousness, cannot be adequately represented in spatial terms. Or rather, the film, having only arrangements of space to work with, cannot render thought, for the moment thought is externalized it is no longer thought. The film, by arranging external signs for our visual perception, or by presenting us with dialogue, can lead us to *infer* thought. But it cannot show us thought directly. It can show us

[5]*Saturday Review*, XXXVIII (April 25, 1955), 19.
[6]J. P. Mayer, *Sociology of Film* (London, 1946), p. 278.

characters thinking, feeling, and speaking, but it cannot show us their thoughts and feelings. A film is not thought; it is perceived.[7]

That is why pictorial representations of dreams or memory on the screen are almost always disappointing. The dreams and memories of *Holiday for Henrietta* and *Rashomon* are spatial references to dreams and memories, not precise renditions. To show a memory or dream, one must balloon a separate image into the frame (Gypo remembering good times with Frankie in *The Informer*); or superimpose an image (Gypo daydreaming about an ocean voyage with Katie); or clear the frame entirely for the visual equivalent (in *Wuthering Heights*, Ellen's face dissolving to the house as it was years ago). Such spatial devices are always to some degree dissatisfying. Acting upon us perceptually, they cannot render the conceptual feel of dreams and memories. The realistic tug of the film is too strong. If, in an effort to bridge the gap between spatial representation and nonspatial experience, we accept such devices at all, we accept them as cinematic conventions, not as renditions of conceptual consciousness.

Given the contrasting abilities of film and novel to render conceptual consciousness, we may explore further the media's handling of time.

Chronological Time

The novel has three tenses; the film has only one. From this follows almost everything else one can say about time in both media. By now, we are familiar with Bergson's distinction between two kinds of time: chronological time measured in more or less discrete units (as in clocks and metronomes); and psychological time, which distends or compresses in consciousness, and presents itself in continuous flux. What are the comparative abilities of novel and film to render these types of time?

To begin with, Mendilow describes language as "a medium consisting of consecutive units constituting a forward-moving linear form of expression that is subject to the three characteristics of time—transience, sequence, and irreversibility." But we must remember that Mendilow is here referring to chronological time only. And chronological time in the novel exists on three primary levels: the chronological duration of the reading; the chronological duration of the narrator's time; and the chronological span of the narrative events. That the three chronologies may harmonize in the fictive world is due entirely to the willingness of the reader to suspend disbelief and accept the authority of convention. As

[7]See Maurice Merleau-Ponty, "Le Cinéma et la Nouvelle Psychologie," *Les Temps Modernes*, No. 26 (November, 1947), pp. 930–943.

long as the novelist is not troubled by the bargain into which he enters with his reader, the three levels do not come into any serious conflict.

But Laurence Sterne saw a long time ago the essential paradox of the convention. If the novelist chooses to chronicle a series of events up to the present moment, he discovers that by the time he commits a single event to paper, the present moment has already slipped away. And if the novelist discovers that it takes a chronological year to record a single fictional day, as Sterne did, how is one ever to overcome the durational lag between art and life? If the present moment is being constantly renewed, how can prose, which is fixed, ever hope to catch it? Whenever a novelist chooses for his province a sequence of events which cannot be completed until the present moment, the three levels come into open conflict. In Sterne and Gide, that conflict becomes more central than conflicts between the characters.

The film is spared at least part of this conflict because one of the levels is omitted. Since the camera is always the narrator, we need concern ourselves only with the chronological duration of the viewing and the time-span of the narrative events. Even when a narrator appears in the film, the basic orientation does not change. When Francis begins to tell the story of Dr. Caligari, the camera shows his face; then the camera shifts to the scene of the story and there takes over the telling. What has happened is not so much that Francis has turned over the role of narrator to the omniscient camera as that the omniscient camera has included Francis as part of the narrative from the beginning.

The ranges of chronological time for reader and viewer are rather fluid, yet more or less fixed by convention. Where a novel can be read in anywhere from two to fifty hours, a film generally runs for one or two. *Intolerance* runs over two hours; the uncut version of *Les Enfants du Paradis* over three; and *Gone with the Wind* and *War and Peace* slightly less than four. Since the fictional events depicted in both novel and film may range anywhere from the fleeting duration of a dream (*Scarlet Street* and *Finnegans Wake*) to long but finite stretches of human history (*Intolerance* and *Orlando*), the sense of passing time is infinitely more crucial than the time required for reading or viewing.

We may note, of course, that a fifty-hour novel has the advantage of being able to achieve a certain density, that "solidity of specification" which James admired, simply because the reader has lived with it longer. Further, because its mode of beholding allows stops and starts, thumbing back, skipping, flipping ahead, and so lets the reader set his own pace, a novel can afford diffuseness where the film must economize. Where the mode of beholding in the novel allows the reader to control his rate, the film viewer is bound by the relentless rate of a projector which he cannot control. The results, as may be expected, are felt in the contrast between the loose, more variegated conventions of the novel and the tight, compact conventions of the film. . . .

Psychological Time: The Time-Flux

As soon as we enter the realm of time-in-flux, however, we not only broach all but insoluble problems for the novel but we also find a sharp divergence between prose and cinema. The transient, sequential, and irreversible character of language is no longer adequate for this type of time experience. For in the flux, past and present lose their identity as discrete sections of time. The present becomes "specious" because on second glance it is seen as fused with the past, obliterating the line between them.

Discussing its essential modernity, Mendilow lends support to the idea that the whole of experience is implicit in every moment of the present by drawing from Sturt's *Psychology of Time*. For Sturt tries to work out the sense in which we are caught by a perpetual present permeated by the past:

> One of the reasons for the feeling of pastness is that we are familiar with the things or events that we recognize as past. But it remains true that this feeling of familiarity is a *present* experience, and therefore logically should not arouse a concept of the past. On the other hand, a present impression (or memory) of something which is past is different from a present impression of something which is present but familiar from the past.[8]

How this seeming contradiction operates in practice may be seen when we attempt to determine precisely which of two past events is prior, and in what manner the distinction between the memory of a past thing and the impression of a present thing is to be made. At first glance, we seem perfectly able to deduce which of two remembered events is prior. For example, on the way to the store this morning, I met a group of children going to school. I also mailed my letter just as the postman came by. I know that ordinarily the children go to school at nine o'clock and the postman comes by at eleven. Therefore, I deduce that I went to the store *before* I mailed my letter. Although I have not been able to give the act of my going to the store an exact location in the past, I have been able to establish its priority.

On second thought, however, it seems as if (apart from the deductions one makes by deliberate attention to relationships) the memory of a past event comes to me with its pastness already intended. The image I have of my friend *includes* the information that this is the way he looked the year before he died. Similarly, if I have a mental image of

[8]Quoted in Mendilow, p. 98.

myself on a train to Kabul, then summon up an image of myself eating chestnuts. I know that the first is an image of a past thing and the second an image of a present thing because the image of myself on the train includes the information that the event took place last year. At the same time, I know that I am eating chestnuts right now. Here the perceptual witnessing of my present action checks and defines my mental images, confirming both the priority of the train ride and the presentness of the eating.

But suppose I bring my attention to bear on an object which is present now and which was also present yesterday at the same time, in the same place, in the same light. If, for example, I look at the lamp in my room, which fulfills all these requirements, then close my eyes and behold the mental image, how am I to know if that image refers to the lamp which was there yesterday or to the lamp which is there today? In this instance, which is tantamount to fusing a thing's past with its present, my present image, for all practical purposes, no longer respects the distinction between past and present. It offers me no way of knowing the exact location of its temporal existence.

This obliteration between past and present is precisely the problem which faces the novelist who wishes to catch the flux in language. If he is faced with the presentness of consciousness on the one hand, and the obliteration of the discrete character of past and present on the other, how is he to express these phenomena in a language which relies on tenses?

Whether we look at William James' "stream of consciousness," Ford Madox Ford's "chronological looping," or Bergson's "*durée*," we find the theorists pondering the same problem: language, consisting as it does of bounded, discrete units cannot satisfactorily represent the unbounded and continuous. We have a sign to cover the concept of a thing's "becoming"; and one to cover the concept of a thing's "having become." But "becoming" is a *present* participle, "become" a *past* participle, and our language has thus far offered no way of showing the continuity between them.

So elusive has been the *durée* that the novelist has submitted to the steady temptation of trying to escape time entirely. But here, too, the failure has served to dramatize the medium's limitations. Speaking of Gertrude Stein's attempt to emancipate fiction from the tyranny of time, E. M. Forster notes the impasse: "She fails, because as soon as fiction is completely delivered from time it cannot express anything at all."

To be sure, there seem to be intuitive moments of illumination in Proust and Wolfe during which a forgotten incident floats up from oblivion in its pristine form and seems thereby to become free of time. Proust's involuntary memory fuses the experience of his mother's madeleine cake with the former experience of Aunt Léonie's, and the intervening time seems, for the moment, obliterated. But it is the precise point of Proust's agonizing effort that—despite our ability, through involuntary memory, to experience simultaneously events "with countless intervening days between"—there is always a sense in which these events remain "widely separated from one another in Time." The recognition of this conflict helps us understand why every formulation which attempts to define a "timeless" quality in a novel seems unsatisfactory, why Mendilow's attempt to find an "ideal time" in Kafka seems to say little more than that Kafka was not plagued by the problem. In the end, the phrase "timeless moment" poses an insuperable contradiction in terms.

We can see the problem exemplified concretely in a passage from Thomas Wolfe's *The Hills Beyond*. The passage describes Eugene Gant's visit to the house in St. Louis where his family had lived thirty years before. Eugene can remember the sights, shapes, sounds, and smells of thirty years ago, but something is missing—a sense of absence, the absence of his brother, Grover, of his family away at the fair:

> And he felt that if he could sit there on the stairs, once more, in solitude and absence in the afternoon, he would be able to get it back again. Then would he be able to remember all that he had seen and been—that brief sum of himself, the universe of his four years, with all the light of Time upon it—that universe which was so short to measure, and yet so far, so endless, to remember. Then would he be able to see his own small face again, pooled in the dark mirror of the hall, and discover there in his quiet three years' self the lone integrity of "I," knowing: "Here is the House, and here House listening; here is Absence, Absence in the afternoon; and here in this House, this Absence, is my core, my kernel—here am I!"[9]

The passage shows the characteristic, almost obsessive longing of the modern novel to escape the passage of time by memory; the recognition that the jump, the obliteration, cannot be made; the appropriation of non-space as a reality in the novel—not the feeling of absence alone, but the absence of absence.

We arrive here at the novel's farthest and most logical remove from the film. For it is hard to see how any satisfactory film equivalents can be found for such a paragraph. We can show Eugene waiting in the house, then superimpose an image of the boy as he might have looked thirty years before, catch him watching a door as if waiting for Grover to return. But as in all cinematic attempts to render thought, such projection would inevitably fail. How are we to capture that combination of past absence and present longing if both are conditions contrary to spatial fact?

The filmmaker, in his own and perhaps more acute way, also faces the problem of how to render the flux of time. "Pictures have no tenses,"

[9]Thomas Wolfe, *The Hills Beyond* (New York, 1941), pp. 37–38. In *Thomas Wolfe: The Weather of His Youth* (Baton Rouge, 1955), pp. 28–53, Louis D. Rubin, Jr. analyzes in some detail Wolfe's handling of time.

says Balázs. Unfolding in a perpetual present, like visual perception itself, they cannot express either a past or a future. One may argue that the use of dialogue and music provides a door through which a sense of past and future may enter. Dialogue, after all, is language, and language does have referential tenses. A character whose face appears before us may *talk* about his past and thereby permeate his presence with a kind of pastness. Similarly, as we saw in our discussion of sound in editing, music may be used to counterpoint a present image (as in *High Noon* and *Alexander Nevsky*) and suggest a future event. In this way, apparently, a succession of present images may be suffused with a quality of past or future.

At best, however, sound is a secondary advantage which does not seriously threaten the primacy of the spatial image. When Ellen, the housekeeper, her withered face illumined by the fire, begins telling her story to Lockwood in *Wuthering Heights,* we do sense a certain tension between story-teller and story. But in the film we can never fully shake our attention loose from the teller. The image of her face has priority over the sound of her voice. When Terry Malone tells Edie about his childhood in *On the Waterfront,* the present image of his face so floods our consciousness that his words have the thinnest substance only. The scars around his eyes tell us more about his past than any halting explanation. This phenomenon is essentially what Panofsky calls the "principle of coexpressibility," according to which a moving picture—even when it has learned to talk—remains a picture that moves, and does not convert itself into a piece of writing that is enacted. That is why Shakesperian films which fail to adapt the fixed space of the stage to cinematic space so often seem static and talky.

In the novel, the line of dialogue stands naked and alone; in the film, the spoken word is attached to its spatial image. If we try to convert Marlon Brando's words into our own thought, we leave for a moment the visual drama of his face, much as we turn away from a book. The difference is that, whereas in the book we miss nothing, in the film Brando's face has continued to act, and the moment we miss may be crucial. In a film, according to Panofsky, "that which we hear remains, for good or worse, inextricably fused with that which we see." In that fusion, our seeing (and therefore our sense of the present) remains primary.

If, however, dialogue and music are inadequate to the task of capturing the flux, the spatial image itself reveals two characteristics which at least permit the film to make a tentative approach. The first is the quality of familiarity which attaches itself to the perceptual image of a thing after our first acquaintance. When I first see Gelsomina in *La Strada,* I see her as a stranger, as a girl with a certain physical disposition, but without a name or a known history. However, once I identify her as a character with a particular relationship to other characters, I am able to include information about her past in the familiar figure which now appears before me. I do not have to renew my acquaintance at every moment. Familiarity, then, becomes a means of referring to the past, and this past reference fuses into the ensemble which is the present Gelsomina. The spatial image of Gelsomina which I see toward the end of the film includes, in its total structure, the knowledge that she has talked to the Fool and returned to Zampano. In a referential sense, the pastness is built in.

That the film is in constant motion suggests the second qualification of film for approximating the time-flux. At first glance, the film seems bound by discrete sections, much as the novel is bound by discrete words. At the film's outer limit stands the frame; and within the frame appear the distinct outlines of projected objects, each one cut as by a razor's edge. But the effect of running off the frames is startlingly different from the effect of running off the sentence. For whether the words in a novel come to be as nonverbal images or as verbal meanings, I can still detect the discrete units of subject and predicate. If I say, "The top spins on the table," my mind assembles first the top, then the spinning, then the table. (Unless, of course, I am capable of absorbing the sentence all at once, in which case the process may be extended to a paragraph composed of discrete sentences.) But on the screen, I simply perceive a shot of a top spinning on a table, in which subject and predicate appear to me as *fused*. Not only is the top indistinguishable from its spinning, but at every moment the motion of the top seems to contain the history of its past motion. It is true that the top-image stimulated in my mind by the sentence resembles the top-image stimulated by the film in the sense that both contain the illusion of continuous motion. Yet this resemblance does not appear in the *process* of cognition. It appears only after the fact, as it were, only after the component words have been assembled. Although the mental and filmic images do meet in rendering the top's continuity of motion, it is in the mode of apprehending them that we find the qualitative difference.

In the cinema, for better or worse, we are bound by the forward looping of the celluloid through the projector. In that relentless unfolding, each frame is blurred in a total progression. Keeping in mind Sturt's analysis of the presentness of our conceptions, a presentness permeated by a past and therefore hardly ruled by tense at all, we note that the motion in the film's *present* is unique. Montage depends for its effects on instantaneous successions of different spatial entities which are constantly exploding against each other. But a succession of such variables would quickly become incomprehensible without a constant to stabilize them. In the film, that constant is motion. No matter how diverse the moving spaces which explode against each other, movement itself pours over from shot to shot, binding as it blurs them, reinforcing the relentless unrolling of the celluloid.

Lindgren advances Abercrombie's contention that completeness in art has no counterpart in real life, since natural events are never complete: "In nature nothing at any assignable point begins and nothing at any assignable point comes to an end: all is perfect continuity." But Abercrombie overlooks both our ability to perceive spatial discreteness in natural events and the film's ability to achieve "perfect continuity." So powerful is this continuity, regardless of the *direction* of the motion, that at times we tend to forget the boundaries of both frame and projected object. We attend to the motion only. In those moments when motion alone floods our attention and spatial attributes seem forgotten, we suddenly come as close as the film is able to fulfilling one essential requirement of the time-flux—the boundaries are no longer perceptible. The transience of the shot falls away before the sweeping permanence of its motion. Past and present seem fused, and we have accomplished before us a kind of spatial analogue for the flux of time.

If the film is incapable of maintaining the illusion for very long, if its spatial appeal to the eye overwhelms its temporal appeal to the mind, it is still true that the film, above all other nonverbal arts, comes closest to rendering the time-flux. The combination of familiarity, the film's linear progression, and what Panofsky calls the "Dynamization of Space" permits us to intuit the *durée* insofar as it can, in spatial art, be intuited at all.

The film, then, cannot render the attributes of thought (metaphor, dream, memory); but it can find adequate equivalents for the kind of psychological time which is characterized by variations in rate (distension, compression; speed-up, *ralenti*); and it approaches, but ultimately fails, like the novel, to render what Bergson means by the time-flux. The failure of both media ultimately reverts to root differences between the structures of art and consciousness.

Our analysis, however, permits a usable distinction between the two media. Both novel and film are time arts, but whereas the formative principle in the novel is time, the formative principle in the film is space. Where the novel takes its space for granted and forms its narrative in a complex of time values, the film takes its time for granted and forms its narrative in arrangements of space. Both film and novel create the illusion of psychologically distorted time and space, but neither destroys time or space. The novel renders the illusion of space by going from point to point in time; the film renders time by going from point to point in space. The novel tends to abide by, yet explore, the possibilities of psychological law; the film tends to abide by, yet explore, the possibilities of physical law.

Where the twentieth-century novel has achieved the shock of novelty by explosions of words, the twentieth-century film has achieved a comparable shock by explosions of visual images. And it is a phenomenon

which invites detailed investigation that the rise of the film, which preëmpted the picturing of bodies in nature, coincides almost exactly with
the rise of the modern novel which preëmpted the rendition of human
consciousness.

Finally, to discover distinct formative principles in our two media
is not to forget that time and space are, for artistic purposes, ultimately
inseparable. To say that an element is contingent is not to say that it is
irrelevant. Clearly, spatial effects in the film would be impossible without
concepts of time, just as temporal effects in the novel would be impossible
without concepts of space. We are merely trying to state the case for a
system of priority and emphasis. And our central claim—namely that time
is prior in the novel, and space prior in the film—is supported rather than
challenged by our reservations.

CONCLUSION

What Griffith meant by "seeing," then, differs in quality from
what Conrad meant. And effecting mutations from one kind of seeing to
another is necessary not only because the materials differ but also because
the origins, conventions, and audiences differ as well.

What happens, therefore, when the filmist undertakes the adaptation of a novel, given the inevitable mutation, is that he does not convert
the novel at all. What he adapts is a kind of paraphrase of the novel—
the novel viewed as raw material. He looks not to the organic novel, whose
language is inseparable from its theme, but to characters and incidents
which have somehow detached themselves from language and, like the
heroes of folk legends, have achieved a mythic life of their own. Because
this is possible, we often find that the film adapter has not even read the
book, that he has depended instead on a paraphrase by his secretary or
his screen writer. That is why there is no necessary correspondence between the excellence of a novel and the quality of the film in which the
novel is recorded.

Under these circumstances, we should not be surprised to find a long
list of discontented novelists whose works have been adapted to motion
pictures. The novelist seems perpetually baffled at the exigencies of the
new medium. In film criticism, it has always been easy to recognize how
a poor film "destroys" a superior novel. What has not been sufficiently
recognized is that such destruction is inevitable. In the fullest sense of the
word, the filmist becomes not a translator for an established author, but a
new author in his own right.

Balázs has, perhaps, formulated the relationship most clearly. Recognizing the legitimacy of converting the subject, story, and plot of a novel

into cinematic form, Balázs grants the possibility of achieving successful results in each. Success is possible because, while "the subject, or story, of both works is identical, their content is nevertheless different. It is this different *content* that is adequately expressed in the changed form resulting from the adaptation." It follows that the raw material of reality can be fashioned in many different forms, but a *content* which determines the form is no longer such raw material. If I see a woman at a train station, her face sad, a little desperate, watching the approach of a hissing engine, and I begin to think of her as a character in a story, she has already, according to Balázs, become "semi-fashioned" artistic content. If I begin to think of how to render her thoughts in words, I have begun to evolve a character in a novel. But if, returning to my impression of that woman at the station, I begin to imagine Garbo in the role of Anna Karenina, I have again transformed her into a new artistic content.

In these terms, says Balázs, the fully conscious film-maker who sets out to adapt a novel

> . . . may use the existing work of art merely as raw material, regard it from the specific angle of his own art form as if it were raw reality, and pay no attention to the form once already given to the material. The playwright, Shakespeare, reading a story by Bandello, saw in it not the artistic form of a masterpiece of story-telling but merely the naked event narrated in it.

Viewed in these terms, the complex relations between novel and film emerge in clearer outline. Like two intersecting lines, novel and film meet at a point, then diverge. At the intersection, the book and shooting-script are almost indistinguishable. But where the lines diverge, they not only resist conversion; they also lose all resemblance to each other. At the farthest remove, novel and film, like all exemplary art, have, within the conventions that make them comprehensible to a given audience, made maximum use of their materials. At this remove, what is peculiarly filmic and what is peculiarly novelistic cannot be converted without destroying an integral part of each. That is why Proust and Joyce would seem as absurd on film as Chaplin would in print. And that is why the great innovators of the twentieth century, in film and novel both, have had so little to do with each other, have gone their ways alone, always keeping a firm but respectful distance.

[1957]

A. R. FULTON

From Novel to Film

Discussion of a film based on a novel or a play arrives sooner or later at a comparison of the film with its source. This kind of criticism may have its advantages. But somehow it leads to the mistaken conclusion that the excellence of the film depends on similarity to the novel or the play from which it is adapted.

It is relevant to observe that the method of the motion pictures is more like that of the novel than of the play. The way a novel tells a story —primarily by description and narration—is comparable to the way a film does—primarily by pictures—whereas the dramatic method is primarily dialogue. It is true of course that a more literal adaptation can be made of a play than of a novel. A film resembles a play in manner of presentation; that is, it can be seen and heard. A play might therefore be so recorded by camera and microphone as to be almost identical to the play produced on the stage. The more faithfully a film "follows the play," the more like the play it becomes—and the less cinematic. A novel, on the other hand, is faithfully adapted to the screen by a translation of the novelistic terms into cinematic ones and thus by being different. For these reasons a film adapted from a play is seldom better than, or even as good as, the original play, whereas a film adapted from a novel is frequently as good as the original novel, and occasionally better. With few exceptions, films made from novels are better than films made from plays. They are invariably better than films adapted from plays literally—and they are better because of the ways in which they are different.

From *Motion Pictures: The Development of an Art from Silent Films to the Age of Television*, by A. R. Fulton. Copyright 1960 by the University of Oklahoma Press.

151

Although a film made from a novel is sometimes praised for "following" the book, literal likeness is of course impossible. Even von Stroheim failed to put *McTeague* "completely on the screen just as it was originally written." It is ironic, however, that frequently the conspicuous differences between a film and its source are due not to the cinematic way of storytelling, but to changes imposed arbitrarily. First of all, there is censorship, the screen unfortunately being denied the freedom permitted the printed word or even the stage. Then because the movies are Big Business and a film must therefore appeal to as wide an audience as possible, concessions are made in a work of literary merit to this mass audience, which, it has somehow been determined, has the capacity to understand equivalent to that of a child of fourteen. A comparison of a film with the novel from which it is adapted usually reveals that in the film certain incidents and characters are left out. These deletions are due less to the cinematic method of storytelling than to the convention of the trade that a film should be ninety minutes long.

The changes may be as minor, for example, as the one in *Great Expectations* (1946) in which the sound of the mice rattling behind a panel in Miss Havisham's dining room in Dickens' novel becomes, in the film, a mouse seen nibbling the wedding cake on the table. Or the changes may be as radical as the one in *The Informer* in which the motivation for Gypo's informing, that is, a half-realized need of money for a night's lodging, becomes in the film Gypo's wanting money for two steamship tickets to America. Although it might be argued that on the screen a mouse is more effective seen than heard or that the hero's wanting to take his girl to America is a more plausible motive than wanting shelter, such changes are for the most part not dictated by the necessities of the medium.

Considerably less arbitrary, however, is the matter of style. In the adaptation of a play, the playwright's style can be retained only in whatever dialogue is carried over verbatim into the film. However, the extent to which a film in this way retains the author's style implies the motion pictures only as a machine. What, though, if the adaptation be that of a novel? The film *Great Expectations* begins with a shot of a book being opened and the voice of John Mills, the actor who plays the older Pip, reading the first paragraph of *Great Expectations* as Dickens wrote it. This literal injection of the paragraph into the film, however, is hardly cinematic. A film adapted from a novel cannot naturally retain the author's style. In describing a scene in the estuary Dickens writes:

> . . . some ballast-lighters, shaped like a child's first rude imitation of a boat, lay low in the mud; and a little squat shoal-lighthouse on open piles, stood crippled in the mud on stilts and crutches; and

> slimy stakes stuck out of the mud, and slimy stones stuck out of the
> mud, and an old landing-stage and an old roofless building slipped
> into the mud, and all about us was stagnation and mud.

But, for all the reality in which the scene in the estuary was shot, the film
here cannot approximate the style in Dickens' description. On the other
hand, if the passage were merely recited on the sound track, it would be
as extrinsic as the recitation of Auden's poem in *Night Mail*.

Although it has become standard practice for films to be only about
ninety minutes long, there are of course exceptions. But because a film
like a play, implies an audience, its length is affected by the length of
time an audience can be expected to sit still in a theatre. That time is
about three hours. The running time of *Great Expectations* is two hours.
Dickens' novel runs to about five hundred pages. On the assumption that
one can read a page a minute, it might be estimated that the reading time
of *Great Expectations* is eight hours, although one would not ordinarily
read five hundred pages continuously at this rate. In one respect it may
be said, then, that the film adaptation of *Great Expectations* is only a
quarter as long as the novel. What accounts for the contraction?

Consider Dickens' description of Miss Havisham's dining room:

> I crossed the staircase landing, and entered the room she indicated.
> From that room, too, the daylight was completely excluded, and it
> had an airless smell that was oppressive. A fire had been lately
> kindled in the damp old-fashioned grate, and it was more disposed
> to go out than to burn up, and the reluctant smoke which hung in
> the room seemed colder than the clearer air—like our own marsh
> mist. Certain wintry branches of candles on the high chimney-piece
> faintly lighted the chamber; or, it would be more expressive to say,
> faintly troubled its darkness. It was spacious, and I dare say had once
> been handsome, but every discernible thing in it was covered with
> dust and mould, and dropping to pieces. The most prominent object
> was a long table with a tablecloth spread on it, as if a feast had been
> in preparation when the house and the clocks all stopped together.
> An epergne or centre-piece of some kind was in the middle of this
> cloth; it was so heavily overhung with cobwebs that its form was
> quite indistinguishable.

A picture, according to the Chinese proverb, is worth a thousand words.
Excepting the airless smell and the temperature, not to mention Dickens'
style, the description of Miss Havisham's dining room can be represented
on the screen—and in only a few seconds. Although it happens that in
depicting this particular scene in the film the camera probes about the
room for more than a few seconds, the time could be reduced to nothing.
For whereas in a novel the action ceases whenever the novelist stops to
describe, in a film the description can be effected while the action is

progressing. For example, Dickens takes a page to describe Miss Havisham. In the film we *see* Miss Havisham while Pip is entering the room, and we continue to see her throughout most of the scene. Since a film takes less time to describe than a novel, it cannot be said that a film is shortened by a curtailing of description.

On the other hand, a film takes more time to narrate than a novel. Suppose, for example, the novelist writes that the hero went to London. The narration is effected as briefly as that. But if the hero's going to London were presented in a film, even if the action were reduced to a minimum, as for example, just the hero's departure and arrival, it would require more time than that for a reading of the statement. In *The Informer* O'Flaherty narrates McPhillip's death in hardly more than a hundred words:

> At thirty-five minutes past seven Francis Joseph McPhillip shot himself dead while trying to escape from No. 44 Titt Street, his father's house. The house had been surrounded by Detective-Sergeant McCartney and ten men. Hanging by his left hand from the sill of the back-bedroom window on the second floor, McPhillip put two bullets into McCartney's left shoulder. While he was trying to fire again, his left hand slipped and lost its hold. The pistol muzzle struck the edge of the sill. The bullet shot upwards and entered McPhillip's brain through the right temple.

In the film this incident comprises a sequence lasting more than three minutes. "At thirty-five minutes past seven," the novel briefly states. The sequence opens with a scene representing the interior of the McPhillip kitchen. The camera shoots down at a clock on the wall by a door. The hands indicate sixteen minutes after six. In the immediately preceding scene another clock has also been made conspicuous—the clock on the wall of the police station. In this scene Gypo is sitting, his back to the camera, looking up at a clock, the hands of which indicate five minutes after six. There is an intervening shot, and then Gypo is again shown looking up at the clock. The hands now indicate six minutes after six. Then there is a lap dissolve to the clock in the McPhillip kitchen. In directing attention to the clocks the film links the sequences, but it also helps to expand the phrase "at thirty-five minutes past seven." The rest of the passage is correspondingly expanded. Thus although in the adaptation of a novel to the screen, description implies contraction, narration implies expansion.

But in terms of time the contraction by no means compensates for the expansion. Whereas description may be reduced in a film to no time at all, narration expands. Furthermore a novel comprises more narration than description. Thus even three hours would be too short a time in which to include all of the characters, incidents, scenes, details, etc. of an average-length novel. A film adapted from a novel therefore implies deletions.

When *Great Expectations* was adapted to the screen, Orlick, Joe's journeyman, was left out and therefore all of that part of the plot which depends on him. Other characters were omitted—Mr. Wopsle's great aunt, Trabb, Trabb's boy, the Avenger, Miss Skiffins, and Clara—and the film is accordingly narrower in scope than the novel. Episodes are abridged: Pumblechook's taking Pip to Miss Havisham's, Pip's preparation for leaving home, Mrs. Joe's death, and the return of Magwitch. In the novel Mr. Jaggers finds Pip and Joe at the Three Jolly Bargemen and then accompanies them home, where Pip's great expectations are revealed. In the film, all of the scenes at the public house having been deleted, the incident is compressed into a single scene at the forge.

This kind of contraction tends to make a film like a play not only in scope, for it results in fewer characters, scenes, incidents, and plots than in a novel, but also in detail, for when a novel is adapted to the screen, detail is elaborated as in a play. The brief passage in *The Informer* narrating Frankie's death is expanded in the film to present, in detail, Frankie's arriving home, his conversation with his mother and his sister, the police surrounding the house. Frankie's attempt to escape, etc. Furthermore the film presents the setting and the appearance of the characters in as much detail as in a play produced on the stage.

In being adapted to the screen a novel, then, is both contracted and expanded. It is contracted in scope and expanded in detail, according to Mortimer Adler's dictum. Whereas a play in being adapted to the screen takes on certain aspects of a novel, a novel in being adapted takes on certain aspects of a play. However, because the cinematic way is more like the novelistic than like the dramatic, a film is more like a novel than like a play. It cannot of course be exactly like a novel. It is something less than a novel. But it is also something more. . . .

[1960]

GEORGE W. LINDEN

The Storied World

Most novels do not begin "Once upon a now." Most films do.
Novels are almost invariably written in the past; films are delibly shot in
the present. Novels are tied to the past because narrative is the form of
fictional prose, and the essence of narrative form is the past remembered
as history. Thus, Henry James was quite right when he defined the novel
as art and as history. He was mistaken, however, as Susanne K. Langer
points out, in not seeing that art and history fail to coincide. James consequently confused the novel with actual history or at least conceived it
as a history of the actual. It is neither. A novel is a history of a possible
world. A novel is a history of an illusion.

Film, like the novel or the heart of Columbus, is also concerned with
the possible. It provides us with an illusion, an illusion that could be true.
It provides us with a possible world, which we feel we might inhabit. In
doing so, film follows the heart's surmise, penetrates to meanings hidden
in the illusion, and reveals to us hitherto undisclosed aspects of the world
and of ourselves. In film, aspects emerge from visibility to feeling to
awareness that we would not ordinarily have perceived, had we merely remained at the level of the natural standpoint. All art transcends the natural standpoint to create an illusory world of emotional depth. It then
negates itself as illusion and leaves us with altered eyes to view our everyday world. Film, being an art, and a public one at that, participates in
this dialectical movement. Unlike the novel, however, film does not so
much pose a world as ex-pose one. It takes us, transports us, into a land
of "Once upon a time," then returns us to our common world. But be-

cause of the peculiar nature of time and space in film, because it collapses all its elements into a fluid present, film's "Once upon a time" is *now*. A novel is a remembrance of things past; a film is a remembrance of things present.

While the novel is a narrative that deploys past events moving toward a present, a film directly displays the present. It presents the present. Even though a novel may be concerned with the present almost exclusively, it is still written and experienced in the reflective mode and hence never quite reaches the present. A film, on the other hand, never quite reaches the past. Hence, where the novelist describes, a director shoots; where a novelist is forced to explain, a director exhibits. Thus, while the novelist constructs the present as past, the director presents the past as present. Although film may borrow certain devices from drama to establish distance (such as scenery, costumes, and archaic language) or may use certain techniques of its own (such as a dissolve into a monologue or a flashback to evoke the past), it never quite succeeds in coinciding with or establishing the past as past. The essence of film is its immediacy, and this immediacy is grounded in its tenselessness. In fact, a film might be defined as a tension without tense.

Moving pictures are composed of pictures, and pictures have no tenses. Béla Balázs states:

> They show only the present—they cannot express either a past or a future tense. In a picture itself there is nothing that would compellingly and precisely indicate the reasons for the picture being what it is. In a film scene we see only what is happening before our eyes.

One may at first be conscious of the fact that Olivier is portraying Henry the Fifth; but, once the soliloquy is over and the battle of Agincourt begins, one sees the battle taking shape before his eyes, and the conviction carried by the images, this immediacy of the present, later leads the spectator to reject the painted castles as props and as phony. The fact that these pictures are moving also adds to their condensation into the present. Through motion there is a kind of spatializing of time and it becomes difficult, if not impossible, to say "then" on film. Condensation also changes the status of relation; thus, relations in the novel tend to be causal, whereas relations in film tend to be casual.

The novel can be much more precise in its treatment of time than can the film. Being more abstract, it can be more exact. Hence the novelist can write: "*Before* John and Mary were married . . . *After* the second anniversary . . . *In November* they discovered she was pregnant . . . *June 12th*, the baby was born . . . *In August* he was baptized. . . ." But, as Stephenson and Debrix point out,

> Film has no words like these; film has no tenses—past, present, or future. When we watch a film, it is just something that is happening —*now*. . . . The immediacy of what film shows us consequently surpasses anything in other arts, and it can have a terseness and a pace that literature cannot match.

One can, of course, always find borderline cases. Ernest Hemingway's style, for example, by its short punching quality, comes close to the terseness of film. The spatialization of time in James Joyce's *Ulysses* or the shifting "camera angles," "zooms," "pans," and "set-ups" in William Faulkner's *As I Lay Dying* also come close to film, not merely through similarity of technique but through the movement toward emotional intensity in a fluid present. Nevertheless, the basic orientation of the novel is to what has happened. Film *is* what's happening.

Just as the novel and film are alike and different in their relations to time, so they are also alike and different in their relations to space. Unlike drama, both the novel and film utilize a space that is intangible and nontangential to the standpoint of the spectator-participant. The space of the novel is a construct of words; it is a space that is engendered by the imagination of the reader, once he has become moved by description to envision. The space of film, however, is immediately given to the eye by the flickering visual image. Both the novel and the film tell stories, but one tells by saying and the other by presenting. Hence, the reader of the novel must conjure up the author's posed world through his own active imagination. But the moviegoer is presented a story already given in image. In this sense, his imagination is more passive, for the film presents its own pace and space; and the shifts in either are controlled, not by his imagination, but by the camera. It is probably fair to conclude, then, that the novel is primarily a representational medium, whereas film is primarily a presentational medium.

Perhaps it should be obvious that moving pictures are not novels. Certainly this is what I have been arguing in emphasizing the immediate presence of the film and the basic mnemonic character of novels. But this is not obvious to everyone. To the layman, the relation between the novel and the film appears to be one of absolute identity. Or rather, one might call it moral identity, since the average man insists that though the film and novel may not be the same, they *ought* to be. To the respected critic Brendan Gill, the relation seems to be one of substance and attribute, though it is quite arbitrary which one picks as substance and which as attribute. To Marshall McLuhan, the relation is one of formal or structural identity. Let us examine these three specific points of view before returning to a general discussion of the relations of films and novels.

Most surveys reveal that the useful fiction, the average layman, simply does not buy many books. If he does, few of them are novels; and, of those, even fewer are ever read. It is probably safe to assume that most people buy books for the look of their living rooms rather than to add new furniture to the mansions of their minds. The motto seems to be "Buy the book if you must, but see the movie." And, perhaps, for sound pragmatic reasons. It takes less time to see the film. Furthermore, it often takes much less effort. One does not have to think as much to experience the film and, besides, it is continuous. As far as the average man is concerned, the novel and the film are practically identical. But practical identity for him means identity. Hence, if he has not read the novel, he will consider himself to have read it after watching the film. If he has previously read the novel, he will either criticize the film for not being faithful to the book or praise it for being a fine rendering of the original. It takes someone more subtle—say, a professional critic—to condemn a film for being too faithful to a novel. This, of course, is exactly what many critics do, although it is far more common even for the professionals to condemn a film for violating the novel. The basic assumption of the ordinary layman, then, and of some critics, is that for a motion picture to be faithful to a novel it must simply be the novel.

One contemporary critic, Brendan Gill, has the distinction of downgrading two films in the same review for contradictory reasons. He rejects the film *Reflections in a Golden Eye* on the basis that John Huston did not follow the novel with greater fidelity and made the film realistic, whereas the terrain of the novel is a purely fictional land. Huston, he claims, has been unfaithful to Carson McCullers' intention and to her work. At the same time, Gill rejects *Far from the Madding Crowd* because it too slavishly follows Thomas Hardy's novel. Not only the director but also the producers, writers, and actors are condemned for excessive reverence. Huston is accused, therefore, either of good faith that has been misplaced or of bad faith, and John Schlesinger is condemned for having displayed good faith with too much fidelity.

If one takes Mr. Gill's critiques literally, he appears to be contradicting himself or at least to be outlining an almost impossible task for a director. He is also overlooking the fact that both the novel and the film are types of fiction. They simply happen to be different kinds of fiction. Huston's film is not more real than the novel on which it is based. Though it may give the illusion of greater reality, the film is also an illusion, a visual instead of a verbal one. That there is a sense in which the film and the novel exist on somewhat the same plane is evidenced by the fact that we speak of the film *version* of the book or we say "the novel on which the film is *based*." But the idea of "basing" and the word "version" also connote differences. There must be some sense, then, in asserting that a film can be a translation or, even more accurately, a transformation of a novel. The question is still open, however, as to what should be kept, what should be thrown out, what should be transformed, and how.

Gill explicitly rejects the theory that films should be judged strictly as films without regard to their novelistic antecedents when he states: "This is an old and not very intelligent theory, and, significantly, is nearly always employed as a device for defending a movie that has failed, rather than paying tribute to one that has succeeded." Not because of but in spite of Mr. Gill's dogmatism and pejorative language, there is some truth in what he says. But there is also some truth in asserting that it is more fruitful to compare films with films than to compare films with novels. Because of the intimate organic relations of form and content, no matter how faithful the film, it can never express the content of the novel as the novel expresses it. Different materials demand different modes of expression. The novel, after all, projects a world from words; the film presents one in images.

Some forms of expression, Mr. Gill seems to feel, such as Hardy's, should stay safely ensconced between dead covers and should never be resurrected by adaptation. Presumably what he means is that it is most difficult, if not impossible, to transform Hardy's pessimistic value world into visual terms. In assuming that it is the value world of the novel, not the characters, events, or plot, that is of central importance for film, Mr. Gill is essentially correct. A motion picture should make us see the world the author has envisioned.

Another novel champion, Marshall McLuhan, is convinced that film is linear and print oriented and that television images are nonlinear—in fact, antilinear. Thus, he attempts to prove that the decline in the popularity of baseball is due to television because baseball is a game of specialists who play a game that proceeds one-thing-at-a-time, whereas television demands generalists with everything happening at once. This evidence is simply not evidence. Football has as great an amount of, perhaps more, specialization than baseball, and it has been enhanced by TV. In recent years, no sport has made more dramatic strides in popularity than golf, and this rise in popularity is due almost entirely to television coverage. It would be difficult to imagine a more linear game than golf, either in the literal or the figurative sense. Baseball is declining probably because it is a highly intellectual game in which most of the time nothing is going on; and, unlike golf, it is difficult if not impossible to edit. Hence, long lapses exist and they cannot be compressed. But this is not due to its linearity, as opposed to the nonlinearity of football.

McLuhan is attempting, via TV, to assimilate the film to the novel, not only in the sense of its supposed print orientation (why he missed the pun that filmstrips are printed is a puzzle), but also in the sense of narrative. He does not look to see whether films are in fact linear and ABCED-minded; he assumes that they must be, then attempts to prove his point. He first attempts to collapse film into literature by asserting that both the filmmaker and the writer try to transfer the "reader or viewer from one world, his *own*, to another, the world created by typography and film." This is, of course, true, but it does not show that print and film are therefore identifiable in some specific and significant manner. It is the function of all art—whether film, painting, sculpture, or drama—to transport the viewer to another world, to give him another temporary world to live in. McLuhan's assertion that movies are a form of "statement without syntax" is slipshod and false. Film images may be tenseless, but they are not without syntax. In fact, the Russian school has long held that film is little else but syntax, a formalist point of view, which McLuhan ought logically to hold if he were consistent with his assertion that the "medium is the message"—an assertion that puts the entire emphasis and value on form and declares that content is irrelevant at best and pernicious at worst. One can attempt to assimilate film to literature; but, in order to make the attempt, one should be more accurate and more subtle than McLuhan— one must be a Jean Cocteau, a Robert Bresson, or an Alexandre Astruc. Even then, one should remember that what he is doing is describing analogies, not reducing one art to the other.

Thus, while McLuhan tries to draw sharp distinctions between the film and television, he attempts to blur the distinctions between the film and the novel. He claims that the viewing of film demands a high degree of and training in literacy. This is merely a half truth. The film experience does demand a definite amount of visual literacy but does not necessarily demand verbal literacy. This can be observed quite clearly in children, who can grasp the flow of images and the reference of one to another even though they have not as yet learned to read. A little reflection will show that the following McLuhan assertion is false: "The close relation, then, between the reel world of film and the private fantasy experience of the printed word is indispensable to our Western acceptance of the film form." In fact, a slight knowledge of history will show it false. The audiences who were shocked by D. W. Griffith's first use of the close-up and fled from the theatre when the first face filled the entire screen were *verbally* literate. Newspapers and books, after all, were not invented after the Griffith films. The difficulty was that the audiences were *visually* illiterate in a new form: film.

But McLuhan continues: "Film, both in its reel form and in its scenario or script form, is completely involved with book culture. All one need do is to imagine for a moment a film based on newspaper form in order to see how close film is to the book." One does not need to imagine, one has simply to see. Look at Jean-Luc Godard's *Breathless* or Richard Lester's *A Hard Day's Night,* and you will see films based, not on newspaper content, but on newspaper form. Or look at the verbal version of

Federico Fellini's *Juliet of the Spirits*. The printed version consists of a long interview and two scripts: the original script and the shooting script. The film itself differs from both written scripts.

It may be that McLuhan is correct, though he does not identify his authorities and grandly personifies the film industry in general, when he states that "even the film industry regards all of its greatest achievements as derived from novels, nor is this unreasonable." It may not be unreasonable, but it is doubtful. If one reflects for a few moments on some of the great films, he will find that they can be classified into three categories with respect to the novel: fine films not based on novels, fine films based on poor novels, and fine films based on fine novels. The same categories, of course, could hold for poor films. But if one confines himself to the set which McLuhan pinpoints as "the greatest achievements" of film, he will find that either McLuhan or the "industry" or both are probably wrong. In fact, it is highly doubtful that the greatest films are derived from novels. There even seems to be a kind of basic antagonism or inverse relationship between the novel and the film. It seems almost as though the greater the novel, the less likely that the resulting film will be great.

It is difficult to think of a truly revolutionary film that was derived from a novel. The word "revolutionary" here is intended to refer to both those films that changed the course of the development of film art and also those films that stand as examples, *par excellence*, of the medium. *The Great Train Robbery, The Birth of a Nation, Intolerance, The Cabinet of Doctor Caligari, Grand Illusion, Citizen Kane, La Strada, The Bicycle Thief, Potemkin, Zero for Conduct, Alexander Nevsky, Children of Paradise, Shoeshine, Umberto D, Hiroshima Mon Amour, Wild Strawberries, Last Year at Marienbad, The Four Hundred Blows, L'Avventura, The Young and the Damned, The Seven Samurai, On the Waterfront*— one could go on almost indefinitely naming films that were written specifically for the screen, insofar as writing was involved. Many of the great directors have avoided making any films based on novels but have preferred, as Bergman and Fellini have, either to collaborate on scripts or to do all their own writing.

Fine films made from poor or at least mediocre literary works are not difficult to list, either. Such films as *Treasure of the Sierra Madre, The Postman Always Rings Twice, Gone with the Wind, The Informer, Double Indemnity, The African Queen, Rashomon, The Ox-Bow Incident, Greed, The Maltese Falcon, The Graduate* are all cases in point. But it is much more difficult to list fine films made from fine novels. There are a few, such as *Tom Jones, Ulysses, The Grapes of Wrath, Lolita, The Red Badge of Courage;* and it should be noted that these films often deviate drastically from the novels on which they were based. *The*

Grapes of Wrath, for example, contains as a film none of the mystic uncertainty of the novel and completely changes the ending of the novel in
order that the film may be upbeat and may end on a note of optimism,
not despair. It is not difficult at all, of course, to remember poor films
made from fine novels. Almost any film version of *Crime and Punishment*
is hardly worth watching, and the same may be said for *The Red and the
Black, The Brothers Karamazov, Moby Dick, Huckleberry Finn*, and many
other screen disasters. Some cases that are moot come to mind. For example, *The Old Man and the Sea* is not a great novel nor is the film a great
film. One could no doubt draw up innumerable lists of this type; and it
must be granted that no matter how many films might be listed, such
inventories would probably prove little.

Nevertheless, it is worth noting that many films considered the high
points of the various genres in the history of the motion picture were not
adaptations of novels nor did they depend primarily upon novelistic
technique. The American discoveries of film possibilities made by Griffith
and exploited in the silent comedies, the Russian films of socialist realism
and non-heroes, the German cinema of expressionism, and Italian neo-
realism all avoided dependence upon the novel. The same can be said for
most of the great creators of personal films, whether from primarily silent
times, such as Chaplin, or from the new age of alienation, such as Bergman, Fellini, and Antonioni. At the very least, then, we must conclude
that McLuhan's attempt to identify film with the novel, like the attempt
of the layman, is suspect. In all probability, it is false.

These reflections should make it evident that the relations between
the quality of novels and the resulting quality of the film are not simple.
No doubt the film companies pay enormous funds for famous novels;
whether they happen to be fine novels is irrelevant. It is the fame, after
all, that is important, for the motive behind such purchases is not artistic
but commercial. It is the producer who usually "buys" the novel, and,
once bought, it ceases to be a novel and becomes a property. It may well
be that those films based on novels with reputations, notorious or otherwise, do in fact make more money. This may have been what McLuhan
meant, but it was far from what he said. And even then, few would accuse
Chaplin or Fellini of having become poverty-stricken by the film. It would
appear, then, that films are not so easily identified with the novel as both
the ordinary layman and Marshall McLuhan assume. As Professor Baum-
bach has remarked, many college students can barely read or write, but
they are filmically literate.

What the camera can provide is the richness of immediate presence,
and this very complexity of quality makes film "the most difficult of all
arts both to practice and appreciate." This richness of presence must be
unified by taste and sensitivity, by an awareness of the emotional rightness

of visual images, and it cannot be reduced to verbal rules René Clair was quite aware that—although, from the viewpoint of intellect, one could set up a strict metre of shot structure on the basis of shot length, scene alternation, and internal movement—from a practical point of view, it would not work. " 'I am resigned,' he concluded, 'to find neither rules nor logic in this world of images. The primitive wonder of this art enchants me.' " Had Marshall McLuhan been as sensitive as René Clair to the differences that lie at the base of every analogy, he might not have mistaken presence for sequence and tried to reduce film to a linear succession of static parts.

The theory of aesthetics resulting from McLuhan's prior positions is one of sheer formalism and rests upon a constant confusion of the verbal and the visual. It is summed up in his most famous phrase: "The medium is the message." What this means, if it is taken to be meaningful, is that meaning is purely a function of syntax and is completely independent of content. Hence, it is the sheer how of things and not their way that is important. It must be admitted that McLuhan tries to base the reduction of film to words on the structural similarities of shot sequence and verbal construction. He has to depend upon sequence, of course, since he has already claimed that a shot is without syntax. That such an analogy does not appear applicable has already been noted. It is difficult for McLuhan himself to avoid depending upon content. His belief in the importance of plot brings him to the posture that film is a closed medium.

The arguments in *Understanding Media* that film is medieval are false in one sense and true in another. They are false insofar as they argue that film is composed of static essences and true when they claim that a film is a kind of two-hour cathedral. The assertions of stability are McLuhan's attempt to express a belief in a set universe of clear categories and Thomistic essences. This same attitude brings him to utilize Henri Bergson's contrast of the living and the static to misinterpret the nature of film. While it is true that in one frame a camera captures only the static, it is untrue that what the human eye perceives on the screen is a series of changes of states and essences. What one perceives is the flow and patterning of images. This patterning is in part done by the spectator. During a ninety-minute film, about forty minutes is composed of a black screen; yet the persistence of vision negates the darkness and allows us to perceive a continuously flowing phenomenon. McLuhan's analogy of the building of cathedrals and the construction of film, however, is a medievalism that bears some truth. The truth it carries, however, negates his attempt to assimilate film to the novel.

McLuhan is quite right in stating that the creation of film is a corporate activity. The creation of a film, like the building of a cathedral, depends upon the coordinated interplay of activities among a large group of specialists. The products of the activities of each particular group of specialists must be governed with a view to the whole, and the quality of the part must be so constructed as to enhance the unity and the impact of the whole. Thus, the sculptor who worked on the cathedral did not create free-standing works but elements that were designed to enhance and enliven the architecture. In the same way, the costume designer or the make-up man who works in films contributes elements that should help constitute the revelation of character and situation, only a part of which is contributed by the written script. Like the construction of the cathedral, the film demands a hierarchy of coordinated activity and one overriding authority in charge, usually the producer or, more effectively, the director. Both the film and the cathedral are incredibly expensive and depend upon complex economic relationships. Both provide a temporary haven for those seeking communion and temporary escape from the real evils of the world. But, of course, they differ greatly as to time. It may take centuries to build a cathedral, and it is designed to last for centuries more. No film could afford to take so long to shoot, it rarely lasts more than a few years, and the solace it is designed to provide is usually confined within the span of two hours, not an eternity. It is precisely the corporate character of film production, of course, that has been such a painful reality for most writers.

The task of a writer is an exercise in loneliness; in fact, writing is almost narcissistic in its singularity. Everything the writer creates, everything he includes or fails to include in his novel, must, one way or another, come out of the depths of his own experience and being. The agonizing solitude of the writer provides him with a control over his work that is perhaps as absolute as anything can be in this life. This means that the viewpoint of the author is basic, and his perspective determines the theme, the style, the form, the tone, and the content of his work. Whether the narrator is a character in the story, as he usually is, or the author himself, the point of view of the narrator and his rendition of past events lie at the heart of the novel. He is not subject to the revisions of the continuity director, the cameraman, the sound technicians, or the prop man. Ultimately, in the novel, the author and the author alone is responsible for the characters and the scene. But the film is not primarily scene but something immediately seen. Hence, even if it is a highly personal film, stamped with the style and characteristics of the director, even this viewpoint is submerged by what is immediately seen and heard. If the writer has simply been hired to work on a film, his impact on the end result will be even less, and it is not at all unusual to find a film that has had many scriptwriters. It is most unusual to find a novel with more than one author, and it would be a rare publisher indeed who would hire several authors to write and revise the same work. This process, of course, is quite normal in the film. And it is often successful. Films are not composed of words. A motion picture is composed of images. And the images move.

The altered relation to words is one reason that the motion-picture experience exists on a lower level of imagination than that of the novel. The author of the novel uses the bulge and nuzzle of language to move the reader onto an imaginary plane. And what is imagination except seeing as if present that which is not present? The world the novelist describes may be enchanting or enchanted, but it is not now actually present in sensation. A novel is something thought, not something seen. The world the motion-picture director displays, on the other hand, is one which appears present in the visibility and urgency of immediacy. Through the rhythmic tension of images and depth, the director elicits the visibility of the actual and projects it, both literally and figuratively, into an immediate possible present, not an imaginary past. Worlds, not words, are important in film. Without words, the novel could not manifest itself, it could not be. But film can and does exist without words. Admittedly, it is better with them (if one excludes the avalanche of excessively talky films that succeeded the technical breakthrough of *The Jazz Singer*). But the true function of words in film is not to portray but to punctuate vision.

Usually an author writes his novel in sequential order; he writes the first chapter followed by the second, and so on. Sometimes, he may write a climactic scene, and then write up to and away from it. If he is writing a mystery novel, he may well write the ending first, then plan the rest of the book and write it to meet the final revelation. It is a rare author, however, such as James Joyce, who works on three or four different chapters at the same time or in alternate sequences. Such a mode of shooting is the normal procedure in film; and if one ever watches a film being shot, the one overwhelming feeling he has is that it will be a miracle if all of this chaos is ever brought into any semblance of order. The order of composition of the film is from the outside in; the order of composition of a novel is from the inside out. Very few significant films are shot in sequence, and the resulting cut product, of course, is always much, much less than the amount of film used. This will vary with the director and his character. During the first thematic phase of Akira Kurosawa's *High and Low*, the spectator is conscious of the careful composition and the extended length of the scenes. These takes last about ten minutes on the screen, yet each was edited from one hour's shooting. The shot/film ratio of this sequence is thus six to one. My guess would be that Fellini's shot/finished film ratio is probably three or four times that of Ingmar Bergman for the simple reason that Fellini is more emotional, more flamboyant, more in love with happy accidents, whereas Bergman is more theatrical, more intellectual, and more controlled.

The status and functions of the writer, then, differ considerably with respect to the film and the novel. In some films, such as *8½*, the writer may serve as an intellectual foil and as an alter ego for the main character. Sometimes he may be a disembodied narrator, as in *Tom Jones*, or an embodied one, as in the framing device of *Quartet*. Usually, however, the writer is not in the film in any form at all, though he is almost always in the novel in one form or another. The main difference in the relations of the writer to film and to the novel is the element of control. With respect to the novel, the writer is a mortal and singular god; whatever is there, he created. In film, he is merely one worker among many. For his novel to become a film, it must undergo "treatment" and become a shooting script. And a film script, as we said in Chapter 1, is merely the skeleton for an aural-visual world and not a full-fleshed creature. Since the skills needed to transform a novel into a shooting script differ from those of the novelist proper, few novelists become successful screenwriters. Some, such as Faulkner, have made their bread and butter by screenwriting, but we remember them for their novels, not for their sharp shooting scripts.

If we turn to the experience of the reading of the novel, we find that the reader's experience is analogous to that of the writer: he has much more control. We have already described the bearable democracy of attending the movies. When one reads a novel, he usually reads it in familiar surroundings, that is, in his own home. Since one's lived environment is familiar and known, it is seldom an object of sensation. It is simply assumed; and being assumed, it can much more easily slip into a surrounding ambience and become an unperceived, or at least dimly perceived, horizon of the self. Hence, when one takes up the novel and begins reading in his easy chair, the surrounding room soon begins to slip away. One becomes unaware of the place and ground of his own body and imaginatively becomes excarnate, inhabiting—omnisciently, of course— the world of the novel. This easy slip into externalized subjectivity is evidence that McLuhan is right in asserting that the founder of modern thought was not Descartes but Gutenberg. At any rate, as soon as one is imaginatively engaged in the novel, he feels himself to be nowhere and nowhen in relation to the actual world. But he has much more control over the pace and direction of his experience than he has in film. He can dwell on this situation or that, this character or that, and he can thumb his way back to a previous passage to confirm an image or impression. The reader's vision and ability to envision consequently follow his attention, whereas in film our attention follows our vision. We cannot stop the flow of the film, reverse its order, or dwell on a scene since its directionality is forced upon us. We can be and are selective, but the degree of control the movie spectator can exert is much less than that of the novel reader.

One has the feeling when reading the novel that he is in direct communion with the author. The novel reader's experience, then, is like that of the moviegoer and unlike that of the member of the audience in the stage play in that his own persona, his self as a generalized other, is bypassed. It is the function of all media, whether the motion picture, radio, television, the novel, or the telephone, to bypass the self-as-other and to negate the natural standpoint. For this reason, films and novels can be both intimate and impersonal, for the persona of the individual is not involved. This, I take it, is why children with speech defects usually become avid readers, and why children who stutter seldom do so on the telephone. It also explains why my teen-aged daughters are so addicted to the telephone; it allows them to reach the aural being of the other without having to suffer from his gaze. Media provide the possibility for immediate participation without the concomitant defect of embarrassment. They provide us with another way to be. And that other way to be is an experience of excarnation.

The experience of the reader is analogous to that of the director in another sense: it is intermittent. One usually reads a novel, then puts the book aside for the press of everyday life before once again resuming the illusory world. But the illusory world of experiencing the film is continuously present. One reason that it is possible for the reader to experience the novel intermittently is because the novel is a narrative. It is something he must think together in imagination. The verbal symbols are constant and fairly simple to resume. The task of the director is much more difficult. He is working, not primarily with thoughts or with the verbal, but with the aural and visual; hence, he must be able to draw these disparate elements together on the basis of emotional rhythm. The necessity for emotional unity varies according to the type of film involved, of course. Hence, a documentary tends to be thought, while a fictional film is much more dependent upon feeling. In the novel, feeling is a precipitate of thought. In film, thought is a precipitate of feeling engendered by vision. In the novel, we see because we remember; in film, we remember because we see.

The experience of the reader of the novel is much more singular than that of the spectator of the film. The word "singular" is used here in various senses. The experience is singular in the sense that it is more rare and less frequent. At least in the modern world more people view films more often than read the novels on which those films are based, however loosely. The experience is also singular in the sense that one usually reads a novel alone. Rarely is novel reading a group experience; and, although in a very real sense each individual watching a film is in a theatre of his own, films are nevertheless a group experience. The reading of a novel is singular in the still further meaning that only one sense is usually involved: vision. One rarely reads a novel aloud; hence, the written symbols must carry the force to create the entire imaginary world. But it is precisely the counterpoint and fusion of sight and sound that are basic to the impact of film.

While the film and the novel are alike in that they are not primarily concerned with the imitation of an action, as is drama, but with the development of events, their approaches to the event differ due to their different demands and emphases. The novelist tends to reveal what people do through what they are; the director, to reveal what they are through what they do. What the novelist deploys, the director must display. It is exactly here that the film based on the novel usually fails. For a film to be an adequate rendition of a novel, it must not only present the actions and events of the novel but also capture the subjective tones and attitudes toward those events. This the novelist can do quite freely by using description and point of view. It is much more difficult for the director, since he must either discover or create visual equivalents for the narrator's evaluations. . . .

The film, then, must capture the feeling-tone of the novel and translate this basic quality into its appropriate medium. Sometimes the director follows the novelist with extreme exactitude as, for example, Richardson does in the eating scene with Tom and Mrs. Waters. At other times, he includes scenes which are not in the novel at all but are implied by its characters and descriptive structure; for example, the brutal stag chase. At other times, he concretizes visually the implied analogues of the author; for example, the dull grey shots of the prison scenes, which render in immediate visual quality the analogues to Hogarth's *The Rake's Progress* implied by Fielding. Once the director has a firm grasp of the central emotional quality of the novel, he has the end in view. He must then discover or create the means appropriate both to his medium and to his message.

If a film is to be an adaptation of a novel, then, the film director has a more difficult task before him than if the film script is an original. He must learn to walk a fine line between excess reverence for the author's work (see Luchino Visconti's *The Stranger*) and disregard (*The Long Hot Summer*). Sometimes a film may deviate radically from the book and still be an engaging and interesting film; for example, *To Have and Have Not*. Usually such deviations, however, since they are due to commercial, patriotic, or other such nonartistic reasons, end in disaster. The narrative line of the novel can be incorporated into the film script and will emerge as plot and incident. But the tone, the stance, the voice of the author may be much more difficult to translate. A successful film adaptation of a novel should not *be* the book. Nor should it be a substitute for the book. If it is truly successful, it should be a work of art in its own right, which excites the reader to go reexperience that world in another medium: the novel. . . .

In this chapter, I have been reflecting upon some of the family differences between novel and film. I have used the novel as an analogical example of the structural or formal dimension of film. What these reflections reveal is that film incorporates characters and narrative line from the novel. Because of the inevitable differences of the two media, however, the narrative line of the novel becomes transformed by film into plot. But plot is merely a subplan in movies. Plot in film is but an element in theme. Thus, the director must be able to translate the novelist's verbal system—his tone or stance—into a visual theme if he is to capture the novel. Theme expresses the artist's view of the nature of existence.

Akira Kurosawa's film *High and Low* was mentioned earlier in the chapter. An analysis of his films would show the thematic, as distinguished from plotted, nature of film. Kurosawa's films have the following phases of form: (1) thematic statement, (2) bridge, (3) dominant theme, (4) development of dominant theme, (5) secondary theme, (6) development of secondary theme and articulation of dominant, (7) coda for reflection. In *High and Low*, of course, the secondary theme—a business struggle—is introduced first. Still, this analysis would fit almost all his films. It will also fit the films of many other modern directors. The reason is simple. Novels begin in imagination. Films end in it.

[1970]

4

Film and Poetry

OUTTAKES

. . . "cinema is the true poetic language." It's much closer to poetry than to theater.

BERNARDO BERTOLUCCI

The cinema should always be the discovery of something. I believe that the cinema should be essentially poetic; that is why during the shooting and not during the preparation, I try to plunge myself into a poetic development, which differs from narrative development and dramatic development.

ORSON WELLES

. . . the cinema offers the language arts a salutary example of the spirit of sacrifice. By its very nature, literature supports the two-thousand-year-old prejudice of Western civilization in favor of clarity. This is because in order for something to be in literature, it has to be expressed. Because nothing that is not clearly perceived is effective, we are led to belittle the value of indirect suggestion and to consider as unimportant those aesthetic effects that take place outside the center of interest and are more or less unperceived by intelligence. Literature normally tends toward pure prose—that is, toward a form of expression perfectly identical with itself, equally devoid of both mystery and implications, in which there is nothing beyond what is said and immediately understood.

Fortunately, during the course of history several arts have come to the rescue and protected literature from itself, preserving in it some areas of silence and safeguarding the rights of poetry. At the end of the nineteenth century such was the function of music in relation to the symbolist movement. Today this may be the role of the movies. Valéry, thinking of Wagner, dreamed of a literature that would, like the latter's orchestration, know how to create "in the shadow of the auditory sense, in the distant and defenseless regions of the sensitive soul, the far-off events, the presentiments, the questions, the enigmas, the undefinable stirrings . . ." He wanted an art that would, like music, know how to speak to the unconscious. But the cinema, no less than music, acts directly on the "sensitive soul": like music, it speaks to the senses without having to pass through the intermediary of understanding; it is, in the etymological sense of the word, aesthetic rather than intellectual. And that is why it is able to

Luis Bunuel explores the unconscious by linking potent images in this series of stills from the beginning of *Un Chien Andalou* (1928) (figures 4.1-4.3).

Figure 4.1   Museum of Modern Art/Film Stills Archive.

Figure 4.2   Museum of Modern Art/Film Stills Archive.

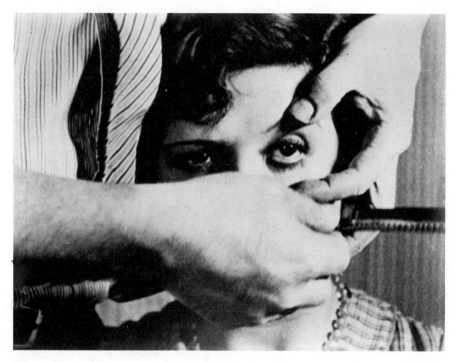

Figure 4.3   Museum of Modern Art/Film Stills Archive.

Figure 4.4   Maya Deren uses superimpositions for poetic effect in this still from Meshes of the Afternoon *(1943). Museum of Modern Art/Film Stills Archive.*

avoid the error that constantly threatens the language arts—the error of reducing human consciousness to only its most rational part and speaking to that part alone.

CLAUDE-EDMONDE MAGNY

Despite critical biases, few theoreticians of film avoid speaking of poetry in cinema. Like the word *narrative, poetry* is a term which seems as natural to cinema as to literature. It is clear that poetry existed in oral form long before it appeared in writing and that from the beginning poetry was associated with the arts of music and dance as part of communal ceremonies. Perhaps this clear and long interaction of poetry with, and within, other art forms explains our implied acknowledgment that poetry exists independently of any one medium and that therefore film, too, can be poetry. Poetry is, of course, difficult to define. Most definitions, including those by print-oriented commentators, emphasize the rhythmic expression which people give to their most imaginative and intense perceptions of the world, themselves, and one another.

In "Poetry and the Film: A Symposium" various poets of the cinema and of literature grapple with definitions and relationships. The symposium, which took place on October 28, 1953, includes Maya Deren, Parker Tyler, Dylan Thomas, and Arthur Miller, with Willard Maas acting as chairman. Their interchange of ideas is loose and open, as one would expect from a symposium, but challenging and fruitful in its insights. Tyler begins with the assumption that poetry exists apart from any particular medium (especially print), and Deren follows with what becomes the reference point (as well as the dissension point) for the symposium. After defining poetry as an approach to experience defined by rhythm, color, and so on, she distinguishes between a (poetic) vertical approach which illuminates the moment and a (dramatic) horizontal attack which involves narrative development. Thomas attempts to deflate her ideas. (Elsewhere Thomas has defined poetry as "the rhythmic, inevitably narrative, movement from an overclothed blindness to a naked vision.") Miller voices his concern with establishing a firmer understanding of how film works before coming to aesthetic conclusions, and Maas returns to his concern with the relationship of sound to visuals.

In "The Other Direction," Jonas Mekas, the leading spokesman for the New American Cinema, offers a plea for poetic cinema. He deplores the tendency to consider only narrative cinema, suggesting that such critical recognition would be like ignoring printed poetry in favor of narrative. The indirect, intuitive expression of cinematic poetry offers a "meditation on life" which Mekas suggests is no less valuable than the contributions of narrative cinema.

Robert Richardson, the author of *Literature and Film,* examines the relationship of printed contemporary poetry to the modern cinema. Contending that the effect of montage on literature has been extensive, he suggests that modern poetry and film have been evolving along similar lines. Concentrating on such mutual concerns as design, interest in sight and sound, and making a viewer or reader experience feelings or realizations for himself rather than achieve them through the intellect, Richardson suggests that cinema is an extension of modern literature.

Offering a print poet's view of the subject, Richard Wilbur examines the effects cinema has on the poet, and specifically upon himself. Using his poetry for examples, he contemplates the uses a modern poet may put to his cinematic exposure.

MAYA DEREN, WILLARD MAAS,
ARTHUR MILLER, DYLAN THOMAS,
PARKER TYLER

Poetry and the Film:
A Symposium

Maas: In a prepanel discussion earlier this week with the majority of the panel, we decided that maybe the best way to start this discussion would be to try to have the members of the panel outline . . . some of the basic aesthetic principles of the poetic film; and, therefore, I think I would like to call on Mr. Tyler first. . . .

Tyler: Thank you. My thought was that the question, rather than the assumption, by which the symposium will proceed tonight is that of what poetry, in and outside the film, actually is. Perhaps it would be necessary, for such a demonstration, to conceive the question at the start, and honestly, as faced with the two horns of a dilemma. Now that dilemma is: On the one hand, there's the *theory* of poetry, its possibilities as such in the film medium, and on the other hand the *practice* of poetry, as concentrated in the avant-garde film. It should be hoped that we don't snag on either of these but will steer a just course between them. Now I thought we might get an over-all picture of the field to be surveyed, and to that end I'd like to give you a memorandum, so to speak, of the types of poetical expression that do appear in films today; that is, these expressions may be whole or fragmentary, they may be pure or impure, but at least they exist, and they are to be recognized as such, Now, poetical expression falls rather automatically into two groups: that is, poetry as a visual medium and poetry as a verbal medium, or, in a larger sense, as auditory, and that would, of course, include music. We might well begin with some of the shorter films that concentrate on poetry as a visual medium, and this, of course, leads right to Cocteau's *Blood of a Poet*, and to Buñuel-Dali's *Andalusian Dog,* and to Watson's *Lot in Sodom.* All these are classics now, and they emphasized a surrealist poetry of the image and gave rise to schools and styles of avant-garde all over the world. Cinema 16 patrons are familiar with some of these outstanding works—those of Maya Deren, of James Broughton, of Kenneth Anger, of Curtis Harrington. All these film-makers concentrated on what might be called pure cinema—entirely without words as a rule, although sometimes with music. Then to go back (after all, the avant-garde movement in poetry in America goes rather far back, at least to the 1920's) I know there was a type of film which got the name of cine-poem, and these films were impressionistic, but they concentrated on pictorial conceptions of city life, of nature, and, importantly, they stressed abstract patterns. Then, of course, there's the poetry of painting in motion—the pure abstract film—which also has a considerable history (there are Norman McLaren, the Whitney brothers, and many others). Then, also as a candidate in this list (perhaps disputable, but at any rate certainly worth mentioning), a school of naturalistic poetry of which Robert Flaherty was the pioneer. And we presume that his films can be considered integral without the commentary. And, finally, I would include the dream and hallucination sequences, with sound effects sometimes, that appear in commercial films.

Now poetry as a visual-verbal medium: We have the fantasy films of Jean Vigo (these films are primarily visual); and we have the avant-garde films that are set to poems or to poetic prose (those of Sidney Peterson, of Willard Maas, of Ian Hugo); then there's what I would term the "severe formalism" of Sergei Eisenstein, whose montage borders on pure poetry. There are, of course, the Cocteau myth films: *Beauty and the Beast, The Eternal Return,* and *Orpheus.* And we might also include a special class of naturalistic poetry documents, such as *The River* and *The Blood of the Beasts* . . . of course they had commentary. And, then, to conclude, the fifty-fifty fusion; that is, Shakespeare's plays, Eliot's *Murder in the Cathedral,* and the numerous operas that have been filmed. Now these are, admittedly, only the main leads of a very broad field, indeed. Many definitions are required in order to isolate the poetic content and the poetic potentialities in these various manifestations . . . Above all, there's the indications of value that have to be made. I'm sure that the members of the panel, including myself, have a number of significant distinctions and perhaps even more important opinions on these aspects.

Maas: Well, Miss Deren, will you take over from there?

Deren: I'm going to do something I think is a bit risky, and that is to go a little bit into the question of what is poetry, and what distinguishes what we would call poetry from anything else, because I think that only if we can get this straight, can we sensibly discuss poetry in film, or the poetic film, or anything else. Now I say that it's risky, because this is a subject that has been discussed for many, many centuries, and it's been very difficult to pin down. But the reason I'm going into it is not because I think distinctions are important as formulae and as rigidities, but I think they're important in the sense that they give an audience, or any *potential* audience, a preparation, an approach, to what they're going to see. In the sense that if they're thinking they are going to see an adventure film, and if they are confronted with a poetic film, that's not going to go very well. I don't think one is always predisposed toward poetry; the whole notion of distinguishing and, if you will, labeling things is not a matter of defining them so much as a matter of giving a clue to the frame of mind you bring to them. In other words, what are you going to be watching as this unrolls? What are you going to be listening for? If you're watching for *what* happens, you might not get the point of some of the retardations because they're concerned with *how* it happens. Now poetry, to my mind, consists not of assonance; or rhythm, or rhyme, or any of these other qualities we associate as being characteristic of poetry. Poetry, to my mind, is an approach to experience, in the sense that a poet is looking at the same experience that a dramatist may be looking at. It comes out differently because they are looking at it from a different point of view and because they are concerned with different elements in it. Now, the characteristics of poetry, such as rhyme, or color, or any of those emotional qualities which we attach to the poetic work, also may be present in works which are not poetry, and this will confuse us. The distinction of poetry is its construction (what I mean by "a poetic structure"), and the poetic construct arises from the fact, if you will, that it is a "vertical" investigation of a situation, in that it probes the ramifications of the moment, and is concerned with its qualities and its depth, so that you have poetry concerned, in a sense, not with what is occurring but with what it feels like or what it means. A poem, to my mind, creates visible or auditory forms for something that is invisible, which is the feeling, or the emotion, or the metaphysical content of the movement. Now it also may include action, but its attack is what I would call the "vertical" attack, and this may be a little bit clearer if you will contrast it to what I would call the "horizontal" attack of drama, which is concerned with the development, let's say, within a very small situation from feeling to feeling. Perhaps it would be made most clear if you take a Shakespearean work that combines the two movements. In Shakespeare, you have the drama moving forward on a "horizontal" plane of development, of one circumstance—one action—leading to another, and this delineates the character. Every once and a while, however, he arrives at a point of action where he wants to illuminate the meaning to *this* moment of drama, and, at that moment, he builds a pyramid or investigates it "vertically," if you will, so that you have a "horizontal" development with periodic "verti-

cal" investigations, which are the poems, which are the monologues. Now
if you consider it this way, then you can think of any kind of combination being possible. You can have operas where the "horizontal" development is virtually unimportant—the plots are very silly, but they serve as
an excuse for stringing together a number of arias that are essentially
lyric statements. Lieder are, in singing, comparable to the lyric poems, and
you can see that all sorts of combinations would be possible.

It seems to me that in many films, very often in the opening passages, you get the camera establishing the mood, and, when it does that,
cinematically, those sections are quite different from the rest of the film.
You know, if it's establishing New York, you get a montage of images,
that is, a poetic construct, after which what follows is a dramatic construct
that is essentially "horizontal" in its development. The same thing would
apply to the dream sequences. They occur at a moment when the intensification is carried out not by action but by the illumination of that moment. Now the short films, to my mind (and they are short because it is
difficult to maintain such intensity for a long period of time), are comparable to lyric poems, and they are completely a "vertical," or what I
would call a poetic construct, and they are complete as such. One of the
combinations that would be possible would be to have a film that is a
dramatic construct, visually, accompanied by a commentary that is essentially poetic; that is, it illuminates the moments as they occur, so that you
have a chain of moments developing, and each one of them is illuminated.
It's things of this sort that, I believe, occur in the work of Mr. Maas, who
has done that to a certain extent in his last film, *Image in the Snow*,
where the development of the film is very largely "horizontal," that is,
there is a story line, but this is illuminated constantly by the poetic commentary so that you have two actions going on simultaneously. Now this,
I think, is one of the great potentials of film and something that could
very well be carried and developed much further, and I think that one
of the distinctions of that film and also of *Geography of the Body*, is that
it combines these principles. I think that this is a way of handling poetry
and film, and poetry *in* film . . . I don't know how the other people feel
about it.

Maas: Well, Mr. Thomas, being a poet, what do you feel about it?

Thomas: Well, I'm sure that all Maya Deren said was what I would
have said, had I thought of it or understood it (*laughter and slight applause*). I was asked, on the side, whether that meant that I thought that
the audience didn't understand what Miss Deren was saying. I'm sure
they did, and I wish I was down there. But it sounds different from that
side, you know. Now I'm all for (I'm in the wrong place tonight) . . . I'm
all for horizontal and vertical (*laughter*), and all for what we heard about
in the avant-garde. The only avant-garde play I saw in New York was in

a cellar, or a sewer, or somewhere (laughter). I happened to be with Mr. Miller over there. We saw this play going on . . . I'm sure it was fine. And, in the middle, he said, "Good God, this is avant-garde." He said, "In a moment, the hero's going to take his clothes off . . ."

Maas: Did he?

Thomas: He did. (*Laughter.*)

Maas: All to the good.

Thomas: But I don't know. I haven't a theory to my back, as they say. But there are, all through films that I've seen all my life . . . there have always been . . . bits that have seemed to me . . . Now, this is a bit of poetry. They might have been in the UFA films or something that I saw as a child. Or somebody coming down some murderous dark, dark, silent street, apart from the piano playing. Or it might have been a little moment when Laurel and Hardy were failing to get a piano up or down a flight of stairs. That always seemed to me the poetry . . . when those moments came. Well, I have to go a step beyond those UFA films, now, to the non-silent films. In the best of those moments, the words seemed to fit. They were really the right words, even though the right word might only be a grunt. I'm not at all sure that I want such a thing, myself, as a poetic film. I think films, fine as they are, if only they were better! And I'm not quite sure that I want a new kind of film at all. While I'm recharging an almost empty mind with an almost empty battery, perhaps Mr. Miller would say something. (*Applause.*)

Maas: Well, I don't think I'll let it go at that, Mr. Thomas. Surely you must realize that the film is a popular medium, and you, more than anybody else, have tried to bring poetry to the public from the platform. Don't you think, in the popular art, in the way that the Elizabethan theater was a popular art, don't you think it would be possible in some way to weld poetry to the film? Do you think that it's just a verbal thing? That it would not be possible in the way that Elizabethan drama somehow welded language to the film?

Thomas: Well, just as a poem comes out . . . one image makes another in the ordinary dialectic process (somebody left out the word "dialectic," well I may as well bring it in, you know). So, as in a poem one image breeds another, I think, in a film, it's really the visual image that breeds another—breeds and breathes it. If it's possible to combine a verbal image to a visual image in this sort of horizontal way, I'd rather see horizontal films, myself. I like stories. You know, I like to see something going on (laughter and applause).

Maas: I shouldn't be saying anything; I'm the moderator. So, Mr. Miller, you talk about it.

Miller: Well, there've been about forty different ideas that have come across this table. It seems to me that to create a poetic film is, at bottom, the same problem as the drama presents when you contrast what is normally called naturalism with what is generally called a poetic drama. The only criticism I would have of such a discussion as this is that it is not tied to what anybody wishes to say. If I'm speaking to you now with a reasonable amount of confusion, I will sound confused, and I will speak in this tone of voice. If, on the other hand, I was clearly imbued with something very emotionally important to me, I would start speaking in a different rhythm. I would possibly use some images and so forth, so that to speak in the blue without reference to our lives, without references really to the age in which we live, about this problem is an endless talk. Ah, that's the first place. On the question of technique, there's one obvious thing to me: The motion picture image is an overwhelming fact; it is different from any other experience we have in the arts because it is so much larger than we are. The possibility for the poet or the writer to tell a story or to transmit an emotion in their films, it seems to me, is contained within the image, so that I'm afraid, even though I'm much in sympathy with Willard's desire to join poetic speech with images, that, possibly, in the long run, it will be discovered to be a redundancy—that the poetry is in the film just as it is in the action of the play first. I was gratified to see that the poet's poet, T. S. Eliot, not long ago said as much, that, after pushing the drama around on his desk for many years, he had come to the conclusion that if the structure of the drama was not complete and beautiful, nothing he could do in the way of technical manipulation of words could get him out of the hole. I think, at bottom, that the structure of the film is the structure of the man's mind who made it, and if that is a mind that is striving for effect because it is striving for effect, the film will be empty, however interesting it happens to be on the surface. If it is a mind that has been able to organize its own experience, and if that experience is cohesive and of one piece, it will be a poetic film. Mr. Thomas has said, as (Mr. Tyler) has said, too, that the commercial film is full of poetic things because, at certain moments, in almost any poor structure, certain accidental qualities come into synchronization, so to speak, where, as in life sometimes, one needs only to drop a package of cigarettes, and the world explodes. Symbolic action is the point of all organization in the drama as well as in the film. To get back to the first proposition again . . . I think that it would be profitable to speak about the special nature of any film, of the fact of images unwinding off a machine. Until that's understood, and I don't know that it's understood (I have some theories about it myself), we can't begin to create, on a methodical basis, an aesthetic for that film. We don't understand the psychological meaning of images—any images—coming off a machine.

There are basic problems, it seems to me, that could be discussed here. I've probably added no end to the confusion, but that's what I have to say at the moment. (*Applause.*)

Maas: Well, it seems to me that we have to start thinking about the image—the visual image and the verbal image. Can they be welded in some way?

Miller: I think that the basis for my remarks is perhaps almost physiological. I think that the reason why it seems to many of us that the silent film is the purest film and the best is because it mimics the way we dream. We mostly dream silent, black and white. A few of us claim to dream in technicolor, but that's disputed by psychologists. It's sort of a boast: Certain people want to have more expensive dreams . . . I think that the film is the closest mechanical or aesthetic device that man has ever made to the structure of the dream. In a dream, montage is of the essence, as a superimposition of images in a dream is quite ordinary. The cutting in a dream is from symbolic point to symbolic point. No time is wasted. There is no fooling around between one important situation and the most important moment in the next situation. It seems to me that if we looked at the physiology of the film, so to speak, and the psychology of the film, the way it actually turns off the machine, we begin to get the whole question of style and the whole question of aesthetics changing when one sees it that way. In other words, sound in films and speech seem, perhaps, like the redundancy they so often are in films. I'll just leave it at that for the moment; maybe somebody else will have something to say about it.

Maas: Maya, I'm sure you have something to say about it.

Deren: If everyone will forgive me, Mr. Miller has made several references to "the way it comes out of the machine," he obviously hasn't made a film because first you have to put it in the machine, and that's awfully hard. It does begin before the machine. And it begins in the mind of the creator. And your reference to montage, and so on, is, if I may be permitted to return to my "vertical"—that is, the relationship between the images in dreams, in montage, and in poetry—is . . . they are related because they are held together by either an emotion or a meaning that they have in common, rather than by the logical action. In other words, it isn't that one action leads to another action (this is what I would call a "horizontal" development), but they are brought to a center, gathered up, and collected by the fact that they all refer to a common emotion, although the incidents themselves may be quite disparate. Whereas, in what is called a "horizontal" development, the logic is a logic of actions. In a "vertical" development, it is a logic of a central emotion or idea that attracts to itself even disparate images which contain that central core, which they have in common. This, to me, is the structure of poetry, so that, for example, you could have a dramatic development, in the sense of a "horizontal" development, for a while, as I said, in Shakespeare, and let us take the monologoues where, in a poetic or a "vertical" structure, he brings together all various images that relate to the feeling, let us say, of indecision. Now what I mean there by being essentially a "horizontal" development, is that it would have sufficed for Hamlet to say, "I can't make up my mind," and that's all, and that would not have affected the drama of the play, do you see? The poetic monologue there is, as it were, outside it or built upon it as a pyramid at that point as a means of intensifying that moment in the "horizontal" development. That is why film, I believe, lends itself particularly to the poetic statement, because it is essentially a montage and, therefore, seems by its very nature to be a poetic medium. . . .

Tyler: We *are* snagged on the horns of a dilemma in a way, although I'm sure we've covered a lot of ground. I think one of the most interesting things is the shape and the character of these horns—that is, Miss Deren, who is a professional artist in the poetic film, started out by using a rather complex, a rather difficult, technical vocabulary in order describe her theory about what she does. Now that's perfectly all right. But it struck Mr. Thomas as not precisely all right, and he then proceeded to talk about his very spontaneous reactions to films in terms of what he thought was poetic in them, various little incidents, certain aspects, just points of emotion. And then Mr. Miller took over and started to talk about dreams and the pure medium of the film. Now the fact is that both these gentlemen—both of whom are professional writers, and one a professional poet—expressed the very view of life, the cinematic attitude toward life that Miss Deren and a number of other film-makers started out with and, in this primitive way, are simply reflecting, perhaps, the first stage of her development when she had the impulse to make poetic films—that is, to create meaningful images through the medium of moving photography. Now, it becomes the problem, especially here tonight, as to why she started out by using a very difficult vocabulary, a technical vocabulary, to express a sort of intellectual specialty in the way she regarded her art. As a matter of fact, the surrealists started out by excerpting parts of commercial films, jumbling them up, and making little poems out of them. It is simply a question of the editing, the montage, as Mr. Miller intelligently hinted a moment ago, a question of integrating a series of photographs, of spontaneous shots into a form, a shape, and then you have something. That is, you have a feeling about reality—which is what art is. So I think that the rudimentary ground is present; that is, poetic film means using the film as a conscious and exclusive means of creating ideas through images. As for poets and other artists collaborating with film-makers, the method of Eisenstein was one of strict collaboration in a technical sense. It was also one of literature in that he wrote out very elaborate, very detailed scripts, action for action, shot for shot, beforehand, and then, when he was in the field, since he was an artist, he remained open so that his technical advisors were always listened to. It was a question of using an original script, which was really literature, which was written as a starting point and, out of this kind of literature, creating a film. Certainly, among big film-makers and artists who created full length films, and films that were commercially distributed, Eisenstein was, in the history of films, the most conscious artist. So it seems to me just a little strange that Mr. Miller, in particular, being a dramatist, should take a purist point of view toward the film. I mean, that's his privilege, if he feels that way. But the hard part, at least to me, is that this is the way that the little film-makers, the poets of the film such as Miss Deren, feel—this is their approach to life. So now I don't know where we are! It's a question of what role literature, what role verbal poetry, should have in film. I don't know why Mr. Thomas and Mr. Miller should insist, and I'm waiting to find out if they will insist, why poetry as literature should not, or cannot, collaborate with poetry as film.

Deren: I wish mainly to say that I'm a little bit flabbergasted at the fact that people who have handled words with such dexterity as Mr. Thomas and Mr. Miller and Mr. Tyler, should have difficulty with such a simple idea as the "vertical" and the "horizontal" (applause).

Thomas: (*aside*) Here we go up and down again.

Deren: These seem to me the most elementary movements in the world and really quite fundamental.

Maas: I don't think you ought to get vulgar.

Deren: That has really flabbergasted me to the extent that I am unable to develop the idea any further . . . I don't see anything so difficult in the notion that what I called a "horizontal" development is more or less of a narrative development, such as occurs in drama from action to action, and that a "vertical" development such as occurs in poetry, is a part of plunging down or a construction that is based on the intent of the moment, so that, for example, from a short story, one should be able to deduce the life of the hero before and after. In other words, the chosen moment should be of such significance that one can deduce all history from it. So, in a poem, in a way, from the emotion one can particularize to the incidents that might contain it, whereas in a drama, one generalizes the emotion from the particular instant. That is, the actions of the drama may not be personally known, but one generalizes the emotion that comes from it, and then it becomes possible to identify with it as a generalized emotion. I still don't know what's so difficult about those two differences, and I think I'd like to hear something from the floor myself.

Miller: Let me just say, I didn't intend to make it so difficult; it isn't. It's just not separate. There is no separation in my mind between a horizontal story and the plumbing of its meaning in depth. (*Applause*).

Maas: Well, surely, Mr. Miller, you must see the difference between presenting something by words or dialogue, as you do and I do and Mr. Thomas does, and presenting something·by the visual image. Now Ezra Pound said, in a definition of the image, that it is an emotional and intellectual complex caught in an instant of time. It's a very direct and quick way of saying things, a lyric way of saying things, whereas the way a dramatist says things is by putting the characters that speak back and forth in conflict. We know that you can't have any sort of situation, poetic or otherwise, without dramatic conflict. I agree with that, but it's quite different in developing a narrative action from presenting it imagistically and quickly, and I think in the film you can do that. You can do it by word; you can do it by visual image, and by the combination of the two, which is a very complicated thing. Though mentioned, no one here tonight has talked very extensively about Jean Cocteau's *Blood of a Poet*. Anybody who sees that, sees the perfect welding of the two. It can be done. Though he is the father of the poet film, Jean Cocteau does not have many forebears. Still, I know that is a technique that could be done, and is essentially different, I'm afraid, from one of presenting things imagistically and presenting them narratively, and by statement and by dramatic action. There's a great difference there.

* * *

Miller: (*answering a question from the floor*) To hell with that "vertical" and "horizontal." It doesn't mean anything. (*Applause*.) I understand perfectly what it means, but the point is, if an action is worth anything emotionally, it proceeds to get deeper into its meaning as it progresses, as it reveals. The whole intent of any good playwright is to construct such action as will finally achieve the greatest depths of meaning. So that it is simply a question of, here again, an image, which is, in one case, when you speak of "vertical" and "horizontal," rather mechanical. And I'm sure the lady didn't mean it that way, and that's why it was taken so absurdly. But it isn't absurd; it's just that they aren't separated in any way. A perfectly prosaic play, as we all know, can sometimes arrive at a point which creates a very high poetic feeling. Now, it's a different problem; you have the whole question of verse structure and so on. But the verse structure will never come without that plumbing, without that going deep. You can't implant it on a vacuous piece of material. My only point is that it's of one piece. The technique cannot be used simply because one wishes to use it. (*Applause*.) It's all a question of the degree. But you might say that the best example of the relationship between words and action is that while we're talking here, all these people are walking out. (*Laughter, applause*.)

Maas: We spent most of our time talking about what Miss Deren called "vertical" and "horizontal." I think in a way she was talking about narrative and lyric. Is that right?

Deren: Yes. The gentleman who brought it up, brought up the question here as to the fact that he thought poetry and film were different ways of doing the same thing. That is why I went into the whole nature of what I call the poetic structure, because I believe that this poetic structure can be present in any one of the forms. For example, in dance, you would have a narrative ballet or you would have an essentially lyric ballet; or you might have a *pas de deux,* in it, which was an exploration of a moment that occurred. The *pas de deux* is over, and you go back to the line of your plot. So that I'm not thinking of the poetic structure as referring to poetry simply as a verbal form; I'm thinking of it as a way of structuring in any one of a number of mediums, and (I think) that it is also possible to make the dramatic structure in any one, or that it is also possible to combine them. When Mr. Miller says he doesn't think they are different, it is another way of saying that they can be combined, in which sense he is contradicting his rather purist insistence that they should not be combined. To me, this comes out a contradiction. I think that they can. Now I am speaking for a combination, although personally, in my films, there has not been such a combination. I'm speaking of other films and of the way poetry occurs in them, either as an image—the sudden development of a poetic image, which you might have in a dream sequence of a film that was otherwise narrative in its structure, and the whole narrative stops while the hero has a dream which illuminates the particular moment in the story, and then he goes back to the narrative, somebody wakes him up or something like that, and you go on with the narrative development. It's this sort of nightmare that was present in *Death of a Salesman,* which was a moment in which, in effect, the action almost stopped, and you had this poetic illumination of the moment.

Miller: That's a good point because I know something about that. You see, that's precisely the point; it didn't stop. It never stopped. This has been confused with a flashback. It was never a flashback. The design of that play is concurrent stories. Now we can get right to the movie, and here's a good example. I am wedded to action; I can't bear "narrative drama." It's to me an impossibility; it bores me to tears. There's a difference between narrative and dramatic, obviously. Now the place that you would speak, I presume, of the "vertical" investigation, let's call it, is in those sections of the play where the man goes back into time. To be sure, the present moment vanishes in the sense that he goes back in time, but every word that is in those memories changes the situation that will arise as soon as those things are over. They are not, in other words, excursions, for the sake of reaching outside the structure of the play to bring in some information. They are incorporated, completely wedded to the action. They *are* action. Now the only argument I have here at all, and the reason I have a feeling that verse, possibly, doesn't belong in the movies, is that if you have on the screen an image . . . an image is a bad word because it seems static . . . an action. Now it can be an action that is seemingly real or a fantastic one. And then, on top of it, you have an unseen narrator who is speaking—I'm afraid that the spoken word will be a kind of narrative, or lyrical, nondramatic verse. And that is going to stop the motion of the motion picture. And I'm against that. I think it's an intrusion on the medium. That's all I mean, I'm speaking for an organic art, that's all. (*Applause.*) . . . There's a good example in the making of the movie of *Death of a Salesman*. This was a very fascinating problem, and it is right to the point here. On the stage, it seemed perfectly all right to most people that the man should move into his memories which were evoked by the action in the present. I didn't like the script of the movie, and I quarreled very much with it. One would think, offhand, that it would be much easier in a movie to dissolve the present, because the very word dissolve is so natural to the camera and simply throws the man into the past. When the present was dissolved, the meaning of what happened in the past was less. And the reason for it was that, on stage, you had the present with you all the time. We couldn't remove the set. The man had his dreams in relation to the real set that he was standing on, so there was a tension involved. There was, in other words, a reproduction of reality, because when we talk to ourselves on the street, the street is still there, and we don't vanish in thin air. But, in the movie, they made the terrible mistake of evaporating his surroundings, so that he was thrust completely into his dream. And what happened was: It became a narrative. The conflict was that this man—after all, it's not quite as bad to talk to yourself when you're alone in the desert as it is when you're standing in front of a girl at Macy's counter—that has an entirely different meaning. In one case, the man can be quite balanced; in the other case, he begins to look as though he's losing his balance. This, to my mind, is an analogy between anything that stops action, that is bad in a picture. I think, in the movie of *Death of a Salesman*, the action was stopped because the visual thing that kept the tension of those memories was evaporated. And I'm afraid that the same thing would happen with speech in a picture.

[1953]

JONAS MEKAS

The Other Direction

What do we mean when we say films are *avant-garde, experimental, underground, personal?* What we mean, what it is, is that every art has two extremes, two ends. On one end, man expresses himself by telling stories, by retelling myths. He reenacts certain situations, experiences through characters—protagonists—and then goes to the other end of himself, where it becomes vaguer and vaguer, more abstract, where man can express himself only very indirectly, by suggestions, where he doesn't exactly *know* really how to express things. It all becomes very intuitive and very indirect—symbols, metaphors. Here we enter the area of non-narrative poems, poetry. Then we come to the extreme end, where it becomes totally abstract. Take storytelling painting and take Mondrian; take Faulkner, and then go to the real extreme of poetry, that is, to Concrete Poetry.

In cinema we were—and still are as far as I can see—only at the narrative end; that is, one end, one part of man. This part of man expresses itself in cinema through narrative forms. We are interested in only one part of man. But this is a complete misdirection of our attitude toward cinema, a misdirected conception of cinema that we have, and we take this as normal. What about the other part, which expresses itself through non-narrative forms, through poetry? That seems to us just like fooling around. The experimental film, the avant-garde film—that isn't cinema, that's only fooling around. Imagine a man who is teaching literature and is only teaching the novel, only the narrative forms of literature, and ignoring poetry, ignoring Ezra Pound, ignoring Blake, ignoring almost every poet who ever existed unless he wrote epic poems in which there are characters. That's okay. That we should teach in schools and universities. That is literature. But Blake, haiku—three lines, a few syllables—that's not serious. Yet that's exactly our attitude in cinema, and we take it as normal. In literature, it would be ridiculous; in music, it would be ridiculous; in painting, it would be ridiculous. In cinema— normal.

What the avant-garde is and what the avant-garde did during the last ten years developed those non-narrative forms. I say ten years because those ten years were really a concentrated period of attention in that direction. The roots always go much further, to the twenties, to the very beginning of the cinema. But the vocabulary, the forms, and the technology of the non-narrative cinema, of the poetic cinema, have been worked out during the last ten years.

When we go to see a narrative film (and I am not now talking about journalistic or all other forms of film), we expect certain plots, certain excitement, certain suspense to hold our interest. We are dealing with a very strange area of entertainment when we consider the reasons why we go to the cinema. We go to a gallery to see paintings for reasons which are not always very clear, but it isn't always for entertainment. We see something, deduce something from those paintings, those colors, those forms. Something attracts us. We keep coming back to certain paintings, certain artists, for reasons that we don't even know. They do something to us that makes us feel we should see them again. In music, there are certain compositions we want to listen to again and again.

In cinema, we feel that if it really holds us there for those ninety or a hundred minutes with climaxes, constant suspense, then it is okay. But if we have to put some effort of our own into the viewing, that is already bad. Take our newspapers, our reviewers—I can imagine Bosley Crowther or somebody sitting there as if behind a steel wall. He protects himself totally from what is there. And we have to work very hard to get him. But he wouldn't put himself into that film. Now when we come to poetry, to the avant-garde film—films which are there—there are no obvious climaxes, no suspense, no excitement, no thrill on the surface that would really "grab" you. They don't attack you. They're very simple, inoffensive, unobtrusive. They don't want to impose anything on you. To get anything from these films, in the first place, you have to get yourself in a certain attitude. You have to put yourself into it, open yourself completely so that something, whatever it is, in that work, will begin to float, talk, come in to you. There will be contact between that film and you. If you can get yourself into that very open, receptive attitude, you can abandon your preconceptions and expectations and just see whatever there is on the screen.

Cinema has so many ends, directions, so many uses—like words and literature. You can write a poem, you can write a short story, you can write haiku, or a journalistic piece about a bridge that has just been built or about the war in Vietnam—any subject you want. You can write a textbook. So we have cinema put to all these uses. Bruce Baillie's *All My Life*, for instance, is like a haiku. Just one simple image. There are many filmmakers who are concerned today with this form of very short film—one image, one idea. (I say haiku as the easiest of references.) Taking any subject, any object, and making it the center of the work. Against those who say that film needs a big subject, a big theme, we say that anything could be a subject of a film, of a poem. A scent, a flower—like Andy Warhol making a film on a man eating a mushroom for forty minutes or Michael Snow with water dripping into an enamel plate for ten minutes. But as you watch it, it becomes a meditation on that subject. One feels the subject is invested with great love, that whatever is around you is worth that attention and that love. Not only those happenings and situations in which there is action, plot, and climax, but *anything* under the sun—perhaps even having nothing to do with life, with human beings. But how can we love human beings if we don't love water drips or a fence surrounded with roses? These films, their subjects, their themes, are very small. Just maybe a feeling, a mood. When we go to a commercial film, a theatrical narrative or art film, and when we ask what is the subject of that film, we usually have many obvious, "important" themes we can point out. But these other films are very unpretentious. They don't want to change you by force. They don't work, they do not plot, to undermine you so you will be this or that. One mood, one feeling—but it's a mood or a feeling that the artist who made the film had and considers important. The artist believes it is important that man has these moods, that they survive, that man doesn't become too simple, too mechanized. He believes that there are certain areas which the narrative film with its melodrama and its action, plot and suspense, does not descend to, and that it's up to the non-narrative forms—to poetry, to certain forms of painting or of music—to express these feelings or emotions, thoughts or movements, that are on some deeper levels of our existence. And these films are there to register them on film for us.

When one cannot express something directly and clearly, one uses indirect means. The rhythm, the movement of a film is one of those means whereby man can express certain things that he doesn't really know how to express. Pacing and rhythm become very important in film. There are rhythms and speeds of excitement, there are rhythms and speeds of meditation, of loving, of gentle feelings. There are certain rhythms you respond to immediately without knowing what it is all about. You respond to the movement, to the rhythm, and it does something—

you may not even be able to describe it clearly. The same thing happens when you are standing in front of certain paintings. There are loud, crying paintings that work on some very entertaining level, and there are also others in which certain shapes, lines, nuances, colors touch something on certain levels in you, which begin to wake up in you areas that are not too clear but that are there, crying to be developed.

Any comparison—as when I say that in avant-garde film there is a parallel to poetry and literature—cannot be taken literally, because these are different media. But there was a time when cinema was much younger, when filmmakers were afraid to be in the same room with any other art. They wanted to be independent; they stressed their independence from all other arts. But today that is not necessary. Cinema has established itself and doesn't have to have that kind of inhibition. We know that all the arts are expressions of man expressing different aspects of our being, so that somewhere and at some point each of the arts touches. They come to some one center from which it can be said that the same idea, or the same feeling, the same thought, can be expressed through *any* other art. But, you see, one must descend into the very seed where that thought or feeling begins and man wants to express it. It is then directed to that area where man is most capable, the area he has mastered—movement, sound, cinema, or words. And already that depends on the path of one's life.

The basis of all creation is the restructuring of reality. Restructured reality becomes different depending on which art you use. There are large areas; there are traditions. There are materials; there is technology. There are all the past works. Then we come to the theories, the aesthetics, the practices. And then we begin to find out really what it is that "grabs" you. Something can grab you even if you are not ready—certain colors, certain surface things that stand out. Later you come back and you find out that that was not the essence of the particular work, that there is something more subtle, much deeper there.

We know that there is poetry and there are poets, and we find that some people are interested in poetry, some not. Some react to a poet; some do not. Or I find nothing in this poem or in this film or in this painting, and then someone else comes and says this poem or film or painting is the greatest, it changed my life. So it always comes back to you, to where you yourself are, what stage of your life you are in. For instance, there are certain composers that one prefers, and others one just doesn't get anything from and yet may come to later in life when one's life direction has changed. A number of things are involved. It always depends on the viewer.

One could say it is like a pyramid. At the top there are those who are most developed in sensitivities, in intelligence and experiences—both quantitative and qualitative—and then on the very bottom those who are like minerals and vegetables. Each of the levels has a different kind of art, different kind of food, different kind of people, and these change as one grows. For that growth—and I believe that we should constantly develop and grow, or, rather, that we have no choice, for those are the laws of life—for that growth one always goes through stages, abandons certain art which for somebody else will be of value but which to you is no longer of value as you look forward to more and more subtle forms, as you grow. Of course it is possible that you are "growing" backwards. Hollywood has tried to influence growth by its insistence on certain kinds of film. For a long time Hollywood had control of all the theaters across the country—four or five thousand—and there was no choice. Man was reduced to one kind of visual or cinematic food. Again, we know the laws of life. If one is exposed for too long to the same primitive kind of "underground" cinema—because that's what Hollywood is, a true underground cinema which gives primitive, gross reality simplified emotions and feelings—one will be dragged down to the ground and under the ground.

Today we have certain art theaters and we have the universities, so we have a certain choice. We don't have to show only the lowest kind of film. We can begin to show Bergman. And eventually come to Brakhage, because before we come to Brakhage we have to go through all kinds of other stages.

We usually think only in extremes, and the usual attitude is that the avant-garde film ignores other cinema. The avant-garde has never opposed the other cinema. It's the newspapers that distorted what the avant-garde really is all about, our attitudes. We are not against Hollywood. Hollywood is there. We are not against narrative cinema. We are doing different things. Poetry is not opposed to narrative. A short piece of music is not opposed to a symphony. There is no opposition; each does a different thing. A cow is one, a horse another, and a sheep another. They are not opposed, but each of them *is* a different animal. So it's important to remember that when we are speaking of this cinema, we don't mean to cut out the rest. We take cinema as a whole. Each film, each area, each rung does its job in a different field of experience.

There are poems that are needed to make certain moral points. There are occasional poems which can be read and presented to a wide public and read in a loud voice. But then there are poems which you read only by yourself, at home, in the evening, when you don't want any disturbance. You read and deal with just that poem because it concerns more private, more personal, more subtle areas of experience. One area the avant-garde film deals with is the private, personal area. You will not always react to these films. They may look like nothing to you. You may be open to them, find something in them, only if you are watching by yourself or with two or three friends in your own home, or perhaps on seeing the film for the third, fourth, fifth, or even tenth time. We are looking forward to the days when you will be able to have your own private libraries—when the technology of cinema will allow it. That will change your understanding of what the avant-garde is all about, what film poetry is all about, what non-narrative film is all about, and what narrative film is all about—because that will change too. You will discover that many of the narrative films you preferred, found great, that grabbed you, will fall to pieces on the second or third viewing. They will not give you anything any more. But you will also turn to some other narrative films (like Dreyer's) which give you, no matter how many times you look at them, something else each time.

I keep talking about small films, films that do not force anything upon you. As the cinema progresses, the latest preoccupation of some filmmakers in the vanguard of film is with very limited subjects—the window, the flower, the fence. Sort of Minimal Film. Some filmmakers are going into great detail; some are dealing just with patterns. They don't even show the pot or the window, they just stick to the flower. In a sense, the farther man jumps into space, the more he also goes to the other extreme (and really one needs the other). He becomes more and more private. He finds joy in details. He invests every detail with love and attention. There is no end to how small that detail can be. This personal approach to everything, this feeling that everything can be beautiful and important, that no matter how small or insignificant it is, it can be a subject for a work of art—this direction inwards then bounces back to the other extreme. I would say that our flight to the moon is only a crystallized opposite. The spiritual direction that is transformed into matter. The farther we want to fly into space, the deeper we have to go inward. That's how it happened. It's no coincidence that we are landing on the moon just when the interest in bio-chemical and mystical explorations is at its highest in this country and around the world; besides the very stagnant, very mechanical attitudes and systems of today, there is this opposite pole, this other direction.

[1969]

ROBERT RICHARDSON

The Question of Order and Coherence in Poetry and Film

The film's basic technique, the method of composition by jux-taposition which can be called cutting, editing, or montage and which is the most characteristic feature of film form, is also the aspect of film that has had the greatest impact on literature. The excesses into which this technique can lead are most evident in the work of Robbe-Grillet and the numerous writers who see as he does a mandate for chaos in the film's technique of juxtaposition, while the greatest constructive uses of mon-tage in literature are to be found in modern poetry.

Early in the century, Vachel Lindsay wrote a long poem called "The Trial of the Dead Cleopatra in Her Beautiful and Wonderful Tomb," and in his *Art of the Moving Picture* suggested that the poem be made into a film. It is I think a poor poem, but Lindsay's idea is arresting. Pursuing his claim that the picture language of the silent film is analo-gous to the hieroglyphics of the Egyptians, Lindsay pushes the comparison even further. Like Melville before him, Lindsay came to believe that man's myths and religions can all be traced to Egypt. Melville noted that the "awful idea of Jehovah" was born in the pyramids, and Lindsay wrote that "Man is an Egyptian first, before he is any other type of civilized being." Thus Lindsay proposed to take the *Book of the Dead*, which he translated as "On Coming Forth by Day," to retell the Cleopatra story through the form and rituals of this book and thus produce a sort of prototype or archetype of resurrection. The Christian and Egyptian myths are crucial, of course, but one also gets the impression that Lindsay thought the film capable of a sort of visible, if mechanical, proof or dem-onstration of the idea of immortality.

Reprinted from *Literature and Film* by Robert Richardson, copyright ©
1969 by Indiana University Press, Bloomington, by permission of the publisher.

As Shakespeare could urge in his sonnets that the writing of poetry combats time, denies ruin, and confers a renewal of sorts because artistic creation is itself a process of renewal, so Lindsay seems to have felt that the motion picture was itself a pattern or a paradigm of rebirth or renewal. Emerson once wrote that "genius is the activity that repairs the decay of things," and Lindsay's poem, odd and flawed as it appears, still represents a noble example of such activity.

Perhaps the best of the scattering of poems that owe an obvious debt to films in one way or another is Hart Crane's "Chaplinesque." Not only has Crane here, as in so many other places, used the condensed elliptical style which is so similar to the flow of images in a film, but more importantly, it is the visible humanity, the sense of grace, perceived and conveyed in what Lindsay called a "quietness of light," that shows how deeply the films had affected Crane:

> The game enforces smirks; but we have seen
> The moon in lonely alleys make
> A grail of laughter of an empty ash can,
> And through all sound of gaiety and quest
> Have heard a kitten in the wilderness.

Crane also used the image of the cinema at the very start of his most ambitious poem, *The Bridge*. In the third stanza of the "Proem" occur these lines:

> I think of cinemas, panoramic sleights
> With multitudes bent toward some flashing scene
> Never disclosed, but hastened to again,
> Foretold to other eyes on the same screen.

Crane seems to suggest here that the poem itself will be a series of flashing scenes and panoramic sleights, a poem of film-like images easier to witness than to comprehend. Crane's poetry remains difficult, but if it is thought of as using certain elements of cinema style, it becomes a little easier to make out.

Interesting as the above poems—and others like them—may be in their obvious attempts to include film forms and film subjects in poetry, the actual significance of such overt influence is small by comparison with some other and much broader matters of style which have deeply marked both modern poetry and the film without its being at all easy to say which has influenced which. However one manages to explain it, though, it can be argued that modern poetry and the film have been evolving along surprisingly similar lines.

Earlier it was suggested that Whitman's poetry can be considered a step toward cinema style. But it is, of course, true that Whitman's example was not widely followed in the nineteenth century, nor did his increasingly bardic pose, nor his later and inflated verse, encourage imitation, and poetry in America from the Civil War to the turn of the century continued to grope with problems of form in a world that seemed to have less and less form itself. Sidney Lanier tried to push poetry into pure music; Poe had also worked to this end; Emily Dickinson created her magnificent poems in part by resorting to a form that was based on hymnody; Melville tried all sorts of strange verse forms; and Stephen Crane experimented with a harsh gnomic style. Meanwhile the poets who inherited the genteel tradition of Bryant, Longfellow, Whittier, and Lowell stayed within conventional forms and styles while their work grew increasingly weak and unreal. By the 1890's a poet such as Edwin Arlington Robinson could look around him and see nothing but what he called the "little sonnet men," the gentlemen poets with three names and tired themes. Robinson's own work, which continued up into the thirties, but which remained characteristic of his earliest writings, is in some ways very revealing about the general state of poetry from 1890 to 1910. Robinson's ruling image, one which occurs over and over in his poems, is the image of the loss of light. One sees it clearly in "Credo," written in 1896:

> *I cannot find my way: there is no star*
> *In all the shrouded heavens anywhere . . .*
> *No there is not a glimmer, nor a call,*
> *For one that welcomes, welcomes when he fears*
> *The black and awful chaos of the night.*

The idea is worked out in greater detail in "The Man Against the Sky," in which the loss of light is quite clearly an image of the loss of certainty and direction. Robinson himself, as Robert Frost remarked, was a poet who "stayed content with the old way to be new," meaning that Robinson avoided radical formal innovation, preferring to treat new problems with forms that had been in use for hundreds of years. But Robinson's reflective, almost Wordsworthian temperament had difficulty even with the old forms, and his work lacks color, lacks visibility, prefers to present endless dialogue and colloquy rather than scene, or action, or picture, and is heavily verbose and abstract. His poems are poems of discursive rationality, dominated by the logic of prose, though they are set, rather uneasily one feels, in the form of verse. Thus Robinson's theme, the waning of the light, and his practice, the pervasive haunting and intentional flatness of what one constantly feels ought to be better seem to mark, between them, a sort of low point in modern poetry. The problem, I think, was essentially one of form, and Robinson's shrewd insistence on the fading light constitutes a brilliant diagnosis of what was wrong. For if the image for the technical sterility of the turn of the century was darkness, the new poetry of the period roughly from 1912 to 1925 signalized its arrival by a fresh insistence on light. The poetry of Pound, the Imagists and Amygists, Eliot, Williams, Stevens, and others used new forms, sought new voices, and insisted on highly visual imagery; through it all crept the image of light as a counterforce to Robinson's image of darkness.

At the same time the film began to find itself, and it too was working with new forms, and insisting on high visibility. Because its art consists of painting with light, it was also, in its way, flushed with optimism and fascinated with the phenomenon and even the imagery of light. By 1920, the new poetry had more in common with film than it had with Robinson and all that Robinson stood for in poetic expression. The new poetry and the film had both found fresh and exciting ways to approach their material, and both seemed, at the time, to have found a way around the questions of meaning that had so tormented, say, "The Man against the Sky." For neither the film nor the new poetry seemed to care to explain about what things meant. It was enough, as it had often been enough for Whitman, simply to present images, to celebrate life. Wallace Stevens dramatized the problem of conventional meaning and a possible solution or way round the problem in a poem which begins:

> *Twenty men crossing a bridge,*
> *Into a village,*
> *Are twenty men crossing twenty bridges,*
> *Into twenty villages,*
> *Or one man*
> *Crossing a single bridge into a village*
>
> *This is old song*
> *That will not declare itself . . .*

If one asks what twenty men crossing a bridge mean or what they really are, one can reply by saying that since each man sees the bridge differently, then for each the experience is different and therefore cannot be generalized. Or one can say that all men are essentially alike and therefore any man's experience in crossing a bridge is the same as any other man's. But neither of these psychological explanations really tells us anything worth knowing; they are abstract formulations. The poem continues:

> *Twenty men crossing a bridge,*
> *Into a village,*
> *Are*
> *Twenty men crossing a bridge*
> *Into a village.*
>
> *That will not declare itself*
> *Yet is certain as meaning . . .*

One could explain by saying that the thing means itself. Twenty men crossing a bridge are no more and no less and no other than twenty men crossing a bridge. That then is clear enough, but it still doesn't justify all the fuss, nor does it get us anywhere. If things are what they are, then there is nothing to do except, with Gertrude Stein, to go round and round. Finally Stevens' poem finds, and illustrates, the way out of the problem:

> *The boots of the men clump*
> *On the boards of the bridge.*
> *The first white wall of the village*
> *Rises through fruit-trees.*
> *Of what was it I was thinking?*
> *So the meaning escapes.*
>
> *The first white wall of the village . . .*
> *The fruit-trees . . .*

Stevens cuts into the scene below the abstract or generalized statement. A particular sound and a particular sight serve instead to create an image in the mind, a remembered scene composed of remembered details. It is the experience, the actuality of the scene, that matters; and as the scene becomes visible and audible, it becomes enough, it is sufficient in and of itself, and so it is no matter, and perhaps even a good thing, that the meaning escapes. This is not to say, of course, that the poem is without significance or importance, for it has both. The poem's close brings to mind an image like those of the impressionist painters, and the world, when it is seen by such men and passed on for us to see without what Keats called the "irritable reaching after fact and reason" is a marvelous and splendid place, rich and full in itself, making it enough just to be alive and aware.

As it has been explored and presented, this strong and widespread interest in the sights and sounds of the world, and the accompanying decrease of interest in explaining or reasoning it all out, has given modern poetry and film a whole world, one that is quite new in that it is now for the first time widely seen and shared. And both film and poetry have contributed to our understanding of this realm, which is essentially one of sight and sound; in which significance arises from all sorts of things but rarely from plain statement. Significance arises from context, from juxtaposition, from irony, from image, from overtones, or hints. Both film and modern poetry seem to agree that the point is not to tell the spectator or reader what things mean, but to make him find, feel, or realize the meaning for himself. Thus the realm in which film and poetry now move is not a realm of fixed values, not a realm of prose logic or discursive intelligence.

Just how close the techniques of the experimental or innovative line of modern poetry are to those of film, particularly the silent film, may be seen by considering T. S. Eliot's preface to and translation of St. John Perse's *Anabasis*. Eliot describes the poem as a "series of images of migration, of conquest of vast spaces in Asiatic wastes, of destruction and foundation of cities and civilizations. . . ." Eliot speaks of the poem's "logic of imagery" and he explains that "any obscurity of the poem, on first readings, is due to the suppression of 'links in the chain,' of explanatory and connecting matter, and not to incoherence, or to the love of cryptogram. The justification of such abbreviation of method is that the sequence of images coincides and concentrates into one intense impression of barbaric civilization. The reader has to allow the images to fall into his memory successively without questioning the reasonableness of each at the moment; so that, at the end, a total effect is produced." *Anabasis*, as Eliot so clearly points out, is not built upon meter or rhyme or other forms of verbal regularity; its order, like that of a film, is a "logic of imagination," a logic of carefully arranged sequences of images in Whitmanesque lines. The poem, in Eliot's version, begins:

> I have built myself, with honour and dignity have I built myself on three great seasons, and it promises well, the soil whereon I have established my Law.
> Beautiful are bright weapons in the morning and behind us the sea is fair. Given over to our horses this seedless earth,
> delivers to us this incorruptible sky. The Sun is unmentioned but his power is amongst us,
> and the sea at morning like a presumption of the mind.

After the initial sentence, which gives us a speaker, a premise, and a purpose, the lines turn to the business of simply delivering images of arms, of morning, of the sea, of horses, earth, sky, and sun, much as a good film lays out its significant spaces and forces at the start. It is by no means clear that *Anabasis* shows any actual or demonstrable film influence, yet its remarkable closeness to techniques and approaches made familiar in this century by the film makes this poem, and a good deal of modern poetry, close kin to film.

The tendency of both modern poetry and film to display, disclose, or reveal their subjects rather than to explain or judge them can also be seen clearly in the steadily increasing importance of documentary styles in film and in poetry. Russian directors in the twenties often used citizens rather than actors in an effort to avoid the appearance of artifice; war films use newsreel clips for action sequences; *Citizen Kane* exhibits an

overtly documentary technique, while Italian Neorealism and the movement known as *Cinéma Vérité* show that this emphasis on authenticity
and simplicity through documentation is far from spent. Documentary
film undertakes to edit reality. It avoids clever or tricky shots, concentrates on sober camerawork, relying for its effect on the authenticity of its
material, and depends more on the perception of the cameraman than on
the skill of the editor. Poems such as William Carlos Williams' *Paterson*,
Ezra Pound's *Cantos*, MacLeish's *Conquistador*, Berryman's *Homage to
Mistress Bradstreet*, and even such poems as Lowell's "The Quaker Graveyard in Nantucket" and Eliot's "The Waste Land" share this technique.
All depend heavily on written documents which are inserted into the
text, often making up a substantial part of the text. Each of the poems
is reaching for greater authenticity by including historical records, diary
entries, and fragments of other poems, but of equal importance with the
documentary material is the arrangement of such material in the poem.
In film, documentary techniques are usually intended to bring out or
stress the actual, real, or tangible qualities of the subject. In literature,
documentary techniques serve this purpose too, but it is less noticed than
its other effect, which is to provide some sort of connection between past
and present. But despite the apparent realism of film documentary and
the apparent historicism of documentary poetry, the so called documentary approach need be neither realistic nor historical, for in the film,
material is rigorously selected to illustrate the film maker's point and in
poetry the past is presented and documented with a very careful, not to
say loaded, selectivity. In each form, though, an appearance of realism or
historicism is given to the modern work of art, whose essential principle
may be neither realistic nor historical. Indeed, in documentary as in other
respects, both modern poetry and film seem to insist primarily on the integrity of the design of any given work.

William Carlos Williams' "Classic Scene" is an example of one
rather obvious concern with design:

> *A power-house*
> *in the shape of*
> *a red brick chair*
> *90 feet high*
>
> *on the seat of which*
> *sit the figures*
> *of two metal*
> *stacks—aluminum—. . .*

Robert Frost wrote a number of poems that make conscious use of design, one of them a little-known sonnet:

She is as in a field a silken tent
At midday when a sunny summer breeze
Has dried the dew and all its ropes relent,
So that in guys it gently sways at ease,
And its supporting central cedar pole,
That is its pinnacle to heavenward
And signifies the sureness of the soul,
Seems to owe naught to any single cord,
But strictly held by none, is loosely bound
By countless silken ties of love and thought
To everything on earth the compass round,
And only by one's going slightly taut
In the capriciousness of summer air
Is of the slightest bondage made aware.

Yeats' concern for design led eventually to the extravagance of *A Vision*, with its perfect symmetry and its elaborate detail. The book is a vast design, almost a cosmology, that Yeats said served to give him a source for metaphors. And Wallace Stevens has carried on this attention to design in such poems as "The Anecdote of the Jar":

I placed a jar in Tennessee,
And round it was, upon a hill.
It made the slovenly wilderness
Surround that hill. . .

This sense of design, of pattern, which I suppose can be thought of as some sort of organizing principle other than the narrative or linear, has been equally evident in the film. The four stories and the keystone image of *Intolerance* are an attempt, if not a wholly successful one, to make design dominate the material. Eisenstein's *Strike* and his *Potemkin* show a strong sense of design; Eisenstein once noted that the latter film came to him as he was gazing one day at the great Odessa steps, and the film was then built around those steps. The same director's *Ivan the Terrible* has an even greater, almost oppressive, sense of design. *Citizen Kane* also works because of its careful design; if it is a film about men, its design is organized around buildings. The list could be extended indefinitely; the work of Disney, McLaren, Hitchcock, Cocteau, and Resnais is all marked by as strong an insistence on design as that in modern poetry.

Closely allied with this sense of design, and strongly reinforced by a critical movement loosely called the New Criticism, is the idea, most easily observed in poetry and in film, that a work of art is, and should be, largely self-sufficient. The poem, or the film, the argument goes, provides its own context, encloses its own world, is its own frame of reference. Its own arrangement, its tensions and structure, its text alone constitute it whole, and one need not refer beyond the text to history, biography, or the real world. Thus in a famous phrase, Archibald MacLeish has said "A poem should not mean/But be." A simple enough example is a poem of Richard Wilbur's called "Piazza di Spagna."

> I can't forget
> How she stood at the top of that long marble stair
> Amazed, and then with a sleepy pirouette
> Went dancing slowly down to the fountain-quieted square;
>
> Nothing upon her face
> But some impersonal loneliness—not then a girl,
> But as it were a reverie of the place,
> A called-for falling glide and whirl;
>
> As when a leaf, petal, or thin chip
> Is drawn to the falls of a pool and, circling a moment above it,
> Rides on over the lip—
> Perfectly beautiful, perfectly ignorant of it.

The poem catches a moment. It does not matter who the girl is, what her relation to the speaker is, when or where it happens, what preceded, or what is to follow this one moment. The title is a sort of connection between the poem and the world, but it is not much of one. Any flight of steps would do as well. The girl gains nothing from Rome. The delight of such a poem is in the way the lines themselves create and contain the momentary preoccupation perfectly. The verse is light, as is the girl's movement. The poem is not sonorous or ponderous because to be so would contradict the tone of the moment. The poem's economy is perfect, and it itself is as graceful and pleasing as the moment described. One could go on, working with more complicated matters of diction, rhythm, and so forth, but the point is clear enough. The poem is designed to be self-sufficient and it is. The film has not gone as far as poetry has toward the ideal of the self-contained work, but such films as the various parts of *Fantasia*, Bergman's *The Magician*, Resnais's *Last Year at Marienbad*, and Cocteau's *Blood of a Poet* are in this same tradition.

To be thus self-sufficient, a given work must have a strong design to hold it together. The result, whether in film or poetry, is a tendency to regard a given movie or a given poem more as an artifact, as a verbal or pictorial construct, than as a work meant primarily to communicate something to someone. As Frank Kermode has pointed out, with the elegant simplicity and common sense that mark his work, "Information cannot be conveyed where there is no scope for choice between understood alternatives." So when Michael Drayton begins a sonnet with—

> Since ther's no helpe, Come, let us kisse and part,
> Nay, I have done: You get no more of Me,

And I am glad, yea glad with all my heart,
That thus so cleanly, I my Self can free. . .

—the reader knows at once what is going on, since he is aware not only of what Drayton says, but of what he does not say, of what is sayable about the situation. Everything is clear because we understand the alternatives. But can a reader grasp, in a similar way, a poem which goes:

so much depends
upon
a red wheel
barrow

glazed with rain
water

beside the white
chickens.

The poem has a point, of course, for much does depend on our ability and our willingness to see the world around us, to be aware of color, of contrast, of unpretentious things, to appreciate the difference between design and accident. But none of this is quickly or even surely communicated, no alternatives are visible or even imaginable. We do not know where to start. If so much depends on this, what might be an example of something on which nothing depends?

No doubt the weakening of poetry as a communicative art (and as a narrative art) is offset to some extent by the heightened beauty and interest of the poem as artifact, but it remains true that such an ideal of self-sufficiency depends heavily upon the order and design that can be achieved in the individual work, and it is ironical that one of the great themes of modern poetry and film as well has been the theme of the breakdown of order and design.

[1969]

RICHARD WILBUR

A Poet and the Movies

It is hard to say offhand how much one's art may have been tinctured by one's seeing of motion pictures, because watching film is (for me, for most) so much less judicial and analytic than other art experience. The conventions are transparent, the molding of the imagination is insidious. Even the worst movie has much of the authority of the actual, and quite without knowing it one comes out of the theater brainwashed into scanning the world through the norms of the camera. The enthusiasts of the pittoresco at the close of the eighteenth century, rapturously arrang-ing the landscape in their Claude glasses, were conscious of the imposi-tion; the moviegoer walks about taking shots and sequences unaware. The same entrancement characterizes the moviegoer's acquisition of per-sonal style; to put on an Old Vic accent, to ape the gestures of a stage actor or actress—these involve some deliberate imposture, but to smoke like George Raft, to lift the eyebrows like Cary Grant—that is another and more hypnotized order of imitation. The mannerisms of movie stars, unconsciously borrowed and recognized without specific reminiscence, have for us something of the universality of the Italian vocabulary of ges-tures, though of course they are more transitory.

Knowing how far my mind's eye must have been conditioned by motion pictures, I venture with diffidence the opinion that certain pre-Edison poetry was genuniely cinematic. Whenever, for example, I read *Paradise Lost*, I, 44–58 (the long shot of Satan's fall from Heaven to Hell, the panorama of the rebels rolling in the lake of fire, the sudden close-up of Satan's afflicted eyes), I feel that I am experiencing a passage which, though its effects may have been suggested by the spatial surprises of Baroque architecture, is facilitated for me, and not misleadingly, by my familiarity with screen techniques. If this reaction is not anachronistic foolishness, it follows that one must be wary in attributing this or that aspect of any contemporary work to the influence of film.

But glancing at my own poems, as the editor has invited me to do, I find in a number of pieces—"Marginalia" for instance—what may owe as much to the camera as to the sharp noticing of poets like Hopkins and Ponge: a close and rapid scanning of details, an insubordination of authenticating particulars, abrupt shifting in lieu of the full-dress rhetorical transition. Here is a bit of the poem mentioned:

> Things concentrate at the edges; the pond-surface
> Is bourne to fish and man and it is spread
> In textile scum and damask light, on which
> The lily-pads are set; and there are also
>   Inlaid ruddy twigs, becalmed pine-leaves,
>   Air-baubles, and the chain mail of froth . . .

I notice in the first line of another poem ("Haze, char, and the weather of all souls") what may be an effort at the instant scenic fullness of an opening shot. Move as it may, the picture on the screen gives enviably much at once, and the moviegoing poet, impatient of his prolix medium, may sometimes try for a lightning completeness, a descriptive *coup*. Finally, I wonder if the first four lines of "An Event" are not indebted to trick photography:

> As if a cast of grain leapt back to the hand,
> A landscapeful of small black birds, intent
> On the far south, convene at some command
> At once in the middle of the air . . .

All of the above is doubtful, but there is no doubt about two of my poems, "Beasts" and "The Undead." Each owes something to a particular horror film, in respect of mood, matter, and images. "Beasts" takes some of its third and fourth stanzas from *Frankenstein Meets the Wolf Man*, and "The Undead" obviously derives in part from Bela Lugosi's *Dracula*. Neither of these films is great art, though the latter comes close, but both are good enough to haunt the memory with the double force of reality and dream, to remind one of a deeper Gothic on which they draw, and to start the mind building around them. One would have to be brooding on a film to produce such a visual pun as "Their black shapes cropped into sudden bats."

The Undead

Even as children they were late sleepers,
Preferring their dreams, even when quick with monsters,
   To the world with all its breakable toys,
      Its compacts with the dying;

From the stretched arms of withered trees
They turned, fearing contagion of the mortal,
   And even under the plums of summer
      Drifted like winter moons.

Secret, unfriendly, pale, possessed
Of the one wish, the thirst for mere survival,
   They came, as all extremists do
      In time, to a sort of grandeur:

Now, to their Balkan battlements
Above the vulgar town of their first lives,
   They rise at the moon's rising. Strange
      That their utter self-concern

Should, in the end, have left them selfless:
Mirrors fail to perceive them as they float
   Through the great hall and up the staircase;
      Nor are the cobwebs broken.

Into the pallid night emerging,
Wrapped in their flapping capes, routinely maddened
   By a wolf's cry, they stand for a moment
      Stoking the mind's eye

With lewd thoughts of the pressed flowers
And bric-a-brac of rooms with something to lose,—
   Of love-dismembered dolls, and children
      Buried in quilted sleep.

Then they are off in a negative frenzy,
Their black shapes cropped into sudden bats
   That swarm, burst, and are gone. Thinking
      Of a thrush cold in the leaves

Who has sung his few summers truly,
Or an old scholar resting his eyes at last,
   We cannot be much impressed with vampires,
      Colorful though they are;

Nevertheless, their pain is real,
And requires our pity. Think how sad it must be
   To thirst always for a scorned elixir,
      The salt quotidian blood

Which, if mistrusted, has no savor;
To prey on life forever and not possess it,
   As rock-hollows, tide after tide,
      Glassily strand the sea.   [1967]

5

Authorship and Auteurship

Figure 5.1 Death and the knight play chess in Ingmar Bergman's The Seventh Seal (1956). Courtesy of Janus Films.

OUTTAKES

Secondly, those people who deny that there can be any connection between the scenario and literature seem to me to have a wrong conception, so much of the film as of literature. Literature they seem to regard as something polite and academic, in other words, as something god-forsaken and superannuated, compounded of correct grammar and highsounding ciceronian phrases. Such a conception reveals the feebleness of their sensibility. If you ask me to give you the most distinctive quality of good writing, I would give it to you in this one word: VISUAL. Reduce the art of writing to its fundamentals and you come to this single aim: to convey images by means of words. But to convey images. To make the mind see. To project onto that inner screen of the brain a moving picture of objects and events, events and objects moving towards a balance and reconciliation of a more than usual state of emotion with more than usual order. That is a definition of good literature—of the achievement of every good poet—from Homer and Shakespeare to James Joyce or Ernest Hemingway. It is also a definition of the ideal film.

HERBERT READ

. . . the old forms of communication are not unaffected by the development of new ones, nor do they survive alongside them. The filmgoer develops a different way of reading stories. But the man who writes the stories is a filmgoer too. The mechanization of literary production cannot be thrown into reverse. Once instruments are used even the novelist who makes no use of them is led to wish that he could do what the instruments can: to include what they show (or could show) as part of that reality which constitutes his subject-matter; and above all, when he writes, to assume the attitude of somebody using an instrument.

BERTOLT BRECHT

You will see that this little clicking contraption with the revolving handle will make a revolution in our life—in the life of writers. It is a direct attack on the old methods of literary art. We shall have to adapt ourselves to the shadowy screen and to the cold machine. A new form of writing will be necessary. I have thought of that and I can feel what is coming. But I rather like it. The swift change of scene, this blending of emotion and experience—it is much better than the heavy, long-drawn-out kind of writing to which we are accustomed. It is closer to life. In life, too, changes and transitions flash by before our eyes, and emotions of the soul are like a hurricane. The cinema has divined the mystery of motion. And that is greatness.

LEO TOLSTOY

[It is] almost impossible to write a film play without first writing a story. One can reproduce an effect caught in another medium, but one cannot make the first act of creation in script form. One must have the sense of more material than one needs to draw on.

GRAHAM GREENE

Creation must take place between the pen and the paper, not before in a thought or afterwards in a recasting.

GERTRUDE STEIN

It is under the director's guidance that the film is created, transformed from the inadequately expressed idea of the script to a living sequence of sound and images. And for the appearance of every image he is dependent on the cameraman. It would be simpler if we could regard the cameraman as a "technician" merely who complies with the director's demands; but, to demand specific effects, a director must be a cameraman himself, which is rare. It is not perhaps generally appreciated that composition, lighting and movement are very often the cameraman's responsibility, and yet these are among the chief means of expression in the cinema.

LINDSAY ANDERSON

The creator of a novel, a poem, or a painting can almost always be identified as a specific, nameable person. Some other creators, however, must share credit for the realization of a work of art. A composer may create a piece of music, but the performing orchestra and its conductor are necessary for the music's coming into being. An architect depends upon builders. A play requires a director and actors.

Like music and drama, film is most often a performance-based art. It requires numerous specialized contributors for existence. But films do not usually move through the well-defined two-step process of creation and performance in the same fashion as do plays or pieces of music. In music and drama the creator receives primary credit for a work while the conductor and musicians, or director and actors, achieve secondary notice as interpretative artists. In film, the creator (the scriptwriter) is often overlooked, as some of the articles in this section point out. The director and the star (or stars) normally vie for the critical spotlight, and others such as the cinematographer and the editor often receive more notice for the finished work than does the writer. Frequently, however, the director, actors, cinematographer, and editor contribute more to the creation of a film than does the scriptwriter.

Unfortunately, space in this section does not permit exploring the contributions of many of those responsible for a film. Instead, the focus is upon those involved with creation (hence the notion of authorship) rather than with performance. (One could argue, though, and rightly, that the editor is often involved with creation, with conceptualization, rather than performance, and the literary dimensions of this situation would be well worth considering. The creative contribution of the editor is, for example, at the core of Eisenstein's aesthetics.) In some cases, all too few, a filmmaker assumes the spectrum of tasks necessary to bring a film into being. But until this becomes commonplace, questions and concerns with authorship will continue.

Ingmar Bergman, who writes his own scripts, provides the point of view of a recognized *auteur** who has control of his films at all stages. Bergman has strong feelings about the process of filmmaking; he considers the script only "a very imperfect and *technical* basis for a film." The subtleties, rhythms, and mood of a film, even of the dialogue, cannot be realized on paper. Bergman declares firmly that "film has nothing to do with literature." Connecting literature with words, he maintains that words interact with the intellect and films with the imagination. (Ironically, Bergman is regarded as one of the chief contemporary makers of intellectual cinema.) Bergman does not see himself as an author nor does he want to be one. Although one of the world's most recognized names in filmmaking, he would prefer to be one of the anonymous artists working on a film, like the artists who worked unnamed on the old cathedrals.

Béla Balázs boldly argues for the significance of the script and the scriptwriter. The script provides the literary foundation for a film and is an independent literary form in its own right, equaling the written stage play. Balázs compares the scripts for play and film, observing little differences between them as independent art forms. He does see functional differences between them, however. A film script must articulate the film's "subtle visual ideas with intricate plots," making a play script word-oriented and a film script visually oriented. Balázs, however, talks about

*French for "author," the title *auteur* implies that the director is the equivalent of a literary author because he or she has primary control and responsibility for the final product; an *auteur* earns that title, according to auteurist critics, by displaying a unique cinematic style.

213

scripts primarily from a European perspective. (He assumes, for example, a single scriptwriter.) As if fulfilling Balázs's prophecies, though, most bookstores today display numerous scripts. At the time Balázs wrote (prior to 1945), scant attention was paid the film script.

Dudley Nichols, a Hollywood scriptwriter of distinction, offers a less hyperbolic view of the subject. Painfully conscious of the assembly-line nature of Hollywood film production, he places more emphasis than does Balázs on the script as a step and not a finished product. According to Nichols, the screenplay is a far less completed work than the stageplay, which ultimately relies on words throughout. Nichols goes on to explain the process leading to the creation and realization of a script, the challenges of adaptation, and the problems faced by a creative writer working in an industry devoted to entertainment. Like Bazin, Nichols believes that serious novels aid the developing art of cinema by furnishing complex materials which those within the industry would not be allowed to create.

The debate over the value of an *auteur* approach to cinema has flourished for well over a decade. And it has been an instructive debate. Francois Truffaut threw down the gauntlet in an intentionally polemical and exploratory article in *Cahiers du Cinema* in which he used the phrase "politique des auteurs" and argued that a viewer could distinguish the "signature" of the auteur in his films. Sarris became the American spokesman for the movement, providing the word "theory" to suggest that auteur thought had a formulated critical approach to offer. (Numerous critics have pointed out that Sarris was advancing a series of propositions or notions, but certainly not a theory.) Sarris's proposition has three sections which he views as concentric circles. The outer circle involves technique, followed in order by personal style and interior meaning. Sarris then goes on to show how auteurist criticism can provide insights otherwise missed by critics.

BÉLA BALÁZS

The Script

Not so very long ago it was still difficult to convince the Philistines that the film was an independent, autonomous new art with laws of its own. To-day this is scarcely ever questioned and it is also admitted that the literary foundation of the new art, the script, is just as much a specific, independent literary form as the written stage play. The script is no longer a technical accessory, not a scaffolding which is taken away once the house is built, but a literary form worthy of the pen of poets, a literary form which may even be published in book form and read as such. Of course scripts can be good or bad, like any other literary work, but there is nothing to prevent them from being literary masterpieces. That the literary form of the film script has not yet had a Shakespeare, a Calderón, a Molière, an Ibsen is no matter—it will have some day. In any case, we do not even know whether there may or may not have been some great masterpiece lost among the thousands of film scripts to which we paid not the slightest attention. We never searched for masterpieces among them, often even denied the very possibility of one being found in such an unlikely place.

Most cinema-goers do not realize that what they are watching is the staging of a film script, very much as they would be watching the staging of a play in the theatre. And even in the theatre, how many spectators think of this? If the newspaper reviews did not discuss the play itself and the performance of it as two distinct subjects, few theatre-goers would think of the literary creative work that has to precede every stage performance of a play.

From Béla Balázs, *Theory of the Film*, Dover Publications, Inc., New York, 1970. Reprinted through the permission of the publisher.

215

That public opinion distinguishes more easily between play and stage performance than between script and screened film is due to the fact that a play can be performed in many ways in many theatres, thus demonstrating that the play has an existence of its own apart from the performance. The film on the contrary mostly absorbs the script completely so that it is not preserved as an independent object which could be used again for a different film production. In most cases it is not available in print; it is not yet an accepted custom to publish scripts for reading.

The film script is an entirely new literary form, newer even than the film itself, and so it is scarcely surprising that no books on the æsthetics of literature mention it as yet. The film is fifty years old, the script as a literary form only twenty-five at most. It was in the twenties of this century, in Germany, that specially interesting scripts first began to be published.

In this again the film slavishly copied the development of the stage. There had been highly developed and popular theatre, there had been great playwrights for centuries before plays began to be written down and made available for reading outside the theatre. In ancient Greece, in the Middle Ages and in the Renaissance the written play was always a product of a later differentiation. The drama began with ritual or improvisation, or was born on the stage itself out of the permanent characters of the *commedia dell' arte.* The stage is a much older thing than the play. It is well known that Shakespeare's plays were pieced together later from the parts written out for the actors.

In the same way the film is much older than the script. "Much" here means about twenty years—but that is nearly half of the whole history of the film.

When the film began, there was no script; the director improvised each scene on the set, telling each actor what to do during the next shot. The sub-titles were written and cut in later.

The film script was born when the film had already developed into an independent new art and it was no longer possible to improvise its new subtle visual effects in front of the camera; these had to be planned carefully in advance. The film script became a literary form when the film ceased to aim at literary effects, planted itself firmly on its own feet and thought in terms of visual effects. The picture sequences of the photographed theatre could be written down in the form of a stereotyped stage play; but a film using specific visual effects could no longer be pressed into the form of the drama, nor of the novel. A new form was needed. Its terms of reference and its novelty were determined by the paradoxical task it had to fulfill, which was to present in words the visual experiences of the silent film, that is, something that could not be adequately expressed in words.

The first scripts were in fact mere technical aids, nothing but lists of the scenes and shots for the convenience of the director. They merely indicated what was to be in the picture, and in what order, but said nothing about how it was to be presented.

In the days of the silent film the importance of the literary script grew in the same measure in which the adventurous film stories were simplified and the films themselves given a deeper meaning. The type of imagination the adventure-story writers possessed was no longer suitable; a special filmic imagination was required, subtle visual ideas without intricate plots. The intensity of the close-up drove out the complicated story and brought a new literary form into being.

Such a simplification of the story did not, however, simplify the film at all. There was less adventure, but more psychology. The development turned inward and script-writing was now a task worthy of the pen of the best writers.

It should be said here that this decline of the adventure story was not the only trend in the development of the silent film. There was at the same time a leaning towards the most exotic romanticism—and both these trends can be traced to the same origins. They were both escapist trends, but running in opposite directions. On the one hand the film provided escape into exotic, romantic adventure, on the other escape to some particle of reality entirely isolated from the rest.

With the birth of the talkie the script automatically came to be of paramount importance. It needed dialogue, as a play did, but it needed very much more than that. For a play is only dialogue and nothing else; it is dialogue spoken, as it were, in a vacuum. The stage, though indicated by the author's directions, is not presented in literary form. In the abstract spiritual space of the drama the visual surroundings of the *dramatis personae* were a mere background which could not influence their state of mind and hence could not take part in the action. But in the film visible and audible things are projected on to the same plane as the human characters and in that pictorial composition common to them all they are all equivalent participants in the action. For this reason the script-writer cannot deal with the scene of action by means of a few stage directions. He must present, characterize, depict the visual aspect as well as the rest, express it by literary means, but in much greater detail than for instance the novelist, who may leave a great deal to the imagination of his readers. In the script the script-writer must define the part played by the images of things every bit as carefully as all the other parts, for it is through them that the destinies of the human characters fulfill themselves.

Thus the now fully developed and mature film art had borne a new fruit, a new literary form, the film script. By now many scripts are available in print and soon they may be more popular reading than the more abstract stage play. It is difficult to say how much time must elapse before our literary critics finally notice this new phenomenon born before their eyes; for this reason we shall try to define the laws governing this new literary form.

The problem is: in what respect does the film script differ from the stage play or the novel? The question is put in this form because it will be easiest to define the specific principles and laws of the script by defining the essential qualities which distinguish it from the other forms most closely related to it.

The present-day script is not an unfinished sketch, not a ground-plan, not a mere outline of a work of art, but a complete work of art in itself. The script can present reality, give an independent, intelligible picture of reality like any other form of art. True, the script puts on paper scenes and dialogues which later are to be turned into a film; but so does the drama put on paper the stage performance. And yet the latter is regarded as a literary form superior to the former.

Written music is only a symbol of the music to be produced by the instruments, but nevertheless no one would call a Beethoven sonata 'unfinished' or a 'sketch' because of this. We even have film scripts now which are intended for reading and could not be shot—just as there are 'book' plays which could never be staged. Nevertheless such scripts are not novels or short stories or stage plays—they are film scripts. They belong to a new literary form.

The basic fact which underlies every form of film and determines the laws governing the script is that the film is an audible spectacle, a motion picture, i.e. an action played out in the present, before our eyes.

One of the things that follow from this basic fact is that the script, like the drama, can present only "real time." The author cannot speak for himself in the script, just as he cannot in the drama. The author cannot say "meanwhile time passed . . .," he cannot say ". . . After many years . . ." or ". . . after this . . ." The script cannot refer to the past, cannot tell us about something that happened long ago or in some other place, it cannot summarize events, as the epic forms can. The script can only present what can be enacted before our eyes, in the present, in a space and time accessible to our senses; in this it is similar to the drama.

How, then, does the script differ from the drama?

In the film, as on the stage, the action is visible and audible, but on the stage it is enacted in real space (the space of the stage) by live human beings (the actors). The film on the other hand shows only pictures, images of that space and of those human beings. The film does not present some action played out in the imagination of a poet, but an actual event enacted in real space by real human beings in nature or in a studio, but presents only a picture, a photograph of these events. Thus it is neither a figment of the brain nor immediate reality.

The upshot of this is that the script as a literary form can contain only what is visible and audible on the screen. This appears to be a truism if we do not examine the bounds set by this rule. But it is on this that everything turns.

In one of the finest Soviet films, *Chapayev,* the political commissar attached to Chapayev's partisan troop arrests one of the partisan leaders for stealing a pig. But why lock him up on the farm where they are staying? There is only a dilapidated barn with a broken door that cannot be locked. We see this because the giant partisan more than once pushes his tiger-like head through the door. He could of course come out at will. What prevents him from kicking down the whole tumbledown contraption? That Furmanov, the political commissar, has placed a sentry to guard the door? But the sentry is even more decrepit than the barn; he is a hollow-chested short-sighted, pitiful little figure, a clerk who scarcely knows one end of his rifle from the other. The giant, savage partisan could blow the funny little man away with a breath of his mighty lungs. But he does not do so. It is thus made obvious that what holds the giant captive is not physical force but a moral influence. And we can *see* this moral influence, it is quite unmistakably manifested in a pictorial effect.

Then Chapayev himself comes to release his friend. But the ridiculous, miserable little private who is guarding the prisoner, bars his way. Whose way? The way of the commander, the tremendously strong, fierce, dangerous Chapayev, who rages, flings his sword away—but does not shove the ridiculous little soldier out of the way. Why? Here again it is not physical force that stops Chapayev, but a moral power rendered evident by the visible, pictorial presentation; a moral force incarnated in the hollow-chested, short-sighted, clumsy little man put there on guard by the representative of the Party. It is the authority of the Communist Party which even the undisciplined, unruly, fierce partisans respect and which endows the ridiculous little sentry with a conscious dignity.

Here the authority of the Party, although it may seem an abstract idea, has been rendered visible in a dramatic scene, and thus something that can be photographed. It is to be particularly noted that in this example there are no symbolic or "metaphorical" shots, they are all quite real, ordinary, pictures with nothing improbable about them and yet they radiate a "deeper meaning."

LESSING AND THE FILM

In analysing the basic difference between the drama and its stage presentation, Lessing outlined the difference between the film script and the film a century and a half before their time. His definition of the nature and laws governing the stage were so brilliant that now, 150 years later, they helped us to define the different laws and the different nature of a different although not entirely unrelated art.

At the beginning of his *Hamburgische Dramaturgie* he speaks of plays made from novels and says: "It is not at all difficult . . . to expand single emotions into scenes . . . but to be able to transpose oneself from the point of view of a narrator to the true point of view of each character and instead of describing their passions make these come into existence under the eyes of the spectator and develop without a break in an illusory continuity—that is what is needed here." In this passage all is said about the most essential difference between drama and epic. The same difference exists between the film script and the epic. Like the drama, the script does not describe the passions but makes them come into being and develop under the eyes of the spectator. But in this same passage Lessing also defined the difference between the drama and the film script and has helped us to understand one of the basic principles of film art. He says that the drama presents the passions without a break, in an illusory continuity. And truly this is the specific quality of the drama; such continuity is a necessary consequence of the fact that the drama is written for the stage. For a character coming on to the stage is under our eyes in uninterrupted continuity, without a break, until it leaves the stage again.

PARALLEL ACTIONS

The novelist can take his readers into a large gathering and then deal with only one person of all the company. He can tell the whole life-story of that one person without informing the reader of what the other people present were doing all that time. The reader may easily forget that they are there at all. In the epic forms such "jumps" are possible and the illusion of an unbroken continuity of scene is not imperative as it is on the stage. This is the basic difference between epic and dramatic forms.

In this respect, however, the film script is related to the epic rather than the dramatic form. The film, like the epic, is not bound to maintain the illusion of unbroken continuity,—such continuity is not even possible. In a film scene all the persons present at the same place not only need not all be visible in every shot but to show them all, all the time, would even be contrary to the style and technique of the film. The public has the illusion that the participants in the scene are present, but they are not always all of them visible. In ceaselessly changing short shots and close-ups we see only those whose face or words happen to be needed just then. The film can lift such a figure out of the greatest crowd and devote special attention to it, penetrate deeply into its emotions and psychology. In this the film and the film script are related to the epic.

The film can interrupt the continuity of a scene not only by not showing all the persons in a scene all the time—the whole scene itself can be interrupted, the film show a different scene enacted in quite a different place, and then the previously interrupted scene can be continued. This is inconceivable on the stage. The possibility of showing in parallel sequence more than one simultaneous action is a quite specific feature of the film and hence a specific possibility of the film script as an art form.

The unity of space thus binds the film even less than the least form-bound of dramas. For the drama cannot in the middle of a scene show another scene enacted in quite a different place and then return to continue the original scene. The law of the unity of space does not apply to the film at all. But the unity of time all the more so. For even if we interrupt a scene and the interpolated scene is enacted *elsewhere,* it must not be enacted at another *time.* It must happen neither sooner nor later, but at the same time, else the audience would either not understand what was going on or would not believe it.

TECHNICAL CONDITIONS AND
ARTISTIC PRINCIPLES

The question now arises: if there are several characters on the stage but only one or two of them are really engaged in speech or action, do not the others pale into mere lifeless properties? (This is what the technique of the film enables us to avoid.) In a good play this cannot happen, because a good play always has a central problem which organically binds together all the *dramatis personae*. Whatever is said on the stage, whoever says it, always concerns questions vital to all the characters and therefore they all remain alive and interesting. Thus the technical requirements of the stage determine the literary structure of the drama.

As we have seen, the technical requirements of the film are different and therefore the literary structure of the script is different too. The single central problem, the grouping around a single central conflict, which characterizes the structure of the drama, is contrary to the nature of the film, the technical conditions of which are different. The visual nature of the film does not tolerate a structure consisting of a few long scenes. The reason for this is that while long scenes without a change of setting are possible if they are full of internal movement and people can talk in a room for hours if their words express some internal movement or internal struggle, the film, in which the decisive element is always the visual, cannot be content with such long-drawn, merely internal—and hence non-visible—events. The film requires an external, visible, "shootable" picture for every internal happening. For this reason the film script—again like the novel—does not centralize the conflicts but faces the characters with a series of problems in the course of the story.

One of the laws governing the form of the film script is its prescribed length. In this it resembles the drama, the length of which is determined by the duration feasible on the stage. Of course there are also dramas which are not intended to be performed and which disregard this condition. In the same way it is possible to write fine film scripts intended only for reading and not for shooting as a film.

The film, too, has by now developed a standard length, partly for business reasons, to enable the motion picture theatres to give several shows daily; but there are also physiological reasons which have limited the length of films. For the time being, films longer than ten thousand feet tire the eye.

These are merely external, technical considerations. But it often happens in art that external technical conditions harden into laws governing the internal artistic composition of the work. The short story was created by the predetermined length of the newspaper feature and this art form then brought forth such classics as the short stories of Maupassant or Chekhov. Architectural forms dictated many a composition of sculpture.

The predetermined length may also determine the content. The prescribed length of the sonnet determines its style. No one is forced to write sonnets or film scripts. But if one does, the predetermined length must not become a bed of Procrustes which curtails or draws out the required content. The theme, content and style of the film script must be inspired by the predetermined length of it. This predetermined length is in itself a style, which the script-writer must master.

By now the script has come to be an independent literary form. It was born of the film as the drama was born of the stage play. In the course of time the drama gained precedence over the stage play and now it is the drama that prescribes the tasks and style of the stage, and the history of the stage has long been merely an appendage to the history of the drama.

In the film there is as yet no trace of a similar development. But it will come in time. Up to now the history of the film script has been merely a chapter in the history of the film. But soon the script may in its turn determine the history of the film. . . .

[1945]

INGMAR BERGMAN

Bergman Discusses Film-Making

. . . A film for me begins with something very vague—a chance remark or a bit of conversation, a hazy but agreeable event unrelated to any particular situation. It can be a few bars of music, a shaft of light across the street. Sometimes in my work at the theater I have envisioned actors made up for yet unplayed roles.

These are split-second impressions that disappear as quickly as they come, yet leave behind a mood—like pleasant dreams. It is a mental state, not an actual story, but one abounding in fertile associations and images. Most of all, it is a brightly colored thread sticking out of the dark sack of the unconscious. If I begin to wind up this thread, and do it carefully, a complete film will emerge.

This primitive nucleus strives to achieve definite form, moving in a way that may be lazy and half asleep at first. Its stirring is accompanied by vibrations and rhythms which are very special and unique to each film. The picture sequences then assume a pattern in accordance with these rhythms, obeying laws born out of and conditioned by my original stimulus.

If that embryonic substance seems to have enough strength to be made into a film, I decide to materialize it. Then comes something very complicated and difficult: the transformation of rhythms, moods, atmosphere, tensions, sequences, tones and scents into words and sentences, into an understandable screenplay.

This is an almost impossible task.

The only thing that can be satisfactorily transferred from that original complex of rhythms and moods is the dialogue, and even dialogue is a sensitive substance which may offer resistance. Written dialogue is like a musical score, almost incomprehensible to the average person. Its interpretation demands a technical knack plus a certain kind of imagination and feeling—qualities which are so often lacking, even among actors. One can write dialogue, but how it should be delivered, its rhythm and tempo, what is to take place between lines—all this must be omitted for practical reasons. Such a detailed script would be unreadable. I try to squeeze instructions as to location, characterization and atmosphere into my screenplays in understandable terms, but the success of this depends on my writing ability and the perceptiveness of the reader, which are not always predictable.

Now we come to essentials, by which I mean montage, rhythm and the relation of one picture to another—the vital third dimension without which the film is merely a dead product from a factory. Here I cannot clearly give a key, as in a musical score, nor a specific idea of the tempo which determines the relationship of the elements involved. It is quite impossible for me to indicate the way in which the film "breathes" and pulsates.

I have often wished for a kind of notation which would enable me to put on paper all the shades and tones of my vision, to record distinctly the inner structure of a film. For when I stand in the artistically devastating atmosphere of the studio, my hands and head full of all the trivial and irritating details that go with motion-picture production, it often takes a tremendous effort to remember how I originally saw and thought out this or that sequence, or what was the relation between the scene of four weeks ago and that of today. If I could express myself clearly, in explicit symbols, then this problem would be almost eliminated and I could work with absolute confidence that whenever I liked I could prove the relationship between the part and the whole and put my finger on the rhythm, the continuity of the film.

Thus the script is a very imperfect *technical* basis for a film. And there is another important point in this connection which I should like to mention. Film has nothing to do with literature; the character and substance of the two art forms are usually in conflict. This probably has something to do with the receptive process of the mind. The written word is read and assimilated by a conscious act of the will in alliance with the intellect; little by little it affects the imagination and the emotions. The process is different with a motion picture. When we experience a film, we consciously prime ourselves for illusion. Putting aside will and intellect, we make way for it in our imagination. The sequence of pictures plays directly on our feelings.

Music works in the same fashion; I would say that there is no art form that has so much in common with film as music. Both affect our emotions directly, not via the intellect. And film is mainly rhythm; it is inhalation and exhalation in continuous sequence. Ever since childhood, music has been my great source of recreation and stimulation, and I often experience a film or play musically.

It is mainly because of this difference between film and literature that we should avoid making films out of books. The irrational dimension of a literary work, the germ of its existence, is often untranslatable into visual terms—and it, in turn, destroys the special, irrational dimension of the film. If, despite this, we wish to translate something literary into film terms, we must make an infinite number of complicated adjustments which often bear little or no fruit in proportion to the effort expended.

I myself have never had any ambition to be an author. I do not want to write novels, short stories, essays, biographies, or even plays for the theater. I only want to make films—films about conditions, tensions, pictures, rhythms and characters which are in one way or another important to me. The motion picture, with its complicated process of birth, is my method of saying what I want to my fellow men. I am a filmmaker, not an author.

Thus the writing of the script is a difficult period but a useful one, for it compels me to prove logically the validity of my ideas. In doing this, I am caught in a conflict—a conflict between my need to transmit a complicated situation through visual images, and my desire for absolute clarity. I do not intend my work to be solely for the benefit of myself or the few, but for the entertainment of the general public. The wishes of the public are imperative. But sometimes I risk following my own impulse, and it has been shown that the public can respond with surprising sensitivity to the most unconventional line of development.

When shooting begins, the most important thing is that those who work with me feel a definite contact, that all of us somehow cancel out our conflicts through working together. We must pull in one direction for the sake of the work at hand. Sometimes this leads to dispute, but the more definite and clear the "marching orders," the easier it is to reach the goal which has been set. This is the basis for my conduct as director, and perhaps the explanation of much of the nonsense that has been written about me.

While I cannot let myself be concerned with what people think and say about me personally, I believe that reviewers and critics have every right to interpret my films as they like. I refuse to interpret my work to others, and I cannot tell the critic what to think; each person has the right to understand a film as he sees it. Either he is attracted or repelled. A film is made to create reaction. If the audience does not react one way or another, it is an indifferent work and worthless.

I do not mean by this that I believe in being "different" at any price. A lot has been said about the value of originality, and I find this foolish. Either you are original or you are not. It is completely natural for artists to take from and give to each other, to borrow from and experience one another. In my own life, my great literary experience was Strindberg. There are works of his which can still make my hair stand on end—*The People of Hemsö,* for example. And it is my dream to produce *Dream Play* some day. Olof Molander's production of it in 1934 was for me a fundamental dramatic experience. . . .

People ask what are my intentions with my films—my aims. It is a difficult and dangerous question, and I usually give an evasive answer: I try to tell the truth about the human condition, the truth as I see it. This answer seems to satisfy everyone, but it is not quite correct. I prefer to describe what I *would like* my aim to be.

There is an old story of how the cathedral of Chartres was struck by lightning and burned to the ground. Then thousands of people came from all points of the compass, like a giant procession of ants, and together they began to rebuild the cathedral on its old site. They worked until the building was completed—master builders, artists, laborers, clowns, noblemen, priests, burghers. But they all remained anonymous, and no one knows to this day who built the cathedral of Chartres.

Regardless of my own beliefs and my own doubts, which are unimportant in this connection, it is my opinion that art lost its basic creative drive the moment it was separated from worship. It severed an umbilical cord and now lives its own sterile life, generating and degenerating itself. In former days the artist remained unknown and his work was to the glory of God. He lived and died without being more or less important than other artisans; "eternal values," "immortality" and "masterpiece" were terms not applicable in his case. The ability to create was a gift. In such a world flourished invulnerable assurance and natural humility.

Today the individual has become the highest form and the greatest bane of artistic creation. The smallest wound or pain of the ego is examined under a microscope as if it were of eternal importance. The artist considers his isolation, his subjectivity, his individualism almost holy. Thus we finally gather in one large pen, where we stand and bleat about our loneliness without listening to each other and without realizing that we are smothering each other to death. The individualists stare into each other's eyes and yet deny the existence of each other. We walk in circles, so limited by our own anxieties that we can no longer distinguish between true and false, between the gangster's whim and the purest ideal.

Thus if I am asked what I would like the general purpose of my films to be, I would reply that I want to be one of the artists in the cathedral on the great plain. I want to make a dragon's head, an angel, a devil—or perhaps a saint—out of stone. It does not matter which; it is the sense of satisfaction that counts. Regardless of whether I believe or not, whether I am a Christian or not, I would play my part in the collective building of the cathedral.

[1960]

DUDLEY NICHOLS

The Writer and the Film

Ours is the age of the specialist. In older times, before the Machine, men did specialize of course in the various arts and crafts—but those arts and crafts were not themselves subdivided into specialized functions. The man who painted did the whole job himself: he was a painter. So with the silversmith and the shoemaker and the sculptor. But the Machine changed all that. The painter today has his materials prepared by other people, by specialized craftsmen or tradesmen, and only wields those materials in the final function of creating pictures. The etcher buys his copper plates already prepared and seldom pulls his own prints. The sculptor models in clay and leaves to others the pouring of the mould or the work of the pointing-machine. The writer no longer turns out beautiful manuscripts that may be passed from hand to hand: he pounds out a script on the typing machine and passes it on to his publisher's printing factories. In science and art we have become specialized, narrowing our fields of study and work because those fields have grown too enormous for the single mind to embrace. We are all specialized, for better or worse, and it is only natural that the one new art form which the Machine has produced should be the most highly specialized of all. For the motion picture *is* an art form, whether it be so regarded or not.

By rights this new art form should be controlled by individuals who include all functions in themselves. They should be film-makers. But the functions are too diversified and complex to be handled by the creative energy of one individual. So we break them down into separate

Taken from *Twenty Best Film Plays* by Dudley Nichols. Copyright © 1943, 1971 by Crown Publishers, Inc. Used by permission of Crown Publishers, Inc.

crafts—writing, directing, photography, scenic designing, optical printing and camera effects, cutting and assembly of film, composing music, recording, mixing and re-recording, the making of *dissolves* and *fades* and other transitions: into an immense field of works which require the closest and most harmonious collaboration to produce excellent results.

This in effect is detrimental to film as an art form and an obstacle to the development of artists who wish to work in film. It is too much the modern factory system: each man working on a different machine and never in an integrated creation. It tends to destroy that individuality of style which is the mark of any superior work of art. Individual feeling gets lost in the complicated process and standardized products come off the assembly line. I make these remarks by way of preface to point out that there is only one way to overcome the impediments—and that is to learn the whole process, to be a master craftsman within the factory system; to be, in short, a film-maker first and a writer or director or whatever-you-will afterwards.

Of course this poses a dilemma: one cannot under our present system make films without first learning to make films: and the only way to learn film-making is by making films. Hence by subterfuge of one sort or another one must enter the field as a specialized apprentice and try to learn all the other specialized functions, so that the individual may return to his specialty with the full equipment of an artist. A screenwriter should have knowledge of direction, of cutting, of all the separate functions, before his imagination and talent can be geared effectively and skillfully to his chosen line of work. Fortunately we are none of us so competent as we might be, if for no other reason than that Hollywood is too bent on turning out films to take the time to train its artisans to the top of their bent. As a result there is always room for the interested new worker. A writer can find a place, even without knowing much about film-making, and if he has a secret star he may glitter into sudden prominence even without knowing the slightest thing about film-making.

Hollywood is used to taking works of fiction in other forms and translating them into film; and for this and other reasons the talented writer does not feel encouraged to write directly for the screen. This is to be regretted because the screenplay might easily become a fascinating new form of literature, provided the studio heads acquired sufficient taste to recognize and desire literary quality. Yet there have been, there are, and there will continue to be written, screenplays of quality and sincerity; if only because of the dogged efforts of writers and directors who set themselves high goals and persist frequently against their own material interests.

There is one other circumstance which makes it difficult for the screenplay to be enjoyed as a literary form in itself: it is not and never can be a finished product. It is a step, the first and most important step, in the process of making a film. One might also say that a play is not a finished product for the theatre; yet a play relies entirely on the word; idea, character and action are projected by means of the word; and a skillful playreader can enjoy wonderful performances within the theatre of his own imagination. The screenplay is far less a completed thing than the play, for the skilled screenwriter is thinking continuously in terms of film as well as of the word. The filmwriter must be a film-maker at heart, and a film-maker thinks and lives and works in film. That is the goal, the end-result—eight or ten thousand feet of negative patched together to reproduce, upon its unreeling, an illusion of a par-ticular kind and quality. It is that illusion which the film-maker—and in this instance the filmwriter—is pursuing when he begins to gather together his first nebulous conception.

The truth is that a motion picture undergoes a series of creations: first it is a novel, a short story, or a conception in the mind of the screenwriter. That is the point of departure. Next the filmwriter takes the first plunge toward the finished negative by building the story in screenplay form. This rough draft, at least in the case of the present writer, will undergo two or three revisions, each nearer to the peculiar demands of cinema. With luck the director, who must have an equal sympathy for the drama to be unfolded, will be near at hand during the groundwork, contributing cinematic ideas here and there, many of which will not appear in the script but will be remembered or recorded in other notes to be used when the time comes.

Ordinarily, when all ideas of cinematic treatment have been un-earthed and the final draft completed, the writer's work is ended and the creation of the projected film moves on into the hands of the director and other specialists; which is most unfortunate for the writer, for his education ceases in the middle of an uncompleted process. Let us, how-ever, follow along with the writer who is able to follow the progress toward film. The second creation of the film is in its casting, which can help or hinder the designed illusion. The novelist is a fortunate artist who creates his characters out of the flesh and spirit of his own imagina-tion; they need never be distorted by being embodied by living beings who necessarily have other traits and characteristics. But the playwright and the filmwriter must have real persons to present their characters— and identity is not to be found. There have been ideal casts, but even the most perfect will alter indefinably the shape and mood and meaning of an imagined drama. Now each of the actors chosen must create his part of the film; and the sum of their parts creates another phase of the film. Implicated in this is the personality of the director, who creates the film by combining (in his own style which may not be the style of the writer) the contributions of the writer and actors.

It is at this point that a peculiar thing occurs, which must be understood to discriminate between the stage and screen. I have never seen this pointed out before, even by film-makers, and it needs to be set down; stage and screen are entirely different media because the audience participates in quite opposite ways. The theatre—and I use the term to embrace both stage and screen—demands an audience. It is not complete without its audience and even derives much of its power from its audience. Every stage actor knows this and has experienced it. The audience identifies itself with the actor, its collective emotions rush out in sympathy or buffet against him with antipathy like an unseen electric discharge—which increases the actor's potential so to speak, permitting him to give back his feelings with increased power, which again returns to him, like the oscillating discharge of an electric machine. It is these heightened moments that create unforgettable experiences in the theatre when the drama is great both in its literary power and in its acting. Here the relationship between the actor and the audience is direct and the intelligent actor can grow by what he experiences, just as the audience grows.

Now, curiously, this does not at all exist in the cinema; but it does exist at the stage of cinema-making we are discussing. On the stage of a film studio the actor still has an audience, though a small one: the half-hundred people who comprise "the crew"—grips, juicers, cameramen, script girl, and all the familiar others. But if he acts in such a style as to affect this audience solely he is lost, for his actual audience is miles away and they will see him only through the uncaring single eye of the camera that looks on like a tripod man from Mars. The significant thing is that at this point there is an invisible transition taking place that will break all the rules of the stage and impose new ones of the screen.

The actors are creating a film, not a stageplay, even though it appears they are making a stageplay. We are not cameras, we are living beings, and we cannot see things with the detachment of a lens. In the early days of sound-film I observed many failures because this was not understood. The action seemed good on the sound-stage, but it did not come off on the screen.

The reason is that the audience, the film-theatre audience, participates in an entirely different way with the projected images of a film. This is not so strange if we remember that a motion picture film will give just as good a performance in an empty theatre as in a full one. It will not, of course, be so moving or so amusing to a single spectator as it will to that same spectator in a crowded theatre: members of an audience need each other to build up laughter, sorrow and joy. But the film is unaffected, it does not in itself participate as do the actors on a stage. It is a complete illusion, as in a dream, and the power of identification (which you must have in any form of theatre) must be between audience and the visually projected re-actor.

Unthinking people speak of the motion picture as the medium of "action"; the truth is that the stage is the medium of action while the screen is the medium of reaction. It is through identification with the person *acted* upon on the screen, and not with the person acting, that the film builds up its oscillating power with an audience. This is understood instinctively by the expert film-makers, but to my knowledge it has never been formulated. At any emotional crisis of a film, when a character is saying something which profoundly affects another, it is to this second character that the camera instinctively roves, perhaps in close-up; and it is then that the hearts of the audience quiver and open in release, or rock with laughter or shrink with pain, leap to the screen and back again in swift growing vibrations. The great actors of the stage are actors; of the screen, re-actors.

If anyone doubts this let him study his own emotions when viewing a good film; an experienced film-maker can do this automatically at the first showing of a film, but very likely others will have to go a second time, or check it over in mental review. I recently did this with some lay friends after a showing of Noel Coward's *In Which We Serve,* and it was illuminating to find out that they had been most deeply moved by reactions, almost never by actions: the figure of a woman when she gets news her husband has been lost at sea, the face of an officer when told his wife had died. (And how cunningly Noel Coward had that officer writing a letter to his wife when the radioman entered with the news; the reaction then was continued to the point where the officer goes on deck and drops the letter into the sea, a reaction extended into action, so to speak.) In the same film one of the most affecting scenes was the final one where the captain bids goodbye to the remainder of his crew; and while this appears to be action, the camera shrewdly presented it as reaction: It is the faces of the men, as they file past, that we watch, reaction to the whole experience even in their laconic voices and in the weary figure of the captain.

Now this brings us to the next phase in the making of a film, or next "creation" if you prefer. I have said that a film ensues from a series of consecutive creations, which were enumerated from the first stage of concept to the point where the first recording on film is made. The director, the actors, the art director, the cameraman, the whole crew in fact, have followed after a fashion (but with many inevitable departures in which the writer, if he is fortunate, has collaborated) the final draft of the screenplay. Now you have perhaps a hundred thousand feet of film, the negative of which is safely tucked away in the laboratory while you have for your study a "work print." Now the film is in the cutting room, in a thousand strips or rolls, some strips perhaps only a few feet long, some four or five hundred. Every foot-and-a-half is a second of time in the projection room, and you do not want your finished film to be one second longer than is determined by dramatic necessity. Every good artist, every good workman, has a passion for economy: if you can do a thing in one stroke, don't use two; if a certain mood or atmosphere is essential to the illusion you are after and it requires a hundred strokes, use them. By elimination and rough assembly the cutter patches together a work-print, say, fourteen thousand feet long: two or three miles of strips of film, assembled consecutively on seventeen or eighteen reels. That is the first creation of the cutter.

Now another job begins, one of the most delicate and sensitive jobs of all. Rough cutting was determined by the screen writer but this did not and could not include the interior cutting of the director and cameraman. Since terminology is not yet standardized in film-making, I designate the cutting of the director on the set the "montage," using a word which the Russians apply for all cutting or editing. It is determined by the style of the director, his feeling for photographed images, the way he rests the eye of the audience or gives it sudden pleasures, moving in at different angles on his scenes and characters. Had the writer attempted to anticipate the director and set down all this montage on paper, his script would have become a useless mess; for this interior cutting cannot be determined precisely (though many attempt to do so) before arriving on the set. This manner of shooting and handling the camera must be guided by spontaneous feeling and by discoveries made on the set. I for one have no patience with the growing method of having every camera-shot sketched beforehand so that director, cameraman and actors can work by rote. It destroys that spontaneity of feeling which is the essence of film art; though of course many films are so unimportant that it does not matter how they are shot: they never were alive at any moment.

To continue following our film through to its finish, you now have a rough assembly which is far overlength, the cutting of which was largely determined by the script and direction. But this is only a provisional arrangement. Everything depends on the final cutting, elimination and rearrangement. And the only compass to guide you in this final orchestration of images is your own feeling. The final test is to project the film on the screen and see how the arrangement you have made affects you. By this time you have grown weary of every foot of the film but you doggedly keep your feeling fresh as the only touchstone, until you have wearily said, "That's the best we can make of it." And I promise you disappointment in every film, for it is far removed from the perfection of imagination, as is everything that is realized.

Yet you have not finished with this scratched-and-tattered work-print, which now looks as tired as yourself. There are two final stages, sound and music recording, and finally the re-recording of the whole thing. Sound is a magic element and part of your design as a screen-writer or director has been the effect of sound. In the case of *This Land Is Mine,* which was directed by a great film-maker, Jean Renoir, one of the focal points of the drama was a railroad yard, and as we could not shoot the action in an actual railroad yard we determined to create it largely by sound. We spent endless days gathering sound-tracks and trying to orchestrate our sounds as carefully as if they were music. And finally came the scoring of the music itself, not a great deal of it but every bar important: choosing Mendelssohn here, Mehul there, original composition for the rest, and getting it re-recorded in a harmonious whole.

At last you have, say nine or ten thousand feet of image-film and a second sound-film of the same length synchronized to the split-second. Every frame of both films is numbered, corresponding with the thousands of feet of negative in the laboratory. You send your final work-prints to the laboratory, the negative is cut, the sound track printed alongside— and you receive your first composite print. And, if the composite print checks, your work is finished and the negative is shipped, ready for countless prints to be made and released through the theatres of the world. This is what you set out to make—or rather help to make—when you began writing your rough draft of a screenplay. And this is what you had to keep in mind all the wearisome while.

All the foregoing must sound tedious—and yet it has been only lightly touched upon. What it shows, and what I meant to show, is why film-makers must specialize. You could not have done this work alone, carried the film through all its successive creations. A hundred specialists have aided you and carried through the work. It is a vast collaboration in which, if you have ever achieved a satisfactory film, you must accept a humble part. Yet the collaboration must always have a dominant will and personality if the work is to be good. Sometimes two people can work together with such sympathy and shared attitude that they can achieve a common style; and these two people must, I believe, be the writer and director.

Undoubtedly this all seems to be an exhausting introduction to an anthology of screenplays, but I feel it is essential to an understanding of what screenplays are and what their intention is. They are not complete works in themselves, they are blueprints of projected films. Many factors may have intervened to make the finished films different from the designed illusion, for better or worse.

The most noticeable feature of a skillful screenplay is its terseness and bareness. This is because the eye is not there, the eye which fills and enriches. Nor does the screenwriter waste time with much descriptive matter or detailing of photographic moods. These have all been discussed at length with the director, art director and others. It is the writer's job to invent a story in terms of cinema or to translate an existing story into terms of cinema. He creates an approximate continuity of scenes and images, suggesting cinematic touches where he can. He will write "close-up" of a character without setting down the most important thing, which is what that character is feeling during that close-up. That is because the context will take care of that. If he is an artist the director will submit the actor to that experience while photographing the close-up, by playing the actual scene out of range of the camera.

Writing for the screen, if long practiced, also seduces one to write dialogue in a synoptic fashion, which may show itself to the eye when printed on a page, but should never reveal itself to the ear when spoken from the screen. Stage dialogue, no matter how wonderful in quality, cannot be directly shifted to the screen; it must be condensed, synopsized. The reason is obvious; on the stage the actor depends for projection upon the word: on the screen he relies upon visual projection. And it is hard to describe visual projection in a screenplay; that must be left to the director and cast. . . .

However, almost everyone who is seriously interested in the cinema has seen *The Informer* on the screen, and as the film projects the screenplay with great fidelity I am prompted by Mr. Gassner to explain the method by which I translated Mr. O'Flaherty's novel into the language of film. In 1935 this was in a certain sense an experimental film; some new method had to be found by which to make the psychological action photographic. At that time I had not yet clarified and formulated for myself the principles of screenwriting, and many of my ideas were arrived at instinctively. I had an able mentor as well as collaborator in the person of John Ford and I had begun to catch his instinctive feeling about film. I can see now that I sought and found a series of symbols to make visual the tragic psychology of the informer, in this case a primitive man of powerful hungers. The whole action was to be played out in one foggy night, for the fog was symbolic of the groping primitive mind: it is really a mental fog in which he moves and dies. A poster offering a reward for information concerning Gypo's friend became the symbol of the evil idea of betrayal, and it blows along the street, following Gypo; it will not leave him alone. It catches on his leg and he kicks it off. But still it follows him and he sees it like a phantom in the air when he unexceptedly comes upon his fugitive friend.

So it goes all through the script; some of the symbolism is obvious, much of it concealed except from the close observer. The officer uses a stick when he pushes the blood-money to Gypo at headquarters, symbolic of contempt. The informer encounters a blind man in the dark fog outside and grips his throat in sudden guilt. The blind man is a symbol of the brute conscience, and Gypo releases him when he discovers the man cannot see. But as Gypo goes on to drown his conscience in drink, the tapping of the blind man's stick follows him; we hear it without seeing the blind man as Gypo hears his guilt pursuing him in his own soul. Later when he comes face to face with his conscience for a terrifying moment he tries to buy it off—by giving the blind man a couple of pounds, a lordly sum. . . . But I shall not continue this account of a screenplay that cannot be presented in this book. Sufficient to say that the method of adaptation in this instance was by a cumulative symbolism, to the very last scene where Gypo addresses the carven Christ, by which the psychology of a man could be made manifest in photographic terms. In this case I believe the method was successful.—I might add that I transferred the action of the drama from its original, rather special setting to a larger and more dramatic conflict which had national connotations. Whether that was any gain I do not know. Size of conflict in itself I hold to be unimportant. It is the size of characters within a conflict and how deeply they are probed that matters.

So much for the adaptation. For an example of an original screenplay you may examine *This Land Is Mine*. It is not easy to trace the origin of a story. It is easier to say that a work of fiction happens. But that is not exact, for a story comes into existence because of some inner necessity of the individual. Every human being contains creative energy, he wants to make something. A man may make a chair, or a pair of shoes, a masterpiece of painting, or a pulp-magazine story; precisely what he makes is dictated by his imagination, temperament, experience and training. But the act of creation is dictated by desire. I should imagine this runs through the universe as a law, since it is so with man, and man is part of the universe. If the Supreme Will desires to build a Universe, the Universe will "happen." It is all a matter of the degree of intensity of desire. A story-teller is passionately interested in human beings and their endless conflicts with their fates, and he is filled with desire to make some intelligible arrangement out of the chaos of life, just as the chairmaker desires to make some useful and beautiful arrangement out of wood. Frustrate those creative desires in man and his forces will be turned toward destruction: for energy cannot remain unexpended, it is not static, it must swing one way or another.

That is one aspect of the motivation of the story-teller. Another motive is the desire to entertain, to communicate one's own personality by holding the delighted attention of others. This might appear to be nothing more than egotism, yet it can rise above self and have an exalted purpose. Jesus of Nazareth could have chosen simply to express Himself in moral precepts; but like a great Poet he chose the form of the parable, wonderful short stories that entertained and clothed the moral precept in an eternal form. It is not sufficient to catch man's mind, you must also catch the imaginative faculties of his mind.

Yet stories for the purpose of entertainment alone are commonplace fiction and can only be redeemed by a dazzling style, a sheer delight in the materials of story-telling, a touch of the poet. The cinema is only in its infancy as an art form, and its usual fate so far has been to be used only for entertainment and making money. Because it is a very costly medium it will continue to be employed for making money until money ceases to be the great desire of the people of the world. Most motion pictures are mere entertainment and accordingly the screenwriter can work only with half of himself: his satisfaction must usually be in artistry of manner, skill in the way he accomplishes his work, without much regard for the content of the film. For this reason the story of serious intention can rarely be written within a film studio; and for this reason serious writers in other fields, novelists and dramatists, have given great aid to the development of the cinema. For the powers-that-be will buy the film rights of a serious novel if it seems to have enough readers, and though the contents of the novel are sometimes perverted by film censorship or bad taste, enough remains to make a notable motion picture. But the screenwriter who desires to make an original story has no readers, at least not for the projected story. If the story proposes to make a serious statement beyond mere entertaining it will seem off the beaten track and the writer will very likely meet opposition. It is for this reason and this reason alone that so few stories of any account *originate* within Hollywood. In France, before the war, the film-makers were largely their own entrepreneurs and for this reason produced many brilliant original works. They were story-tellers functioning freely in the new medium of film.

Nevertheless the serious film-writer cannot resign himself to Hollywood's barriers against original work designed for the screen. The average Hollywood entrepreneur is an intelligent man, and it is up to writers and directors to prove to him that films which probe into the chaos of life can be successful. John Ford made *The Informer* in spite of studio resistance; even after its completion it was held to be a failure and a waste of money by certain entrepreneurs. But the film did go out and make a profit. There *was* an audience for the realistic film. In spite of this and other instances I will say in all fairness that usually the studio heads have been right and the film-makers wrong: because usually the film-makers have not measured up to their task and their responsibilities when granted freedom. They have not measured up or they have wanted both money and freedom, which are incompatible. It is an axiom that no one will pay you to be a free artist. You are hired for profit—that is common sense. Very well, then, you must stop working for salary, you must devote yourself to the task in hand as do the novelist and dramatist, and only be recompensed if the film makes a profit. Economically I believe the writer and director will fare even better with this arrangement than under the salary system. Spiritually they will become whole men and work with integrity.

[1959]

ANDREW SARRIS

Notes on
the Auteur Theory in 1962

I call these sketches Shadowgraphs, partly by the designation to remind you at once that they derive from the darker side of life, partly
because, like other shadowgraphs, they are not directly visible. When
I take a shadowgraph in my hand, it makes no impression on me,
and gives me no clear conception of it. Only when I hold it up opposite the wall, and now look not directly at it, but at that which
appears on the wall, am I able to see it. So also with the picture I
wish to show here, an inward picture that does not become perceptible until I see it through the external. This external is perhaps not
quite unobtrusive, but, not until I look through it, do I discover that
inner picture that I desire to show you, an inner picture too delicately drawn to be outwardly visible, woven as it is of the tenderest
moods of the soul.

SøREN KIERKEGAARD, in *Either/Or*

An exhibitor once asked me if an old film I had recommended
was *really* good or good only according to the *auteur* theory. I appreciate
the distinction. Like the alchemists of old, *auteur* critics are notorious
for rationalizing leaden clinkers into golden nuggets. Their judgments
are seldom vindicated, because few spectators are conditioned to perceive
in individual works the organic unity of a director's career. On a given
evening, a film by John Ford must take its chances as if it were a film by
Henry King. Am I implying that the weakest Ford is superior to the
strongest King? Yes! This kind of unqualified affirmation seems to reduce
the *auteur* theory to a game of aesthetic solitaire with all the cards turned
face up. By *auteur* rules, the Fords will come up aces as invariably as the

From *Film Culture*, no. 27 (Winter, 1962–63). Reprinted by permission
of Andrew Sarris.

Kings will come up with deuces. Presumably, we can all go home as soon as the directorial signature is flashed on the screen. To those who linger, *The Gunfighter* (King 1950) may appear worthier than *Flesh* (Ford 1932). (And how deeply one must burrow to undermine Ford!) No matter. The *auteur* theory is unyielding. If, by definition, Ford is invariably superior to King, any evidence to the contrary is merely an optical illusion. Now what could be sillier than this inflexible attitude? Let us abandon the absurdities of the *auteur* theory so that we may return to the chaos of common sense.

My labored performance as devil's advocate notwithstanding, I intend to praise the *auteur* theory, not to bury it. At the very least, I would like to grant the condemned system a hearing before its execution. The trial has dragged on for years, I know, and everyone is now bored by the abstract reasoning involved. I have little in the way of new evidence or new arguments, but I would like to change some of my previous testimony. What follows is, consequently, less a manifesto than a credo, a somewhat disorganized credo, to be sure, expressed in formless notes rather than in formal brief.

I. AIMEZ-VOUS BRAHMS?

Goethe? Shakespeare? Everything signed with their names is considered good, and one wracks one's brains to find beauty in their stupidities and failures, thus distorting the general taste. All these great talents, the Goethes, the Shakespeares, the Beethovens, the Michelangelos, created, side by side with their masterpieces, works not merely mediocre, but quite simply frightful.

LEO TOLSTOY, *Journal*, 1895–99

The preceding quotation prefaces the late André Bazin's famous critique of "*la politique des auteurs*," which appeared in the *Cahiers du Cinéma* of April, 1957. Because no comparably lucid statement opposing the *politique* has appeared since that time, I would like to discuss some of Bazin's arguments with reference to the current situation. (I except, of course, Richard Roud's penetrating article "The French Line," which dealt mainly with the post-*Nouvelle Vague* situation when the *politique* had degenerated into McMahonism.)

As Tolstoy's observation indicates, *la politique des auteurs* antedates the cinema. For centuries, the Elizabethan *politique* has decreed the reading of every Shakespearean play before any encounter with the Jonsonian repertory. At some point between *Timon of Athens* and *Volpone*, this procedure is patently unfair to Jonson's reputation. But not really. On the most superficial level of artistic reputations, the *auteur* theory is merely a figure of speech. If the man in the street could not invoke Shakespeare's name as an identifiable cultural reference, he would probably have less contact with all things artistic. The Shakespearean scholar, by contrast, will always be driven to explore the surrounding terrain, with the result that all the Elizabethan dramatists gain more rather than less recognition through the pre-eminence of one of their number. Therefore, on balance, the *politique*, as a figure of speech, does more good than harm.

Occasionally, some iconoclast will attempt to demonstrate the fallacy of this figure of speech. We will be solemnly informed that *The Gambler* was a potboiler for Dostoyevsky in the most literal sense of the word. In Jacques Rivette's *Paris Nous Appartient*, Jean-Claude Brialy asks Betty Schneider if she would still admire *Pericles* if it were not signed by Shakespeare. Zealous musicologists have played *Wellington's Victory* so often as an example of inferior Beethoven that I have grown fond of the piece, atrocious as it is. The trouble with such iconoclasm is that it presupposes an encyclopedic awareness of the *auteur* in question. If one is familiar with every Beethoven composition, *Wellington's Victory*, in itself, will hardly tip the scale toward Mozart, Bach, or Schubert. Yet that is the issue raised by the *auteur* theory. If not Beethoven, who? And why? Let us say that the *politique* for composers went Mozart, Beethoven, Bach, and Schubert. Each composer would represent a task force of compositions, arrayed by type and quality with the mighty battleships and aircraft carriers flanked by flotillas of cruisers, destroyers, and mine sweepers. When the Mozart task force collides with the Beethoven task force, symphonies roar against symphonies, quartets maneuver against quartets, and it is simply no contest with the operas. As a single force, Beethoven's nine symphonies, outgun any nine of Mozart's forty-one symphonies, both sets of quartets are almost on a par with Schubert's, but *The Magic Flute, The Marriage of Figaro,* and *Don Giovanni* will blow poor *Fidelio* out of the water. Then, of course, there is Bach with an entirely different deployment of composition and instrumentation. The Haydn and Handel cultists are moored in their inlets ready to join the fray, and the moderns with their nuclear noises are still mobilizing their forces.

It can be argued that any exact ranking of artists is arbitrary and pointless. Arbitrary up to a point, perhaps, but pointless, no. Even Bazin concedes the polemical value of the *politique*. Many film critics would rather not commit themselves to specific rankings ostensibly because every film should be judged on its own merits. In many instances, this reticence masks the critic's condescension to the medium. Because it has not been firmly established that the cinema is an art at all, it requires cultural audacity to establish a pantheon for film directors. Without such audacity, I see little point in being a film critic. Anyway, is it possible to honor a work of art without honoring the artist involved? I think not. Of course, any idiot can erect a pantheon out of hearsay and gossip. Without specifying any work, the Saganesque seducer will ask quite cynically, "Aimez-vous Brahms?" The fact that Brahms is included in the pantheon of high-brow pickups does not invalidate the industrious criticism that justifies the composer as a figure of speech.

Unfortunately, some critics have embraced the *auteur* theory as a short-cut to film scholarship. With a "you-see-it-or-you-don't" attitude toward the reader, the particularly lazy *auteur* critic can save himself the drudgery of communication and explanation. Indeed, at their worst, *auteur* critiques are less meaningful than the straight-forward plot reviews that pass for criticism in America. Without the necessary research and analysis, the *auteur* theory can degenerate into the kind of snobbish racket that is associated with the merchandising of paintings.

It was largely against the inadequate theoretical formulation of *la politique des auteurs* that Bazin was reacting in his friendly critique. (Henceforth, I will abbreviate *la politique des auteurs* as the *auteur* theory to avoid confusion.) Bazin introduces his arguments within the context of a family quarrel over the editorial policies of *Cahiers*. He fears that, by assigning reviews to admirers of given directors, notably, Alfred Hitchcock, Jean Renoir, Roberto Rossellini, Fritz Lang, Howard Hawks, and Nicholas Ray, every work, major and minor, of these exalted figures is made to radiate the same beauties of style and meaning. Specifically, Bazin notes a distortion when the kindly indulgence accorded the imperfect work of a Minnelli is coldly withheld from the imperfect work of Huston. The inherent bias of the *auteur* theory magnifies the gap between the two films.

I would make two points here. First, Bazin's greatness as a critic, (and I believe strongly that he was the greatest film critic who ever lived) rested in his disinterested conception of the cinema as a universal entity. It follows that he would react against a theory that cultivated what he felt were inaccurate judgments for the sake of dramatic paradoxes. He was, if anything, generous to a fault, seeking in every film some vestige of the cinematic art. That he would seek justice for Huston vis-à-vis Minnelli on even the secondary levels of creation indicates the scrupulousness of his critical personality.

However, my second point would seem to contradict my first. Bazin was wrong in this instance, insofar as any critic can be said to be wrong in retrospect. We are dealing here with Minnelli in his *Lust for Life* period and Huston in his *Moby Dick* period. Both films can be considered failures on almost any level. The miscasting alone is disastrous. The snarling force of Kirk Douglas as the tormented Van Gogh, the brutish insensibility of Anthony Quinn as Gauguin, and the nervously scraping tension between these two absurdly limited actors, deface Minnelli's meticulously objective decor, itself inappropriate for the mood of its subject. The director's presentation of the paintings themselves is singularly unperceptive in the repeated failure to maintain the proper optical distance from canvases that arouse the spectator less by their detailed draughtsmanship than by the shock of a *gestalt* wholeness. As for *Moby Dick*, Gregory Peck's Ahab deliberates long enough to let all the demons flee the Pequod, taking Melville's Lear-like fantasies with them. Huston's epic technique with its casually shifting camera viewpoint then drifts on an intellectually becalmed sea toward a fitting rendezvous with a rubber whale. These two films are neither the best nor the worst of their time. The question is: Which deserves the harder review? And there's the rub. At the time, Huston's stock in America was higher than Minnelli's. Most critics expected Huston to do "big" things, and, if they thought about it at all, expected Minnelli to stick to "small" things like musicals. Although neither film was a critical failure, audiences stayed away in large enough numbers to make the cultural respectability of the projects suspect. On the whole, *Lust for Life* was more successful with the audiences it did reach than was *Moby Dick*.

In retrospect, *Moby Dick* represents the turning downward of Huston as a director to be taken seriously. By contrast, *Lust for Life* is simply an isolated episode in the erratic career of an interesting stylist. The exact size of Minnelli's talent may inspire controversy, but it does represent something in the cinema today. Huston is virtually a forgotten man with a few actors' classics behind him surviving as the ruins of a once-promising career. Both Eric Rohmer, who denigrated Huston in 1957, and Jean Domarchi, who was kind to Minnelli that same year, somehow saw the future more clearly on an *auteur* level than did Bazin. As Santayana has remarked: "It is a great advantage for a system of philosophy to be substantially true." If the *auteur* critics of the 1950's had not scored so many coups of clairvoyance, the *auteur* theory would not be worth discussing in the 1960's. I must add that, at the time, I would have agreed with Bazin on this and every other objection to the *auteur* theory, but subsequent history, that history about which Bazin was always so mystical, has substantially confirmed most of the principles of the *auteur* theory. Ironically, most of the original supporters of the *auteur* theory have now abandoned it. Some have discovered more useful *politiques* as directors and would-be directors. Others have succumbed to a European-oriented pragmatism where intention is now more nearly equal to talent in critical relevance. Luc Moullet's belated discovery that Samuel Fuller was, in fact, fifty years old, signaled a reorientation of *Cahiers* away from the American cinema. (The handwriting was already on the wall when Truffaut remarked recently that, whereas he and his colleagues had "discovered" *auteurs,* his successors have "invented" them.)

Bazin then explores the implications of Giraudoux's epigram: "There are no works; there are only authors." Truffaut has seized upon this paradox as the battle cry of *la politique des auteurs.* Bazin casually demonstrates how the contrary can be argued with equal probability of truth or error. He subsequently dredges up the equivalents of *Wellington's Victory* for Voltaire, Beaumarchais, Flaubert, and Gide to document his point. Bazin then yields some ground to Rohmer's argument that the history of art does not confirm the decline with age of authentic geniuses like Titian, Rembrandt, Beethoven, or nearer to us, Bonnard, Matisse, and Stravinsky. Bazin agrees with Rohmer that it is inconsistent to attribute senility only to aging film directors while, at the same time, honoring the gnarled austerity of Rembrandt's later style. This is one of the crucial propositions of the *auteur* theory, because it refutes the popular theory of decline for aging giants like Renoir and Chaplin and asserts, instead, that, as a director grows older, he is likely to become more profoundly personal than most audiences and critics can appreciate. However, Bazin immediately retrieves his lost ground by arguing that, whereas the senility of directors is no longer at issue, the evolution of an art form is. Where directors fail and fall is in the realm not of psychology but of history. If a director fails to keep pace with the development of his medium, his work will become obsolescent. What seems like senility is, in reality, a disharmony between the subjective inspiration of the director and the objective evolution of the medium. By making this distinction between the subjective capability of an *auteur* and the objective value of a work in film history, Bazin reinforces the popular impression that the Griffith of *Birth of a Nation* is superior to the Griffith of *Abraham Lincoln* in the perspective of timing, which similarly distinguishes the Eisenstein of *Potemkin* from the Eisenstein of *Ivan the Terrible,* the Renoir of *La Grande Illusion* from the Renoir of *Picnic in the Grass,* and the Welles of *Citizen Kane* from the Welles of *Mr. Arkadin.*

I have embroidered Bazin's actual examples for the sake of greater contact with the American scene. In fact, Bazin implicitly denies a decline in the later works of Chaplin and Renoir and never mentions Griffith. He suggests circuitously that Hawks's *Scarface* is clearly superior to Hawks's *Gentlemen Prefer Blondes,* although the *auteur* critics would argue the contrary. Bazin is particularly critical of Rivette's circular reasoning on *Monkey Business* as the proof of Hawks's genius. "One sees the danger," Bazin warns, "which is an aesthetic cult of personality."

Bazin's taste, it should be noted, was far more discriminating than that of American film historians. Films Bazin cites as unquestionable classics are still quite debatable here in America. After all, *Citizen Kane* was originally panned by James Agee, Richard Griffith, and Bosley Crowther, and *Scarface* has never been regarded as one of the landmarks of the American cinema by native critics. I would say that the American public has been ahead of its critics on both *Kane* and *Scarface*. Thus, to argue against the *auteur* theory in America is to assume that we have anyone of Bazin's sensibility and dedication to provide an alternative, and we simply don't.

Bazin, finally, concentrates on the American cinema, which invariably serves as the decisive battleground of the *auteur* theory, whether over *Monkey Business,* or *Party Girl.* Unlike most "serious" American critics, Bazin likes Hollywood films, but not solely because of the talent of this or that director. For Bazin, the distinctively American comedy, western, and gangster genres have their own mystiques apart from the personalities of the directors concerned. How can one review an Anthony Mann western, Bazin asks, as if it were not an expression of the genre's conventions. Not that Bazin dislikes Anthony Mann's westerns. He is more concerned with otherwise admirable westerns that the *auteur* theory rejects because their directors happen to be unfashionable. Again, Bazin's critical generosity comes to the fore against the negative aspects of the *auteur* theory.

Some of Bazin's arguments tend to overlap each other as if to counter rebuttals from any direction. He argues, in turn, that the cinema is less individualistic an art than painting or literature, that Hollywood is less individualistic than other cinemas, and that, even so, the *auteur* theory never really applies anywhere. In upholding historical determinism, Bazin goes so far as to speculate that, if Racine had lived in Voltaire's century, it is unlikely that Racine's tragedies would have been any more inspired than Voltaire's. Presumably, the Age of Reason would have stifled Racine's neoclassical impulses. Perhaps. Perhaps not. Bazin's hypothesis can hardly be argued to a verifiable conclusion, but I suspect somewhat greater reciprocity between an artist and his *zeitgeist* than Bazin would allow. He mentions, more than once and in other contexts, capitalism's influence on the cinema. Without denying this influence, I still find it impossible to attribute X directors and Y films to any particular system or culture. Why should the Italian cinema be superior to the German cinema after one war, when the reverse was true after the previous one? As for artists conforming to the spirit of their age, that spirit is often expressed in contradictions, whether between Stravinsky and Sibelius, Fielding and Richardson, Picasso and Matisse, Chateaubriand and Stendhal. Even if the artist does not spring from the idealized head of Zeus, free of the embryonic stains of history, history itself is profoundly affected by his arrival. If we cannot imagine Griffith's *October* or Eisenstein's *Birth of a*

Nation because we find it difficult to transpose one artist's unifying conceptions of Lee and Lincoln to the other's dialectical conceptions of Lenin and Kerensky, we are, nevertheless, compelled to recognize other differences in the personalities of these two pioneers beyond their respective cultural complexes. It is with these latter differences that the *auteur* theory is most deeply concerned. If directors and other artists cannot be wrenched from their historical environments, aesthetics is reduced to a subordinate branch of ethnography.

I have not done full justice to the subtlety of Bazin's reasoning and to the civilized skepticism with which he propounds his own arguments as slight probabilities rather than absolute certainties. Contemporary opponents of the *auteur* theory may feel that Bazin himself is suspect as a member of the *Cahiers* family. After all, Bazin does express qualified approval of the *auteur* theory as a relatively objective method of evaluating films apart from the subjective perils of impressionistic and ideological criticism. Better to analyze the director's personality than the critic's nerve centers or politics. Nevertheless, Bazin makes his stand clear by concluding: "This is not to deny the role of the author, but to restore to him the preposition without which the noun is only a limp concept. 'Author,' undoubtedly, but of what?"

Bazin's syntactical flourish raises an interesting problem in English usage. The French preposition "de" serves many functions, but among others, those of possession and authorship. In English the preposition "by" once created a scandal in the American film industry when Otto Preminger had the temerity to advertise *The Man with the Golden Arm* as a film "by Otto Preminger." Novelist Nelson Algren and the Screenwriters' Guild raised such an outcry that the offending preposition was deleted. Even the noun "author" (which I cunningly mask as *"auteur"*) has a literary connotation in English. In general conversations, an "author" is invariably taken to be a writer. Since "by" is a preposition of authorship and not of ownership like the ambiguous "de," the fact that Preminger both produced and directed *The Man with the Golden Arm* did not entitle him in America to the preposition "by." No one would have objected to the possessive form: "Otto Preminger's *The Man with the Golden Arm*." But, (even in this case, a novelist of sufficient reputation is usually honored with the possessive designation. Now, this is hardly the case in France, where *The Red and the Black* is advertised as "un film de Claude Autant-Lara." In America, "directed by" is all the director can claim, when he is not also a well-known producer like Alfred Hitchcock or Cecil B. deMille.

Since most American film critics are oriented toward literature or journalism, rather than toward future film-making, most American film criticism is directed toward the script instead of toward the screen. The writer-hero in *Sunset Boulevard* complains that people don't realize that someone "writes a picture; they think the actors make it up as they go along." It would never occur to this writer or most of his colleagues that people are even less aware of the director's function.

Of course, the much-abused man in the street has a good excuse not to be aware of the *auteur* theory even as a figure of speech. Even on the so-called classic level, he is not encouraged to ask "Aimez-vous Griffith?" or "Aimez-vous Eisenstein?" Instead, it is which Griffith or which Eisenstein? As for less acclaimed directors, he is lucky to find their names in the fourth paragraph of the typical review. I doubt that most American film critics really believe that an indifferently directed film is comparable to an indifferently written book. However, there is little point in wailing at the Philistines on this issue, particularly when some progress is being made in telling one director from another, at least when the film comes from abroad. The Fellini, Bergman, Kurosawa, and Antonioni promotions have helped push more directors up to the first paragraph of a review, even ahead of the plot synopsis. So, we mustn't complain.

Where I wish to redirect the argument is toward the relative position of the American cinema as opposed to the foreign cinema. Some critics have advised me that the *auteur* theory only applies to a small number of artists who make personal films, not to the run-of-the-mill Hollywood director who takes whatever assignment is available. Like most Americans who take films seriously, I have always felt a cultural inferiority complex about Hollywood. Just a few years ago, I would have thought it unthinkable to speak in the same breath of a "commercial" director like Hitchcock and a "pure" director like Bresson. Even today, *Sight and Sound* uses different type sizes for Bresson and Hitchcock films. After years of tortured revaluation, I am now prepared to stake my critical reputation, such as it is, on the proposition that Alfred Hitchcock is artistically superior to Robert Bresson by every criterion of excellence and, further, that, film for film, director for director, the American cinema has been consistently superior to that of the rest of the world from 1915 through 1962. Consequently, I now regard the *auteur* theory primarily as a critical device for recording the history of the American cinema, the only cinema in the world worth exploring in depth beneath the frosting of a few great directors at the top.

These propositions remain to be proven and, I hope, debated. The proof will be difficult because direction in the cinema is a nebulous force in literary terms. In addition to its own jargon, the director's craft often pulls in the related jargon of music, painting, sculpture, dance, literature, theatre, architecture, all in a generally futile attempt to describe the indescribable. What is it the old jazz man says of his art? If you gotta ask what it is, it ain't? Well, the cinema is like that. Criticism can only attempt an approximation, a reasonable preponderance of accuracy over inaccuracy. I know the exceptions to the *auteur* theory as well as anyone. I can feel the human attraction of an audience going one way when I am going the other. The temptations of cynicism, common sense, and facile culture-mongering are always very strong, but, somehow, I feel that the *auteur theory* is the only hope for extending the appreciation of personal qualities in the cinema. By grouping and evaluating films according to directors, the critic can rescue individual achievements from an unjustifiable anonymity. If medieval architects and African sculptors are anonymous today, it is not because they deserved to be. When Ingmar Bergman bemoans the alienation of the modern artist from the collective spirit that rebuilt the cathedral at Chartres, he is only dramatizing his own individuality for an age that has rewarded him handsomely for the travail of his alienation. There is no justification for penalizing Hollywood directors for the sake of collective mythology. So, invective aside, "Aimez-vous Cukor?"

II. WHAT IS THE *AUTEUR* THEORY?

As far as I know, there is no definition of the *auteur* theory in the English language, that is, by any American or British critic. Truffaut has recently gone to great pains to emphasize that the *auteur* theory was merely a polemical weapon for a given time and a given place, and I am willing to take him at his word. But, lest I be accused of misappropriating a theory no one wants anymore, I will give the *Cahiers* critics full credit for the original formulation of an idea that reshaped my thinking on the cinema. First of all, how does the *auteur* theory differ from a straightforward theory of directors. Ian Cameron's article "Films, Directors, and Critics," in *Movie* of September, 1962, makes an interesting comment on this issue: "The assumption that underlies all the writing in *Movie* is that the director is the author of a film, the person who gives it any distinctive quality. There are quite large exceptions, with which I shall deal later." So far, so good, at least for the *auteur* theory, which even allows for exceptions. However, Cameron continues: "On the whole, we accept the cinema of directors, although without going to the farthest-out extremes of the *la politique des auteurs*, which makes it difficult to think of a bad director making a good film and almost impossible to think of a good director making a bad one." We are back to Bazin again, although Cameron naturally uses different examples. That three otherwise divergent critics like Bazin, Roud, and Cameron make essentially the same point about the *auteur* theory suggests a common fear of its abuses. I believe there is a misunderstanding here about what the *auteur* theory actually claims, particularly since the theory itself is so vague at the present time.

First of all, the *auteur* theory, at least as I understand it and now intend to express it, claims neither the gift of prophecy nor the option of extracinematic perception. Directors, even *auteurs*, do not always run true to form, and the critic can never assume that a bad director will always make a bad film. No, not always, but almost always, and that is the point. What is a bad director, but a director who has made many bad films? What is the problem then? Simply this: The badness of a director is not necessarily considered the badness of a film. If Joseph Pevney directed Garbo, Cherkassov, Olivier, Belmondo, and Harriet Andersson in *The Cherry Orchard*, the resulting spectacle might not be entirely devoid of merit with so many subsidiary *auteurs* to cover up for Joe. In fact, with this cast and this literary property, a Lumet might be safer than a Welles. The realities of casting apply to directors as well as to actors, but the *auteur* theory would demand the gamble with Welles, if he were willing.

Marlon Brando has shown us that a film can be made without a director. Indeed, *One-Eyed Jacks* is more entertaining than many films with directors. A director-conscious critic would find it difficult to say anything good or bad about direction that is nonexistent. One can talk here about photography, editing, acting, but not direction. The film has personality, but, like *The Longest Day* and *Mutiny on the Bounty*, it is a cipher directorially. Obviously, the *auteur* theory cannot possibly cover every vagrant charm of the cinema. Nevertheless, the first premise of the *auteur* theory is the technical competence of a director as a criterion of value. A badly directed or an undirected film has no importance in a critical scale of values, but one can make interesting conversation about the subject, the script, the acting, the color, the photography, the editing, the music, the costumes, the decor, and so forth. That is the nature of the medium. You always get more for your money than mere art. Now, by the *auteur* theory, if a director has no technical competence, no elementary flair for the cinema, he is automatically cast out from the pantheon of directors. A great director has to be at least a good director. This is true in any art. What constitutes directorial talent is more difficult to define abstractly. There is less disagreement, however, on this first level of the *auteur* theory than there will be later.

The second premise of the *auteur* theory is the distinguishable personality of the director as a criterion of value. Over a group of films, a director must exhibit certain recurring characteristics of style, which serve as his signature. The way a film looks and moves should have some relationship to the way a director thinks and feels. This is an area where American directors are generally superior to foreign directors. Because so much of the American cinema is commissioned, a director is forced to express his personality through the visual treatment of material rather than through the literary content of the material. A Cukor, who works with all sorts of projects, has a more developed abstract style than a Bergman, who is free to develop his own scripts. Not that Bergman lacks personality, but his work has declined with the depletion of his ideas largely because his technique never equaled his sensibility. Joseph L. Mankiewicz and Billy Wilder are other examples of writer-directors without adequate technical mastery. By contrast, Douglas Sirk and Otto Preminger have moved up the scale because their miscellaneous projects reveal a stylistic consistency.

The third and ultimate premise of the *auteur* theory is concerned with interior meaning, the ultimate glory of the cinema as an art. Interior meaning is extrapolated from the tension between a director's personality and his material. This conception of interior meaning comes close to what Astruc defines as *mise en scène*, but not quite. It is not quite the vision of the world a director projects nor quite his attitude toward life. It is ambiguous, in any literary sense, because part of it is imbedded in the stuff of the cinema and cannot be rendered in noncinematic terms. Truffaut has called it the temperature of the director on the set, and that is a close approximation of its professional aspect. Dare I come out and say what I think it to be is an *élan* of the soul?

Lest I seem unduly mystical, let me hasten to add that all I mean by "soul" is that intangible difference between one personality and another, all other things being equal. Sometimes, this difference is expressed by no more than a beat's hesitation in the rhythm of a film. In one sequence of *La Règle du Jeu*, Renoir gallops up the stairs, turns to his right with a lurching movement, stops in hop-like uncertainty when his name is called by a coquettish maid, and, then, with marvelous postreflex continuity, resumes his bearishly shambling journey to the heroine's boudoir. If I could describe the musical grace note of that momentary suspension, and I can't, I might be able to provide a more precise definition of the *auteur* theory. As it is, all I can do is point at the specific beauties of interior meaning on the screen and, later, catalogue the moments of recognition.

The three premises of the *auteur* theory may be visualized as three concentric circles: the outer circle as technique; the middle circle, personal style; and the inner circle, interior meaning. The corresponding roles of the director may be designated as those of a technician, a stylist, and an *auteur*. There is no prescribed course by which a director passes through the three circles. Godard once remarked that Visconti had evolved from a *metteur en scène* to an *auteur,* whereas Rossellini had evolved from an *auteur* to a *metteur en scène*. From opposite directions, they emerged with comparable status. Minnelli began and remained in the second circle as a stylist; Buñuel was an *auteur* even before he had assembled the technique of the first circle. Technique is simply the ability to put a film together with some clarity and coherence. Nowadays, it is possible to become a director without knowing too much about the technical side, even the crucial functions of photography and editing. An expert production crew could probably cover up for a chimpanzee in the director's chair. How do you tell the genuine director from the quasi-chimpanzee? After a given number of films, a pattern is established.

In fact, the *auteur* theory itself is a pattern theory in constant flux. I would never endorse a Ptolemaic constellation of directors in a fixed orbit. At the moment, my list of *auteurs* runs something like this through the first twenty: Ophuls, Renoir, Mizoguchi, Hitchcock, Chaplin, Ford, Welles, Dreyer, Rossellini, Murnau, Griffith, Sternberg, Eisenstein, von Stroheim, Buñuel, Bresson, Hawks, Lang, Flaherty, Vigo. This list is somewhat weighted toward seniority and established reputations. In time, some of these *auteurs* will rise, some will fall, and some will be displaced either by new directors or rediscovered ancients. Again, the exact order is less important than the specific definitions of these and as many as two hundred other potential *auteurs*. I would hardly expect any critic in the world fully to endorse this list, especially on faith. Only after thousands of films have been revaluated, will any personal pantheon have a reasonably objective validity. The task of validating the *auteur* theory is an enormous one, and the end will never be in sight. Meanwhile, the *auteur* habit of collecting random films in directional bundles will serve posterity with at least a tentative classification.

Although the *auteur* theory emphasizes the body of a director's work rather than isolated masterpieces, it is expected of great directors that they make great films every so often. The only possible exception to this rule I can think of is Abel Gance, whose greatness is largely a function of his aspiration. Even with Gance, *La Roue* is as close to being a great film as any single work of Flaherty's. Not that single works matter that much. As Renoir has observed, a director spends his life on variations of the same film.

Two recent films—*Boccaccio '70* and *The Seven Capital Sins*—unwittingly reinforce the *auteur* theory by confirming the relative standing of the many directors involved. If I had not seen either film, I would have anticipated that the order of merit in *Boccaccio '70* would be Visconti, Fellini, and De Sica, and in *The Seven Capital Sins* Godard, Chabrol, Demy, Vadim, De Broca, Molinaro. (Dhomme, Ionesco's stage director and an unknown quantity in advance, turned out to be the worst of the lot.) There might be some argument about the relative badness of De Broca and Molinaro, but, otherwise, the directors ran true to form by almost any objective criterion of value. However, the main point here is that even in these frothy, ultracommercial servings of entertainment, the contribution of each director had less in common stylistically with the work of other directors on the project than with his own previous work.

Sometimes, a great deal of corn must be husked to yield a few kernels of internal meaning. I recently saw *Every Night at Eight*, one of the many maddeningly routine films Raoul Walsh has directed in his long career. This 1935 effort featured George Raft, Alice Faye, Frances Langford, and Patsy Kelly in one of those familiar plots about radio shows of the period. The film keeps moving along in the pleasantly unpretentious manner one would expect of Walsh until one incongruously intense scene with George Raft thrashing about in his sleep, revealing his inner fears in mumbling dream-talk. The girl he loves comes into the room in the midst of his unconscious avowals of feeling and listens sympathetically. This unusual scene was later amplified in *High Sierra* with Humphrey Bogart and Ida Lupino. The point is that one of the screen's most virile directors employed an essentially feminine narrative device to dramatize the emotional vulnerability of his heroes. If I had not been aware of Walsh in *Every Night at Eight*, the crucial link to *High Sierra* would have passed unnoticed. Such are the joys of the *auteur* theory.

[1962]

6

Message, Medium,
and Literary Art

The following sequence of stills illustrates some of the ways in which a filmmaker can manipulate the cinematic image to render mental state and to create tropes.

Figure 6.1 The Cabinet of Dr. Caligari, *an early expressionist film directed by Robert Wiene (1919). Museum of Modern Art/Film Stills Archive.*

Figure 6.2 The Cabinet of Dr. Caligari. *Museum of Modern Art/Film Stills Archive.*

Figure 6.3 The Trial *(1962), directed by Orson Welles. Museum of Modern Art/Film Stills Archive.*

Figure 6.4 The Trial. *Museum of Modern Art/Film Stills Archive.*

Figure 6.5 The Trial. *Museum of Modern Art/Film Stills Archive.*

OUTTAKES

What we are watching is, perhaps, the cinema's diversification into a variety of idioms. For the cinema's equivalent is not *literature*; its equivalent is *print*. The cinema is not an art-form. It is a medium, comprising art forms as diverse as print—i.e., ranging from the stream-of-consciousness novel and concrete poetry. It also includes communicating styles which have no connection whatsoever with art (in the usual sense of the word), or even entertainment, and correspond to journalism, technical manuals or textbooks. Soon, perhaps, such a thing as a "film critic" will seem as ridiculous as a "print-critic." There is no art of the cinema. Long live the cinema arts!

RAYMOND DURGNAT

Some time ago I travelled from York to London. In my compartment were an enterprising young English lady and a few American soldiers. They sang film songs from York to London. They never repeated themselves. I was amazed at such memory and I reflected sadly on the future of the human race.

J. P. MAYER

Of course [the cinema is] a marvelous toy. But I cannot bear it, because perhaps I am too "optical" by nature. I am an Eye-man. But the cinema disturbs one's vision. The speed of the movements and the rapid change of images force men to look continually from one to another. Sight does not flood one's consciousness. The cinema involves putting the eye into uniform, where before it was naked. . . . Films are iron shutters. . . . Real life is only a reflection of the dreams of poets. The strings of the lines of modern poets are endless strips of celluloid.

FRANZ KAFKA

The fact seems to be this: so long as we remain within one shot or scene and have no cut or dissolve, therefore no montage, the criteria of a moving picture are relevant, and painting and photography offer valuable suggestions; but once we cut, edit, and construct the film, the whole effort is to break down the quality of painting or photography, to effect something else. To effect what?

PAUL GOODMAN

259

The story goes that Thamus said many things to Theuth in praise or blame of the various arts . . . but when they came to the letters, "this invention, O king," said Theuth, "will make the Egyptians wiser and will improve their memories; for it is an elixir of memory and wisdom that I have discovered." But Thamus replied, "Most ingenious Theuth, one man has the ability to beget arts, but the ability to judge of their usefulness or harmfulness to their users belongs to another; and now you, who are the father of letters, have been led by your affection to ascribe to them a power the opposite of that which they really possess. For this invention will produce forgetfulness in the minds of those who learn to use it, because they will not practice their memory. Their trust in writing, produced by external characters which are no part of themselves, will discourage the use of their own memory within them. You have invented an elixir not of memory, but of reminding; and you offer your pupils the appearance of wisdom, not true wisdom, for they will read many things without instruction and will therefore seem to know many things, when they are for the most part ignorant and hard to get along with, since they are not wise, but only appear wise.

SOCRATES

There is no need to regard the cinema as a completely new art; in its fictional form it has the same purpose as the novel, just as the novel has the same purpose as the drama. Chekhov, writing of his fellow novelists remarked: "The best of them are realistic and paint life as it is, but because every line is permeated, as with a juice, by awareness of a purpose, you feel, besides life as it is, also life as it ought to be, and this captivates you." This description of an artist's theme has never, I think, been bettered. . . . Life as it is and life as it ought to be: let us take that as the only true subject for a film.

GRAHAM GREENE

How shall we incorporate some of our potential readers into our actual public? Books are inert. They act upon those who open them, but they can not open by themselves. There can be no question of popularizing; we would be literary morons, and in order to keep literature from falling into the pitfalls of propaganda we would be throwing it right in ourselves. So we must have recourse to new means. They already exist; the Americans have already adorned them with the name of "mass media"; these are the real resources at our disposal for conquering the virtual public—the newspaper, the radio, and the movies. Naturally, we have to squelch our scruples. To be sure, the book is the noblest, the most ancient of forms; to be sure, we will always have to return to it. But there is a literary art of radio, film, editorial, and reporting. There is no need to popularize. The film, by its very nature, speaks to crowds; it speaks to them about crowds and about their destiny. . . . We must learn to speak in images, to transpose the ideas of our books into these new languages.

JEAN-PAUL SARTRE

Good motion picture direction has little to do with literacy or cultivation in its conventional sense. Several of the most cultivated and literate gentlemen in the movies are among the most prosaic directors. They have brought with them a knowledge of other arts, which has blinded them to the essential quality of the camera. They think of the movies as a form of the theater, of literature, or of painting. It is none of these things. It demands at best a unique kind of imagination which parallels these arts but does not stem from them. It is true that the rigid economic organization of the modern studio demands the same kind of prevision and preparation on the part of the directors as on the part of any other creator. Even aside from urgencies of this kind, the St. Clairs, Lubitschs, Duponts, Eisensteins, are under the same imaginative necessity to organize their material as a Cézanne or Beethoven. But there the similarity ceases. Directors of this kind know that their greatest need is the power to seize reality—in its widest sense—and make it significant in forms of motion. This power, this understanding, is a gift by itself. It requires a special kind of eye, a special kind of feeling about the relationship between things and things, events and events, and an intuitive as well as empirical knowledge of how to make the camera catch what that eye sees and that imagination feels. It has nothing to do with words, as such, nor with history or politics or any of the traditional matters which are politely assumed to represent cultivation, and which so often debase the metal of the imagination.

The movie is in other words a new way in which to see life. It is a way born to meet the needs of a new life. It is a way of using the machine to see what the machine has done to human beings. It is for this reason that the best motion picture directors arise from strange backgrounds, with a secure grasp on techniques of living rather than on academic attitudes. They are not always preoccupied with proving that life is so small that it can be caught in the net of art. It is the pragmatic sanction hovering over them which offends academicians.

Ralph Block

The medium in which a work appears affects and shapes that work. The writers in this section examine the effects a medium has on an artist and how a medium influences the relationship of word and image, style and content, and artistic technique and practice. The attitudes of the writers in this section toward media vary widely: one will use issues of media to distinguish between film and literature and to warn against attempts by filmmakers to achieve with an image what can only be communicated through words; another sees communication through images signaling a new kind of cultural communication or art; yet another questions the whole notion that simple distinctions between verbal and visual art are valid at all.

261

In an article written in 1926 (just before the advent of sound), Virginia Woolf calls attention to the differences between words and the images in films, contending that cinematic images cannot have access to the suggestive and connotative power of words. Film's dependence on literature can only be disastrous to both since the alliance creates an unnatural division between eye and mind. Movies, she believes, provide thrills and sensations for the vulgar of society and ought not to attempt more.

W. R. Robinson sees the relationship between words and cinematic images in much the same way as Virginia Woolf but comes to somewhat different conclusions. Robinson connects the word (and the Word) to the notion of order and suggests that words form a self-enclosed system not directly perceptible to the senses. Movies, on the other hand, are all surface and provide an emotional rather than an intellectual experience. Like Woolf, he sees movies as without complexity and with no secondary level of significance. At the same time, Robinson sees both literature and film as enriched by the tension between word and image, and the rise of the movies he perceives as a sign of a larger struggle in culture between word and light.

George Bluestone focuses on a specific artistic device, the trope, and examines the way this device is manifested in print and film. Like Woolf, Bluestone points to the sophistication of the verbal metaphor ("packed symbolic thinking") and suggests that this kind of metaphor is peculiar to imaginative rather than visual activity. When made visual and literal, verbal metaphors become absurd. Although film is unable to render linguistic tropes, he explains that film has discovered a metaphoric ability of its own. Through editing, the film artist can use his plastic materials to render tropes which can emerge from a film's own setting.

First published in 1934, Erwin Panofsky's "Style and Medium in the Motion Pictures" provides the classic defense of film as a visual medium. Tracing the art of film from its beginning in non-literary sources, Panofsky explores the unique qualities within film itself which must be developed in the process of cinema's evolution. The qualities he finds most individual to film are the dynamization of space and the spatialization of time. Against the primary attributes of film form and style he juxtaposes the techniques and procedures of the dramatist, asking that film develop its own "unique and specific" resources.

Marshall McLuhan, on the other hand, sees parallels between watching movies and reading. Literary culture paves the way for the ability to accept the sequential advances of film, with book culture aiding film in its development. Those whose cultures are non-literate do not know how to "read" film. McLuhan finds that it is the business of the writer or the filmmaker to bring a person into the creator's own world, and the ability to enter a created world depends upon the kind of literary training provided by a culture.

Charles Eidsvik also suggests that films and books provide similar experiences, but points out that fuzzy semantics have prevented critics from recognizing literature as an art with more than one medium and film as a medium capable of containing many arts. Eidsvik contends that literature has never been a one-medium art; on the contrary, literature began as an oral art and then contributed to new media as they developed. Similarly, no single art form for film can be identified even though the narrative mode dominates by way of volume. Eidsvik strongly disagrees with Bluestone's distinctions between film as a perceptual art and print as a conceptual one, suggesting that scholars do not yet know enough to compare the structures of perception and the structures of verbal language.

VIRGINIA WOOLF

The Movies And Reality

People say that the savage no longer exists in us, that we are at
the fag-end of civilization, that everything has been said already, and
that it is too late to be ambitious. But these philosophers have presumably
forgotten the movies. They have never seen the savages of the twentieth
century watching the pictures. They have never sat themselves in front
of the screen and thought how, for all the clothes on their backs and the
carpets at their feet, no great distance separates them from those bright-
eyed, naked men who knocked two bars of iron together and heard in
that clangor a foretaste of the music of Mozart.

The bars in this case, of course, are so highly wrought and so covered over with accretions of alien matter that it is extremely difficult to
hear anything distinctly. All is hubble-bubble, swarm and chaos. We are
peering over the edge of a cauldron in which fragments of all shapes and
savors seem to simmer; now and again some vast form heaves itself up,
and seems about to haul itself out of chaos. Yet, at first sight, the art of
the cinema seems simple, even stupid. There is the King shaking hands
with a football team; there is Sir Thomas Lipton's yacht; there is Jack
Horner winning the Grand National. The eye licks it all up instantane-
ously, and the brain, agreeably titillated, settles down to watch things
happening without bestirring itself to think. For the ordinary eye, the
English unaesthetic eye, is a simple mechanism, which takes care that the
body does not fall down coal-holes, provides the brain with toys and
sweetmeats to keep it quiet, and can be trusted to go on behaving like a
competent nursemaid until the brain comes to the conclusion that it is
time to wake up. What is its surprise, then, to be roused suddenly in the
midst of its agreeable somnolence and asked for help? The eye is in difficulties. The eye wants help. The eye says to the brain, "Something is hap-

pening which I do not in the least understand. You are needed." Together
they look at the King, the boat, the horse, and the brain sees at once that
they have taken on a quality which does not belong to the simple photograph of real life. They have become not more beautiful, in the sense in
which pictures are beautiful, but shall we call it (our vocabulary is mis-
erably insufficient) more real, or real with a different reality from that
which we perceive in daily life? We behold them as they are when we are
not there. We see life as it is when we have no part in it. As we gaze we
seem to be removed from the pettiness of actual existence. The horse will
not knock us down. The King will not grasp our hands. The wave will
not wet our feet. From this point of vantage, as we watch the antics of
our kind, we have time to feel pity and amusement, to generalize, to en-
dow man with the attributes of the race. Watching the boat sail and the
wave break, we have time to open our minds to beauty and register on
top of it the queer sensation—this beauty will continue, and this beauty
will flourish whether we behold it or not. Further, all this happened ten
years ago, we are told. We are beholding a world which has gone beneath the wave. Brides are emerging from the Abbey—they are now
mothers; ushers are ardent—they are now silent; mothers are tearful;
guests are joyful; this has been won and that has been lost, and it is
over and done with. The War sprung its chasm at the feet of all this innocence and ignorance, but it was thus that we danced and pirouetted,
toiled and desired, thus that the sun shone and the clouds scudded up to
the very end.

But the picture-makers seem dissatisfied with such obvious sources
of interest as the passage of time and the suggestiveness of reality. They
despise the flight of gulls, ships on the Thames, the Prince of Wales, the
Mile End Road, Piccadilly Circus. They want to be improving, altering,
making an art of their own—naturally, for so much seems to be within
their scope. So many arts seemed to stand by ready to offer their help. For
example, there was literature. All the famous novels of the world, with
their well known characters, and their famous scenes, only asked, it
seemed, to be put on the films. What could be easier and simpler? The
cinema fell upon its prey with immense rapacity, and to this moment
largely subsists upon the body of its unfortunate victim. But the results
are disastrous to both. The alliance is unnatural. Eye and brain are torn
asunder ruthlessly as they try vainly to work in couples. The eye says:
"Here is Anna Karenina." A voluptuous lady in black velvet wearing
pearls comes before us. But the brain says: "That is no more Anna
Karenina than it is Queen Victoria." For the brain knows Anna almost
entirely by the inside of her mind—her charm, her passion, her despair.
All the emphasis is laid by the cinema upon her teeth, her pearls, and her
velvet. Then "Anna falls in love with Vronsky"—that is to say, the lady

in black velvet falls into the arms of a gentleman in uniform, and they kiss with enormous succulence, great deliberation, and infinite gesticulation on a sofa in an extremely well appointed library, while a gardener incidentally mows the lawn. So we lurch and lumber through the most famous novels of the world. So we spell them out in words of one syllable written, too, in the scrawl of an illiterate schoolboy. A kiss is love. A broken cup is jealousy. A grin is happiness. Death is a hearse. None of these things has the least connection with the novel that Tolstoy wrote, and it is only when we give up trying to connect the pictures with the book that we guess from some accidental scene—like the gardener mowing the lawn—what the cinema might do if it were left to its own devices.

But what, then, are its devices? If it ceased to be a parasite, how would it walk erect? At present it is only from hints that one can frame any conjecture. For instance, at a performance of *Dr. Caligari* the other day, a shadow shaped like a tadpole suddenly appeared at one corner of the screen. It swelled to an immense size, quivered, bulged, and sank back again into nonentity. For a moment it seemed to embody some monstrous, diseased imagination of the lunatic's brain. For a moment, it seemed as if thought could be conveyed by shape more effectively than by words. The monstrous, quivering tadpole seemed to be fear itself, and not the statement, "I am afraid." In fact, the shadow was accidental, and the effect unintentional. But if a shadow at a certain moment can suggest so much more than the actual gestures and words of men and women in a state of fear, it seems plain that the cinema has within its grasp innumerable symbols for emotions that have so far failed to find expression. Terror has, besides its ordinary forms, the shape of a tadpole; it burgeons, bulges, quivers, disappears. Anger is not merely rant and rhetoric, red faces and clenched fists. It is perhaps a black line wriggling upon a white sheet. Anna and Vronsky need no longer scowl and grimace. They have at their command—but what? Is there, we ask, some secret language which we feel and see, but never speak, and, if so, could this be made visible to the eye? Is there any characteristic which thought possesses that can be rendered visible without the help of words? It has speed and slowness; dartlike directness and vaporous circumlocution. But it has also, especially in moments of emotion, the picture-making power, the need to lift its burden to another bearer; to let an image run side by side along with it. The likeness of the thought is, for some reason, more beautiful, more comprehensible, more available than the thought itself. As everybody knows, in Shakespeare the most complex ideas form chains of images through which we mount, changing and turning, until we reach the light of day. But, obviously, the images of a poet are not to be cast in bronze, or traced by pencil. They are compact of a thousand suggestions of which the visual is only the most obvious or the uppermost. Even the simplest image: "My luve's like a red, red rose, that's newly sprung in June," presents us with impressions of moisture and warmth and the glow of crimson and the softness of petals inextricably mixed and strung upon the lilt of a rhythm which is itself the voice of the passion and hesitation of the lover. All this, which is accessible to words, and to words alone, the cinema must avoid.

Yet if so much of our thinking and feeling is connected with seeing, some residue of visual emotion which is of no use either to painter or to poet may still await the cinema. That such symbols will be quite unlike the real objects which we see before us seems highly probable. Something abstract, something which moves with controlled and conscious art, something which calls for the very slightest help from words or music to make itself intelligible, yet justly uses them subserviently—of such movements and abstractions, the films may, in time to come, be composed. Then, indeed, when some new symbol for expressing thought is found, the filmmaker has enormous riches at his command. The exactitude of reality and its surprising power of suggestion are to be had for the asking. Annas and Vronskys—there they are in the flesh. If into this reality he could breathe emotion, could animate the perfect form with thought, then his booty could be hauled in hand over hand. Then, as smoke pours from Vesuvius, we should be able to see thought in its wildness, in its beauty, in its oddity, pouring from men with their elbows on a table; from women with their little handbags slipping to the floor. We should see these emotions mingling together and affecting each other.

We should see violent changes of emotion produced by their collision. The most fantastic contrasts could be flashed before us with a speed which the writer can only toil in vain; the dream architecture of arches and battlements, of cascades falling and fountains rising, which sometimes visits us in sleep or shapes itself in half-darkened rooms, could be realized before our waking eyes. No fantasy could be too farfetched or insubstantial. The past could be unrolled, distances annihilated, and the gulfs which dislocate novels (when, for instance, Tolstoy has to pass from Levin to Anna, and in so doing jars his story and wrenches and arrests our sympathies) could, by the sameness of the background, by the repetition of some sense, be smoothed away.

How all this is to be attempted, much less achieved, no one at the moment can tell us. We get intimations only in the chaos of the streets, perhaps, when some momentary assembly of color, sound, movement suggests that here is a scene awaiting a new art to be transfixed. And sometimes at the cinema in the midst of its immense dexterity and enormous technical proficiency, the curtain parts and we behold, far off, some unknown and unexpected beauty. But it is for a moment only. For a strange thing has happened—while all the other arts were born naked, this, the youngest, has been born fully clothed. It can say everything before it has anything to say. It is as if the savage tribe, instead of finding two bars of iron to play with, had found, scattering the seashore, fiddles, flutes, saxophones, trumpets, grand pianos by Erard and Bechstein, and had begun with incredible energy, but without knowing a note of music, to hammer and thump upon them all at the same time.

[1926]

W. R. ROBINSON

The Movies, Too,
Will Make You Free

. . . That the movies possess the depth and breadth necessary
for articulating contemporary moral reality, or the aesthetic means to
bring it into vivid relief, is borne out by the difference between them and
literature. Both are predominantly narrative arts employing images—one
directly, the other indirectly—as vehicles for storytelling. Because of that
slight difference, however, they are worlds apart. Literature and the literary imagination are metaphorical; they seek to make explicit a reality
hidden to the senses. From one point of view literature, an art of words,
duplicates the acts of creation by the Greek Logos or the Christian God:
through it the Word, the primordial ontological power in Greek and
Christian metaphysics, brings order into the world by imposing itself upon
chaos. Since words are not natural or material entities, literature is inherently deductive—words issuing from the Word—both alienated from the
physical and constituting a self-enclosed system which locates the source
of the Good outside the physical world, within the Word, an a priori
realm which validates particular words. But from another, a human, point
of view, literature, originating within a worldly predicament, arises either
from the longing of words to be themselves or from man's hunger to dwell
in the realm of ideas or reason. Not inherently inclined to be denotative,
words much prefer to consort among their own kind and, indeed, ar-
dently long to return to their source. In any case, the literary imagination
works from a fallen state and, nostalgically lamenting its paradise lost,
aspires to regain verbal heaven.

Drama nicely illustrates the bias of literature and one of the ways in which it functions. In drama, at least when it is authentic art, words turn characters inside out, manifesting their inner being with language. For this reason the dialogue, in, say, *Who's Afraid of Virginia Woolf?* can be heard from a recording and still be aesthetically effective. With neither the theatrical nor cinematic spectacle distracting from the words, they intensively activate the hearer's imagination and turn him, too, inside out. Characters serve as the metaphorical vehicles by which the Word is made manifest. In a verbal medium such as drama the visual element complements the words and is eventually dispensable. Poetry—lyric poetry in particular—reigns supreme among the literary arts because the words are relatively unencumbered by the sensory, although in poetry, too, imagery is indispensable as metaphorical agency. Its object is, of course, to let the human spirit sing out. Verbal narrative on the other hand relies more heavily on the referential dimension of language, and words as a consequence tend to function analytically, pointing to underlying patterns, causes, or essences. Not by accident fiction favors temporal and historical explanations. Read in solitude, it cultivates the mind, and whatever the circumstances it proffers the intellectual satisfaction attained through comprehending the abstractions governing life. Nevertheless, despite being more abstract than drama or poetry, verbal narrative is also governed by the principle that literature be concrete and specific or "make sense"; and with drama and poetry it paradoxically employs words as the instrument by which man can penetrate through the mask of phenomena to the Word beyond it and transcend his finite condition. Literature and the literary imagination are bound by the laws of language, which is always metaphorical; through postulating likenesses, they put the mind in contact with intangible intellectual essences not directly perceptible.

In contrast to literature, the movies and the cinematic imagination are literal. A visual medium in which the word is complementary and dispensable, the movies illuminate sensory reality or outer form. They are empirical revelations lighting the thing itself and revealing change as nothing more than it appears to be. In their world there is no becoming, only being, or pointless change, no innate potential to be realized in time, no essence to be released from original darkness, no law to be learned and obeyed. For this reason analysis is rarely successful in the movies, *Citizen Kane* being the most famous of the very few exceptions. Even the Russian intellectual cinema, which on first impression seems analytical, at its best is hortatory—it inspires the viewer to be. Or, more specifically, in individual frames, by composition and photographic style, it endows the lowly and exploited with splendid being. Whatever a movie illuminates it has already celebrated, saying, in effect, "So be it." Its atomic constituents seem to have a greater life than the enclosing forms, while order, causality, and pattern appear arbitrarily imposed. And, with the atomistic quality so pronounced in them, the movies evoke an emotional rather than an intellectual response—the thing directly perceived is directly felt, and intellectual reflection follows upon the emotion, whereas in literature the emotion follows upon the word after the mind has made the initial encounter. Understandably, movies more perfectly satisfy Tolstoy's requirement that art appeal to the universal innate feelings in man. Consequently, they tend to be egalitarian, and literature elitist—only those who know how to read and think are admitted to its domain, while anyone with eyes qualifies as a citizen of the movie world. From these differences it is clear that literature testifies, while the movies witness. As a verbal medium, literature gives voice to the mind's lust for meaning. In seeking to commit the mind to what is not at once evident to the senses, literature demands belief; it insists that its report, always an interpretation, be trusted. The movies, on the other hand, a visual art, are immersed in the sensory, physical world, viewing it from within as a passing parade ceaselessly coming and going. They have no way, except for words, to gain a vantage point outside it. In this respect they are the archetype for the contemporary intellectual predicament characterized by the twilight of absolutes—they have no revealed word or a priori ideas, nor any criterion within experience itself, by which to ascertain reality or value; they are face to face with what is in its full multiplicity and glory. They dwell in the present, in a world all surface. Lacking a second level of reality, they are without complexity—without irony, meaning, or necessity. On the face of things appear process, activity, energy, and behind this mask is nothingness. Whereas the word is mysterious, the image is evident; everything it has is showing. Thus for movies the created world is good, not fallen; they offer no salvation through belief, as Christianity and rationalism do, but instead regard the given world as redeemed. They are existentialist, valuing the concrete, existence, or what is.

Little wonder, then, that the literary sensibility is not at home in the cinematic world and suspects movies of being superficial—without soul, intellectually impotent, and morally frivolous. One devoted to ideas, the other to particulars, one committed to transcendent truth, the other to ever-present reality, the verbal and visual modes are fated to eternal hostility. Yet despite this inherent hostility, the movies have their inevitable literary aspect—in their title and dialogue, and in the property or scenario from which they are derived. (Perhaps this literary origin raises major obstacles to successful film-making, since the film is in effect a translation and the viewer is invited—or does so out of habit—to translate it back into its original, and truer, literary prototype. The film functions, in this case, as literature did in classical theory, as a decorative illustration for a truth known through a prior and more authoritative faculty.)

There are those who lament the fact that movies must have a literary aspect; purists of a sort, they long for a return to the era of the silent film, when movies were movies and that's all there was to them. That nostalgia is understandable, for the pure movie demands a less complex response and poses less complex critical problems. The fact is, however, that the movies, allowing for the proper dominance, are an image-word medium, as is literature, and all for the better. For, despite the invidious criticism which can arise from a bias favoring either the intellect or the senses, the presence of the antagonistic elements reflects the human predicament. The tension generated between images and words in an impure movie and our ambivalent response to their interaction beget a truth that would otherwise be lost. As literature is enriched by the tension between word and image, so are the movies. The beneficent effects of this tension can be readily observed in many movies, but it has become consciously explicit in such recent ones as *Alfie,* in which a narrator terrified of death tries unsuccessfully, through directly addressing the audience or from a verbal point of view, to determine what his life comes to within a cinematic context; and *Fahrenheit 451,* in which a French director flatly and ludicrously repudiates his own art in lamenting the demise of book man.

The tension in these movies also appears, reversed, in recent literature, perhaps most notably in the work of Alain Robbe-Grillet. Words are being adapted to cinematic reality, with the result that they no longer mean anything. Readers trained in the traditional ways of words, predictably, are deeply frustrated by the literature of nothingness. Paradoxically, the impurity of the movies makes them a more perfect art, capable of more extensively exploring its own possibilities and limitations, and thereby of more profoundly and more precisely giving body to man's truth.

Once the movies are acknowledged to be art and what they unveil is taken seriously, we have to face the fact, extensively argued by Existentialists, that the word has been superseded by sensation. The movies define better than any other art what we feel today to be the relation between the intellect and the senses. Among other things they make it quite clear, to the verbalist's distress, that the word is an adjunct of the image. In their version of the play between the eye's truth and the mind's, the ancient theme of appearance versus reality is reversed. In contrast to, say, Elizabethan poetry, in which images decorate a rational framework, in the movies reason rides on the tiger back of images in motion.

This new relation between the senses and the mind is the contemporary form assumed by an ancient and enduring antagonism. For at stake ultimately in the difference between literature and the movies are the prerogatives of two moral universes, two cultures, and two ideas of creation. Both art forms, just by existing, pay tribute to their source, the power which makes them possible—literature to the Word, the movies to the Light. Beyond that, by implication when not directly, literature celebrates a God transcendent, the movies a god immanent; one affirms creation by fiat, the other creation by emanation. These inevitably hostile alternatives, if Joseph Campbell's account in *The Masks of God* is correct, led to the division of East from West some eight thousand years ago —the East following the way of the Light and the West the way of the Word—and has been the source of their mutual suspicion ever since. But the Light and the Word have also vied with one another for supremacy within Christendom. The Old and New Testament offer conflicting accounts of the instrument responsible for creation, and St. John indiscriminately mixes creation by the Word with creation by the Light. St. John's confusion, a careless mixture of Judaic and Greek attitudes, may well be the source of the traditional friction in Western culture between the Light and the Word. At any rate Judaism's existential, worldly faith has persistently contended with Greek rationalistic idealism for dominance in Western culture. The Word has been clearly dominant until recently, but as a result of science's corrosive effect upon Christianity, the Light is now in the ascendant. So the difference between the movies and literature is rooted in a fundamental antithesis in man's being, and the rise of the movies as an art is one sign of a profound change taking place in Western culture—a transformation begetting what pundits have been variously calling a post-Christian, post-rationalistic, post-typographical, or post-literary period.

The movies derive their aesthetic stature, obviously, from being a closer analogue to reality than is literature. For the alert film-maker and his audience today a movie can and should be a microcosm of life. All the world's a movie screen. Thus the director's medium is inherently closer than any other to life, and he is the most advantageously equipped artist for adventuring in moral reality.

The movies at their best have always performed the task of art, even when film-makers, critics, and theorists claimed that, paradoxically, the movies could be art only if the imagination was weighed down by materiality. Accepting this condition in *Greed*, Erich von Stroheim created serious art in spite of the inherent bias against the medium. Nonetheless this assumption hurt the movies in the pressure it exerted on moviemakers to honor piously the dominion of the mechanical, material, and casual over their art. And theorists, including such sophisticated ones as Erwin Panofsky and Susanne Langer, in their turn were impaled on a dichotomy which forced them to choose between conceptions of the movie as dream or as bound to physical reality.

The movie of the last decade, along with developments elsewhere in thought and the arts, has put this realistic assumption to rest. It was a period's taste, time has made evident—a corruption of reality. Today the movie is explicitly and confidently committed to freedom as the supreme value and truth, and the moral dialogue it is now participating in is probing the career of man's good in that direction—whether in great, good, bad or indifferent films, in parts of films or in their entirety; in the character of the emancipated female: Mrs. Waters in *Tom Jones*, Jeanne Moreau or Brigette Bardot in *Viva Maria*, Jean Seberg in *Breathless*, or the various roles played by Natalie Wood; or the cool, resilient male: Belmondo in *Breathless* and elsewhere, Anthony Quinn in *Zorba the Greek*, or Vittorio Gassman in *The Easy Life*; or as a theme in the work of Bergman and Fellini.

The free camera, moreover, supports the free character. It has always been understood that the camera used with skill is a projection of an individual's sensibility, not a mechanical eye; foreign films especially, coming out of visual traditions different from our own, have been constant reminders of this fact. Today there is not even a shadow of a doubt that the movies, instead of being by nature or moral precept enslaved to physical reality, are a technological vehicle by which the human spirit can escape material limitations once thought to be narrowly restrictive. Not too long ago regarded as man's nemesis, technology, in the movies as well as in the airplane, enlarges his power of flight. The movies, consequently, need no longer be an illusion of the "real" but are at liberty to be artifice and even to call attention to their fictional character, as Tony Richardson does in *Tom Jones* and as Richard Lester does in *A Hard Day's Night*. A still more striking example is Mario Monicelli's *The Organizer*, in which, although the movie is ostensibly a realistic treatment of capitalistic inhumanity, the artistry draws attention to itself, contradictorily and ironically proclaiming the dominion of the imagination over substance.

But the movies' greatest contribution to today's moral dialogue over freedom does not lie in characters or camera technique. It lies, rather, in the emancipation of the image. Not long ago it was excitedly argued that the camera gave painting a new life by freeing it from photographic representation, but the camera has done even more than that: it has freed itself, too, at least from all debilitating forms of representation. This child of empiricism, repudiating its parent, has liberated form from the physical world. Marilyn Monroe, never a physical actuality for moviegoers, lives on every time the camera projects her image on the screen, and so, although physically dead, she has gained immortality. She has been released, as has the moviemaker and the viewer, and, indeed, man's mind everywhere, to dance in the imagination's heaven. Actually physics is mainly responsible for destroying the idea of substance, but the movies have done more to set the imagination free to dream upon human moral possibilities within a substanceless universe. By conclusively demonstrating that an image does not necessarily signify substance, they have destroyed the last vestige of our materialistic mental habits. Unburdening us of the hunger for and anxiety about meaning, the free movie teaches us that to be is enough; existence needs no justification. Ironically, in the new intimacy between the senses and the mind which the movie achieves, Plato's realm of forms is realized through physical vision.

Once regarded as a puerile, cowardly escape from life because they begot and simulated dreaming, the movies are now recognizable as an extension of the supreme power inherent in a universe of energy, chance, evolution, explosiveness, and creativity. In such a youthful, exuberant universe the movies' kind of dreaming gives concrete probability and direction to the ongoing drive of energy, and as a consequence what at one time was thought to be a vitiating defect is now their greatest virtue. The new freedom they reflect and extend is freedom within the world, contingent and not absolute, a heightened vision of existence through concrete form beyond abstraction. In a world of light and a light world—unanalyzable, uninterpretable, without substance or essence, meaning or direction—being and non-being magically breed existence. Out of the darkness and chaos of the theater beams a light; out of nothingness is generated brilliant form, existence suspended somewhere between the extremes of total darkness and total light. Performing its rhythmic dance to energy's tune, the movie of the imagination proves, should there be any doubt, that cinema, an art of light, contributes more than any other art today to fleshing out the possibilities for good within an imaginative universe.

[1967]

GEORGE BLUESTONE

The Trope in Literature
and Cinema*

THE TROPE IN LANGUAGE

The film, then, making its appeal to the perceiving senses, is free to work with endless variations of physical reality. "Literature on the other hand," Mendilow points out, "is dependent entirely on a symbolic medium that stands between the perceiver and the symbolised percepta . . . ." Perhaps nothing better illustrates this root difference between language and photographed image than an appraisal of each medium's ability to render literary tropes.

Carrying Mendilow's statement a step further, we observe that word-symbols must be translated into images of things, feelings and concepts through the process of thought. Where the moving picture comes to us directly through perception, language must be filtered through the screen of conceptual apprehension. And the conceptual process, though allied to and often taking its point of departure from the percept, represents a different mode of experience, a different way of apprehending the universe.

The distinction is a crucial one, for it generates differences which run all the way down the line from the media's ability to handle tropes, affect beholders, render states of consciousness (including dreams, memories, feelings, and imagination), to their respective methods of handling conventions, time, and space.

*Editor's title.

The linguistic trope is the novel's special way of rendering the shock of resemblance. By juxtaposing similar qualities in violently dissimilar things, language gets its revenge on the apparent disorder of life. It binds together a world which seems atomized and therefore chaotic to the primitive mind. Modern theories of symbolic thinking demonstrate that we necessarily see resemblances in the most ordinary perceptions. Arnheim points out that an illusion, to be strong, does not have to be complete in every detail: "everyone knows that a clumsy childish scribble of a human face consisting of two dots, a comma, and a dash may be full of expression and depict anger, amusement, fear . . . ." A kind of basic tropism is involved in such a process: the mind sees resemblances in the disparate sources of scribbled drawing and angry face.

So similar are linguistic and cognitive processes in finding resemblances that critics like Cleanth Brooks build their analytical systems around the metaphor. The difference between the artist who coins metaphors and the ordinary mind which classifies objects derives largely from the fact that the artist casts his net much wider. Where the cognitive mind finds common traits in collies and boxers and calls them dogs, the maker of tropes finds common qualities in slings, arrows, and outrageous fortune. Literary tropes, however, are distinguished from cognitive classification, first, by their verbal origins and, second, by a kind of connotative luxuriance. Not only does the power of the trope inhere in its figurative character but in its ability to compound itself without damage to intended meanings. Virginia Woolf, contrasting the novel and film, is especially sensitive to the unique power of the figure of speech. The images of a poet, she tells us, are compact of a thousand suggestions, of which the visual is only the most obvious:

> Even the simplest image: "my luve's like a red, red rose, that's newly sprung in June," presents us with impressions of moisture and warmth and the flow of crimson and the softness of petals inextricably mixed and strung upon the lift of a rhythm which is itself the voice of the passion and the hesitation of the love. All this, which is accessible to words, and to words alone, the cinema must avoid.[1]

We have already seen that a special kind of film trope is possible, but only when it is confined to cinematic terms: it must arise naturally from the setting (as Lillian Gish's knitting in *Way Down East,* or Marlon Brando's horse in *Viva Zapata*). If disparate objects are compared, the

---

[1]Virginia Woolf, "The Movies and Reality," *New Republic,* XLVII (August 4, 1926), 309.

film metaphor must be predicated upon a clear suspension of realistic demands (as the invasion montage in the Marx Brothers' *Duck Soup*). Since the latter is rarely successful (the notable failure of the cradle linkage in *Intolerance*), the former technique must carry the burden of metaphor. James Agee, speaking of the metamorphic mobility of the silent-screen comedian, his ability to assume physical shapes suggesting objects or emotions, is able to say, "It was his business to be as funny as possible physically, without the help or hindrance of words. So he gave us a figure of speech, or rather a vision . . . ."[2] But if such figures work at all, they do so by becoming appropriated to the peculiar laws of the film, and not by simple conversion. The final and most central cinematic analogy to the metaphor may be found in the special case of editing (discussed below), where two disparate elements, as in the trope, are linked together to create a *tertium quid*.

That film tropes are enormously restricted compared to literary tropes is indicated by the character of the compacted imagery in almost any passage by Marcel Proust. Watching the aged Duc de Guermantes, Marcel marvels to find him showing his age so little, and understands why

> . . . as soon as he rose and tried to stand erect, he had tottered on trembling limbs (like those aged archbishops who have nothing solid on them except their metallic cross . . .) and had wavered as he made his way along the difficult summit of his eighty-three years, as if men were perched on giant stilts, sometimes taller than church spires, constantly growing and finally rendering their progress so difficult and perilous that they suddenly fall.[3]

The images of metallic cross, men on stilts, in turn taller than church spires and still growing, depend for their effect precisely on the fact that they are not to be taken literally. The quality of precarious summits common to stilts and years is the resemblance which yokes these things together. In the process a new thing is created which resides neither in octogenarians nor in stilts. The moment such relationships lose their novelty and become habitual, they become cliches. So that besides conceptual appeal and figurative luxuriance the final property of the trope is its insistence on perpetual renewal. It is a way, then, of packed symbolic thinking which is peculiar to imaginative rather than to visual activity. Converted into a literal image, the metaphor would seem absurd. In such attempts, to adopt Virginia Woolf's formulation, "Eye and brain are torn asunder ruthlessly as they try vainly to work in

---

[2] James Agee, "Comedy's Greatest Era," *Life*, XXVII (September 5, 1949), 70.
[3] Marcel Proust, "The Past Recaptured," *Remembrance of Things Past*, trans. Frederick A. Blossom, II (New York, 1932), 1123.

couples." She is right in concluding that the results of conversion from linguistic to visual images are disastrous to both. The difference is too great to overcome.

Just as the cinema exhibits a stubborn antipathy to novels, the novel here emerges as a medium antithetical to film. Because language has laws of its own, and literary characters are inseparable from the language which forms them, the externalization of such characters often seems dissatisfying. The distinction between the character who comes to us through a screen of language and the character who comes to us in visual images may account, perhaps, for the persistent disclaimers of film commentators like Michael Orme[4] and Thomas Craven.[5] Protesting De Mille's butchering of *Four Frightened People* by E. Arnot Robinson, Orme reflects, "you cannot transpose any one character from page to screen and hope to present him entirely as the novelist created him or as the novelist's public knew him . . . . who can really recall having seen a screen performance which really and truly portrayed his favourite character as he knew it?"

EDITING: THE CINEMATIC TROPE

If the film is thus severely restricted in rendering linguistic tropes (despite dialogue which will be discussed presently), it has, through the process of editing, discovered a metaphoric quality all its own. We have already noted how the spatial liberation of the cinema was its unique achievement. But film editing, combining the integrity of the shot with the visual rhythm of the sequence, gives the director his characteristic signature.

"The first thing to be observed about the technique of editing," Lindgren observes, "is that it affords the film-maker a new field for his powers of selection." Since the complete action of any given scene is made up of a large number of moving components, the director must constantly choose which detail he will emphasize at a given moment. Selection, however, can go much farther than this. Through editing, the film-maker can eliminate meaningless intervals, concentrate on significant details, ordering his design in consonance with the central line of his narrative.

[4]Michael Orme, "The Bookshelf and the Screen," *Illustrated London News,* CLXXXVI (March 10, 1934), 368.

[5]Craven's statement reads, "I doubt if the most astute and sympathetic reader ever visualizes a character; he responds to that part of a created figure which is also himself, but he does not actually see his hero. . . . For this reason all illustrations are disappointing." In "The Great American Art," *Dial,* LXXXI (December, 1926), 489–490.

For example, Pudovkin poses the problem of presenting a man falling from a window five stories high. The director, in this case, would take one shot of a man falling from a window in such a way that the net (into which he safely falls) is not visible on the screen; then a shot of the same man falling from a slight height to the ground. Joined together, the shots would give the desired impression of continuous fall. It is precisely this technique that Griffith used in the Babylonian episode of *Intolerance,* which Pudovkin had seen and admired. The camera, it should be noted, has not followed nature. Instead, the director has selected two points in the process, leaving the intervening passage to be filled in by the mind of the spectator. This extraordinary power of suggestion is indeed unique in the dramatic arts. "It is not correct," Pudovkin warns us, "to call such a process a trick; it is a method of filmic representation exactly corresponding to the elimination of five years that divides a first from a second act upon the stage." The method corresponds roughly to the temporal gap between one panel and another in Renaissance frescoes depicting the lives of saints, except that in the film the action seems continuous.

In cinematic terms, then, the method of connecting the film strips becomes the basic formative function. For the two strips, joined together, become a *tertium quid,* a third thing which neither of the strips has been independently. This is the essence of that much abused concept of Eisenstein's which we have come to know as montage.

Given the transition, the relationship between shots as the center of the creative process, a high degree of discipline must be exercised in the editing. Long shots must dovetail with close shots. There must be a logical connection between the shots, a kind of visual momentum, or transference. We see a man about to cross a street. In a close-up, we see his face twist in horror. We cut immediately to a scene in front of him. A car is bearing down on a small child. We accept the instantaneous shift because, interested as we are in the cause of the horror, we are propelled visually to the next significant detail. Different points of view must thus be carefully blended to suggest a continuous action.

Building his design out of individual strips, always thinking plastically, the film-maker may use almost endless spatial combinations. He may, for example, use contrast ironically. When Alec Guinness, in *The Promoter,* achieves a social triumph by dancing with the Countess of Chell, the film cuts to a shot of greasy sausage frying in a skillet. It is the next day and the "card's" mother is preparing his meal in their dingy kitchen. Or the director may use what the Feldman brothers call parallel editing.[6] A wife, to make her husband jealous, is seen flirting

---

[6] Joseph and Harry Feldman, *Dynamics of the Film* (New York, 1952), p. 86.

with a willing lover. We cut to an office where the husband is seen making advances to his secretary. The director may use symbolism. In *Strike,* the shooting down of workers is punctuated by shots of the slaughter of a steer in a stockyard. In *The Blue Angel,* birds are used with consummate artistry as a kind of leitmotif. In the opening scene, Professor Unrat coos at a caged canary. Later, having devoted himself to Lola, a music-hall singer, he watches pigeons flying up against a clock whose bronze figures ominously mark the passage of time. And at the height of his degradation, the Professor crows like a cock. The possibility for plastic comments like these, as distinct from verbal renditions of the same effects, is unprecedented in the arts.

A new kind of relationship between animate and inanimate objects springs up, a relationship which becomes the key to plastic thinking. Pudovkin points out quite cogently that relationships between human beings are, for the most part, illumined by conversation, by words. No one carries on conversation with objects, and that is why an actor's relationship to objects is of special interest to the film technician.

Within the composition of the frame, the juxtaposition of man and object becomes crucial. "The performance of an actor linked with an object and built upon it will always be one of the most powerful methods of filmic construction."[7] We have only to think of Chaplin to see the principle in operation. The dancing rolls in *The Gold Rush,* the supple cane, the globe dance in *The Great Dictator,* the feeding machine in *Modern Times,* the flowers and drinks in *Monsieur Verdoux,* the flea skit in *Limelight*—these are only isolated examples of Chaplin's endless facility for inventing new relationships with objects. He leans on a doorman as on a lamppost, and the animate becomes inanimate. The spring of the watch in *The Pawnshop* comes alive, and the inanimate becomes animate. The confusion dynamizes the relationship, and the distinction between man and object is obliterated. Man and object become interchangeable, and the inanimate joins the animate as an actor. Certainly this accounts for a good part of Chaplin's filmic genius.

Not only has the film discovered new ways to render meanings by finding relationships between animate and inanimate objects, but the human physiognomy itself has been rediscovered. So pervasive has been the power of the close-up to convey emotion that in *"Der Sichtbare Mensch"* Béla Balázs places the film on a par with the invention of the printing press. The method of conveying meaning by facial expression, a

---

[7]Pudovkin, p. 115. A telling account of a familiar phenomenon appears in Lindsay, p. 15: ". . . there came to our town not long ago a film of a fight between Federals and Confederates, with the loss of many lives, all for the recapture of a steam-engine that took on more personality in the end than private or general on either side, alive or dead."

method which according to Balázs fell into desuetude with the advent of printing, has been revived by the "microphysiognomy" of the screen image. The face becomes another kind of object in space, a terrain on which may be enacted dramas broad as battles, and sometimes more intense. Physiognomy preempts the domain of nonverbal experience: "The gestures of visual man are not intended to convey concepts which can be expressed in words, but such inner experiences, such nonrational emotions which would still remain unexpressed when everything that can be told has been told."[8]

Just as words are not merely images expressing our thoughts and feelings, but in many cases their *a priori* limiting forms, the subtleties of the mobile face not only render hitherto unrecorded experiences but also create the conditions for new experiences to come into being. If, then, "the film increases the possibilities for expression, it will also widen the spirit it can express." If Balázs goes too far in calling for an "encyclopedia of comparative gesturology," he at least draws attention to the unprecedented possibilities of the human face. These possibilities have given rise to a wholly different kind of acting. The microdrama of the human countenance permits the reading of the greatest conflicts in the merest flicker of an eye. Understatement becomes the key to film characterization. The subtleties of Mme. Falconetti's face in Dreyer's *The Passion of Joan of Arc,* or of Giulietta Massina's in Fellini's *La Strada* would have been incomprehensible to anyone in the dramatic arts before 1900.

In a real sense, then, Pudovkin is right when he says, "In the discovered, deeply imbedded detail there lies an element of perception, the creative element that gives the event shown its final worth." By selecting and combining, by comparing and contrasting, by linking disparate spatial entities, photographed images of "the deeply imbedded detail" allow the film-maker, through editing, to achieve a uniquely cinematic equivalent of the literary trope.

[1957]

[8]Béla Balázs, *Theory of the Film,* trans. Edith Bone (New York, 1953), p. 40.

ERWIN PANOFSKY

Style and Medium
in the Motion Pictures

Film art is the only art the development of which men now living have witnessed from the very beginnings; and this development is all the more interesting as it took place under conditions contrary to precedent. It was not an artistic urge that gave rise to the discovery and gradual perfection of a new technique; it was a technical invention that gave rise to the discovery and gradual perfection of a new art.

From this we understand two fundamental facts. First, that the primordial basis of the enjoyment of moving pictures was not an objective interest in a specific subject matter, much less an aesthetic interest in the formal presentation of subject matter, but the sheer delight in the fact that things seemed to move, no matter what things they were. Second, that films—first exhibited in "kinetoscopes," viz., cinematographic peep shows, but projectable to a screen since as early as 1894—are, originally, a product of genuine folk art (whereas, as a rule, folk art derives from what is known as "higher art"). At the very beginning of things we find the simple recording of movements: galloping horses, railroad trains, fire engines, sporting events, street scenes. And when it had come to the making of narrative films these were produced by photographers who were anything but "producers" or "directors," performed by people who were anything but actors, and enjoyed by people who would have been much offended had anyone called them "art lovers. . . . "

In the beginning, then, there were the straight recordings of movement no matter what moved, viz., the prehistoric ancestors of our

Originally appeared in the *Bulletin of the Department of Art and Archaeology*, Princeton University, 1934. Reprinted by permission.

"documentaries"; and, soon after, the early narratives, viz., the prehistoric ancestors of our "feature films." The craving for a narrative element could be satisfied only by borrowing from older arts, and one should expect that the natural thing would have been to borrow from the theater, a theater play being apparently the *genus proximum* to a narrative film in that it consists of a narrative enacted by persons that move. But in reality the imitation of stage performances was a comparatively late and thoroughly frustrated development. What happened at the start was a very different thing. Instead of imitating a theatrical performance already endowed with a certain amount of motion, the earliest films added movement to works of art originally stationary, so that the dazzling technical invention might achieve a triumph of its own without intruding upon the sphere of higher culture. The living language, which is always right, has endorsed this sensible choice when it still speaks of a "moving picture" or, simply, a "picture," instead of accepting the pretentious and fundamentally erroneous "screen play."

The stationary works enlivened in the earliest movies were indeed pictures: bad nineteenth-century paintings and postcards (or waxworks à la Madame Tussaud's), supplemented by the comic strips—a most important root of cinematic art—and the subject matter of popular songs, pulp magazines and dime novels; and the films descending from this ancestry appealed directly and very intensely to a folk art mentality. They gratified—often simultaneously—first, a primitive sense of justice and decorum when virtue and industry were rewarded while vice and laziness were punished; second, plain sentimentality when "the thin trickle of a fictive love interest" took its course "through somewhat serpentine channels," or when Father, dear Father returned from the saloon to find his child dying of diphtheria; third, a primordial instinct for bloodshed and cruelty when Andreas Hofer faced the firing squad, or when (in a film of 1893–94) the head of Mary Queen of Scots actually came off; fourth, a taste for mild pornography (I remember with great pleasure a French film of *ca.* 1900 wherein a seemingly but not really well-rounded lady as well as a seemingly but not really slender one were shown changing to bathing suits—an honest, straightforward *porcheria* much less objectionable than the now extinct Betty Boop films and, I am sorry to say, some of the more recent Walt Disney productions); and, finally, that crude sense of humor, graphically described as "slapstick," which feeds upon the sadistic and the pornographic instinct, either singly or in combination.

Not until as late as *ca.* 1905 was a film adaptation of *Faust* ventured upon (cast still "unknown," characteristically enough), and not until 1911 did Sarah Bernhardt lend her prestige to an unbelievably funny film tragedy, *Queen Elizabeth of England*. These films represent the first conscious attempt at transplanting the movies from the folk art level to that of "real art"; but they also bear witness to the fact that this commendable goal could not be reached in so simple a manner. It was soon realized that the imitation of a theater performance with a set stage, fixed entries and exits, and distinctly literary ambitions is the one thing the film must avoid.

The legitimate paths of evolution were opened, not by running away from the folk art character of the primitive film but by developing it within the limits of its own possibilities. Those primordial archetypes of film productions on the folk art level—success or retribution, sentiment, sensation, pornography, and crude humor—could blossom forth into genuine history, tragedy and romance, crime and adventure, and comedy, as soon as it was realized that they could be transfigured—not by an artificial injection of literary values but by the exploitation of the unique and specific possibilities of the new medium. Significantly, the beginnings of this legitimate development antedate the attempts at endowing the film with higher values of a foreign order (the crucial period being the years from 1902 to *ca.* 1905), and the decisive steps were taken by people who were laymen or outsiders from the viewpoint of the serious stage.

These unique and specific possibilities can be defined as *dynamization of space* and, accordingly, *spatialization of time*. This statement is self-evident to the point of triviality but it belongs to that kind of truths which, just because of their triviality, are easily forgotten or neglected.

In a theater, space is static, that is, the space represented on the stage, as well as the spatial relation of the beholder to the spectacle, is unalterably fixed. The spectator cannot leave his seat, and the setting of the stage cannot change, during one act (except for such incidentals as rising moons or gathering clouds and such illegitimate reborrowings from the film as turning wings or gliding backdrops). But, in return for this restriction, the theater has the advantage that time, the medium of emotion and thought conveyable by speech, is free and independent of anything that may happen in visible space. Hamlet may deliver his famous monologue lying on a couch in the middle distance, doing nothing and only dimly discernible to the spectator and listener, and yet by his mere words enthrall him with a feeling of intensest emotional action.

With the movies the situation is reversed. Here, too, the spectator occupies a fixed seat, but only physically, not as the subject of an aesthetic experience. Aesthetically, he is in permanent motion as his eye identifies itself with the lens of the camera, which permanently shifts in distance and direction. And as movable as the spectator is, as movable is, for the same reason, the space presented to him. Not only bodies move in space, but space itself does, approaching, receding, turning, dissolving and recrystallizing as it appears through the controlled locomotion and focusing of the camera and through the cutting and editing of the various shots—not to mention such special effects as visions, transformations, disappearances, slow-motion and fast-motion shots, reversals and trick films. This opens up a world of possibilities of which the stage can never dream. Quite apart from such photographic tricks as the participation of disembodied spirits in the action of the *Topper* series, or the more effective wonders wrought by Roland Young in *The Man Who Could Work Miracles,* there is, on the purely factual level, an untold wealth of themes as inaccessible to the "legitimate" stage as a fog or snowstorm is to the sculptor; all sorts of violent elemental phenomena and, conversely, events too microscopic to be visible under normal conditions (such as the life-saving injection with the serum flown in at the very last moment, or the fatal bite of the yellow-fever mosquito) ; full-scale battle scenes; all kinds of operations, not only in the surgical sense but also in the sense of any actual construction, destruction or experimentation, as in *Louis Pasteur* or *Madame Curie;* a really grand party, moving through many rooms of a mansion or a palace. Features like these, even the mere shifting of the scene from one place to another by means of a car perilously negotiating heavy traffic or a motorboat steered through a nocturnal harbor, will not only always retain their primitive cinematic appeal but also remain enormously effective as a means of stirring the emotions and creating suspense. In addition, the movies have the power, entirely denied to the theater, to convey psychological experiences by directly projecting their content to the screen, substituting, as it were, the eye of the beholder for the consciousness of the character (as when the imaginings and hallucinations of the drunkard in the otherwise overrated *Lost Weekend* appear as stark realities instead of being described by mere words) . But any attempt to convey thought and feelings exclusively, or even primarily, by speech leave us with a feeling of embarrassment, boredom, or both.

What I mean by thoughts and feelings "conveyed exclusively, or even primarily, by speech" is simply this: Contrary to naïve expectation, the invention of the sound track in 1928 has been unable to change the basic fact that a moving picture, even when it has learned to talk, remains a picture that moves and does not convert itself into a piece of writing that is enacted. Its substance remains a series of visual sequences held together by an uninterrupted flow of movement in space (except, of course, for such checks and pauses as have the same compositional value as a rest in music), and not a sustained study in human character and destiny transmitted by effective, let alone "beautiful," diction. I cannot remember a more misleading statement about the movies than Mr. Eric Russell Bentley's in the spring number of the *Kenyon Review*, 1945: "The potentialities of the talking screen differ from those of the silent screen in adding the dimension of dialogue—which could be poetry." I would suggest: "The potentialities of the talking screen differ from those of the silent screen in integrating visible movement with dialogue which, therefore, had better not be poetry."

All of us, if we are old enough to remember the period prior to 1928, recall the old-time pianist who, with his eyes glued on the screen, would accompany the events with music adapted to their mood and rhythm; and we also recall the weird and spectral feeling overtaking us when this pianist left his post for a few minutes and the film was allowed to run by itself, the darkness haunted by the monotonous rattle of the machinery. Even the silent film, then, was never mute. The visible spectacle always required, and received, an audible accompaniment which, from the very beginning, distinguished the film from simple pantomime and rather classed it—*mutatis mutandis*—with the ballet. The advent of the talkie meant not so much an "addition" as a transformation of musical sound into articulate speech and, therefore, of quasi pantomime into an entirely new species of spectacle which differs from the ballet, and agrees with the stage play, in that its acoustic component consists of intelligible words, but differs from the stage play and agrees with the ballet in that this acoustic component is not detachable from the visual. In a film, that which we hear remains, for good or worse, inextricably fused with that which we see; the sound, articulate or not, cannot express any more than is expressed, at the same time, by visible movement; and in a good film it does not even attempt to do so. To put it briefly, the play—or, as it is very properly called, the "script"—of a moving picture is subject to what might be termed the *principle of coexpressibility*.

Empirical proof of this principle is furnished by the fact that, wherever the dialogical or monological element gains temporary prominence, there appears, with the inevitability of a natural law, the "close-up." What does the close-up achieve? In showing us, in magnification, either the face of the speaker or the face of the listeners or both in alternation, the camera transforms the human physiognomy into a huge field of action where—given the qualification of the performers—every subtle movement of the features, almost imperceptible from a natural distance, becomes an expressive event in visible space and thereby completely integrates itself with the expressive content of the spoken word; whereas, on the stage, the spoken word makes a stronger rather than a weaker impression if we are not permitted to count the hairs in Romeo's mustache.

This does not mean that the scenario is a negligible factor in the making of a moving picture. It only means that its artistic intention differs in kind from that of a stage play, and much more from that of a novel or a piece of poetry. As the success of a Gothic jamb figure depends not only upon its quality as a piece of literature but also, or even more so, upon its integrability with the architecture of the portal, so does the success of a movie script—not unlike that of an opera libretto —depend, not only upon its quality as a piece of literature but also, or even more so, upon its integrability with the events on the screen.

As a result—another empirical proof of the coexpressibility principle—good movie scripts are unlikely to make good reading and have seldom been published in book form; whereas, conversely, good stage plays have to be severely altered, cut, and, on the other hand, enriched by interpolations to make good movie scripts. In Shaw's *Pygmalion,* for instance, the actual process of Eliza's phonetic education and, still more important, her final triumph at the grand party, are wisely omitted; we see—or, rather, hear—some samples of her gradual linguistic improvement and finally encounter her, upon her return from the reception, victorious and splendidly arrayed but deeply hurt for want of recognition and sympathy. In the film adaptation, precisely these two scenes are not only supplied but also strongly emphasized; we witness the fascinating activities in the laboratory with its array of spinning disks and mirrors, organ pipes and dancing flames, and we participate in the ambassadorial party, with many moments of impending catastrophe and a little counterintrigue thrown in for suspense. Unquestionably these two scenes, entirely absent from the play, and indeed unachievable upon the stage, were the highlights of the film; whereas the Shavian dialogue, however severely cut, turned out to fall a little flat in certain moments. And wherever, as in so many other films, a poetic emotion, a musical outburst, or a literary conceit (even, I am grieved to say, some of the wisecracks of Groucho Marx) entirely lose contact with visible movement, they strike the sensitive spectator as, literally, out of place. It is certainly terrible when a soft-boiled he-man, after the suicide of his mistress, casts a twelve-foot glance upon her photograph and says something less-than-coexpressible to the effect that he will never forget her. But when he recites, instead, a piece of poetry as sublimely more-than-coexpressible as Romeo's monologue, at the bier of Juliet, it is still worse. Reinhardt's *Midsummer Night's Dream* is probably the most unfortunate major film ever produced; and Olivier's *Henry V* owes its comparative success, apart from the all but providential adaptability of this particular play, to so many *tours de force* that it will, God willing, remain an exception rather than set a pattern. It combines "judicious pruning" with the interpolation of pageantry, non-verbal comedy and melodrama; it uses a device perhaps best designated as "oblique close-up" (Mr. Olivier's beautiful face inwardly listening to but not pronouncing the great soliloquy) ; and, most notably, it shifts between three levels of archaeological reality: a reconstruction of Elizabethan London, a reconstruction of the events of 1415 as laid down in Shakespeare's play, and the reconstruction of a performance of this play on Shakespeare's own stage. All this is perfectly legitimate; but, even so, the highest praise of the film will always come from those who, like the critic of the *New Yorker,* are not quite in sympathy with either the movies *au naturel* or Shakespeare *au naturel. . . .*

The evolution from the jerky beginnings to this grand climax offers the fascinating spectacle of a new artistic medium gradually becoming conscious of its legitimate, that is, exclusive, possibilities and limitations—a spectacle not unlike the development of the mosaic, which started out with transposing illusionistic genre pictures into a more durable material and culminated in the hieratic supernaturalism of Ravenna; or the development of line engraving, which started out as a cheap and handy substitute for book illumination and culminated in the purely "graphic" style of Dürer.

Just so the silent movies developed a definite style of their own, adapted to the specific conditions of the medium. A hitherto unknown language was forced upon a public not yet capable of reading it, and the more proficient the public became the more refinement could develop in the language. For a Saxon peasant of around 800 it was not easy to understand the meaning of a picture showing a man as he pours water over the head of another man, and even later many people found it difficult to grasp the significance of two ladies standing behind the throne of an emperor. For the public of around 1910 it was no less difficult to understand the meaning of the speechless action in a moving picture, and the producers employed means of clarification similar to those we find in medieval art. One of these were printed titles or letters, striking equivalents of the medieval *tituli* and scrolls (at a still earlier date there even used to be explainers who would say, *viva voce,* "Now he thinks his wife is dead but she isn't" or "I don't wish to offend the ladies in the audience but I doubt that any of them would have done that much for her child"). Another, less obtrusive method of explanation was the introduction of a fixed iconography which from the outset informed the spectator about the basic facts and characters, much as the two ladies behind the emperor, when carrying a sword and a cross respectively, were uniquely determined as Fortitude and Faith. There arose, identifiable by standardized appearance, behavior and attributes, the well-remembered types of the Vamp and the Straight Girl (perhaps the most convincing modern equivalents of the medieval personifications of the Vices and Virtues), the Family Man, and the Villain, the latter marked by a black mustache and walking stick. Nocturnal scenes were printed on blue or green film. A checkered tablecloth meant, once for all, a "poor but honest" milieu; a happy marriage, soon to be endangered by the shadows from the past, was symbolized by the young wife's pouring the breakfast coffee for her husband; the first kiss was invariably announced by the lady's gently playing with her partner's necktie and was invariably accompanied by her kicking out with her left foot. The conduct of the characters was predetermined accordingly. The poor but honest laborer who, after leaving his little house with the checkered tablecloth, came upon an abandoned baby could not but take it to his home and bring it up as best he could; the Family Man could not but yield, however temporarily, to the temptations of the Vamp. As a result these early melodramas had a highly gratifying and soothing quality in that events took shape, without the complications of individual psychology, according to a pure Aristotelian logic so badly missed in real life.

Devices like these became gradually less necessary as the public grew accustomed to interpret the action by itself and were virtually abolished by the invention of the talking film. But even now there survive—quite legitimately, I think—the remnants of a "fixed attitude and attribute" principle and, more basic, a primitive or folkloristic concept of plot construction. Even today we take it for granted that the diphtheria of a baby tends to occur when the parents are out and, having occurred, solves all their matrimonial problems. Even today we demand of a decent mystery film that the butler, though he may be anything from an agent of the British Secret Service to the real father of the daughter of the house, must not turn out to be the murderer. Even today we love to see Pasteur, Zola or Ehrlich win out against stupidity and wickedness, with their respective wives trusting and trusting all the time. Even today we much prefer a happy finale to a gloomy one and insist, at the very least, on the observance of the Aristotelian rule that the story have a beginning, a middle and an ending —a rule the abrogation of which has done so much to estrange the general public from the more elevated spheres of modern writing. Primitive symbolism, too, survives in such amusing details as the last sequence of *Casablanca* where the delightfully crooked and right-minded *préfet de police* casts an empty bottle of Vichy water into the wastepaper basket; and in such telling symbols of the supernatural as Sir Cedric Hardwicke's Death in the guise of a "gentleman in a dustcoat trying" (*On Borrowed Time*) or Claude Rains's Hermes Psychopompos in the striped trousers of an airline manager (*Here Comes Mister Jordan*).

The most conspicuous advances were made in directing, lighting, camera work, cutting and acting proper. But while in most of these fields the evolution proceeded continuously—though, of course, not without detours, breakdowns and archaic relapses—the development of acting suffered a sudden interruption by the invention of the talking film; so that the style of acting in the silents can already be evaluated in retrospect, as a lost art not unlike the painting technique of Jan van Eyck or, to take up our previous simile, the burin technique of Dürer. It was soon realized that acting in a silent film neither meant a panto-mimic exaggeration of stage acting (as was generally and erroneously assumed by professional stage actors who more and more frequently condescended to perform in the movies), nor could dispense with styliza-tion altogether; a man photographed while walking down a gangway in ordinary, everyday-life fashion looked like anything but a man walking down a gangway when the result appeared on the screen. If the picture was to look both natural and meaningful the acting had to be done in a manner equally different from the style of the stage and the reality of ordinary life; speech had to be made dispensable by establishing an organic relation between the acting and the technical procedure of cinephotography—much as in Dürer's prints color had been made dis-pensable by establishing an organic relation between the design and the technical procedure of line engraving.

This was precisely what the great actors of the silent period ac-complished, and it is a significant fact that the best of them did not come from the stage, whose crystallized tradition prevented Duse's only film, *Cenere,* from being more than a priceless record of Duse. They came instead from the circus or the variety, as was the case of Chaplin, Keaton and Will Rogers; from nothing in particular, as was the case of Theda Bara, of her greater European parallel, the Danish actress Asta Nielsen, and of Garbo; or from everything under the sun, as was the case of Douglas Fairbanks. The style of these "old masters" was indeed comparable to the style of line engraving in that it was, and had to be, exaggerated in comparison with stage acting (just as the sharply incised and vigorously curved *tailles* of the burin are exaggerated in comparison with pencil strokes or brushwork), but richer, subtler and infinitely more precise. The advent of the talkies, reducing if not abolishing this difference between screen acting and stage acting, thus confronted the actors and actresses of the silent screen with a serious problem. Buster Keaton yielded to temptation and fell. Chaplin first tried to stand his ground and to remain an exquisite archaist but finally gave in, with only moderate success (*The Great Dictator*). Only the glorious Harpo has thus far successfully refused to utter a single articulate sound; and only Greta Garbo succeeded, in a measure, in transforming her style in principle. But even in her case one cannot help feeling that her first talking picture, *Anna Christie*, where she could ensconce herself, most of the time, in mute or monosyllabic sullenness, was better than her later performances; and in the second, talking version of *Anna Karenina*, the weakest moment is certainly when she delivers a big Ibsenian speech to her husband, and the strongest when she silently moves along the platform of the railroad station while her despair takes shape in the consonance of her movement (and expression) with the movement of the nocturnal space around her, filled with the real noises of the trains and the imaginary sound of the "little men with the iron hammers" that drives her, relentlessly and almost without her realizing it, under the wheels.

Small wonder that there is sometimes felt a kind of nostalgia for the silent period and that devices have been worked out to combine the virtues of sound and speech with those of silent acting, such as the "oblique close-up" already mentioned in connection with *Henry V;* the dance behind glass doors in *Sous les Toits de Paris;* or, in the *Historie d'un Tricheur,* Sacha Guitry's recital of the events of his youth while the events themselves are "silently" enacted on the screen. However, this nostalgic feeling is no argument against the talkies as such. Their evolution has shown that, in art, every gain entails a certain loss on the other side of the ledger; but that the gain remains a gain, provided that the basic nature of the medium is realized and respected. One can imagine that, when the cavemen of Altamira began to paint their buffaloes in natural colors instead of merely incising the contours, the more conservative cavemen foretold the end of paleolithic art. But paleolithic art went on, and so will the movies. New technical inventions always tend to dwarf the values already attained, especially in a medium that owes its very existence to technical experimentation. The earliest talkies were infinitely inferior to the then mature silents, and most of the present technicolor films are still inferior to the now mature talkies in black and white. But even if Aldous Huxley's nightmare should come true and the experiences of taste, smell and touch should be added to those of sight and hearing, even then we may say with the Apostle, as we have said when first confronted with the sound track and the technicolor film, "We are troubled on every side, yet not distressed; we are perplexed, but not in despair."

From the law of time-charged space and space-bound time, there follows the fact that the screenplay, in contrast to the theater play, *has no aesthetic existence independent of its performance, and that its characters have no aesthetic existence outside the actors.*

The playwright writes in the fond hope that his work will be an imperishable jewel in the treasure house of civilization and will be presented in hundreds of performances that are but transient variations on a "work" that is constant. The script-writer, on the other hand, writes for one producer, one director and one cast. Their work achieves the same degree of permanence as does his; and should the same or a similar scenario ever be filmed by a different director and a different cast there will result an altogether different "play."

Othello or Nora are definite, substantial figures created by the playwright. They can be played well or badly, and they can be "interpreted" in one way or another; but they most definitely exist, no matter who plays them or even whether they are played at all. The character in a film, however, lives and dies with the actor. It is not the entity "Othello" interpreted by Robeson or the entity "Nora" interpreted by Duse; it is the entity "Greta Garbo" incarnate in a figure called Anna Christie or the entity "Robert Montgomery" incarnate in a murderer who, for all we know or care to know, may forever remain anonymous but will never cease to haunt our memories. Even when the names of the characters happen to be Henry VIII or Anna Karenina, the king who ruled England from 1509 to 1547 and the woman created by Tolstoy, they do not exist outside the being of Garbo and Laughton. They are but empty and incorporeal outlines like the shadows in Homer's Hades, assuming the character of reality only when filled with the lifeblood of an actor. Conversely, if a movie role is badly played there remains literally nothing of it, no matter how interesting the character's psychology or how elaborate the words.

What applies to the actor applies, *mutatis mutandis,* to most of the other artists, or artisans, who contribute to the making of a film: the director, the sound man, the enormously important cameraman, even the make-up man. A stage production is rehearsed until everything is ready, and then it is repeatedly performed in three consecutive hours. At each performance everybody has to be on hand and does his work;

and afterward he goes home and to bed. The work of the stage actor may thus be likened to that of a musician, and that of the stage director to that of a conductor. Like these, they have a certain repertoire which they have studied and present in a number of complete but transitory performances, be it *Hamlet* today and *Ghosts* tomorrow, or *Life with Father per saecula saeculorum*. The activities of the film actor and the film director, however, are comparable, respectively, to those of the plastic artist and the architect, rather than to those of the musician and the conductor. Stage work is continuous but transitory; film work is discontinuous but permanent. Individual sequences are done piecemeal and out of order according to the most efficient use of sets and personnel. Each bit is done over and over again until it stands; and when the whole has been cut and composed everyone is through with it forever. Needless to say that this very procedure cannot but emphasize the curious consubstantiality that exists between the person of the movie actor and his role. Coming into existence piece by piece, regardless of the natural sequence of events, the "character" can grow into a unified whole only if the actor manages to be, not merely to play, Henry VIII or Anna Karenina throughout the entire wearisome period of shooting. I have it on the best of authorities that Laughton was really difficult to live with in the particular six or eight weeks during which he was doing—or rather being —Captain Bligh.

It might be said that a film, called into being by a co-operative effort in which all contributions have the same degree of permanence, is the nearest modern equivalent of a medieval cathedral; the role of the producer corresponding, more or less, to that of the bishop or archbishop; that of the director to that of the architect in chief; that of the scenario writers to that of the scholastic advisers establishing the iconographical program; and that of the actors, cameramen, cutters, sound men, make-up men and the divers technicians to that of those whose work provided the physical entity of the finished product, from the sculptors, glass painters, bronze casters, carpenters and skilled masons down to the quarry men and woodsmen. And if you speak to any one of these collaborators he will tell you, with perfect *bona fides,* that his is really the most important job—which is quite true to the extent that it is indispensable. . . .

[1934]

MARSHALL McLUHAN

Movies: The Reel World

In England the movie theater was originally called "The Bioscope," because of its visual presentation of the actual movements of the forms of life (from Greek *bios*, way of life). The movie, by which we roll up the real world on a spool in order to unroll it as a magic carpet of fantasy, is a spectacular wedding of the old mechanical technology and the new electric world. In the chapter on The Wheel, the story was told of how the movie had a kind of symbolic origin in an attempt to photograph the flying hooves of galloping horses, for to set a series of cameras to study animal movement is to merge the mechanical and the organic in a special way. In the medieval world, curiously, the idea of change in organic beings was that of the substitution of one static form for another, in sequence. They imagined the life of a flower as a kind of cinematic strip of phases or essences. The movie is the total realization of the medieval idea of change, in the form of an entertaining illusion. Physiologists had very much to do with the development of film, as they did with the telephone. On film the mechanical appears as organic, and the growth of a flower can be portrayed as easily and as freely as the movement of a horse.

If the movie merges the mechanical and organic in a world of undulating forms, it also links with the technology of print. The reader in projecting words, as it were, has to follow the black and white sequences of stills that is typography, providing his own sound track. He tries to follow the contours of the author's mind, at varying speeds and with various illusions of understanding. It would be difficult to exaggerate the bond between print and movie in terms of their power to generate fantasy in the viewer or reader. Cervantes devoted his *Don Quixote* entirely to this aspect of the printed word and its power to create what James Joyce throughout *Finnegans Wake* designates as "the ABCED-

minded," which can be taken as "ab-said" or "ab-sent," or just alpha-
betically controlled.

The business of the writer or the film-maker is to transfer the
reader or viewer from one world, his *own,* to another, the world created
by typography and film. That is so obvious, and happens so completely,
that those undergoing the experience accept it subliminally and without
critical awareness. Cervantes lived in a world in which print was as
new as movies are in the West, and it seemed obvious to him that print,
like the images now on the screen, had usurped the real world. The
reader or spectator had become a dreamer under their spell, as René
Clair said of film in 1926.

Movies as a nonverbal form of experience are like photography,
a form of statement without syntax. In fact, however, like the print and
the photo, movies assume a high level of literacy in their users and
prove baffling to the nonliterate. Our literate acceptance of the mere
movement of the camera eye as it follows or drops a figure from view
is not acceptable to an African film audience. If somebody disappears
off the side of the film, the African wants to know what happened to
him. A literate audience, however, accustomed to following printed
imagery line by line without questioning the logic of lineality, will
accept film sequence without protest.

It was René Clair who pointed out that if two or three people
were together on a stage, the dramatist must ceaselessly motivate or
explain their being there at all. But the film audience, like the book
reader, accepts mere sequence as rational. Whatever the camera turns
to, the audience accepts. We are transported to another world. As René
Clair observed, the screen opens its white door into a harem of beautiful
visions and adolescent dreams, compared to which the loveliest real
body seems defective. Yeats saw the movie as a world of Platonic ideals
with the film projector playing "a spume upon a ghostly paradigm of
things." This was the world that haunted Don Quixote, who found it
through the folio door of the newly printed romances.

The close relation, then, between the reel world of film and the
private fantasy experience of the printed word is indispensable to our
Western acceptance of the film form. Even the film industry regards
all of its greatest achievements as derived from novels, nor is this unreasonable. Film, both in its reel form and in its scenario or script form,
is completely involved with book culture. All one need do is to imagine
for a moment a film based on newspaper form in order to see how close
film is to book. Theoretically, there is no reason why the camera should
not be used to photograph complex groups of items and events in date-
line configurations, just as they are presented on the page of a news-

paper. Actually, poetry tends to do this configuring or "bunching" more than prose. Symbolist poetry has much in common with the mosaic of the newspaper page, yet very few people can detach themselves from uniform and connected space sufficiently to grasp symbolist poems. Natives, on the other hand, who have very little contact with phonetic literacy and lineal print, have to learn to "see" photographs or film just as much as we have to learn our letters. In fact, after having tried for years to teach Africans their letters by film, John Wilson of London University's African Institute found it easier to teach them their letters as a means to film literacy. For even when natives have learned to "see" pictures, they cannot accept our ideas of time and space "illusions." On seeing Charlie Chaplin's *The Tramp,* the African audience concluded that Europeans were magicians who could restore life. They saw a character who survived a mighty blow on the head without any indication of being hurt. When the camera shifts, they think they see trees moving, and buildings growing or shrinking, because they cannot make the literate assumption that space is continuous and uniform. Nonliterate people simply don't get perspective or distancing effects of light and shade that we assume are innate human equipment. Literate people think of cause and effect as sequential, as if one thing pushed another along by physical force. Nonliterate people register very little interest in this kind of "efficient" cause and effect, but are fascinated by hidden forms that produce magical results. Inner, rather than outer, causes interest the nonliterate and nonvisual cultures. And that is why the literate West sees the rest of the world as caught in the seamless web of superstition.

Like the oral Russian, the African will not accept sight and sound together. The talkies were the doom of Russian film-making because, like any backward or oral culture, Russians have an irresistible need for participation that is defeated by the addition of sound to the visual image. Both Pudovkin and Eisenstein denounced the sound film but considered that if sound were used symbolically and contrapuntally, rather than realistically, there would result less harm to the visual image. The African insistence on group participation and on chanting and shouting during films is wholly frustrated by sound track. Our own talkies were a further completion of the visual package as a mere consumer commodity. For with silent film we automatically provide sound for ourselves by way of "closure" or completion. And when it is filled in for us there is very much less participation in the work of the image.

Again, it has been found that nonliterates do not know how to fix their eyes, as Westerners do, a few feet in front of the movie screen, or some distance in front of a photo. The result is that they move their eyes over photo or screen as they might their hands. It is this same habit of using the eyes as hands that makes European men so "sexy" to American women. Only an extremely literate and abstract society learns to fix the eyes, as we must learn to do in reading the printed page. For those who thus fix their eyes, perspective results. There is great subtlety and synesthesia in native art, but no perspective. The old belief that everybody really saw in perspective, but only that Renaissance painters had learned how to paint it, is erroneous. Our own first TV generation is rapidly losing this habit of visual perspective as a sensory modality, and along with this change comes an interest in words not as visually uniform and continuous, but as unique worlds in depth. Hence the craze for puns and word-play, even in sedate ads.

In terms of other media such as the printed page, film has the power to store and to convey a great deal of information. In an instant it presents a scene of landscape with figures that would require several pages of prose to describe. In the next instant it repeats, and can go on repeating, this detailed information. The writer, on the other hand, has no means of holding a mass of detail before his reader in a large bloc of *gestalt*. As the photograph urged the painter in the direction of abstract, sculptural art, so the film has confirmed the writer in verbal economy and depth symbolism where the film cannot rival him.

Another facet of the sheer quantity of data possible in a movie shot is exemplified in historical films like *Henry V* or *Richard III*. Here extensive research went into the making of the sets and costumes that any six-year-old can now enjoy as readily as any adult. T. S. Eliot reported how, in the making of the film of his *Murder in the Cathedral*, it was not only necessary to have costumes of the period, but—so great is the precision and tyranny of the camera eye—these costumes had to be woven by the same techniques as those used in the twelfth century. Hollywood, amidst much illusion, had also to provide authentic scholarly replicas of many past scenes. The stage and TV can make do with very rough approximations, because they offer an image of low definition that evades detailed scrutiny.

At first, however, it was the detailed realism of writers like Dickens that inspired movie pioneers like D. W. Griffith, who carried a copy of a Dickens novel on location. The realistic novel, that arose with the newspaper form of communal cross-section and human-interest coverage in the eighteenth century, was a complete anticipation of film form. Even the poets took up the same panoramic style, with human interest vignettes and close-ups as variant. Gray's *Elegy*, Burns' *The Cotter's Saturday Night*, Wordsworth's *Michael*, and Byron's *Childe Harold* are all like shooting scripts for some contemporary documentary film.

"The kettle began it. . . ." Such is the opening of Dickens' *Cricket and the Hearth*. If the modern novel came out of Gogol's *The Overcoat*, the modern movie, says Eisenstein, boiled up out of that kettle. It should be plain that the American and even British approach to film is much lacking in that free interplay among the senses and the media that seems so natural to Eisenstein or René Clair. For the Russian, especially, it is easy to approach any situation structurally, which is to say, sculpturally. To Eisenstein, the overwhelming fact of film was that it is an "act of juxtaposition." But to a culture in an extreme reach of typographic conditioning, the juxtaposition must be one of uniform and connected characters and qualities. There must be no leaps from the unique space of the tea kettle to the unique space of the kitten or the boot. If such objects appear, they must be leveled off by some continuous narrative, or be "contained" in some uniform pictorial space. All that Salvador Dali had to do to create a furor was to allow the chest of drawers or the grand piano to exist in its own space against some Sahara or Alpine backdrop. Merely by releasing objects from the uniform continuous space of typography we got modern art and poetry. We can measure the psychic pressure of typography by the uproar generated by that release. For most people, their own ego image seems to have been typographically conditioned, so that the electric age with its return to inclusive experience threatens their idea of self. These are the fragmented ones, for whom specialist toil renders the mere prospect of leisure or jobless security a nightmare. Electric simultaneity ends specialist learning and activity, and demands interrelation in depth, even of the personality.

The case of Charlie Chaplin films helps to illumine this problem. His *Modern Times* was taken to be a satire on the fragmented character of modern tasks. As clown, Chaplin presents the acrobatic feat in a mime of elaborate incompetence, for any specialist task leaves out most of our faculties. The clown reminds us of our fragmented state by tackling acrobatic or special jobs in the spirit of the whole or integral man. This is the formula for helpless incompetence. On the street, in social situations, on the assembly line, the worker continues his compulsive twitchings with an imaginary wrench. But the mime of this Chaplin film and others is precisely that of the robot, the mechanical doll whose deep pathos it is to approximate so closely to the condition of human life. Chaplin, in all his work, did a puppetlike ballet of the Cyrano de Bergerac kind. In order to capture this puppetlike pathos, Chaplin (a devotee of ballet and personal friend of Pavlova) adopted from the first the foot postures of classical ballet. Thus he could have the aura of *Spectre de la Rose* shimmering around his clown getup. From the British music hall, his first training ground, with a sure touch of genius he took images like that of Mr. Charles Pooter, the haunting figure of a nobody. This shoddy-genteel image he invested with an envelope of fairy romance by means of adherence to the classic ballet postures. The new film form was perfectly adapted to this composite image, since film is itself a jerky mechanical ballet of flicks that yields a sheer dream world of romantic illusions. But the film form is not just a puppetlike dance of arrested still shots, for it manages to approximate and even to surpass real life by means of illusion. That is why Chaplin, in his silent pictures at least, was never tempted to abandon the Cyrano role of the puppet who could never really be a lover. In this stereotype Chaplin discovered the heart of the film illusion, and he manipulated that heart with easy mastery, as the key to the pathos of a mechanized civilization. A mechanized world is always in the process of getting ready to live, and to this end it brings to bear the most appalling pomp of skill and method and resourcefulness.

The film pushed this mechanism to the utmost mechanical verge and beyond, into a surrealism of dreams that money can buy. Nothing is more congenial to the film form than this pathos of superabundance and power that is the dower of a puppet for whom they can never be real. This is the key to *The Great Gatsby* that reaches its moment of truth when Daisy breaks down in contemplating Gatsby's superb collection of shirts. Daisy and Gatsby live in a tinsel world that is both corrupted by power, yet innocently pastoral in its dreaming.

The movie is not only a supreme expression of mechanism, but paradoxically it offers as product the most magical of consumer commodities, namely dreams. It is, therefore, not accidental that the movie has excelled as a medium that offers poor people roles of riches and power beyond their dreams of avarice. In the chapter on The Photograph, it was pointed out how the press photo in particular had discouraged the really rich from the paths of conspicuous consumption. The life of display that the photo had taken from the rich, the movie gave to the poor with lavish hand:

> Oh, lucky, lucky me,
> I shall live in luxury,
> For I've got a pocketful of dreams.

The Hollywood tycoons were not wrong in acting on the assumption that movies gave the American immigrant a means of self-fulfillment without any delay. This strategy, however deplorable in the light of the "absolute ideal good," was perfectly in accord with film form. It meant that in the 1920s the American way of life was exported to the entire world in cans. The world eagerly lined up to buy canned dreams.

The film not only accompanied the first great consumer age, but was also incentive, advertisement and, in itself, a major commodity. Now in terms of media study it is clear that the power of film to store information in accessible form is unrivaled. Audio tape and video tape were to excel film eventually as information storehouses. But film remains a major information resource, a rival of the book whose technology it did so much to continue and also to surpass. At the present time, film is still in its manuscript phase, as it were; shortly it will, under TV pressure, go into its portable, accessible, printed-book phase. Soon everyone will be able to have a small, inexpensive film projector that plays an 8-mm sound cartridge as if on a TV screen. This type of development is part of our present technological implosion. The present dissociation of projector and screen is a vestige of our older mechanical world of explosion and separation of functions that is now ending with the electrical implosion.

Typographic man took readily to film just because, like books, it offers an inward world of fantasy and dreams. The film viewer sits in psychological solitude like the silent book reader. This was not the case with the manuscript reader, nor is it true of the watcher of television. It is not pleasant to turn on TV just for oneself in a hotel room, nor even at home. The TV mosaic image demands social completion and dialogue. So with the manuscript before typography, since manuscript culture is oral and demands dialogue and debate, as the entire culture of the ancient and medieval worlds demonstrates. One of the major pressures of TV has been to encourage the "teaching machine." In fact, these devices are adaptations of the book in the direction of dialogue. These teaching machines are really private tutors, and their being misnamed on the principle that produced the names "wireless" and "horseless carriage" is another instance in that long list that illustrates how every innovation must pass through a primary phase in which the new effect is secured by the old method, amplified or modified by some new feature.

Film is not really a single medium like song or the written word, but a collective art form with different individuals directing color, lighting, sound, acting, speaking. The press, radio and TV, and the comics are also art forms dependent upon entire teams and hierarchies of skill in corporate action. Prior to the movies, the most obvious example of such corporate artistic action had occurred early in the industrialized world, with the large new symphony orchestras of the nineteenth century. Paradoxically, as industry went its ever more specialized fragmented course, it demanded more and more teamwork in sales and supplies. The symphony orchestra became a major expression of the ensuing power of such coordinated effort, though for the players themselves this effect was lost, both in the symphony and in industry.

When the magazine editors recently introduced film scenario procedures to the constructing of idea articles, the idea article supplanted the short story. The film is the rival of the book in that sense. (TV in turn is the rival of the magazine because of its mosaic power.) Ideas presented as a sequence of shots or pictorialized situations, almost in the manner of a teaching machine, actually drove the short story out of the magazine field.

Hollywood has fought TV mainly by becoming a subsidiary of TV. Most of the film industry is now engaged in supplying TV programs. But one new strategy has been tried, namely the big-budget picture. The fact is that Technicolor is the closest the movie can get to the effect of the TV image. Technicolor greatly lowers photographic intensity and creates, in part, the visual conditions for participant viewing. Had Hollywood understood the reasons for *Marty*'s success, TV might have given us a revolution in film. *Marty* was a TV show that got onto the screen in the form of low definition or low-intensity visual realism. It was not a success story, and it had no stars, because the low-intensity TV image is quite incompatible with the high-intensity star image. *Marty*, which in fact looked like an early silent movie or an old Russian picture, offered the film industry all the clues it needed for meeting the TV challenge.

This kind of casual, cool realism has given the new British films easy ascendancy. *Room at the Top* features the new cool realism. Not only is it not a success story, it is as much an announcement of the end of the Cinderella package as Marilyn Monroe was the end of the star system. *Room at the Top* is the story of how the higher a monkey climbs, the more you see of his backside. The moral is that success is not only wicked but also the formula for misery. It is very hard for a hot medium like film to accept the cool message of TV. But the Peter Sellers movies *I'm All Right, Jack* and *Only Two Can Play* are perfectly in tune with the new temper created by the cool TV image. Such is also the meaning of the ambiguous success of *Lolita*. As a novel, its acceptance announced the antiheroic approach to romance. The film industry had long beaten out a royal road to romance in keeping with the crescendo of the success story. *Lolita* announced that the royal road was only a cowtrack, after all, and as for success, it shouldn't happen to a dog.

In the ancient world and in medieval times, the most popular of all stories were those dealing with *The Falls of Princes*. With the coming of the very hot print medium, the preference changed to a rising rhythm and to tales of success and sudden elevation in the world. It seemed possible to achieve anything by the new typographic method of minute, uniform segmentation of problems. It was by this method, eventually, that film was made. Film was, as a form, the final fulfillment of the great potential of typographic fragmentation. But the electric implosion has now reversed the entire process of expansion by fragmentation. Electricity has brought back the cool, mosaic world of implosion, equilibrium, and stasis. In our electric age, the one-way expansion of the berserk individual on his way to the top now appears as a gruesome image of trampled lives and disrupted harmonies. Such is the subliminal message of the TV mosaic with its total field of simultaneous impulses. Film strip and sequence cannot but bow to this superior power. Our own youngsters have taken the TV message to heart in their beatnik rejection of consumer mores and of the private success story.

Since the best way to get to the core of a form is to study its effect in some unfamiliar setting, let us note what President Sukarno of Indonesia announced in 1956 to a large group of Hollywood executives. He said that he regarded them as political radicals and revolutionaries who had greatly hastened political change in the East. What the Orient saw in a Hollywood movie was a world in which all the *ordinary people* had cars and electric stoves and refrigerators. So the Oriental now regards himself as an ordinary person who has been deprived of the ordinary man's birthright.

That is another way of getting a view of the film medium as monster ad for consumer goods. In America this major aspect of film is merely subliminal. Far from regarding our pictures as incentives to mayhem and revolution, we take them as solace and compensation, or as a form of deferred payment by daydreaming. But the Oriental is right, and we are wrong about this. In fact, the movie is a mighty limb of the industrial giant. That it is being amputated by the TV image reflects a still greater revolution going on at the center of American life. It is natural that the ancient East should feel the political pull and industrial challenge of our movie industry. The movie, as much as the alphabet and the printed word, is an aggressive and imperial form that explodes outward into other cultures. Its explosive force was significantly greater in silent pictures than in talkies, for the electromagnetic sound track already forecast the substitution of electric implosion for mechanical explosion. The silent pictures were immediately acceptable across language barriers as the talkies were not. Radio teamed up with film to give us the talkie and to carry us further on our present reverse course of implosion or re-integration after the mechanical age of explosion and expansion. The extreme form of this implosion or contraction is the image of the astronaut locked into his wee bit of wrap-around space.

Far from enlarging our world, he is announcing its contraction to village size. The rocket and the space capsule are ending the rule of the wheel and the machine, as much as did the wire services, radio, and TV.

We may now consider a further instance of the film's influence in a most conclusive aspect. In modern literature there is probably no more celebrated technique than that of the stream of consciousness or interior monologue. Whether in Proust, Joyce, or Eliot, this form of sequence permits the reader an extraordinary identification with personalities of the utmost range and diversity. The stream of consciousness is really managed by the transfer of film technique to the printed page, where, in a deep sense it really originated; for as we have seen, the Gutenberg technology of movable types is quite indispensable to any industrial or film process. As much as the infinitesimal calculus that *pretends* to deal with motion and change by minute fragmentation, the film *does* so by making motion and change into a series of static shots. Print does likewise while pretending to deal with the whole mind in action. Yet film and the stream of consciousness alike seemed to provide a deeply desired release from the mechanical world of increasing standardization and uniformity. Nobody ever felt oppressed by the monotony or uniformity of the Chaplin ballet or by the monotonous, uniform musings of his literary twin, Leopold Bloom.

In 1911 Henri Bergson in *Creative Evolution* created a sensation by associating the thought process with the form of the movie. Just at the extreme point of mechanization represented by the factory, the film, and the press, men seemed by the stream of consciousness, or interior film to obtain release into a world of spontaneity, of dreams, and of unique personal experience. Dickens perhaps began it all with his Mr. Jingle in *Pickwick Papers*. Certainly in *David Copperfield* he made a great technical discovery, since for the first time the world unfolds realistically through the use of the eyes of a growing child as camera. Here was the stream of consciousness, perhaps, in its original form before it was adopted by Proust and Joyce and Eliot. It indicates how the enrichment of human experience can occur unexpectedly with the crossing and interplay of the life of media forms.

The film imports of all nations, especially those from the United States, are very popular in Thailand, thanks in part to a deft Thai technique for getting round the foreign-language obstacle. In Bangkok, in place of subtitles, they use what is called "Adam-and-Eving." This takes the form of live Thai dialogue read through a loudspeaker by Thai actors concealed from the audience. Split-second timing and great endurance enable these actors to demand more than the best-paid movie stars of Thailand.

Everyone has at some time wished he were equipped with his own sound system during a movie performance, in order to make appropriate comments. In Thailand, one might achieve great heights of interpretive interpolation during the inane exchanges of great stars.

[1964]

CHARLES EIDSVIK

Soft Edges:
the Art of Literature,
the Medium of Film

Is film a branch of literature? I do not think any of us believe
it for a moment. Yet we go to most films for pretty much the same reasons that we read most novels or go to most plays. We want to imaginatively participate in worlds different from and more interesting than our
own. What we get in most films and novels and plays is similar regardless
of medium: characters with problems in stories with themes, hopefully
in a work with something to say. Film is not literature, but the reason for
being of a lot of films is literary. From that paradox springs the bulk of
film-literature criticism, most of which seems dedicated to showing how
films are different from literature. Such criticism is frequently unsuccessful because critics tend to treat literature as one monolith and film as
another. They forget that literature is an art comprised of more than one
medium and that film is a medium for more than one art. Literature and
film are two sorts of things, each capable of encompassing part of the
other. It is perfectly reasonable to talk of the literary cinema or to call a
particular film a work of literature. But because the films we go to for
literary reasons are merely one use of film, we cannot argue that film *per
se* is a branch of literature.

Film and literary critics alike confuse literature with its dominant
medium, print, and confuse the medium of film with its dominant genre,
the narrative. While the latter confusion leads to a futile search for "the"
art of film, the former confusion has more consequences for film-literature
criticism. Critics accustomed to identifying film by its perceptual mode of

From *Literature/Film Quarterly*, II, no. 1 (Winter, 1974). Copyright ©
1974 by Salisbury State College. Reprinted by permission of Salisbury State College.

apprehension, mistakenly believe that literature can be identified by the conceptual way we apprehend printed verbal language. For example, George Bluestone, in *Novels into Film*, writes of film and literature as "two ways of seeing," which are "overtly compatible, secretly hostile"; he explains that "between the percept of the visual image and the concept of the mental image lies the root difference between the two media."[1] Erwin Panofsky uses words such as "materialistic" and "physical" for film while he calls literature "conceptual."[2] Siegfried Kracauer claims that the cinema, unlike literature, "redeems physical reality" and gives us "life in the raw."[3] And Jean Mitry contends: "the novel is a story which is organized into a world, the film is a world which is organized into a story."[4] Later in this essay I will argue against the democratic assigning of one art to each medium and against the clear opposition between perception and concepts which these writers posit. But first it is necessary to establish that literature is not the same thing as printed verbal language.

Literature has never been a one-medium art. Literature did not spring fully armed from the head of Johann Gutenberg on the day he invented movable type; nor did it arise from the invention of the graphemic alphabet which made writing possible. Literature began with poets, not paper, with performance, not print. The great bardic traditions that gave us Beowulf (and probably Homer's work as well) were aural and theatrical. As Alfred Lord has shown, they were traditions of poets who wrote with their bodies and their voices, and who were (as many poets still are) performing artists. Performance is, in fact, at the heart of literature. *Beowulf* was in the world before a scribe recorded it. Chaucer performed his works. And a printer did not turn *Othello* into literature. Performance was the intended medium for all of Shakespeare's plays, and print is but their poor surrogate memory, their second literary medium. Even a single work can have more than one medium. For example, *The Wasteland* existed in personal performance while Mr. Eliot lived; it exists on paper, and it exists on a phonograph recording. *The Wasteland* is a poem, a poem is poetry, and poetry is literature, no matter the medium. *The Wasteland* might be literature if it were filmed, especially if Eliot had (as he did for *Murder in the Cathedral*) adapted the medium to his intentions. (In a good film adaptation it is sometimes the original and sometimes the medium which is adapted. It depends on which is the

[1]George Bluestone, *Novels into Film* (Berkeley: U. Cal. Press, 1966), pp. 1–2.

[2]Erwin Panofsky, "Style and Medium in the Motion Pictures," *Film: an Anthology*, ed. Daniel Talbott (Berkeley: U. Cal Press, 1969), pp. 15–32.

[3]Siegfried Kracauer, *Theory of Film* (London: Oxford U. Press, 1960). See especially pp. 300–301.

[4]Jean Mitry, *Esthétique et psychology du cinéma*, 2 Vols. (Paris: University Presses, 1963, 1965), I, 59. See also II, 352–354.

more cared about.) Literature is a kind of intentionality, not a kind of artifact.

This is not to say that *The Wasteland* would be better as a film than as a printed poem, or even that *any* film of the poem would be literary. A work is designed for a medium, and its forms are never separate from its means of transmission. Mr. Eliot geared his aural reading to his voice and his printed version to the page. Listening to the poem on a record, and then reading it, I feel as if I have arrived at the same place by two different paths. To judge whether a film of *The Wasteland* were literary, I would have to see the film and judge the place it got me to. Of course the notion of filming *The Wasteland* is far-fetched. That poem was designed for spoken and printed verbal language, and in fact spoken language was *The Wasteland*'s second medium. The *conventional* biases of the medium of film would make a very strange film of Eliot's poem. Though media biases are never absolutes, some literary forms seem most appropriate to a specific medium. Lyrics beg for the music of voice and gesture attainable in personal performance. *Remembrance of Things Past*, because of its length and complexity, would seem odd as anything but a novel. Print makes a work of literature into a portable artifact, and that seems appropriate to Proust. But songs and gestures and voice tones, rhythms, and inflections—all that gets lost in ordinary print. The sounds and sights of Shakespeare's plays and the etchings so integral to Blake's poetry are left out of most printed editions because print is unfriendly to those elements that cannot be symbolized by moveable type. Some *littérateurs* who write for performance, such as George Bernard Shaw, are aware of media biases and rewrite for print. For those who do not rewrite, we can expect that some parts of their work meet tragedy at the print shop. Critics so ready to sneer at what happens when a printed work is filmed never think to ask what happens to a performed work when it is adapted into print.

Print biases are so built into literary criticism that it is difficult to think fairly of literature in any other medium. Since the Renaissance, print has been literature's dominant medium, and it is during print's dominance that literary criticism has matured. The Renaissance encountered the ancients through the medium of print and somehow got the worthiness of the ancients and print so confused that when Ben Jonson printed his plays it became a scandal. By the time Sam Johnson wrote his dictionary (1750), language *meant* printed verbal language. (It has taken modern linguists a half-century to straighten out that error.) In Johnson's "Preface to Shakespeare" he declares as tests of literature "length of duration and continuance of esteem." Although print could not have provided the latter, it gave Shakespeare the former automatically. Johnson's aesthetic (and virtually all of literary criticism since Johnson) is biased against special occasions and biased toward special artifacts which, conveniently for the critic, are forever comparable. "Dated" has become a pejorative term, though all performances are *a priori* dated. The fact that books are artifacts which lose nothing in duplication makes print virtually the only medium which can fare well in an aesthetic which values immortality. The artifact-based aesthetic reached its most monopolistic point with New Criticism's demand that a critic must "go to the text." The only kind of texts a critic can go to easily are those embodied in print form. From the print-bias of criticism has come the common division of labor between literature and theatre departments, with the ludicrous consequence that Shakespeare frequently becomes a disputed property. The sad thing is that few English professors are capable of teaching Shakespeare as a composer of performances. I doubt that more than one-fourth of the professors in the English Department in which I work see more than two plays or attend more than one or two poetry readings per year. Literary critics are usually print critics who paradoxically know nothing about the medium of print.

If literary critics look exclusively to one medium to define their territory, film critics do so to an even greater extent, making film the sole criterion for identifying their domain. Their mistake is in thinking film is one art. They ignore the radical differences between films such as Whitney's computer-made *Permutations* and Arthur Penn's actor-wrought *Bonnie and Clyde*, between journalism such as *An American Family* and what happens when Norman McLaren paints directly onto film stock. I always wonder which of film's arts critics mean when they discuss "the" art of film. I share Raymond Durgnat's view that there are many film arts. Durgnat argues that when we watch a movie we do not look at, but *through* the screen to what is communicated. A medium is something we look through, not at, and it is what we see through a medium that defines which art we are involved in. Etienne Fuzellier, in *Cinéma et littérature,* points out that media such as print and film exist because we need tools with which to communicate, and that communication, being purposive, finds similar outlets in any medium. For example, the lyric, the expository essay, and the narrative occur as both film and print. It is superficial to lump films together as one art when different films have almost irreconcilable intents and effects. We go to Jordan Belson's cosmic animations for different reasons than we go to Eric Rohmer's moral tales and get utterly different things in and from those two artists. Film is a medium with many messages.

The root of film's uniqueness, according to George Bluestone, is in the way we apprehend it. He sees an opposition between "the world perceived on film" and language. For Bluestone, language is a "universe of significations" which "must be filtered through the screen of conceptual apprehension," whereas the visual has "innocence."[5] Bluestone is wrong about both the world we see and about perception. As Edward T. Hall points out repeatedly in *The Silent Language,* "culture communicates." Every culture codifies the significances of not only objects and behavior but also of such elements as time and space. The world encountered by the poet, the novelist, and the filmmaker is prestructured and pre-signified by his culture; he cannot ignore cultural significations if he is to communicate. Without such pre-signification, neither films nor books would make much sense to their audiences. What we see is already a universe of significations.

Further, perception is itself a structured act. We do not listen *at;* we listen *for.* And we do not look *at;* we look *for.* What William James called "a certain blindness in human beings" stems frequently from the way we do not see what is not in our visual vocabulary. To see frequently means "to recognize." When Joseph Conrad wrote that he wanted to make us see, he could well have meant it literally; what we see is frequently clichéd, in part by the intentionality and conceptuality of acts of perception. As Rudolph Arnheim makes clear in *Visual Thinking,* perception involves problem-solving; cognition and perception are inseparable. Vision is a selective process of reaching out for visual objects, separating them from their contexts, and observing their characteristics while watching how they interrelate with their surroundings.[6] Psychology tells us that if vision were not active we literally would not see anything at all because an image fixed on the retina disintegrates.[7] The act of seeing is itself an act of signifying. And because perception occurs in time, our signifying is modified by accretion, which is to say that vision has syntax.

I am not arguing for Benjamin Whorf's notion that language determines perception. Rather I am arguing that perception is itself linguistic, though it remains different from verbal language nevertheless, and though it is very dangerous to attribute the qualities of verbal language to the perceptual. Though one can find perceptual roots in virtually all abstract speech,[8] verbal language functions by conjuring or invoking images which can function as pictures, signs, or symbols. But verbal language unlike perception is incapable of dealing with pictures

[5]Bluestone, pp. 13, 20.

[6]See Rudolf Arnheim, *Visual Thinking* (Berkeley: U. Cal. Press, 1971), pp. 13–15, 37–38.

[7]See R. L. Gregory, *Eye and Brain: the Psychology of Seeing* (New York: McGraw-Hill, 1966), pp. 43–44.

[8]Arnheim, p. 232.

directly and, moreover, must evoke its images one at a time, in a strictly linear order, with each image amending the last and with features like word-order fairly predetermined. If and when semiology reaches maturity, we will be able to better compare the structures of perception and the structures of verbal language. Until then we are best-off keeping our views of the relation between the two soft-edged. In ordinary communication we watch *and* listen *and* converse in a multi-layered way; when we cannot see a speaker, we frequently find it difficult to understand what he is saying. To me, that indicates that verbal language and perception are interlocked parts of a larger linguistic gestalt of which we know very little. Even with the advances made by transformational linguistics, what we know about language is little more than a veneer over a bog of ambiguity. The fact that we know so little about communication makes facile distinctions between communication media highly suspect.

The mythic foundations of media are no less ambiguous than the languages they carry. For André Bazin, the most influential modern French film critic, the cinema is not a product of science but of imagination. In "The Myth of Total Cinema" Bazin argues that the technical developments which make the cinema possible evolved out of man's desire to "recreate the world in its own image." The cinema is the product of the idealist's imagination working in the service of a myth he calls "the myth of total cinema" but which recalls the myths of Narcissus and Dionysius. He sees this myth's relationship to the motion picture as a parallel to the relationship of the myth of Icarus to the airplane: "The myth of Icarus had to wait on the internal combustion engine before descending from the platonic heavens. But it had dwelt in the soul of everyman since he first thought of birds."[9] The myth of total cinema, however, resonates in several arts and several media. As Northrop Frye has observed, lifelikeness is always the primary emphasis in literature; creation for its own sake develops only after an art form reaches maturity. The poet, Shelley said, is the unacknowledged legislator of the world. His purpose is always to recreate and rectify reality. As one critic has written, the artist is "always in sinful competition with God." And that is true whether the artist is a poet, painter, or filmmaker. The myth of total cinema is a resurrection myth. The painter and poet and filmmaker take reality as they see it, embalm it through media, and then make it live again through their art. When we go to the theatre, read a book, or go to a film, we usually partake of the same heretical myth

[9]André Bazin, *What is Cinema*, trans. Hugh Gray, 2 Vols. (Berkeley, U. Cal. Press, 1967, 1972), 1.22.

which expresses the same deep wishes. Every new metamorphosis of the myth which embodies it masterfully reenforces the myth and increases our appreciation of the sin that is art, and every bad work recalls *Frankenstein,* Mary Shelley's embodiment of every artist's fear of failure.

Because one root myth surfaces in all arts, it is no wonder that we usually go to films and read books for pretty much the same reasons. Yet it does not make sense to say that all arts are alike because the myth manifests itself through a series of traditions and rebellions against the inadequacy of those traditions. The literary cinema evolved from a rebellion against the silence of print, the static nature of painting and still photography, and the lack of portability and permanence of live performance. Film is a medium capable of synthesizing a cluster of other media and a cluster of artistic intentions. A film-literature critic must ask what artistic traditions and intentions are most present in a particular film. What is most important in the work? If it is simply the visuals for their own sake, as in the Whitney Brothers' *Lapis,* a critic can hardly illuminate the work by calling on his knowledge of literary traditions. Had the medium of film never been invented, *Lapis* would not have been attempted as a novel or play or performed poem. It might have been a *pointilliste* painting awaiting the art of animation so it could be set to music. If film did not exist, other films might have been attempted in earlier literary media such as print or performance. The fictional narrative, for example, is rooted in a tradition of storytelling which dates from the beginnings of literature; the tradition embodied transcends any one medium. What I am suggesting is that in identifying the affinities of a particular film, the critic would do well to subtract film's existence and ask what artistic traditions the work expresses and continues. On those grounds, a good number of films are works of literature.

Moreover, the literary critic has a lot to offer in criticizing particular films because he knows something about literary traditions which a critic trained only in the history of film would likely be ignorant of. For example, a "pure" film critic would likely find affinities between *Bonnie and Clyde* and earlier films such as John Ford's *The Grapes of Wrath* or gangster films of the 1930's, and those affinities might provide illuminating comparisons and contrasts. A literary critic could find affinities with a whole genre of quest/road works going back to Homer's *The Odyssey.* He would discover that *Bonnie and Clyde* is a modern metamorphosis of the picaresque tale and that it resonates with works as disparate as *Don Quixote* and *Heart of Darkness.* No other critic has more to say about the narrative cinema than the critic trained in both literature and the medium of film.

The job of a critic of film-literature relationships is, then, to discover on whose shoulders a film rests, that is, to ask which traditions illuminate a particular film. Once he has done that he can ask what the individual work does that is unique, that makes it an extension of, rather than merely a part of, an earlier tradition. Ideally that job would involve using total recall and a knowledge of media beyond any of our present dreams. The state of the art of criticism is not that advanced. We are stuck with the choice between modifying old vocabularies and inventing new ones; either way we are likely to be misunderstood. You cannot talk about literature without knowing that literature has been so closely associated with print that scientists ask whether you know a field's "literature." For them, "literature" means "articles about." But you have to start somewhere, and I prefer old language, in part because I feel the distortions it invites are less dangerous than the distortions inherent in cutting oneself off from the languages of the past. Like the artist, the critic *must* depend on others' efforts, even if that makes film-literature criticism not for those who cannot live in a messy house.

It would be easy to just sweep ambiguities under the rug of a one-art-per-medium hypothesis. It would be comfortable, too, except that a B-52 is now taking off close to my house. Even Proust's cork-lined walls could not save me from knowing that if I want literature right now, I've got to go to the movies, because it is too damned noisy to read a book. Given a choice, I prefer ambiguities to the loss of an art I love. When I cannot read, and traffic prevents me from getting to a theatre or large screen, it is comforting to feel that literature will somehow survive, even (God help us) if we have to turn on our television sets to find it.

[1974]

7

Film's Literary Resources

Francois Truffaut offers a variety of moods in this sequence from *Jules and Jim* (1961), although the composition involving three persons is used consistently throughout the film.

Figure 7.1   Courtesy of Janus Films.

Figure 7.2   Courtesy of Janus Films.

Figure 7.3   Courtesy of Janus Films.

Figure 7.4   Courtesy of Janus Films.

Figure 7.5   Courtesy of Janus Films.

Figure 7.6   Courtesy of Janus Films.

OUTTAKES

The more the arts develop the more they depend on each other for definition.

E. M. FORSTER

Literary art differs from non-art in that it stimulates not one idea but an infinity of ideas.

LEO TOLSTOY

All storytelling, whether in folk tales, drama, literature or movies, is based on a projection of fantasies.

HORTENSE POWDERMAKER

Form always has to do with mental qualities, with structures of thought and matter. It's nonsense that lyric is about "nothing." That's how art pulls us into the essence of things, through the form —and the form is thought.

JONAS MEKAS

There is a tendency, in movie criticism, to avoid any comparisons or methods that are either borrowed from other arts or resemble those of the other arts. I think such fears are unnecessary. The fact is, that when you watch a film, you are absorbing various visual impressions.

JONAS MEKAS

Unfortunately, there exists neither a vocabulary nor an intellectual framework in which film as film can be seen; the only tools are literary and art historical, and by a careful juxtapositioning and balancing of the two, it may be possible to approximate a vocabulary of cinematic criticism.

P. ADAMS SITNEY

A film artist's "text" requires the aesthetic participation of the literate spectator; and without the convergence of moviemaker and moviegoer, whose joint effort brings a movie to realization, a movie, like a book, floats in an expanse of air, unfixed and unrecognized, temporary and transient, incapable of being put to use or built upon.

NORMAN SILVERSTEIN

It is the story which fascinates me most. The images are the medium through which a story can be understood.

MICHELANGELO ANTONIONI

The most important element to me is always the idea that I'm trying to express, and everything technical is only a method to make the idea into clear form. I'm always working on the idea whether I am writing, directing, choosing music, or cutting.

JOHN HUSTON

The only thing that is an absolute for any art that deserves the name is point of view (i.e. content). No point of view is sterility. Sterility, no matter how it's dressed up, is the death of theatre and films.

JOSEPH LOSEY

Aesthetic considerations are what concern me most. I believe, for instance, that there are two kinds of cinema, one stemming from Lumière and the other from Delluc. Lumière invented the cinema to film nature or action. Delluc, who was a novelist and critic, thought that one could use this invention to film ideas or actions which have a meaning other than the obvious one, and so, closer to the other arts. . . .

FRANCOIS TRUFFAUT

The orthodox theorists have been unable to formulate criteria which take account of the difference between reality and fiction. Systematically emphasizing the cinema's properties as a visual medium, their theory neglects or denigrates the aspects which the movie shares with narrative forms, especially dramatic ones. Because it is unable to locate what happens on the screen *within* the medium of film, the orthodoxy presents narrative as an alien form which the movie may translate and annotate but not absorb as part of its creative mechanism.
　　The reasoning is false. Story-telling, the representation of imagined action, is not an autonomous form but one which both assumes and informs the character of the medium used in the telling. It is not opposed to poetry, novel, strip-cartoon or theatre, and it cannot reasonably be seen as hostile or irrelevant to cinema. The movie incorporates the real object or fictional event into the medium itself.

V. F. PERKINS

320

By now it is evident that film's bond with literary art is long and extensive. Although not all would agree, many critics, including Susan Sontag, consider narrative film to be one of literature's subdivisions—one operating in a visual medium rather than in print or orally. In this section the various writers look at literary problems which also happen to be film problems. Their concerns are diverse: techniques borrowed from literature, narrative conventions and genres, problems of form and content, and sensitivities to the role of the critic in responsibly and sensitively approaching film and—or as—literature.

Rudolph Arnheim, whose book *Film as Art* remains one of the classic works of film theory, applies to cinema a literary distinction made by Goethe in 1797. Arnheim sees both epic and dramatic forms at work in movies, with the epic providing an outward consideration of a subject which tends toward endlessness, and dramatic film furnishing a style relying on plot, especially suspense, and a hero who deals with a defined problem.

In "The Literary Sophistication of Francois Truffaut," Michael Kline looks at two literary techniques, dislocation and irony, and considers their use in the films of Truffaut. But before taking up Truffaut's films, Kline deals at length with the two techniques, showing how they are manifested in literature. By suggesting how and why Truffaut uses dislocation and irony, Kline indicates one of the ways literary study can help illuminate a person's understanding of film.

Applying psychological criticism to film, Norman N. Holland focuses on what he calls "the dynamics of literary response." Meaning, he suggests, begins in a person's efforts to deal with the fantasy governing a literary work. The "puzzling movie" offers an interesting problem, for it seems to be without meaning. At the same time, an intellectual audience takes pleasure in puzzling movies because they offer a "forbidden content" which is displaced "into aesthetic and intellectual demands for 'meaning.'" Holland is ultimately concerned with why people are drawn to literature, and he parallels the fantasy elements found in films to those of literature.

Looking at some of the larger problems of cinematic art, Raymond Durgnat considers cinema to be a potpourri of art forms, but his chief concern is with the way critics treat form and content. He finds that content is too often regarded as literary content in a narrow sense and that style is merely everything which is not content. He suggests that style is more than embellishment and pleads that style be recognized as inseparable from a work's content.

Susan Sontag is equally cautionary about the relationship between form and content. Sontag extends Durgnat's plea not to regard form as a mere accessory of content, suggesting that at this time in our cultural history interpretation itself is dangerous. By overemphasizing the "translation" of one thing into another, nothing has a chance to be what it is. Art challenges its audience, but interpretation drains away those challenges. Arguing that we need to recover our senses, to see, hear, and feel more, Sontag sees film as the art form most alive because it is the one best able to elude interpreters and at the same time provide something other than content (primarily cinematic technique) to analyze.

RUDOLF ARNHEIM

Epic and Dramatic Film

There are essentially three properties of film as an artistic medium that need to be considered when it comes to deciding which kinds of narrative subject matter are suitable and how they should be presented. First of all, film is a visual art, which tells its stories to the eyes—even when sound is also used. Second, the pictures that tell the story are obtained mechanically by photography, that is, they can portray reality with documentary faithfulness. Third, these pictures can be made to follow each other in an uninterrupted sequence even though they may show the most different settings and actions taken at different times. As an additional and more practical condition the film maker is expected to remember that on the average the telling of the story should not take longer than an hour and fifteen minutes.

Two concepts that have proved to be useful in literary criticism can be applied fruitfully also to the film. In an essay "On Epic and Dramatic Poetry," written in 1797, Goethe asserts: "The epic poem preferably describes man as he acts outwardly: battles, travels, any kind of enterprise that requires some sensuous breadth; tragedy shows man led toward the inside, therefore the plot of a genuine tragedy requires little space." For Goethe this distinction coincided with that between an action told in the form of a poem or novel (epic) and one performed on the stage (dramatic). Indeed, the broad descriptions of varying settings and extensive happenings, which are characteristically epic, hardly suit the theatre. The stage no more than alludes to the setting of the action; it is limited to narrow space and can move from one loca-

From *Film Culture*, III, no. 1 (1957). Copyright © 1957 by Film Culture. Reprinted by permission of Rudolf Arnheim.

tion to the other only by means of clumsy devices. We may say of the film that it has put the epos on the stage. In fact, this is one of the main characteristics of the film medium.

When the two concepts are applied to film, they no longer designate the difference between outwardly and inwardly directed action. What distinguishes the "dramatic" film is rather that it undertakes the solution of a particular problem: it ties the knot by presenting the problem, describes the conflict caused by it, then attempts to find a solution, and finally the catastrophe of the hero wrecked by his failure to solve the insoluble. Dramatic film, just as the dramatic stage play, is dynamic. It presents a plot that proceeds from step to step, and one of its most characteristic effects is "suspense." Also it rigorously limits the presentation to what is needed to explain the motives of the characters and to make the events progress. There is no time for broad description in dramatic film. As much as possible it cuts down on references to what happened before the beginning of the actual story, and it does not linger on the aftermath of the catastrophe. Also, secondary plots are kept in the background of the main conflict.

The epic film, on the other hand, neither deals with a problem nor offers a solution. True, it also can seize upon the great discords of life, which create human suffering, but, unlike the dramatic film, it limits itself to describing their manifestations. *Dr. Jekyll and Mr. Hyde,* a typically dramatic film, poses a problem. A man gravely clashes with his environment because the good and the bad aspects of his nature have produced two independent personalities. The film develops the problem, creates suspense, and finally shows the protagonist killed by his environment, thus indicating that the conflict was insoluble. Compare this kind of treatment with *Don Quixote,* where again a man clashes with his world—this one impelled by ideals of human perfection, nobility, and beauty. But the problem is neither analyzed nor solved. The one permanent and unchanging conflict is shown in a sequence of examples, which, however, do not represent steps toward a solution. More or less accidentally, the story comes to an end—or rather fails to continue—at some point. Epic film is static.

Epic tasks may naturally be expressed through the film because of its capacity to describe reality in all its detail and to ignore the impediments of time and space. There is no documentary theatre, but there are documentary films, and they are epic. On the other hand, the film, just as the theatre, can develop a plot in the dramatic manner and create suspense. Almost invariably, however, the dramatic film will be found also to have epic, descriptive aspects. Even the kind of intimate film play that limits itself strictly to a limited space, a few characters, and a minimum of external action will seem descriptive when compared to similar plays on the stage because the camera inevitably captures with a single sweep so many details of the setting that the stage looks bare and abstract in comparison.

Film describes, but it describes swiftly. It leaps from one place to the other, from small objects seen at close quarters to the encompassing survey of the whole, and thus in a few seconds records hundreds of things which the epic poet could not enumerate in pages. It is for this reason that film can treat an epic subject in little more than an hour.

The epic style of narration has a preference for stringing episodes in sequences. Such chainlike composition stresses the static character of the tale. Don Quixote passes through a series of adventures; so does Ulysses. Sometimes the central figure is a mere pretext, which provides a common denominator for a series of descriptions, or he is a sharply drawn type whose conflicts with his surroundings are shown in ever new examples. The films of Chaplin and Buster Keaton are prototypes of the epic form. These films have been accused of lacking structure, of being episodes patched together. Of course, even an epic work needs unity and structure; but the basic shape of these films merely applies the ancient principle of epic narration. To some extent, the episodes that constitute them are mutually exchangeable, and even the famous endings (Chaplin walks away and disappears on the horizon without having married the pretty girl) are not only a personal expression of resignation but first of all a necessary feature of the epic style, which is not concerned with change and solution but with the presentation of invariable existence.

Occasionally three or four of Chaplin's short films have been combined to a full-sized "feature" film. The result seemed satisfactory because the epic film invites such enumeration whereas dramatic films that deserve the name would be expected to resist the same treatment.

Attempts have also been made to go beyond the narrow span of the movie theatre program and to create larger epic cycles. The films of Chaplin or those of Buster Keaton or Mickey Mouse form together a kind of continuing narrative, which can be presented in installments because each episode is self-contained. This is less true for the continuing adventures of some hero that used to keep the attention of the audiences from chapter to chapter over long stretches of time. The chase after a criminal, for instance, was presented, and the fans would wait for the next chapter as avidly as they were looking forward to the daily installment of a current novel in the newspaper.

A noteworthy variety of the epic film is the biography. Here the central figure does not journey through space as does Ulysses, but through time. We watch a man maintaining himself against afflictions that turn up through the years but remaining basically the same person in spite of the changes time imposes upon him. Externally, a man's entanglement with time appears as dynamic or dramatic because the passing of time suggests a progression; but basically it is static and epic. Therefore, biography suits the film medium well, and so does the historical presentation of several generations as in *Cavalcade*. Here not a single person but a central group of people serves as the nucleus around which a panorama of changing periods, mores, and fashions evolves. In such films the fundamental task of the epic style is clearly revealed: it insists on the unchangeable nature of man.

[1957]

MICHAEL KLEIN

The Literary Sophistication
of Francois Truffaut

Truffaut is not literate merely because his films contain
allusions to Renoir, Hitchcock, Walsh, and Vigo, although they are the
sources of the film conventions he manipulates, nor because *Jules and
Jim* contains references to Shakespeare, Goethe, "Don Quixote," Mozart,
Picasso, Rodin, and Baudelaire. It is also more than a question of
Truffaut being an adaptor of literary sources (Roché, Goodis), a sensitive mediator between life and art. Truffaut's literary sophistication is
a matter of technique and sensibility.

Because most films deal with people and situations and tell some
sort of story, directors cope with problems that dramatists and novelists
face; often they solve them in a way akin to that of their literary
counterparts, Resnais in *Last Year at Marienbad* and Dreyer in *Vampyr*,
for example, maintain a unity of tone that would have pleased Poe.
Antonioni probes small incidents and paces his exploration like Henry
James.

I would like to focus upon two techniques, interesting in themselves, which help us to grasp the meanings of Truffaut's *Shoot the
Piano Player* and *Jules and Jim*. The first technique, used in the modern
novel and in continental drama, is the technique of dislocation. The
second technique, irony, is basic to all forms of literature. Because I
am using these terms in a special sense, especially "dislocation," I will
discuss them before illustrating how they work in Truffaut's films.

Dislocation, like Brecht's alienation, is an effect; it is experienced
by the audience or reader because it is potential in the art object. When

Reprinted by permission of the author.

the spectator is alienated, he is distanced from a play or film or story, so that he may respond with the creative intellect. The artist, in employing the technique of dislocation, attempts to prevent this, because he fears his audience will think in conventional patterns. He may fragment the narrative, use an unreliable narrator, distort space, alter the temporal sequence, etc., to this rhetorical end. The dislocated reader or viewer, confused by distortions in the narrative, has to accept the author's view to make sense out of the material.

Truffaut expresses concern, in his interviews, about audience reaction to his films. Like him, playwrights as diverse as Brecht, Genet, and Pirandello have devised new techniques to overcome the difficult problem of communication with an audience. An *avant-garde* dramatist often assumes that audiences come to a play with a set of commonplace expectations and prejudices that block their relating to the work of art. The artist intends to put his audience in touch with themselves and with the world; that is to say, he wishes to prod and to stimulate by imposing his vision of the world upon their minds and sensibilities. Unfortunately, traditional means of presentation often do not suffice, and the audience has to be lured, tricked, and seduced.

Often this involving of an audience consists of careful manipulation of literary conventions, which are traditional ways of looking at life. This occurs whenever a new literary genre is being created. For example, an eighteenth century reader of Defoe's "Robinson Crusoe," as Virginia Woolf has pointed out, expected an exotic romance and instead was baffled into accepting an island on which life is a series of tasks. On the other hand, film makers like Hawks, Truffaut, and Godard, instead of beginning with a new stylization of life, use old conventions and manipulate the audience's stock responses to achieve their ends. In this their films share a characteristic of twentieth century literature.

For example, seeing Brecht's "The Good Woman of Setzuan," we quickly identify with Shen Te. Like us, she is altruistic and generous; like us, she has a fatalistic attitude toward the privations and social injustices of life. She is good and so, like us, believes that individual acts of charity will remedy social problems. Therefore, when she becomes a shop owner, she devotes herself to helping others. Then, after we are trapped, after we have identified smugly with Shen Te, Brecht has her step in front of the curtain and sing revolutionary anti-capitalist songs.

In modern fiction—for example, in Conrad's "Heart of Darkness" —dislocation is achieved in a more formalist way, through time shifts, changes in the narrative point of view, and by the use of the literary equivalent of montage—paratactic syntax. I can illustrate dislocation, and thus define the tradition in which Truffaut is working, by briefly looking at a shorter work by Joyce, who imposes his vision also by dislocating us in time and space. "Eveline" begins in the evening; the heroine is seated at her apartment window, in Dublin, waiting for her fiancé and thinking about her past. The narrative consists of memories and her judgment of past events. Toward the end, she thinks "Frank would take her in his arms, fold her in his arms. He would save her." And then, the following paragraph: "She stood among the swaying crowd in the station at the north wall. He held her hand. . . ." This seems to be a continuation of her reverie—she is thinking of how it will be when he comes for her. Only when events take a turn for the worse— the point of view (Joyce's) suddenly becomes distanced and objective —do we realize that this is an account of her failure to elope—she is now at the station, not dreaming but unable to act. She is paralyzed.

> He rushed beyond the barrier and called to her to follow. He was shouted at to go on but he still called to her. She set her white face to him, passive, like a helpless animal. Her eyes gave him no sign of love or farewell or recognition.

The conclusion shocks us into a multiple recognition: of Joyce's trick; that Dubliners live in a dream when awake; of Eveline's awful failure; and of the sterility in Dublin life that has made her what she is.

Because reading is a temporal experience, our perception of a story can be viewed as a process. Prior to our recognition, we were confused by Joyce's shift of time and place. At some point between the paragraph that begins "she stood among the swaying crowd" and the concluding paragraph, we, the audience, are uncertain whether the events are taking place in the girl's mind or at the station. Baffled, dislocated, we are receptive to the particular solution that Joyce wishes to give us.

Another example of dislocation. Seeing Renoir's *Rules of the Game,* we relax and enjoy a good comedy. Renoir tells us in the credits that the film will be fun. We may sense implications, but they are not disturbing. We accept the film. The maid's husband is chasing her would-be lover with a gun, upsetting the crowded household. It is very funny. Suddenly, after the *dance macabre,* the gun is fired—a lamp is shattered in the foreground and the main characters become frightened. For a second it seems as if the host is shot. The film becomes serious. But it is unexpected. We're stunned, and the film continues to develop before we can build up our conventional defenses against Renoir's vision.

This last example is similar to Truffaut's use of guns and knives in *Shoot the Piano Player*. But before illustrating this technique in relation to his films, I must briefly discuss irony.

In literature, irony may be achieved by subtle manipulation of language. Shakespeare's "Troilus and Cressida" begins with a speech by a Prologue who, in epic tones, fills in the background of the Trojan War. He speaks a highly formal latinate language; it is like Chapman's "Homer," which praised the war as a moral struggle. "In Troy there lies the scene. And the deep, drawing barks do there disgorge/their warlike fraughtage." However, if we examine the language carefully we discover that it undercuts itself. It is anti-heroic and critical of the war. "Disgorge" suggests vomit; later in the play the Greeks are often associated with disease. "Fraughtage" refers to cargo; later the Greeks are linked with commercial terms. They are not noble warriors. They are merchants out to ransack Troy for plunder and profit.

In the early books of "Paradise Lost" Milton uses a similar technique to ridicule Satan. Like Milton, many authors manipulate their audience in order to make a limited and specific critical statement. At worst, these techniques may serve authoritarian or propagandistic ends. However, they also can function to enlarge the audience's vision of life. In literary terms this is called creating ambiguity. Techniques are used to make the audience accept several meanings of an incident instead of to simplify experience; this is the spirit of plentitude, and is basic to Truffaut.

Perhaps one final example from the drama will be useful. Ionesco's "The Lesson" concludes with a "murder." The Professor stabs the Pupil with an invisible knife because she has a toothache. Up to then the situation has seemed comic. Now the violence of the act impels us to view it as a killing. "Aaah! That'll teach you!" (Striking the Pupil with a very spectacular blow of the knife.) But as the girl falls "her legs spread wide." "A noticeable convulsion shakes" the Professor and he says: "Bitch . . . Oh, that's good, that does me good." It is, as well, a rape.

Truffaut also uses techniques of dislocation and irony, often in the spirit of plentitude. In *Shoot the Piano Player* they tend to be ends in themselves. In *Jules and Jim* they are used to make us recognize the richness and complexity of the characters' lives and to view their experiences with tolerance.

Throughout *Shoot the Piano Player* Truffaut juxtaposes different conventions or genres in order to dislocate the audience. The film begins with a conventional gangster chase that quickly becomes slapstick. Yet at times it seems to be a serious psychological study of Charlie. And during the flashback scene, it appears to be a conventional success-and-fall-of-the-performer film (complete with a shot of the concert pianist from in front of the footlights). At other times it seems to be a story about an honest, tough waitress's attempt to help a laconic, broken piano player. The film concludes in a slapstick gun battle, with a breathtaking Hitchcock form falling down a white hill, and with the killing of the waitress and with Charlie benumbed.

All of this makes us unable to decide what kind of film *Shoot the Piano Player* is. We cease forcing it into our narrow system of classification and instead have to take it on its own terms. Truffaut's use of irony within conventions that are so radically juxtaposed also contributes to this end. Often irony makes us uncertain of how to react to even an isolated section of the film. However, it also guides us to respond in a sensitive way.

For example, consider the flashback scenes. It is a wonderful parody of the Horatio Alger success myth, plus Antonioni. A young boy, whose brothers are hoods, is sent to study with a famous pianist, is discovered by chance in a restaurant, and enjoys a spectacular rise to fame—concerts, interviews, more and more expensive cars. But he and his wife are bored and increasingly estranged. His wife confesses that she slept with the producer to get him discovered. The piano player makes a dramatic exit. She jumps out a window, and we see her corpse on the street.

It is an excellent parody of something that, with variations, has been done so many times. However, ironically, it isn't what we expected. The suicide gives us a jolt and we view the problems raised as serious. In short, Truffaut has rendered a cliché by parodying it. He has made us respond to a situation that, portrayed in a straightforward consistent manner, would have been dismissed easily.

The conclusion of the film works in a similar way. By ironically undercutting the gun battle and making it slapstick, Truffaut is able as well to render it as serious. The bad guys sniff their gun barrels and twirl the guns. They are perturbed and ridiculous. Lena is running. They shoot. Lena is dead. We see Charlie and her corpse in a brutal closeup.

The techniques work to make the film both extremely funny and extremely serious. Parody operates upon a dislocated audience to render meaningful a cinematic cliché. Charlie is not just the conventional Alger hero or the conventional laconic loner made funny. He is also a person to whom we respond with sympathy and horror. *Shoot the Piano Player* is both a gangster comedy and a study of a disillusioned man in a pre-schizoid state of withdrawal.

Truffaut's use of clichés is best studied in *Shoot the Piano Player*. A cliché is an overused convention. It is a symbol that no longer evokes powerful responses in audiences but still stands for something basic. Instead of creating new symbols for universal experiences, Truffaut works to resuscitate traditional signs.

However, the film ultimately is a magnificent exercise in technique, an astounding formalist *tour-de-force,* rather than a dramatic success. The techniques are used better, in a more integrated way, in *Jules and Jim.*

Techniques of dislocation are less obvious but equally effective in *Jules and Jim.* Consider, for example, Dwight Macdonald's response: "I was constantly being buffeted, shocked, puzzled and put off by what seemed to me perverse changes of mood." At times the film seems charming and idyllic. Other sections seem a probing study of love and friendship. Sometimes it appears to be sentimental. But then it becomes sharply satirical. The cremation scene is graphic and brutal. But the car plunge into the river is visual slapstick. Parts of the film are slowly paced and the frames look static. But in the early part of the film the characters are in motion and Truffaut's audacious cutting is sufficient itself to make the audience breathless—to disarm the audience.

While Truffaut buffets and dislocates the audience, he asserts that all these ways of looking at the story of Jules and Jim and Katherine are valid, that life is more complex than the categories with which we attempt to understand it. The form or technique of the film expresses the theme.

Let's see how this works at the conclusion of the film. Most of the scenes in the German chalet are directed in a straightforward manner. Suddenly the cutting becomes more erratic and genres are again mixed. Katherine brandishes a gun and Jim disarms her in detective film style. Albert re-appears—a whacky coincidence, too whacky for a "serious film." Katherine's and Jim's death is slapstick, but their cremation (hot bones and ashes) is sickeningly real. Jules, numb and grief-stricken, is leaving the cemetery. The narrator tells us that Jules feels relieved. The music is gay—a cliché Hollywood crescendo. These shifts in style and tone exhaust the audience's conventional responses.

Our view of Jules at the conclusion is most important because this is the focal point for our response to the whole film. Is Jules relieved or is he sad? Is he relieved *and* in grief? Our answer depends upon whether we are relieved or grieved or both, and this determines our view of Katherine. By making Jim's and Katherine's death slapstick, Truffaut prevents us from responding in a conventional, sentimental way (cry, don't think, quickly forget), which would have been a monstrous over-simplification. Because it is unexpected, the cremation scene makes an impact. We are shocked by "life," not by a serious film. But this is a visceral response. The gay music is then first heard as irritating and puzzling. The music is trite and inappropriate and we attempt to deny it. (It is like jumping on stage and interfering with the action, preventing a murder.) We became involved and respond from within the film. We experience grief and empathy. However, the music and the narrator cannot be completely ignored. As Jules begins to become distanced from his past experience, we also begin to become distanced from the film.

The beginning of the film is as crucial as the conclusion. In the opening scenes Truffaut uses irony to undercut, and it functions to enlarge our conception of life, not to make a specific statement of ridicule. The film is paced fast. The music is gay. Jules and Jim begin an idyllic friendship. Jules meets Katherine. She gets into a tramp outfit and all three go out for a romp. They race across a bridge. Katherine starts early and wins. Jules and Jim are laughing. At first we are charmed by the scenes, but we begin to feel that the music overstates a bit; it is slightly too gay for the action. The cutting is too abandoned, slightly hysteric. We become suspicious—it is a bit forced and overdone. Therefore we take a close look at the bridge scene. It seems significant that Katherine jumps the gun in order to win. We watch her face contort while she is running and mark her ecstatic cry of victory. Katherine must defeat Jules and Jim—she must exert power. She must cheat, and then run hard to beat them. And she knows they are unsuspecting. We are horrified; our expectation of innocence is destroyed. And yet the race isn't just a parable. The music is gay. Jules and Jim are happy. All three are having a good time. They look beautiful. And silly. The scene, then, is *both* an idyll and an ironic rendering of a cold psychological truth. It is *both* innocent and diabolic. Because we *suspect* the idyll, it becomes more important. We are charmed *and* we are horrified. In the same way—Katherine's leap into the river, a mad youthful funny impulse after a dull night at the theater, yet threatening.

The result is ambiguity and plenitude—maturity. We respond to life in the film in a complete way. First of all, we do not judge the characters as we would in life or in a conventional film. We do not wish to punish them. Truffaut admired Renoir's *Rules of the Game* because it was "the first psychological film in which the notion of a good and bad personage had been entirely eliminated." He has qualified his admiration for the gangster film by disliking its simple good/bad dichotomy and its cruel code of justice. His *The 400 Blows* is a protest against our concepts of crime and punishment. Truffaut uses all the techniques at his command to get us to see life as complete, to regard life with tolerance.

Katherine, then, is not just a demonic *über-fraulein* (the term is

Truffaut's) —a self-absorbed, insecure monster (although perhaps a female Frankenstein's monster) who forces people to serve her will. Nor
is she merely a paragon of moral courage and a person of great charm
who brings happiness and catalyzes a "beautiful relationship" (Truffaut
again) while seeking a liberation that is fraught with contradiction.
She embodies *both* polar concepts, and all that is in between. Jules and
Jim are not only silly romantics who overvalue Katherine, frame and
contain her in their image while questing for a childhood idyll and ma-
ternal security. They are not just mature, intelligent, sensitive men
courageously acknowledging the problems of life and attempting to
cope with them. They are both "types" and more.

Jules emerges as the most interesting character because of the role
he plays in relation to the theme of tolerance. Slightly withdrawn, he is
compassionate and accepts life as complex and responds to it on its own
terms. Jules seldom judges Katherine but instead attempts to make the
best of their lives. He is not vindictive; he instead attempts to arrange
for Katherine's and Jim's happiness and to salvage a bit for himself.

Katherine, on the other hand, has a vindictive sense of justice. She
keeps a bottle of vitriol for "lying eyes." She sleeps with a former lover
to punish Jules, whose mother was rude to her, and to punish Jim for
tarrying with Gilberte. She demands justice, simplicity, and a clean slate.
But she believes that the ultimate judge is compassionate toward her.
"She thinks that whatever she does, God will forgive her in advance."

Society, pre-1930, is viewed as tolerant. It nurtured Jules, Jim and
Katherine and the "free life" before the war. In Germany, in the 1920's,
people have a similar spirit of tolerance. The village people were startled
by the *ménage à trois* and by their antics. "The village called them the
three lunatics, *but* respected them." After Hitler, things change and
significantly Truffaut shows us film clips of Nazi book burnings when
Jules, Jim, and Katherine meet in a movie house after long separation.

In the novel Jules was Jewish. This would have complicated the
movie. Truffaut's literary sophistication is evident in the way he adapted
the social and political elements of Henri Pierre Roche's novel. Our
stock responses to Jews and Naziism would have galloped roughshod
over the delicate psychological balance of the film. Truffaut retained a
sense of history but made it function within the film in relation to the
tolerance theme and subordinate to the *ménage à trois* situation.

The progress of the characters' lives reflects the history of the times
during the twenty-plus years of the film. Life is simple before the war,
more complicated after the book-burnings. As we approach the time
of the book burnings the *über-fraulein* aspect of Katherine becomes
stressed. Katherine brandishes a gun at Jim. She wears steel-rimmed

glasses and begins to look "Germanic," especially when we see her immediately after the film-clips. Then follow suicide, immolation, cremation, and the graveyard scene. The cremation might suggest Nazi death-camps—willful Katherine is linked with fascism.

The symbols in *Jules and Jim* are handled with skill and subtlety; for example, Jules' and Katherine's child (Sabine) plays a game at the chalet. It is, first of all, a charming dance and romp. Soon Jim and Katherine appear—more antics. But the game is Sabine (a reflection of Katherine) whipping Jules and making him skip to her lash. It is a concise symbol of Jules' and Katherine's idyllic-demonic relationship.

Truffaut's symbols seldom force themselves upon the viewer. Katherine, who loves power, may be characterized as "Napoleonic." She briefly mentions Napoleon and in Katherine's room there was a photograph of Napoleon on the wall, out of focus and scarcely noticeable. In the chalet Katherine sings a little pop-song about love and missed kisses. It is a light moment. But the song—together we are caught up in life's whirlpool—sums up life in *Jules and Jim*.

And automobiles are obvious symbols of the new technology: a car first appears in *la guerre sociale* scene, while last is Jim's and Katherine's death car. Bicycles represent the old life. But cars are first of all cars, and Katherine's car functions as a device of characterization; it is an extension of one aspect of her personality. Curiously, it resembles a hearse, particularly when she drives it silently, ominously, around and around the little corner square in front of Jim's house.

Aside from the literary aspects of Truffaut's films, other factors are equally important: Truffaut's joy in the process of film making (the home movie spirit of his films); Coutard's photography (horizontal motion—the camera, dance rhythms within the frame). I have focused upon Truffaut's literary sophistication because, in addition to his good heart and a good eye, few film makers have his quality of mind.

In this article I have attempted to work from a critical approach that applies both to film and to the literary arts, and which may also be a guide to film makers. For insofar as an artist is able to structure and to rhetorically manipulate, he or she succeeds in creating a work of art that will haunt the audience. That is the ultimate test of a film, play, novel, or poem.

[1965]

NORMAN N. HOLLAND

Meaning as Defense

Meaning, we have seen, is not static but dynamic: a transformation of the fantasy at the core of a literary work into terms
satisfactory to an adult ego. But meaning is more, as we can see when
meaning is—or seems at first to be—absent, a situation nowhere so visible
as in contemporary cinema. Late in 1958, Janus Films released on a
largely unsuspecting American public Bergman's *The Seventh Seal* and
so started a flood in the art theaters of what seems to be a new genre in
film, "the puzzling movie": *Hiroshima, Mon Amour, Les Amants, Les
Cousins, The Magician, L'Avventura, Juliet of the Spirits, Red Desert,
Blow-Up*—to name but a few of these films, most of which almost dazzle
with their richness, their sheer filmic excellence. As a genre, they represent perhaps the only sustained group of films after the advent of sound
to be truly and overwhelmingly visual: these films look good like a
cinema should.

Arthur Schlesinger, Jr., has suggested they are creating a new
"Movie Generation" to replace those of us who grew up, cinematically,
on the popcorn and cheesecake Hollywood classics of the 'thirties. Another reviewer calls these the "undergraduate movies," and there is much
truth in the adjective, if we extend it to include not only the four-year
kind, but also the perpetual undergraduates on the other side of the
lectern. These are indeed films that make their chief appeal to the
academic and the intellectual.

But why do they appeal to anybody? If you stand outside an art theater as the audience comes out from a "puzzling movie," you will hear over and over again in a variety of phrasings and degrees of profanity, "What was *that* all about?" As an academic joke has it, one sophomore to another, "Have you seen *Last Year at Marienbad?*" The other slowly, thoughtfully, "I—don't know." The feeling these films almost invariably leave us with is, "It means something, but just what I don't know," and the theorist of meaning must ask, Why should that feeling of puzzlement give pleasure to us?

It doesn't, of course, to everyone. Popular as these films may be among intellectuals and academics, there are plenty of people who find them simply boring. At a somewhat more sophisticated level (I am thinking of the usual reviewer for the daily paper), we hear two kinds of complaint. First, these films make just one more statement of the moral and social confusion of the century. Second, we are likely to find a sexual indignation, for these films are rather strikingly casual about such matters. There were, for example, the two proper Bostonian ladies who went to see *The Virgin Spring*. During that appalling rape scene, one leaned over to the other and whispered, "You know, in Sweden, things are like that." And, in fact, sex in these films does tend to be either rape or mere amusement, a kind of bedroom Olympics in which neither the Russians nor the Americans stand a chance—only Common Market countries.

Sex and *mal de siècle*—these films have them in abundance, but the quality that still stands out is the puzzlement they create. Contrast a film-maker like Eisenstein. He uses montage, symbolism, and the rest not very differently from the way the makers of the puzzling movies do, but Eisenstein aims to communicate his socialist and Marxist message, and his symbols serve that end. The maker of the puzzling movie, on the other hand, as much as hangs out a sign that says, "Figure it out—if you can." His symbols serve not so much to communicate as to suggest or even to mystify. (Think, for example, of the devilfish at the end of *La Dolce Vita* and all the different interpretations of it.) Yet, despite the intentional mystification, we take pleasure in them just the same— these films are puzzling in more than one sense.

In particular, there are two ways they puzzle us. They puzzle us as to their meaning in a total sense. They puzzle us scene-by-scene simply as to what is going on in a narrative or dramatic way. Let me consider, first, our puzzlement as to meaning—Why should these films, that seem almost to hide their own meaning, please us?

To answer that question, it helps (as usual) to take a detour by way of the joke, for jokes often have the same riddling quality as, say, a film by Antonioni. Often, we have to solve some little problem before we "get" the joke—for example, the old saw cited by Freud, "A wife is like an umbrella—sooner or later one has to take a taxi." The riddling form draws and holds our attention to the joke. In a puzzling movie, it draws and holds our attention to the film. As Marshall McLuhan puts it:

> Fellini and Bergman pull the story line off the film and the result is that you become much more profoundly involved in the film process. When you put a story line on a novel or a film, you're much less involved. Edgar Allan Poe discovered that if you take the story line off the detective story, the audience has to participate and make the story as it goes. And so, paradoxically, pull the story line off any situation and you get a much higher level of creative participation on the part of the reader, or the audience. Fellini's "8½" is a world where the audience has to work very hard. The same as abstract art.

More specifically, as the mention of Poe's detective stories suggests, the riddling form engages our processes of intellection; in technical terms, the ego's secondary-process or problem-solving thinking. The riddling form busies us with solving the riddle and incidentally enables less relevant, less presentable thoughts prompted by the joke to sneak up on us, to take us unawares, as it were. So with the puzzling film; its enigmatic promise of "meaning" not only draws and holds our attention to the film; it also distracts us from the real source of our pleasure in the film, the thoughts and desires it evokes.

That is, if we think of meaning simply in terms of Freud's early model, a joke's promise that there will be an intellectual meaning, a "point," enables us to relax and enjoy a playing with words and ideas that we would ordinarily dismiss as childish or insane: intellectual content justifies form. At the same time, the play with words and ideas acts as an additional and preliminary source of pleasure. The pleasure in this play unbalances the usual equilibrium between our tabooed impulses and our censoring defenses, and it provides the extra to topple those defenses—we laugh. In other words, the promise of "point" (or intellectual content) in the joke justifies the form; then the pleasure we take in form allows another kind of content to break through, and we gratify through the "point" a disguised version of some sexual or aggressive impulse we would ordinarily hold in check.

The same process seems to operate with the puzzling movie. The feeling we have is: "This means something, but I don't know what." "This means something," the first part of our reaction, acts like intellectual content in the joke—it justifies form; it bribes our reason to accept the incoherent stream of images or the incoherent narrative of the puzzling movie. Then, our pleasure in those images, the sheer visual beauty of the films in this genre, acts like form: it allows us to enjoy the forbidden content of the film.

But what is this forbidden content? In the joke-situation, we can usually identify the hidden impulse of hostility or obscenity that the joke works with. The content of the puzzling movie is not so easy to get at.

We can get a clue, though, from the adverse reactions to the films. Those reviewers and audiences for whom the puzzling quality doesn't work complain of two things: the casual attitude toward sex and the feeling that the films express in a peculiarly negative way the moral confusions of the age. For the disappointed critics of these films, the form didn't work, and the fantasies prompted by the film came through raw and repulsive: sexual promiscuity and a fear of moral confusion.

The sexual angle is the easier (and more pleasurable) to see. These films are extraordinarily free about such matters—I am thinking of such scenes as Jeanne Moreau's taking a bath in *Les Amants* and *La Notte;* the striptease in *La Dolce Vita;* the scenes of lovemaking in *Hiroshima;* rape in *The Virgin Spring, Through a Glass Darkly,* or *Marienbad.* In effect, the puzzling quality of the films gives us an intellectual justification for gratifying the simplest of visual desires, looking at sexy things. This, I hasten to add, is a crude, first-order effect, but nevertheless a very important part of the appeal of even these very sophisticated and intellectual films. Or, for that matter, their lack of appeal—read Bosley Crowther.

The puzzling movies are an intellectual's version of the old De Mille Bible epic, where we gratify our sexual desires by watching the wicked Assyrians, Philistines, Romans, or whomever carry on their grand pagan orgies, but we are justified by the ponderously moral content of the film. The biblical frame allows us to gratify almost shamelessly the seventh and least of the sinful impulses. I say, "us," but no doubt I do you an injustice: no proper intellectual would be fooled by the crudity of the moral sop in the De Mille versions of the Bible, and this is not the kind of justification the puzzling movie gives us. The puzzling movie presents itself as an intellectual and aesthetic problem rather than a moral one, and then perhaps it does fool the intellectual in the same amiable way that jokes and works of art do: the puzzling movie engages his intellectual attention and lets the dark underside of the self (which even intellectuals have) gratify its chthonic wishes.

We can see the process *in statu nascendi,* as it were, in Leslie Fiedler's remarkable review of a "nudie" movie, *The Immoral Mr. Teas.* He looks at this film and finds in it "ambiguity," "irreality," "a world of noncontact and noncommunication." He treats this jolly and ribald movie as an index to the American national character, illustrates from it American attitudes toward the body, and (most strikingly) contrasts the nudity in *The Immoral Mr. Teas* with the more humane nudity in *Room at the Top* and *Hiroshima, Mon Amour.* In other words, Mr.

Fiedler's astute analysis has erected such an intellectual "meaning" for this film (though it is scarcely above the level of a stag movie) that any self-respecting intellectual could go see it with a clear conscience and a blithe spirit—of analysis. Mr. Fiedler does it with criticism; the puzzling film-maker does it with his camera; but, in either case, the intellectual promise of "meaning" justifies the simpler and more primitive pleasure.

Leslie Fiedler treats *The Immoral Mr. Teas* in intellectual and aesthetic terms, whereas the "meaning" that justified the content of the biblical epic was its religious and moral "message." This displacement from moral message to intellectual meaning is itself a source of pleasure in the puzzling movie, particularly for the intellectuals to whom the puzzling movie makes its chief appeal. After all, moral and religious issues have a strong and perhaps frightening emotional overtone. Aesthetic and intellectual "meaning" seems much more manageable. The notion that the moral confusions of this the most trying of centuries can be shifted over to the very kind of aesthetic and intellectual puzzle at which highbrows are adept is itself a very comforting hope indeed. And again, confirmation of this source of pleasure comes from those in the audience who find no pleasure in this displacement: the films clearly deal with moral problems, but for those in the audience who cannot accept the films' translation of moral issues into intellectual ones, the puzzling movies seem merely to express moral problems without answering them, and these critics say the films just prove the sickness of the century.

So far, then, we have found three sources of pleasure in the way these films puzzle us as to meaning. First, we feel that somehow this film "means something," and that promise of content or "point" enables us to take a straightforward sensuous pleasure in the seemingly incoherent and puzzling visual form of the film. That preliminary visual pleasure in form combines with a less acceptable source of visual pleasure in content: peeping at some very erotic scenes. The combination of these pleasures from form and from content unbalance and override our usual inhibitions. At the same time, these films displace moral and social inhibition into aesthetic and intellectual demands for "meaning," something that intellectuals (at least) find much easier to resolve, and the puzzling quality so provides yet a third source of pleasure.

This kind of economic analysis, however, seems highly abstract. Somehow, we are missing some of the essential quality of these films. We can get closer by looking at the second source of puzzlement: not total "meaning," but the scene-by-scene, simple narrative riddle of, What's going on?

I have suggested that one of the brute, root sources of pleasure in these films is simply that of looking at sexual scenes. Yet sex in these films has a peculiar and special quality. Jeanne Moreau's bath scenes in *Les Amants* and *La Notte*—the first occurs in the context of a casual affair; in the second her husband is simply bored by the sight. Similarly, the husband is bored by Romy Schneider's long and lovely bath scene in the Visconti episode of *Boccaccio 70,* a visual feast but an emotional fast. The striptease in *La Dolce Vita* and virtually all the sex in that film is without any emotion but simple desire. Again, there is simply lust or hate in the rape scenes of *The Virgin Spring* or *Rocco and His Brothers.* The same quality shows in those seductions tantamount to rapes by the heroine of *Through a Glass Darkly,* by the nymphomaniac at the hospital in *La Notte,* or the lover of *Red Desert.* The opening love scenes of *Hiroshima, Mon Amour* set out another casual love affair; the woman's voice drones on the sound track throughout the sequence much as the narrator's voice drones on in *Marienbad* debating with himself whether he took the woman by force or not. *The Seventh Seal,* perhaps the finest film in the genre, seems to vary this emotionless pattern, but not really: Bergman isolates sex *cum* love in the juggler and his wife, those who escape Death; while the knight and his wife, the squire and his girl rescued from rape, the blacksmith's wife seduced by the actor, all show the same dogged lovelessness which seems to be the distinctive feature of human relationships in the puzzling movie.

This emotionlessness does not confine itself to sexuality, either. Think, for example, of the cryptic face of Max von Sydow in *The Seventh Seal* or Monica Vitti's classical mask in the Antonioni trilogy. These films are cryptic on the simple level of, What's he thinking? What's he feeling? The suicide of Steiner in *La Dolce Vita* reveals some underlying emotional reality his aesthetic and intellectual life had screened, but what? The disappearance of Anna in *L'Avventura,* her earlier cry of "Sharks!" in the swimming sequence—these tell us something about her inner life, but what? The long, circling walk of the lovers in the last third of *Hiroshima, Mon Amour,* the fashion-plate style of *Marienbad,* the disguises in *The Magician,* all show us cryptic outward actions as a substitute for inner emotions not revealed.

All through the puzzling movies, in other words, we are seeing events without understanding their meaning, particularly their emotional meaning. We are simply not permitted to become fully aware of what is going on emotionally. This sensation, though, is not by any means a new one, special to the puzzling movies. In fact, these films duplicate an experience we have all had, which was at one time irritating, even frightening, a constant reminder of our own helplessness in the face of forces much bigger than we. I am thinking of the child's situation, surrounded by a whole range of adult emotions and experiences he cannot understand. "What's that man doing, Mommy?" is a not inappropriate comment on the whole genre of "puzzling movies."

Typically, the child does not even have the words with which to grasp these adult emotions and experiences, a circumstance these films duplicate by happenstance. That is, they are foreign-language films which put us again in a position where the big people, the ones we see on the screen, have all kinds of complex experiences which they speak about in a language we cannot understand. Even for those of us who spent some time with the tongues, these films make us regress, grow backward into children, a second way by their intentionally visual and filmic quality. They take us back to the picture language of the comic strip, of children, and of dreams.

There is still a third way these films take us back to the child's frame of mind: in sexuality. The child's dim awareness of adult sexuality very much resembles the sexuality of the puzzling movies. He can see or, more usually, imagine the physical act, but he cannot feel the whole range of complex emotions and experiences the adult knows as love. Rather, the child understands the act of sex as something associated with violence and danger, as we see it, for example, in *The Virgin Spring, Rocco and His Brothers, La Dolce Vita, Hiroshima, Mon Amour, Last Year at Marienbad, Les Cousins, Red Desert,* and the rest. The child is aroused at his sexual fantasies and a bit afraid of his own arousal, as indeed we ourselves tend to be at a puzzling movie. Further, the child's general uncertainty about the adult world finds a focus for itself in his uncertainty, arousal, and fear at this particular area of adult life— sexuality. It serves as a nucleus for his total puzzlement at adult emotions and actions, just as the sexuality in the puzzling movies serves as the nucleus of the total atmosphere of mysterious, baffling emotions and motivations.

In various ways, then, the puzzling quality at the story level of these films takes us back to a childhood situation of puzzlement, but presents it now as an intellectual and aesthetic puzzle rather than an emotional one in real life. "This event obviously says something about the emotional life of these people, but I don't know what, and it's only a film anyway." The film puzzles, disturbs, presents us with an emotional riddle, but puts it in an intellectual and aesthetic context.

Further, it transforms the emotional puzzle into precisely the kind of puzzle that an "undergraduate" audience might feel it could solve, an intellectual and aesthetic puzzle instead of an emotional one. In other words, not only do these films take us back to childhood disturbances; they seem to say we can master those disturbances by the strategies of our adult selves, our ability to solve aesthetic and intellectual puzzles. And we dutifully try to puzzle them out.

One way, then, the puzzling movies appeal to their intellectual audiences is by offering the possibility of mastering childish puzzlement by the defenses of the adult intellectual. For example, most intellectuals have a good deal of curiosity. The reason psychologists give is that their early attempts to solve the puzzles of childhood became a way of life. In technical jargon, infantile curiosity became sublimated into the intellectual and aesthetic curiosity of the adult. Now the puzzling movie comes along and enables us to do, or think we can do, just what our life style has been wanting to do all along: solve the riddle of emotions and sexuality by purely intellectual means. Would that we could!

The puzzling movies play into the intellectual's life style in another way. Academics and intellectuals often present the appearance to other people of "cold fish," the reason being that it is typical of the highly intellectualized person that he puts up a barrier between sensuous emotional experience and the intellectual problems with which he concerns himself. The puzzling movie enables him to do this again—to put aside the emotional mysteries of the film and see it coldly, using intellection as a defense. In short, the puzzling movies take us, as any great work of art does, along the whole spectrum of our development from infancy to adulthood; or, at least, they do for most of their "undergraduate" audience.

There is, though, one special reaction that deserves notice: some critics feel no uncertainty at all—at least on the narrative level. The usual review of an Antonioni film for example, in a film magazine or a literary quarterly, will tell you scene by scene and scowl by scowl what each of the characters is thinking at every given moment. For this kind of person, there is no mystery in the puzzling movie, or, more properly, his careful observation of the film enables him to say that he has seen everything there is to be seen. There is no mystery—he understands the emotional riddle. This response offers a variant but no less pleasurable way of overcoming that residue of childish bafflement in us—instead of shifting it to an adult intellectual problem, the critic simply says it doesn't exist at all: there is no puzzle. And this procedure is no less satisfying than the other ways the puzzling movie works.

To bring all these ways together, the puzzling movie turns its puzzling quality into pleasure in two large areas. First, it presents itself as an aesthetic mystery: What does it "mean"? As in a joke, the oblique promise of a "point" enables us to relax our demand for coherence and take sensuous pleasure in the incoherent visual form of the film. Then, that visual form lets us take pleasure in the sexual content and, at the same time, shifts any moral qualms we might have to intellectual and aesthetic qualms. Second, the puzzling movie presents us with a mystery on a simple narrative or dramatic level: What's going on? This second kind of mystery displaces a child's feeling of bafflement into an aesthetic mystery that a sophisticated, intellectual audience, no longer children, can feel confident about solving.

There is a lesson here about movies in general, for all movies take us back to childhood. They give us a child's pleasure in looking at things, which film critics respond to in their demand that the film be true to its medium, that it be visual. Similarly, the film takes us back to a pre-verbal stage of development; and, again, critics demand that the picture make its point, not through words on the soundtrack, but through pictures. Most important, however, there is that certain feeling people have, that looking at a film is somehow "passive." In fact, of course, the film involves no more passivity than reading a novel or watching a play, and yet there is something akin to passivity in the cinematic transaction.

Wolfenstein and Leites, in their classic study of the psychology of the movie audience, find part of that sensation of passivity in the audience's "peering with impunity" at the big people on the screen:

> What novels could tell, movies can show. Walls drop away before the advancing camera. No character need disappear by going off-stage. The face of the heroine and the kiss of lovers are magnified for close inspection. The primal situation of excited and terrified looking, that of the child trying to see what happens at night, is re-created in the theater; the related wish to see everything is more nearly granted by the movies than by the stage. The movie audience is moreover insured against reaction or reproof from those whom they watch because the actors are incapable of seeing them. The onlooker becomes invisible.

The actors, in short, can't fight back, and that is one way the film seems a "passive" medium.

The other side of the coin is that we can't provoke the actor. Unlike the stage situation where the length of our laughter or the solemnity of our listening will affect the actor's performance; unlike the television situation where we can turn the box off, get up for a beer or whatnot, we have no such effect on the film which grinds away its twenty-four pictures a second as relentlessly as Niagara Falls. We are powerless, as we were when we were children, to change the doings of the "big people." Now, though, we are immune, the giants on the screen cannot affect us, either. Our regression is safe, secure, and highly pleasurable.

This regression to the safe but powerless child, it seems to me, is the reason people feel watching a film is somehow "passive": the big people cannot act on us; we cannot act on them. This regression, of course, is a key source of pleasure not only in the puzzling movies, but in all films, and especially those which, like the puzzling movies, make their appeal visually, that is, those in which the pre-verbal element of the film is especially strong.

In fact, we could define cinematic achievement in terms of what it does with this visual, pre-verbal element in the situation of safe help-lessness induced by the motion picture. In the case of silent comedy, the action on the screen says to us, in effect, "This mysterious pre-verbal world of violence and disaster is really harmless—it's all right." Eisen-stein's films and others of the montage school say, "This mysterious pre-verbal world you see is meaningful. You understand it, and you respond to it emotionally and morally." The puzzling movie says to us, "This mysterious pre-verbal world you see, though you don't under-stand it, still it can be solved." The puzzling film pleases us because it is, as in the last analysis all art is, a comfort. . . .

In short, we seem to *need* meaning. We have already considered meaning as the transformation or sublimation of the unconscious fantasy embodied in the work. Presumably, meaning in that sense gratifies us as any sublimation would, with pleasure from the disguised satisfaction of drives. But, evidently, since we seem to need meaning, it must serve defensive as well as pleasurable functions. To see what they are, we must recapitulate.

In these first six chapters, we have been building a model of literary response. We began with a text which is, ultimately, a discrete collection of words to which we, the audience, give meaning and life to the extent we are "absorbed" by it. The metaphor of "absorption," however, reverses the true state of affairs. The reader, or member of the audience, at a rather primitive level, introjects the literary work so that what happens "in" it feels as though it were happening "in" him, more properly, in some undifferentiated "either." When the reader takes the work in, it brings to him its potentialities for fantasy, for defensive trans-formations, and for meaning. The reader in turn brings to it his capacity to fantasy and his own defensive structures (which I have loosely labeled, from Freud's earlier terminology, the "censor"). He also brings—and this is a vital element in his response—his own associations, fantasies, and fears related to the conscious and unconscious content of the literary work. For this, we have been using Simon O. Lesser's term, "analogiz-ing": when we perceive things in life, we bring to them our pre-existing psychic structure and experience; we do the same when we perceive literature. What we bring may be pleasurable fantasies or guilty or anxious ones, defensive structures like form, or intellectual ideas of meaning. And, of course, we bring our "higher" capacity to recognize the literary work as separate from us and to think rationally about it, specifically to explore its meaning. We have spoken of the introjecting and the intellecting reader.

For the purposes of our model, we have "stretched" the text to represent these two different kinds of reading as though these responses were "in" the text itself. Consciously, as described in Chapter 1, we give or find in the text "meaning" by a process of successive abstraction and classification from the words and events of the text. Unconsciously, we introject the text and feel its nuclear fantasy as though it were our own unconscious fantasy—yet we are not aware of it as such.

In consciously analyzing the text for its core of fantasy, though, we arrive at it by a process of abstraction similar to that for intellectual "meaning." However, instead of using the social, moral, or intellectual categories appropriate to theme and meaning in their customary sense, we use a "dictionary" of likely fantasies; and we make connections, not by the logical processes of secondary thought, but by the peculiar shortcuts and associations of the primary process. Both the "meaning" and the fantasy act as "central" ideas that inform the text: if we have analyzed them correctly, they will bring every element in the text to a central focus. Further, "meaning" and fantasy are related: intellectual meaning is an egosyntonic transformation of the unacceptable fantasy content. . . . We have called what does this transforming, "form," that is, what shapes our response and makes it different from our response to the raw fantasy.

That response itself has conscious, unconscious, and preconscious components. Meaning represents our conscious intellection about the text as a separate entity. Form, we are not normally aware of, but we can become aware of it if we concentrate on it—hence it is, roughly, preconscious. The nuclear fantasy we find in a literary work we normally cannot recover without considerable effort, and perhaps not even then—hence, it is unconscious. We are arriving at it here, first, by decoding symbols (a questionable shortcut) ; second, by my finding through self-analysis the nuclear fantasy which I am experiencing and which I assume you share. As for the text itself, each word is, of course, conscious as we perceive it, though a word several hundred pages back may be only preconscious. In that sense, the text as a whole shades off into preconsciousness or even unconsciousness. For the purposes of our model, we have been considering these relations between the reader and the work pictorially:

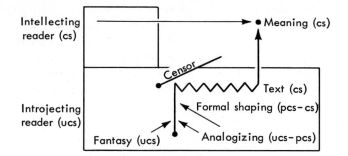

The model describes the potentialities. When we actually become engaged in literary response, when we are "with it," the actuality is the process of transformation, in which each of the levels (fantasy, form, meaning) offers pleasure in itself and modifies the possibilities of pleasure from other levels. We take in the fantasy which is an "hallucinatory gratification." In literature as in life, such a fantasy will typically both give pleasure and provoke anxiety. To the extent it gives pleasure, we simply get pleasure from it. To the extent it provokes anxiety, it must be modified to reduce the anxiety. Form and meaning are the two agents that control and manage the fantasy, and they in turn may be sources of pleasure in themselves.

The devices in the text that we have lumped together as "form" may give pleasure in at least three different ways. First, to the extent the unconscious fantasy evokes guilt or anxiety, form gives pleasure (or, more properly, removes pain) as it defensively manages that part of the fantasy. . . . The defenses built into the literary work enable its unconscious content to get around the reader's censor and achieve imaginary gratification. Not only that, these defenses can manage the fantasies the reader analogizes to the work, and conversely, his own pre-existing defenses may manage the work's fantasy. Second, form as displacement to a verbal level and as verbal play may be pleasurable in itself. . . , and so may, as Freud suggested, overbalance the "censor" (I have shown him tipped). Third, form may in and of itself gratify libidinal or aggressive drives (as [previously] suggested, denial of splitting might satisfy aggressive drives). If so, form represents an extremely powerful multiplier of pleasure to "bribe" the inhibiting censor.

The act of meaning may offer pleasure simply as a disguised version or sublimation of the original fantasied gratification. . . . This chapter, however, somewhat complicates our notion of meaning by finding additional sources of gratification from it, gratifications analogous to those of form. That is, people typically respond to works like the "puzzling movies" or Ionesco's plays by trying to supply the apparently missing meaning: we try to "solve" them. Since we do, meaning must do something for us in the literary experience more complicated than the more or less direct gratifications shown in our preliminary model . . . for we would not "need" the pleasure of our own intellections. Rather, since we do feel a positive need for meaning, meanings must do something for us analogous to what a defense does—if it is missing, we try to supply it.

This is another sense in which form and content are inseparable: form acts like a defense to permit the partial gratification of fantasy; so does meaning. We could represent this more complicated, final model this way:

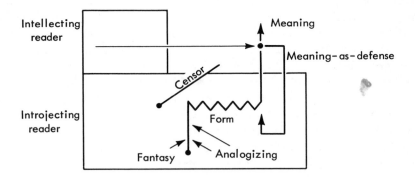

We supply meaning in order to permit expression of and pleasure from the core fantasy. This final model shows meaning's dual role; a sublimation "in" the work itself of its own fantasy content; something analogous to a defense which we supply and without which our egos cannot accept the unintelligible but highly charged work of art. The most explicit and simple works will not ask us to provide meaning-as-defense; the most obscure and difficult will themselves provide little or no sublimatory meaning; but most art will stand between these two extremes. In most art, there will be both kinds of meaning.

The act of meaning—either type—offers three sources of pleasure analogous to the three sources of pleasure in form. First, we have seen in this chapter that (in literature as well as in life) a feeling we are engaged in a socially, morally, or intellectually responsible enterprise assuages guilt and anxiety. In the puzzling movies (or *Mr. Teas*), we can enjoy looking at the sex or nudity, free of guilt or anxiety, provided we feel we are also engaged in making statements about our world. In this sense, meaning or even the mere promise of meaning is a sop thrown to the superego. Second, though I have not tried to demonstrate it in this chapter, it should be fairly obvious that meaning also serves as an economizer. Like rhyme and other formal devices, it makes a condensation. We recognize recurring patterning of theme just as we recognize recurring patterns of sound; they create expectation and trust and gratify them. Like any perceived pattern, meaning also serves to economize the handling of incoming perceptual data. As a result, there would be gratifications associated with the ego. Finally, meaning offers drive gratification to the extent it handles the fantasy materials. Meaning offers mastery, as play does, and, like play, it satisfies whatever libidinal and aggressive drives are involved in turning passive experiences of fantasy into active ones—so, at any rate, Brecht's remarks on passionate commitment would seem to suggest, or Erikson's remarks on play.

That is all, really, that meaning-as-defense need do: offer a mastery of the fantasy content—"make sense" of the text. A reader does not, therefore, need to settle for himself the exact, stringent kind of sublimatory meaning described [previously]. Nor, in this context, need there be only one central meaning. Almost any kind of coherent thought about the work will open up the paths of gratification, so long as it "makes sense" of the text. Historical generalizations about period or genre or style; the resonant pronouncements that American Studies critics are likely to make about the American character; psychological comments about characters, author, or theme; phenomenological statements bringing out the essence of the writer's subjectivity; statements of moral, philosophical, or political import—all are ways different readers may "make sense" of a text, that is, make it acceptable to the conscious ego and so permit the fantasy content a disguised and sublimated gratification.

[1968]

RAYMOND DURGNAT

The Mongrel Muse

The great difficulty in talking about cinema style is that the cinema is a *potpourri* of art forms, sharing elements in common with each, but weaving them into a pattern of its own.

In that it centres on actors, on the human form, it comes closest to the theatre. In its origin, too, it is associated with theatrical forms (the "music hall" act). But it is "deficient" theatre, for the show lacks the actor's presence. Instead of one person physically, constantly, present here and nowhere else in the world, we have only a Polyfoto presence, a pack of images, changing in shape and size—half-way to abstraction.

The cinema can compensate in other ways for its shortcomings in this. It can call on all the resources of photography. It can dispense with the human person altogether (the documentary) or merge him with the landscape (the Western). Its sense of place, in flexibility and realism far beyond theatrical possibility, confers on it something of the novel's narrative fluidity.

But compared with the novel its way with words, and therefore with ideas, is clumsy. The talkie's words take second place to the visual presentation of reality. Film visuals can show a 'lame old black cat sitting on a worn grey mat'. Or a "playful tabby stretched out on a mat with a pattern of roses on it." But they can't say, simply, "the cat sat on the mat." They can show a beautiful statue in sun, then in rain, then in snow, but they can't say simply, "A thing of beauty is a joy for ever." Their powers of abstraction are limited. They can't match the writer's swift, deft way with metaphors. Film is a reasonably good

From Raymond Durgnat, *Films and Feelings*. Reprinted by permission of Faber and Faber Ltd.

350

medium for persuading, but it's a very clumsy one for arguing. And by means of words, which present objective reality through ideas, the novelist can mix visual reality and ideas in a rich, intimate way. Here the cinema is infinitely poorer.

Yet its literary poverty is compensated by its visual richness. It is a visual art, like painting. In the words of Marcel Carné, "One must compose images as the old masters did their canvases, with the same preoccupation with effect and expression. Cinema images have the same needs." The film critic will often need to use the vocabulary of the visual arts rather than of literary criticism. . . . Most film critics (outside Italy) have a literary background, and the fact that films, like novels, tell stories, reinforces their tendency to consider the "core" of film as being somehow "literary." Their indebtedness to a (waning) fashion *in* literary criticism usually leads to the further assumption that the "core" of literature is "psychological insights"—exact definition and motives, and so on. To these displaced persons a film's visual qualities are only "style." The documentarists' influence on film criticism completes the long-dominant emphasis on literary qualities, psychological realism, and social consciousness.

On the other hand, it was also apparent that the dominating creative "charge" of many films was the director's, rather than the writer's or the actor's. So here was a paradox: the *quality* of a film depended less on the writers and actors, who one might have expected to contribute the literary-psychological interest, than on a man whose province was that of "visuals" and "style." "Visual" directors like Eisenstein, Murnau and Dreyer retained their prestige as "geniuses" less, one feels, because these critics really understood or thrilled to their films, than before they were protected by an aura of "prestige." The critics of, for example, *Sight and Sound* whom, for all their individual differences, it is reasonable to consider as a team with a common attitude, typify a fading English critical orthodoxy, with all its confusions and contradictions—summarizable as: "literary content" and "style" are either indistinguishable or the same thing but the first is emphatically more important than the second.

This part attempts to offer some new ideas, to revive some very old ones which fell into disuse when the "literary content" school acquired their stranglehold on film criticism, and to revitalize principles to which it consents in theory but obscures in practice. Space, unfortunately, forbids us from examining each point from as many angles as one would like to. It offers only a series of signposts, rather than a map.

Let us first look at the implications of the antithesis of "content" and "style." Among film critics "content" is equated with "literary content," that is, anything in a film which a novelist could fairly easily put into words if he were writing "the book of the film." And "style" becomes, virtually, anything which isn't "content."

In the other arts the uses of the word "style" are rather different. In painting "literary content" is obviously of minor importance, while much great music is absolutely devoid of all "literary content" whatsoever. By this definition abstract paintings and symphonies would be "pure" style, altogether devoid of meaning—and importance? Clearly then there must be a sense in which "style = content."

The opening definition of "style" in *The Concise O.E.D.* is: "Manner of writing, speaking or doing . . . as opposed to the matter to be expressed or thing done." In other words, an artist's "style" is his answer to the problems with which he is faced in the course of creating his work of art. On the one hand, he has a certain intention, a certain "vision" or "drive," an experience to communicate (even if he isn't himself too sure in his conscious mind of exactly what it is). Similarly, the film director has a scene in a script, or a certain plot point to make. This scene is built around this point, so he thinks of it, for a while, as what the scene "contains," his "content." But his sense of craftsmanship, certain practical exigencies, the need for a slick, easy flow of ideas across the screen, etc., confront him with various practical problems. Should he make the actor walk into shot? or should he pan the camera to pick up the actor? There may be no particular reason for his choice, except, in the case of a dull director, habit or convention, or, in the case of an original director, some intuitive, inexplicable preference. It just feels right to him—more smooth, more elegant, more lively than other possibilities. That choice is his "personal" style. The writer, the actor, the cameraman, the director, will each have such a personal style of his own—favourite, intuitive, unexamined ways of doing things. Often he will be quite unaware that other solutions would have been possible. The director, as *integrator* of everybody's work, has more "stylistic" problems than anyone else; hence his "style" usually flavours the film.

Now let us look at "style" in a medium other than the cinema. Two actors will declaim Shakespeare's words ("content") in altogether different ways ("style"). One makes Hamlet a warrior-hero who can't make up his mind. The other makes him a neurotic intellectual who can't steel himself to action. The "literary content" is exactly the same but the "theatrical content" (gesture, voice) is altogether different. So different that it transforms the meaning of the text. Here, the style is just as much a part of the content as the "content." In fact much of what film critics call "literary content" is in fact "theatrical content," depending less on the text than on acting and staging, and, to this extent, the ordinary fiction film is nearer the theatre than literature.

Of course, not all features of "style" make much difference to the "content." It may make no difference whatsoever whether an actor lifts his left eyebrow before or after he waggles his right finger-tip. This is a change of "content" too, but only a minor one.

From this definition, the question whether style is more important than content is a misleading one. Style is simply those pieces of content which arise out of the way the artist makes his basic points. These may (as often in painting and poetry) be only a pretext, a wire on which to "thread the beads." If style is "manner of doing," then we can say that the way a thing is done is often a way of doing a different thing. To say "sorry" *superciliously* is doing a different thing from saying "sorry" courteously or servilely, etc. Certain tones of voice make "sorry" mean: "Look where you're going, you clumsy imbecile." "It ain't what you do it's the way that you do it." "Le style, c'est l'homme." . . .

The distinction between *"literary* content" and "visual style" is particularly misguided because even in the work of literature much of the "content" comes from the "style." Suppose we call someone "slow but thorough" we feel this is, on the whole, a compliment. His slowness is a trifling disadvantage, the last words acts as a summing-up, an assertion of his value. But if we call him "thorough but slow" there is an implication of criticism. The ideas and the words are exactly the same—but to change their order is like inserting some invisible words. One order says: "We can rely on him." The other: "He should pull his socks up." More often, literary "style" is a matter of choosing different words—different ideas, different content. My friends are "unfaltering," my enemies are "obstinate." I show "intensity of purpose," you are a "fanatic." Our friends are "original," our rivals "eccentric." Writers show such concern over points of "style" (e.g. *le mot juste*) because of their concern over points of "content."

Such nuances of order, sound (especially in poetry), vocabulary, and so on, don't just *colour* the "content" of a passage. They *constitute* its content. The passage may be badly written, but of interest as a description of an interesting event—traffic accident, a battle or a riot. But this event is not its "literary content." It's only the *subject.* Another passage may describe an apparently boring event, but bring to it a wealth of ideas and insights. And in this case we may speak of the author's "style" as enlivening a banal "content." But this wealth of ideas and insights isn't "mere" style—it is "content." And, here, to ask whether style or content is more important is like asking whether water is more important than H_2O. The words are different, the thing's the same, which phrase one uses depends on one's context and emphasis. It is not the importance of their subjects, but the richness of their "content-style" which distinguishes good artists from mediocre ones.

Another quite common and useful sense of the word "style" is to refer to the whole mass of details which go into a film, but which happen to be confusing and difficult to describe in words. Thus a *specific* reaction—horror, joy, etc.—tends to be called "content" because it is easy to define, it offers a nice, solid idea to lean on. On the other hand, an actor's postures, gestures, smiles, the quality of his glance, the tension of his facial muscles, the director's spatial relationships, the tones of grey caught by the cameraman, all these may be very eloquent and forceful in communicating experience (and so are "content"). But because it is difficult to analyze or explain their exact meaning in words they tend to be referred to, vaguely, as "style." But here again "content" and "style" are indissoluble. In fact, here, the "content"—horror, joy—is a spectator's deduction from what the screen actually contains. This is why spectators so often disagree on what a film's content is. The screen contains the style, but not the *content*, which is the spectator's deduction, and not contained on the *screen* at all! . . .

[1965]

SUSAN SONTAG

Against Interpretation

Content is a glimpse of something, an encounter like a flash. It's very tiny—very tiny, content.

WILLEM DE KOONING, in an interview

It is only shallow people who do not judge by appearances. The mystery of the world is the visible, not the invisible.

OSCAR WILDE, in a letter

The earliest *experience* of art must have been that it was incantatory, magical; art was an instrument of ritual. (Cf. the paintings in the caves at Lascaux, Altamira, Niaux, La Pasiega, etc.) The earliest *theory* of art, that of the Greek philosophers, proposed that art was mimesis, imitation of reality.

It is at this point that the peculiar question of the *value* of art arose. For the mimetic theory, by its very terms, challenges art to justify itself.

Plato, who proposed the theory, seems to have done so in order to rule that the value of art is dubious. Since he considered ordinary material things as themselves mimetic objects, imitations of transcendent forms or structures, even the best painting of a bed would be only an "imitation of an imitation." For Plato, art is neither particularly useful

355

(the painting of a bed is no good to sleep on), nor, in the strict sense, true. And Aristotle's arguments in defense of art do not really challenge Plato's view that all art is an elaborate *trompe l'oeil,* and therefore a lie. But he does dispute Plato's idea that art is useless. Lie or no, art has a certain value according to Aristotle because it is a form of therapy. Art is useful, after all, Aristotle counters, medicinally useful in that it arouses and purges dangerous emotions.

In Plato and Aristotle, the mimetic theory of art goes hand in hand with the assumption that art is always figurative. But advocates of the mimetic theory need not close their eyes to decorative and abstract art. The fallacy that art is necessarily a "realism" can be modified or scrapped without ever moving outside the problems delimited by the mimetic theory.

The fact is, all Western consciousness of and reflection upon art have remained within the confines staked out by the Greek theory of art as mimesis or representation. It is through this theory that art as such—above and beyond given works of art—becomes problematic, in need of defense. And it is the defense of art which gives birth to the odd vision by which something we have learned to call "form" is separated off from something we have learned to call "content," and to the well-intentioned move which makes content essential and form accessory.

Even in modern times, when most artists and critics have discarded the theory of art as representation of an outer reality in favor of the theory of art as subjective expression, the main feature of the mimetic theory persists. Whether we conceive of the work of art on the model of a picture (art as a picture of reality) or on the model of a statement (art as the statement of the artist), content still comes first. The content may have changed. It may now be less figurative, less lucidly realistic. But it is still assumed that a work of art *is* its content. Or, as it's usually put today, that a work of art by definition *says* something. ("What X is saying is . . . ," "What X is trying to say is . . . ," "What X said is . . ." etc., etc.)

2

None of us can ever retrieve that innocence before all theory when art knew no need to justify itself, when one did not ask of a work of art what it *said* because one knew (or thought one knew) what it *did.* From now to the end of consciousness, we are stuck with the task of defending art. We can only quarrel with one or another means of defense. Indeed, we have an obligation to overthrow any means of defending and justifying art which becomes particularly obtuse or onerous or insensitive to contemporary needs and practice.

This is the case, today, with the very idea of content itself. Whatever it may have been in the past, the idea of content is today mainly a hindrance, a nuisance, a subtle or not so subtle philistinism.

Though the actual developments in many arts may seem to be leading us away from the idea that a work of art is primarily its content, the idea still exerts an extraordinary hegemony. I want to suggest that this is because the idea is now perpetuated in the guise of a certain way of encountering works of art thoroughly ingrained among most people who take any of the arts seriously. What the overemphasis on the idea of content entails is the perennial, never consummated project of *interpretation*. And, conversely, it is the habit of approaching works of art in order to *interpret* them that sustains the fancy that there really is such a thing as the content of a work of art.

3

Of course, I don't mean interpretation in the broadest sense, the sense in which Nietzsche (rightly) says, "There are no facts, only interpretations." By interpretations, I mean here a conscious act of the mind which illustrates a certain code, certain "rules" of interpretation.

Directed to art, interpretation means plucking a set of elements (the X, the Y, the Z, and so forth) from the whole work. The task of interpretation is virtually one of translation. The interpreter says, Look, don't you see that X is really—or, really means—A? That Y is really B? That Z is really C?

What situation could prompt this curious project for transforming a text? History gives us the materials for an answer. Interpretation first appears in the culture of late classical antiquity, when the power and credibility of myth had been broken by the "realistic" view of the world introduced by scientific enlightenment. Once the question that haunts postmythic consciousness—that of the *seemliness* of religious symbols—had been asked, the ancient texts were, in their pristine form, no longer acceptable Then interpretation was summoned, to reconcile the ancient texts to "modern" demands. Thus, the Stoics, to accord with their view that the gods had to be moral, allegorized away the rude features of Zeus and his boisterous clan in Homer's epics. What Homer really designated by the adultery of Zeus with Leto, they explained, was the union between power and wisdom. In the same vein, Philo of Alexandria interpreted the literal historical narratives of the Hebrew Bible as spiritual paradigms. The story of the exodus from Egypt, the wandering in the desert for forty years, and the entry into the promised land, said Philo, was really an allegory of the individual soul's emancipation, tribulations, and final deliverance. Interpretation thus presupposes a discrepancy between the clear meaning of the text and the demands of (later) readers. It seeks to resolve that discrepancy. The situation is that for some reason a text has become unacceptable; yet it cannot be discarded. Interpretation is a radical strategy for conserving an old text, which is thought too precious to repudiate, by revamping it. The interpreter, without actually erasing or rewriting the text, *is* altering it. But he can't admit to doing this. He claims to be only making it intelligible, by disclosing its true meaning. However far the interpreters alter the text (another notorious example is the Rabbinic and Christian "spiritual" interpretations of the clearly erotic Song of Songs), they must claim to be reading off a sense that is already there.

Interpretation in our own time, however, is even more complex. For the contemporary zeal for the project of interpretation is often prompted not by piety toward the troublesome text (which may conceal an aggression), but by an open aggressiveness, an overt contempt for appearances. The old style of interpretation was insistent, but respectful; it erected another meaning on top of the literal one. The modern style of interpretation excavates, and as it excavates, destroys; it digs "behind" the text, to find a sub-text which is the true one. The most celebrated and influential modern doctrines, those of Marx and Freud, actually amount to elaborate systems of hermeneutics, aggressive and impious theories of interpretation. All observable phenomena are bracketed, in Freud's phrase, as *manifest content*. This manifest content must be probed and pushed aside to find the true meaning—the *latent content*— beneath. For Marx, social events like revolutions and wars; for Freud, the events of individual lives (like neurotic symptoms and slips of the tongue) as well as texts (like a dream or a work of art) —all are treated as occasions for interpretation. According to Marx and Freud, these events only *seem* to be intelligible. Actually, they have no meaning without interpretation. To understand *is* to interpret. And to interpret is to restate the phenomenon, in effect to find an equivalent for it.

Thus, interpretation is not (as most people assume) an absolute value, a gesture of mind situated in some timeless realm of capabilities. Interpretation must itself be evaluated, within a historical view of human consciousness. In some cultural contexts, interpretation is a liberating act. It is a means of revising, of transvaluing, of escaping the dead past. In other cultural contexts, it is reactionary, impertinent, cowardly, stifling.

4

Today is such a time, when the project of interpretation is largely reactionary, stifling. Like the fumes of the automobile and of heavy industry which befoul the urban atmosphere, the effusion of interpretations of art today poisons our sensibilities. In a culture whose already classical dilemma is the hypertrophy of the intellect at the expense of energy and sensual capability, interpretation is the revenge of the intellect upon art.

Even more. It is the revenge of the intellect upon the world. To interpret is to impoverish, to deplete the world—in order to set up a shadow world of "meanings." It is to turn *the* world into *this* world. ("This world"! As if there were any other.)

The world, our world, is depleted, impoverished enough. Away with all duplicates of it, until we again experience more immediately what we have.

5

In most modern instances, interpretation amounts to the philistine refusal to leave the work of art alone. Real art has the capacity to make us nervous. By reducing the work of art to its content and then interpreting *that,* one tames the work of art. Interpretation makes art manageable, conformable.

This philistinism of interpretation is more rife in literature than in any other art. For decades now, literary critics have understood it to be their task to translate the elements of the poem or play or novel or story into something else. Sometimes a writer will be so uneasy before the naked power of his art that he will install within the work itself— albeit with a little shyness, a touch of the good taste of irony—the clear and explicit interpretation of it. Thomas Mann is an example of such an overcooperative author. In the case of more stubborn authors, the critic is only too happy to perform the job.

The work of Kafka, for example, has been subjected to a mass ravishment by no less than three armies of interpreters. Those who read Kafka as a social allegory see case studies of the frustrations and insanity of modern bureaucracy and its ultimate issuance in the totalitarian state. Those who read Kafka as a psychoanalytic allegory see desperate revelations of Kafka's fear of his father, his castration anxieties, his sense of his own impotence, his thralldom to his dreams. Those who read Kafka as a religious allegory explain that K. in *The Castle* is trying to gain access to heaven, that Joseph K. in *The Trial* is being judged by the inexorable and mysterious justice of God. . . . Another *oeuvre* that has attracted interpreters like leeches is that of Samuel Beckett. Beckett's delicate dramas of the withdrawn consciousness—pared down to essentials, cut off, often represented as physically immobilized—are read as a statement about modern man's alienation from meaning or from God, or as an allegory of psychopathology.

Proust, Joyce, Faulkner, Rilke, Lawrence, Gide . . . one could go on citing author after author; the list is endless of those around whom thick encrustations of interpretation have taken hold. But it should be noted that interpretation is not simply the compliment that mediocrity pays to genius. It is, indeed, *the* modern way of understanding something, and is applied to works of every quality. Thus, in the notes that Elia Kazan published on his production of *A Streetcar Named Desire,* it becomes clear that, in order to direct the play, Kazan had to discover that Stanley Kowalski represented the sensual and vengeful barbarism that was engulfing our culture, while Blanche Du Bois was Western civilization, poetry, delicate apparel, dim lighting, refined feelings and all, though a little the worse for wear to be sure. Tennessee Williams' forceful psychological melodrama now became intelligible: it was *about* something, about the decline of Western civilization. Apparently, were it to go on being a play about a handsome brute named Stanley Kowalski and a faded mangy belle named Blanche Du Bois, it would not be manageable.

6

It doesn't matter whether artists intend, or don't intend, for their works to be interpreted. Perhaps Tennessee Williams thinks *Streetcar* is about what Kazan thinks it to be about. It may be that Cocteau in *The Blood of a Poet* and in *Orpheus* wanted the elaborate readings which have been given these films, in terms of Freudian symbolism and social critique. But the merit of these works certainly lies elsewhere than in their "meanings." Indeed, it is precisely to the extent that Williams' plays and Cocteau's films do suggest these portentous meanings that they are defective, false, contrived, lacking in conviction.

From interviews, it appears that Resnais and Robbe-Grillet consciously designed *Last Year at Marienbad* to accommodate a multiplicity of equally plausible interpretations. But the temptation to interpret *Marienbad* should be resisted. What matters in *Marienbad* is the pure, untranslatable, sensuous immediacy of some of its images, and its rigorous if narrow solutions to certain problems of cinematic form.

Again, Ingmar Bergman may have meant the tank rumbling down the empty night street in *The Silence* as a phallic symbol. But if he did, it was a foolish thought. ("Never trust the teller, trust the tale," said Lawrence.) Taken as a brute object, as an immediate sensory equivalent for the mysterious abrupt armored happenings going on inside the hotel, that sequence with the tank is the most striking moment in the film. Those who reach for a Freudian interpretation of the tank are only expressing their lack of response to what is there on the screen.

It is always the case that interpretation of this type indicates a dissatisfaction (conscious or unconscious) with the work, a wish to replace it by something else.

Interpretation, based on the highly dubious theory that a work of art is composed of items of content, violates art. It makes art into an article for use, for arrangement into a mental scheme of categories.

7

Interpretation does not, of course, always prevail. In fact, a great deal of today's art may be understood as motivated by a flight from interpretation. To avoid interpretation, art may become parody. Or it may become abstract. Or it may become ("merely") decorative. Or it may become non-art.

The flight from interpretation seems particularly a feature of modern painting. Abstract painting is the attempt to have, in the ordinary sense, no content; since there is no content, there can be no interpretation. Pop Art works by the opposite means to the same result; using a content so blatant, so "what it is," it, too, ends by being uninterpretable.

A great deal of modern poetry as well, starting from the great experiments of French poetry (including the movement that is mis-leadingly called Symbolism) to put silence into poems and to reinstate the *magic* of the word, has escaped from the rough grip of interpretation. The most recent revolution in contemporary taste in poetry—the revolution that has deposed Eliot and elevated Pound—represents a turning away from content in poetry in the old sense, an impatience with what made modern poetry prey to the zeal of interpreters.

I am speaking mainly of the situation in America, of course. Interpretation runs rampant here in those arts with a feeble and negligible avant-garde: fiction and the drama. Most American novelists and playwrights are really either journalists or gentlemen sociologists and psychologists. They are writing the literary equivalent of program music. And so rudimentary, uninspired, and stagnant has been the sense of what might be done with *form* in fiction and drama that even when the content isn't simply information, news, it is still peculiarly visible, handier, more exposed. To the extent that novels and plays (in America), unlike poetry and painting and music, don't reflect any interesting concern with changes in their form, these arts remain prone to assault by interpretation.

But programmatic avant-gardism—which has meant, mostly, experiments with form at the expense of content—is not the only defense against the infestation of art by interpretations. At least, I hope not.

For this would be to commit art to being perpetually on the run. (It also perpetuates the very distinction between form and content which is, ultimately, an illusion.) Ideally, it is possible to elude the interpreters in another way, by making works of art whose surface is so unified and clean, whose momentum is so rapid, whose address is so direct that the work can be . . . just what it is. Is this possible now? It does happen in films, I believe. This is why cinema is the most alive, the most exciting, the most important of all art forms right now. Perhaps the way one tells how alive a particular art form is, is by the latitude it gives for making mistakes in it, and still being good. For example, a few of the films of Bergman—though crammed with lame messages about the modern spirit, thereby inviting interpretations—still triumph over the pretentious intentions of their director. In *Winter Light* and *The Silence,* the beauty and visual sophistication of the images subvert before our eyes the callow pseudo-intellectuality of the story and some of the dialogue. (The most remarkable instance of this sort of discrepancy is the work of D. W. Griffith.) In good films, there is always a directness that entirely frees us from the itch to interpret. Many old Hollywood films, like those of Cukor, Walsh, Hawks, and countless other directors, have this liberating anti-symbolic quality, no less than the best work of the new European directors, like Truffaut's *Shoot the Piano Player* and *Jules and Jim,* Godard's *Breathless* and *Vivre Sa Vie,* Antonioni's *L'Avventura,* and Almi's *The Fiancés.*

The fact that films have not been overrun by interpreters is in part due simply to the newness of cinema as an art. It also owes to the happy accident that films for such a long time were just movies; in other words, that they were understood to be part of mass, as opposed to high, culture, and were left alone by most people with minds. Then, too, there is always something other than content in the cinema to grab hold of, for those who want to analyze. For the cinema, unlike the novel, possesses a vocabulary of forms—the explicit, complex, and discussable technology of camera movements, cutting, and composition of the frame that goes into the making of a film.

8

What kind of criticism, of commentary on the arts, is desirable today? For I am not saying that works of art are ineffable, that they cannot be described or paraphrased. They can be. The question is how. What would criticism look like that would serve the work of art, not usurp its place?

What is needed, first, is more attention to form in art. If excessive stress on *content* provokes the arrogance of interpretation, more extended and more thorough descriptions of *form* would silence. What is needed is a vocabulary—a descriptive, rather than prescriptive, vocabulary—for forms.* The best criticism, and it is uncommon, is of this sort that dissolves considerations of content into those of form. On film, drama, and painting respectively, I can think of Erwin Panofsky's essay, "Style and Medium in the Motion Pictures," Northrop Frye's essay "A Conspectus of Dramatic Genres," Pierre Francastel's essay "The Destruction of a Plastic Space." Roland Barthes' book *On Racine* and his two essays on Robbe-Grillet are examples of formal analysis applied to the work of a single author. (The best essays in Erich Auerbach's *Mimesis,* like "The Star of Odysseus," are also of this type.) An example of formal analysis applied simultaneously to genre and author is Walter Benjamin's essay, "The Story Teller: Reflections on the Works of Nicolai Leskov."

Equally valuable would be acts of criticism which would supply a really accurate, sharp, loving description of the appearance of a work of art. This seems even harder to do than formal analysis. Some of Manny Farber's film criticism, Dorothy Van Ghent's essay "The Dickens World: A View from Todgers'," Randall Jarrell's essay on Walt Whitman are among the rare examples of what I mean. These are essays which reveal the sensuous surface of art without mucking about in it.

9

Transparence is the highest, most liberating value in art—and in criticism—today. Transparence means experiencing the luminousness of the thing in itself, of things being what they are. This is the greatness of, for example, the films of Bresson and Ozu and Renoir's *The Rules of the Game.*

Once upon a time, (say, for Dante), it must have been a revolutionary and creative move to design works of art so that they might be experienced on several levels. Now it is not. It reinforces the principle of redundancy that is the principal affliction of modern life.

Once upon a time (a time when high art was scarce), it must have been a revolutionary and creative move to interpret works of art. Now it is not. What we decidedly do not need now is further to assimilate Art into Thought, or (worse yet) Art into Culture.

---

*One of the difficulties is that our idea of form is spatial (the Greek metaphors for form are all derived from notions of space). This is why we have a more ready vocabulary of forms for the spatial than for the temporal arts. The exception among the temporal arts, of course, is the drama; perhaps this is because the drama is a narrative (i.e., temporal) form that extends itself visually and pictorially, upon a stage. . . . What we don't have yet is a poetics of the novel, any clear notion of the forms of narration. Perhaps film criticism will be the occasion of a breakthrough here, since films are primarily a visual form, yet they are also a subdivision of literature.

Interpretation takes the sensory experience of the work of art for granted, and proceeds from there. This cannot be taken for granted, now. Think of the sheer multiplication of works of art available to every one of us, superadded to the conflicting tastes and odors and sights of the urban environment that bombard our senses. Ours is a culture based on excess, on overproduction; the result is a steady loss of sharpness in our sensory experience. All the conditions of modern life—its material plenitude, its sheer crowdedness—conjoin to dull our sensory faculties. And it is in the light of the condition of our senses, our capacities (rather than those of another age), that the task of the critic must be assessed.

What is important now is to recover our senses. We must learn to *see* more, to *hear* more, to *feel* more.

Our task is not to find the maximum amount of content in a work of art, much less to squeeze more content out of the work than is already there. Our task is to cut back content so that we can see the thing at all.

The aim of all commentary on art now should be to make works of art—and, by analogy, our own experience—more, rather than less, real to us. The function of criticism should be to show *how it is what it is,* even *that it is what it is,* rather than to show *what it means.*

10

In place of a hermeneutics we need an erotics of art.

[1964]